Wine
Report
2004

Tom Stevenson

LONDON NEW YORK MUNICH
MELBOURNE DELHI

Senior Editor
Gary Werner

Senior Art Editor
Sue Metcalfe-Megginson

Managing Editor
Deirdre Headon

Art Director
Peter Luff

DTP Designer
Louise Waller

Production Controller
Sarah Sherlock

Editors
Sylvia & David Tombesi-Walton
Sands Publishing Solutions
4 Jenner Way, Eccles, Aylesford,
Kent ME20 7SQ

US Editor
Christine Heilman

First American Edition, 2003
Published in the United States by
DK Publishing, Inc.
375 Hudson Street
New York, New York 10014

03 04 05 06 07 08 10 9 8 7 6 5 4 3 2 1

Copyright © 2003 Dorling Kindersley Limited

Text copyright © 2003 Tom Stevenson

**All prices in this guide are
average retail figures expressed
in local currencies.**

All rights reserved under International and
Pan-American Copyright Conventions. No part of this
publication may be reproduced, stored in a retrieval
system, or transmitted in any form or by any means,
electronic, mechanical, photocopying, recording or
otherwise, without the prior written permission of the
copyright owner. Published in Great Britain by
Dorling Kindersley Limited.

A Cataloging-in-Publication record for this
book is available from the Library of Congress.

ISBN 0-7894-9630-5

Printed by Canale in Italy

Discover more at
www.dk.com

CONTENTS

Introduction

Wine Report is the essential reference for the wine lover who has everything.

It is the only guide for the busy wine enthusiast who wants to stay up to speed. And it will be invaluable for members of the wine trade who want to keep abreast of what is going on beyond the wines they deal with on a daily basis, be they wine producers, importers, wholesalers, retailers, or sommeliers.

Each year, *Wine Report* provides a one-stop update on what has happened in the world of wine during the previous 12 months, full of inside information on every wine region.

One person could not possibly keep up with all of this on an annual basis. It takes me several years to update a single edition of *The New Sotheby's Wine Encyclopedia*. This is why I have assembled a team of specialists—and not just any specialists. These are the guys and girls I respect the most in their respective subjects—the ones I would turn to if I needed some inside help. So, it is nothing but the best: Clive Coates MW on Burgundy, David Peppercorn MW on Bordeaux, and Richard Mayson on Portugal, for example. But it is not just full of Brits. I have commissioned two top French experts: Thierry Desseauve on the Rhône and Antoine Gerbelle on the Loire. Thierry is the publisher of *La Revue du Vin de France*, the most influential wine magazine in France, and coauthor with Michel Bettane of the *Classement des Vins de France*, the world's most respected buyer's guide to the best French wines. And Antoine is the Loire contributor for *Classement*.

I have pulled in as many *in situ* experts as I could. Nobody knows more about South Africa than John Platter, for example, and I have Huon Hooke on Australia, Bob Campbell MW on New Zealand, Dan Berger on California, Nick Belfrage MW on Italy (although American, he lives in Italy), Chandra Kurt on Switzerland, Dr. Philipp Blom on Austria, Tony Aspler on Canada, Nico Manessis on Greece, and Daniel Rogov on Israel. All these names will be well known to readers interested in the wines they cover, just as flying viticultural guru Dr. Richard Smart will be, but some are the expert's experts and are known to relatively few outside their spheres of influence, such as Professor Ron Jackson. Ron is, for me, the James Burke of wine science. One of his books—called *Wine Science*, funnily enough—is the only single-volume reference to everything from the grape and viticulture, through wine and oenology (where most books start and stop), to wine tasting and health. It is not dumbed down, but you do not need a science degree to understand it, merely a reasonable level of intelligence. It is the best single-volume book on the subject, making Ron my first choice as contributor, and I am so glad that he accepted.

Health matters

Beverley Blanning, a Master of Wine who specializes in health issues, has been tasked to keep readers up to date with all the latest research into how and why moderate wine consumption can be good for you, protect you against cancer and vascular disease, and extend your life expectancy. This is a vital topic in a world where producers are forbidden to state proven health benefits on the label, while in the US and a growing number of other places, they are forced to print health warnings, some of which are untrue or unproven. However, it is equally vital that *Wine Report* does not lay itself open to the charge of feeding consumers only good news; thus, Beverley has been specifically briefed to highlight research that conflicts with or contradicts any health benefits and to give us the bad news in an unambiguous, unbiased fashion. She has even been asked to provide top 10s of the biggest health hypes and myths!

Wines of Antarctica

Where there are no real experts on an area, region, or country, I have commissioned a professional I respect to specialize in the wines. Take the Jura and Savoie, for example. I knew that Wink Lorch, chairman of AWE (Association of Wine Educators), had a home in the Haut-Savoie, and having worked successfully with Wink on various projects over the past eight years or so, I considered her ideally placed and well qualified to take on the task. Eventually she agreed! And she has dug out a lot of stuff that most of us had no idea about. Doug Frost, one of three people in the world to hold both Master Sommelier and Master of Wine titles, has gamely taken on everything between America's West Coast and the Atlantic Northeast—no fewer than 30 states, but he regularly judges in competitions covering these states and is thus uniquely suited to reveal all. Australian Denis Gastin is the only person I know who could possibly even think of covering Asia—one-third of the planet!

Rough ride

Not that it has been smooth sailing. I have almost 40 contributors, and it is a dream team, but it would have been exactly 40 had I not had to fire a couple of them! They just did not come up with the goods, and you have to be ruthless if you want the best. This first edition covers every well-known wine-producing region in world, all the lesser-known, and many of the most obscure. India, Japan, and China? Old hat. Denis Gastin has them covered in detail, but he also has news on wines from Thailand and South Korea. Even Bali! Next year Chandra Kurt will be including Liechtenstein as an addendum to her Swiss wine report. By comparison, Luxembourg is far more important, but there are very few skilled tasters who know all the small growers, rather than just the few large merchants and cooperatives. Those who do were either not prepared to be critical of any wines (this is what has kept Luxembourg in the backwaters) or could not be relied upon. I have even tried the best local sommeliers. The search goes on, as it does for someone who knows Algiers, Morocco, Tunisia, and other lesser-known African wine-producing countries. I fired a writer here, as I did the person who I had commissioned to research Belgium, the Netherlands, and Denmark (and I am not kidding). When I have those two reports covered, there will just be Ireland and Malta, and that will be it: every square inch of wine-growing in the world.

Contributor's by-line

The problem with annual wine guides that rely on a large number of contributors is that the reader never knows whether something was written by the person on the front cover or one of the plethora of names hidden away in the acknowledgments. In *Wine Report*, however, each contributor is there for all to see, quite literally, with his or her photo heading the report and a full by-line that even credits competing publications. It is about time that figurehead authors gave full credit where due, so hopefully this will set a trend.

Privileged information

Wine Report tells you about important events, incidents, and developments that have happened in each region or subject (in the case of Viticulture, Organic & Biodynamic Wines, Wine Science, Wine & Health, Wine on the Web, and Auctions & Investment). You will be privy to insider information. Some of these topics and news items have not even appeared in the wine trade press. Not only will you discover if, say, a new winemaker has taken over at a *cru classé* Bordeaux château or high-profile New World winery, or somebody has sold up, but you will also find out about new appellations, new wine laws, juicy legal cases, important changes to existing wines, wine launches, the truth behind the hype about the most recent vintage, and any back-pedaling of opinion on previous vintages. I have briefed contributors not to pull any punches, so they will reveal anything currently practiced (legally or not) that should not be, plus, of course, anything that should be happening and yet is not. Last, but not least, each contributor provides listings of producers (greatest, best-value, new, and fastest-improving) and wines (greatest, best bargains, and most exciting or unusual finds). Now you can get inside the head of Clive Coates *et all* and see what they think are the best producers and wines—this year and every year.

- China is now the eighth-largest viticultural country in the world.
- First Native winery opens in Canada.
- Every state in the US has at least one winery.
- Washington wines beat top Napa and Bordeaux growths in two blind taste-offs.
- Frost destroys 80 percent of Champagne harvest.
- Double-whammy fraud uncovered in Champagne.
- Gérard Depardieu succeeds where Robert Mondavi failed.
- Vandals flush a vat of Rémy Pannier down the drain.
- Corrine Mentzelopoulos buys the château everybody thought she owned: Margaux!
- Peppercorn on Parker.
- Horses replace tractors in Burgundy.
- French publication fined for describing Beaujolais as *merde.*
- Casa do Douro, Port's former regulatory body, put out to pasture.
- All Madeira must now be bottled on the island.
- New vintage Madeira appellation established.
- Rumor that Brian Croser might buy Penfolds from Southcorp!
- Pirie kicked out of Pipers Brook.
- Australian wine in "tinnies."
- Zinfandel emerging as a new varietal in southern France.
- Vin de Pays de France mooted.
- Primitivo (Zinfandel) identified in an ancient block of vines in Germany.
- Growers in a Swiss village called Champagne demand the right to their own name.
- Thirteen hybrids declared vinifera to circumvent EU wine law.
- First Greek Master of Wine.
- First Viognier from Israel.
- Soave Superiore, Bardolino Superiore, Greco di Tufo, and Fiano d'Avellino attain DOCG.
- Alleged Cabernetization of Chianti, Barolo, and Barbaresco.
- PRD—the greatest thing since tapwater.

Bordeaux

David Peppercorn MW

Undoubtedly, the topic that is concentrating minds most at present is how the market for Bordeaux wines will react: 2002 is a much smaller crop than 2000 or 2001, and many believe the wines are exceptional.

DAVID PEPPERCORN MW

But how are they to be sold? Prices for the excellent 2001s came down after the great but expensive 2000s, often to the level of the 1999s, which were good but not special. Those who bucked this trend still have stock on their hands, so the question is, "What reduction will be necessary to tempt the buyers?" Not an easy one to answer, in a situation where economic factors combine with political uncertainties to create a position in which many buyers are nervous about committing to any purchases at all. In the vintages 1988, 1989, and 1990, 1988 was the most expensive *en primeur* and 1990 the cheapest; but of course it is the 1990s that are the most highly priced today, and the 1988s are the cheapest.

Perhaps there is a lesson here for today's buyers. If the 2002s are as great as some think, then those brave enough to step in may be rewarded in the mid- to long-term.

DAVID PEPPERCORN MW When David Peppercorn went to Bordeaux as a Cambridge undergraduate in September 1953, it was the beginning of a lifelong love affair. He became a Master of Wine in 1962, and was chairman of the Institute of Masters of Wine from 1968–70. It was while David was a buyer for IDV (International Distillers & Vintners) in the 1970s that he started writing about wine, making his debut as an author with the award-winning *Bordeaux* (Faber & Faber, 1982). His *Pocket Guide to the Wines of Bordeaux* (Mitchell Beazley) has been updated every other year since 1986 (2002 being the latest edition). David is now retired from the wine trade, and spends his time traveling, writing, and lecturing. He is married to Serena Sutcliffe MW.

Absolutely classless

Last autumn, the creation of a new growers' association was announced. Called the Cercle Rive Droite, its concept is quite revolutionary, since its membership crosses the "class" barriers, as can be discerned from the appellations represented: Bordeaux (two properties); Bordeaux Supérieur (six properties); Ste-Foy-Bordeaux (one property); Premières Côtes de Bordeaux (three properties); Côtes de Blaye (three properties); Côtes de Bourg (one property); Côtes de Castillon (eight properties); Côtes de Francs (three properties); Fronsac (nine properties); Canon-Fronsac (four properties); Pomerol (19 properties); Lalande de Pomerol (six properties); St-Emilion Grands Crus (28 properties); St-Emilion Grands Crus Classés (15 properties); Montagne, Puisseguin, and Lussac-St-Emilion (seven properties). The president of this 115-strong association is Alain Reynaud, who owns St-Emilion's new rising star, Château Quinault, as well as various properties in Pomerol and Castillon. The vice president is Alain Moueix of Château Fonroque and Château Mazeyres. They held full-scale *primeur* tastings for 2002 in April 2003.

Grapevine

• The fact that Gianni Agnelli of Fiat fame owned 75 percent of Château Margaux, against Corinne Mentzelopoulos's 25 percent, was not widely known. Agnelli's death in January 2003 led his heirs to circulate their dossier. The word was that the likely asking price for the world's most famous Bordeaux château looked so steep, in today's climate, that many critics wondered whether anyone would even consider making a bid. But Mentzelopoulos obviously thought it was a good deal because she purchased the remaining 75 percent to gain total control.

• The astronomic price offered last year by Gérard Perse for Petit-Village seems to have been too much for his bankers. Perhaps all those unsold stocks of expensive Pavie 2001 the brokers are talking about could have something to do with it. Anyway, AXA Millésimes will be smiling: they did not really want to sell in the first place, and they can now pocket the 10 percent deposit!

• An application has been made to the INAO (Institut National des Appellations d'Origine) for a revision of the classification first made in 1953 and previously revised only once (in 1959). Many of those in the classification do not really want any new members, just extensions to their status, such as classifying Smith-Haut-Lafitte's white wine. This will hardly satisfy La Louvière or recently improved châteaux like Haut-Bergey or Larrivet-Haut-Brion. Such minefields have invigorated St-Emilion, but will they be welcomed in Graves?

• This will be the first vintage for the new management of Nicolas Thienpont. There is no change of ownership, and there is no doubting the excellence of the *terroir* on the Côte de Pavie. After what Thienpont has done for neighboring Pavie-Macquin, expectations must be high.

Opinion:
Parker's influence in decline?

In the ongoing philosophical differences surrounding vineyard management and winemaking that have especially enlivened the Right Bank in recent years, Robert Parker's *Wine Advocate* has wholeheartedly espoused the cause of the *garagistes* and their followers. However, the 2001s suggest that there are limits to his influence. High scores for Gérard Perse's Pavie failed to sell the wine. So it would seem that price does matter, even for the very rich who can afford the *vins de garagistes*. For the next installment, watch the 2002s, where record tannin levels are reported.

Late for class
The new classification of Médoc Crus Bourgeois was announced in 2000 and is promised for VinExpo 2003 in June, which unfortunately falls beyond the deadline of this book. One hopes that some prominent châteaux will not elect to absent themselves.

Grapevine

• **Jean-Pierre Moueix** died on March 28, 2003 in his 90th year. He will always be remembered for almost single-handedly putting Pomerol on the international wine map in the 1950s and 1960s. After World War II, he gradually acquired many leading properties: Magdelaine in St-Emilion; Trotanoy, La Fleur-Pétrus, and Latour à Pomerol in Pomerol; and eventually half the shares in Pétrus itself. As a *négociant*, Moueix was skillful in selecting importers in the US and the UK. He enthused his importers with the magic of Pomerol. As a man, he was a towering personality, combining legendary charm with great determination. His knowledge and understanding of the complex soils of Pomerol was unrivaled at the time. His son, Christian, has run the business for the last 20 years.

• **The gallant octogenarian** owner of Château Belair finally lost her battle with cancer. Madame Dubois-Challon's last days had been clouded by the bitter feud with her nephew, Alain Vauthier. She was co-owner of neighboring First Growth Château Ausone until Vauthier gained managerial control after a long dispute. In 1996, she sold her share to Vauthier, but the end of that particular battle did nothing to end the feud. May she now rest in peace.

Vintage Report

Advance report on the latest harvest

2002

The art of escapology reached new heights in Bordeaux this year. After an exceptionally dry winter, poor weather during the flowering led firstly to widespread *coulure* in the Merlot, especially in vines over 20 years of age, then to *millerandage*, which also affected the Cabernet Franc. This meant a small crop, with some growers on the Right Bank saying it was their smallest vintage since 1991. Prospects by the first week of September were bleak, with warm, showery, humid weather threatening rot; but this danger was averted when, on September 9, a classic high-pressure system delivered strong, cool, northeasterly winds.

The weather gradually got warmer, but it was only because the crop was so small that it ripened within this tiny window of opportunity. The Cabernet Franc and especially the Cabernet Sauvignon and Petit Verdot concentrated rapidly, but the good weather came too late to produce real quality in Merlot, which had already been picked. So, there is the extraordinary spectacle of many properties making Cabernet wines averaging over 13 percent, despite having had no real heat all summer. The best wines are to be found in the Médoc, especially in Pauillac and St-Julien, although there are also many good to excellent wines in Margaux and St-Estèphe, as well as in Pessac-Léognan. The length and elegance of the tannins are reminiscent of 1996, only with more power.

On the Right Bank, those with good proportions of Cabernet Franc have done best. The dry white wines are very fruity with good acidity levels, and in Sauternes there was some excellent botrytis as well as many raisinated grapes. The quality is not up to 2001, but is on the level of 1999 or 1988.

Updates on the previous five vintages

2001

Vintage rating: *90*

It was never going to be easy for this vintage to follow the fabled 2000, but the reds have fine, aromatic fruit quality and great elegance, albeit with less power than 2000. They are also more variable from district to district and from property to property. A handful of growers claim to have made better wines than in 2000, but this is because they failed to maximize the quality of their 2000s. Balance, as always, is vital, and overextracted wines are likely to disappoint, since tannin levels are high. Sauternes made amends for missing out in 2000 with an outstanding year, probably the best since 1990, and matching that year's exceptional richness.

2000

Vintage rating: 96

Nature managed to provide what the market had prayed for, with an exceptional spell of weather from July 29 until October 10. Temperatures were above average, and there was very little rain, hence the thick skins, which gave very powerful, deep-colored wines. A feature of the year is its consistency across the region and the outstanding character and typicity of the wines. The exceptionally high standard of so many of the wines is greater than in 1990 or 1989. Perhaps the potential of the vintage has been better realized than ever before. Unfortunately, Sauternes missed out, yielding about one-third of its normal crop and a quality that is good but not special.

1999

Vintage rating: 85

Heavy outbreaks of rain, combined with higher temperatures than usual from April onward, put a premium on work in the vineyard. Just a few years ago, this would have been a recipe for rot. The record crop of red wines has turned out to have considerable charm, fruit, and elegance, ideal for early drinking. Many St-Emilions and some *cru bourgeois* Médocs are now enjoyable. Some Médoc growers claim to have made better wines than in 1998, but in part this was a reaction against premature press comments on 1998 Médocs. There are more good wines in Margaux, St-Julien, and Pauillac than elsewhere. The best are attractively fruity, but dilute and overextracted ones also exist. Both St-Emilion and Pomerol did well, but the Cabernet Franc was less successful than in 1998. It was, however, the fourth successive fine Sauternes vintage.

1998

Vintage rating: *90*

These are wines of exceptional color and power, rich in tannins, but with an elegant balance. *En primeur*, the Merlots were impressive and seductive, whereas the Cabernets seemed somewhat austere. Yet the Médocs have developed into classic, well-structured wines that improve on every tasting. Many Pomerols and St-Emilions are outstanding, with the marvelous Cabernet Francs giving them added freshness and elegance. The Merlots are dense-textured and opulent. Very fine, rich Sauternes were made in a style similar to 1996.

1997

Vintage rating: *80*

Perceptions of quality were colored by prices that were far too high, and the wines were widely shunned. By 2002, the prices of many wines had halved, and these delicious, early-drinking wines of great charm and style began to be appreciated. Some dilute wines were produced, of course, but all the well-managed properties produced pleasing wines. Sauternes made wines of great finesse and breed, but less weight than 1996 or 1998.

GREATEST WINE PRODUCERS

1. Château Lafite
2. Château d'Yquem
3. Château Ausone
4. Château Pétrus
5. Château Margaux
6. Château Léoville-Las-Cases
7. Château Lafleur
8. Château Cheval Blanc
9. Château Laville Haut-Brion
10. Château Tertre Rôteboeuf

NEW UP-AND-COMING PRODUCERS

1. Château Barde-Haut, St-Emilion
2. Château Laforge, St-Emilion
3. Château Trianon, St-Emilion
4. Château Ste-Colombe, Côtes de Castillon
5. Château Laussac, Côtes de Castillon
6. Château Lezongars, 1er Côtes de Bordeaux
7. Santayne, St-Emilion

FASTEST-IMPROVING PRODUCERS

1. Château Lafite *Very good from 1982 to 1990, but has moved into another gear as of 1996.*
2. Château Ausone *Some of the greatest wines in Bordeaux since 1998; more sensual, yet just as well structured.*
3. Château Berliquet *A sea change since Patrick Valette's consultancy, from 1998 onward.*
4. Château Pontet-Canet *Outstanding wines since 1996.*
5. Château du Tertre *Since 1995, the real potential has at last been realized. The 2000 is spectacular.*
6. Château Duhart-Milon *A great leap forward since 1996.*
7. Château Dauzac *André Lurton's team has worked miracles here since 1996.*
8. Château Rouget *New ownership has transformed this fine Pomerol since 1995.*
9. Château Ferrière *This forgotten Margaux has blossomed since a change of ownership in 1992.*
10. Château Smith-Haut-Lafitte *Both red and white wines have made giant strides in the last decade.*

BEST-VALUE PRODUCERS

1. Château Berliquet, St-Emilion
2. Château Sociando-Mallet, Haut-Médoc
3. Château Pontet-Canet, Pauillac
4. Château Langoa-Barton, St-Julien
5. Château d'Angludet, Margaux
6. Château du Tertre, Margaux
7. Château Beauregard, Pomerol
8. Château Doisy-Daëne, Barsac
9. Château Roc de Cambes, Côtes de Bourg
10. Château La Tour de By, Médoc

GREATEST-QUALITY WINES

1. **Château Pétrus 1990** (€1,330)
2. **Château Lafite 1990** (€212)
3. **Château d'Yquem 1988** (€202)
4. **Château Sociando-Mallet 1989** (€43.50)
5. **Château Tertre Rôteboeuf 1990** (€90)
6. **Château Pichon-Longueville-Lalande 1985** (€103)
7. **Château Latour 1985** (€176)
8. **Château Léoville-Las-Cases 1988** (€60.50)
9. **Domaine de Chevalier Blanc 1988** (€58)
10. **Château Pichon-Longueville-Baron 1989** (€112)

BEST BARGAINS

❶ **Les Ailes de Berliquet 1998** (€18)
❷ **Lafleur de Quinault 1999** (€18.50)
❸ **Carruades de Lafite 1996** (€27)
❹ **Château d'Angludet 1998** (€19.50)
❺ **Château Sociando-Mallet 1996** (€29)
❻ **Pensées de Lafleur 1997** (€33.50)
❼ **Château Roc de Cambes 1997** (€17)
❽ **Château Batailley 1996** (€17.50)
❾ **Château Latour à Pomerol 1997** (€29)
❿ **Château Dauzac 2000** (€21)

MOST EXCITING OR UNUSUAL FINDS

❶ **Reignac Bordeaux Supérieur 1999** (€16.50)
After a decade of hard work, this modest Entre-Deux-Mers vineyard has produced an irresistible old-vine cuvée.

❷ **Trois Moulins Blanc 2001**
Château Lacaussade Saint Martin (€14.10) *One does not expect to find delicious, sumptuous white wines in the Premières Côtes de Blaye. This is 90 percent Sémillon, 10 percent Sauvignon, fermented in 400-liter new oak.*

❸ **Château Pillot 2000**
Côtes de Bourg (€5.50)
Bordeaux is not the easiest place to run an organic vineyard, and at present they are few and far between. This modestly priced sample seems to have everything you could reasonably wish for.

❹ **Château Brown Blanc 2000**
Pessac-Léognan (€17.50)
This well-placed, recently revived vineyard is now producing a white wine to rival some of the big names, but at a far more modest price.

❺ **Château Bonnet 2001**
Entre-Deux-Mers (€9)
My cast-iron standby for a quality, dry white wine when traveling in France!

❻ **Château des Tourtes 2002**
1er Côtes de Blaye (€4)
Another outstanding white from Blaye, but Sauvignon-based.

Burgundy

Clive Coates MW

The most important topic of conversation in Burgundian wine circles is, "What's the latest vintage like?", coupled with, "How are prices moving?"

CLIVE COATES MW

The good news is that 2002 promises to be one of the very best vintages in recent years, and that is for both red and white wines, the length and breadth of the region. Burgundy has been on a roll recently, the last really bad vintage being as long ago as 1984. After the excellent 1999 vintage, 2000 produced very good whites but rather soft reds, while 2001 was the reverse. The 2002 crop was small and has produced wines that are rich in alcohol and tannin, firm in acidity, and with concentrated fruit.

As well as a string of good vintages in the 1990s, burgundy drinkers have benefited from a remarkable degree of price stability. While First-Growth Bordeaux climbed almost 400 percent between 1990 and 2000, and fashionable lesser growths such as Ducru-Beaucaillou went up by more than 300 percent, top burgundy merely doubled over the same period. Good-value burgundy has enjoyed an even greater stability, with good Savigny such as Jean-Marc Pavelot's La Dominode rising by less than 25 percent in 12 years (75FF in 1990, €15.20/99FF in 2002). There has never been a better time to buy burgundy. While it would be rash to predict future prices, with overseas markets quiet and

CLIVE COATES MW is the author of *Côte d'Or* (Weidenfeld & Nicolson, 1997), which has won various awards, including Les Prix des Arts des Lettres from the Confrérie de Tastevin, "the first time that a book on wine and a non-Burgundian have been so honored for 30 years." He is also author–publisher of the award-winning fine-wine monthly magazine *The Vine* (for a free sample issue, write to: *The Vine*, 76 Woodstock Road, London W4 1EQ, UK, or fax 011 44 20 8995 8943). Clive's latest book, *An Encyclopaedia of the Wines and Domaines of France* (Cassell), was published in October 2000.

economic prospects uncertain, there is no reason to believe prices will be pushed too high.

Confusion sexuelle becomes more widespread

Small plastic capsules that excrete female grape-moth pheromones are becoming more and more widespread. This confuses the male *cochilis* and *eudemis* moths, which are then unable to find a female mate, preventing a second generation of moths and, more immediately important, the adolescent form of grape worm, or *vers de la grappe*, which wreaks havoc in vineyards by feeding on unopened flowers, flowers, and young berries. In Europe, the *cochilis* and *eudemis* are considered to be second only to phylloxera in terms of potential damage, but this form of biotechnological control can only be effective if whole *communes* agree on its implementation. Today, the whole of the southern part of the Côte de Nuits, from Bonnes Mares to Nuits-St-Georges Clos de la Maréchale, is covered, as are, in the Côte de Beaune, the white wine *communes* of Meursault, Puligny-Montrachet, Chassagne-Montrachet, and Beaune itself. Visitors to the vineyards will notice these little brown sachets, called Raks, on every fifth vine in every fifth row.

Grapevine

● **Domaine Tollot-Beaut** (Chorey-Lès-Beaune) has bought a further 1.7 hectares (ha) of Chorey-Lès-Beaune. The produce will be incorporated into their export village wine *cuvée* (considered by many to be their best-value burgundy). Additionally, it has just planted a further 2 ha of Bourgogne Blanc. This will give the domaine 40 casks instead of eight as of 2006.

● **Domaine Jean Tardy** of Vosne-Romanée has acquired some Échezeaux: six casks' worth, from very old vines (2002 is the first vintage).

● **Domaine Philippe Charlopin,** based in Gevrey-Chambertin, will be offering Gevrey-Chambertin Premier Cru Bel-Air as of the 2002 vintage.

● **From the 2002 vintage,** Nuits-St-Georges-based Domaine Lecheneaut will have a Morey-St-Denis *premier cru*: three casks of Clos des Ormes.

● **Ghislaine Barthod** now offers Chambolle-Musigny Les Combottes to add to her seven other *premiers crus*. The vines are 15 years old. Until now, the wine has been part of the village blend.

● **The esteemed Domaine Dujac** of Morey-St-Denis, hitherto one of few who still vinify even village wines without destemming, has changed its practices. On average, 40 percent of the fruit is now destemmed. Additionally, there is more *pigeage* during the pre-fermentation cold-soaking, less afterward.

MORE GROWERS BECOME MERCHANTS

There is an increasing trend of growers setting up as merchants, if only in a small way. Growers have the advantage of being on the spot, being able to see how a neighbor tends his vines, and being able to separate the competent from the incompetent. Currently, this trend seems more common in the Côte de Beaune and for white wines. Growers who are also merchants include: Marc Colin & Fils (St-Aubin); Michel Colin-Déléger, Bernard Morey, Jean-Marc Pillot (Chassagne-Montrachet); Étienne Sauzet (Puligny-Montrachet); Pierre Morey under the name of Morey-Blanc, François Mikulski, Jean-Michel Gaunoux, Jean-Philippe Fichet (Meursault); Henri Boillot of Domaine Jean Boillot (Volnay); Jean-Marc Boillot (Pommard); Carré-Courbin (Beaune); and Jean-Jacques Girard (Savigny-Lès-Beaune).

Red-wine grower–merchants include: Louis Boillot of Domaine Lucien Boillot & Fils (Gevrey-Chambertin); Frédéric Magnien of Domaine Michel Magnien (Morey-St-Denis); Michèle & Patrice Rion (Nuits-St-Georges); Alain Burguet (Gevrey-Chambertin); and François Parent (Pommard).

HORSES REPLACE TRACTORS

The search is intensifying for solutions to the increasingly compacted soil between the rows of vines. Since vines were first planted in rows and the shoots trained on wires, some 120 years ago, the soil has been compressed until it almost resembles concrete. This problem has been exacerbated since the advent of tractors in the mid-1950s and the later tendency to use herbicides, rather than plowing, to control weeds between the vines. Compaction has literally squeezed out the microflora and fauna that do so much to help translate the signature of the soil into the wine.

Today, however, all the top growers have returned to plowing, and a new breed of tractor is being developed that can expand its tires on arrival in the vineyard to lessen pressure on the land. Some estates, such as Domaines de la Romanée-Conti and Leroy, have returned to the use of horses. Sadly, the space between the vines being too narrow, these cannot be the carthorses of old, and the small, quasi-ponies that can access the vines rapidly get tired!

LEVELS OF NEW OAK HAVE PEAKED

In the mid-1990s there was a tendency in some Côte de Nuits estates, which were run by the new generation and were media-highlighted, to overdo their vinifications. Extractions were prolonged and the use of new oak high. Fears were expressed by numerous wine writers (including myself) that elegance and the capacity to age with dignity were being sacrificed in the pursuit of high scores, especially from American journals. In an effort to understand this phenomenon, to demonstrate it to others, and to solicit the wider opinions, I conducted extensive tastings, both privately and in public, of some of those wines I feared were vinified to excess. These included the wines of Vincent Girardin, Bernard Dugat-Py, and Denis Mortet in Gevrey-Chambertin, and Christophe Perrot-Minot in Morey-St-Denis. As this exercise progressed, I came to the conclusion that the wines from these four producers were at the very limit but not over it, and when put to the vote at public tastings, many preferred these modern wines to those made by more classic methods. Since 1999, there has been in most cases a deliberate relaxing of this tendency toward overdoing it. Denis Mortet now tells me, "I want to make wines like Charles Rousseau (Domaine Armand Rousseau)."

NEW *PREMIERS CRUS* CREATED

Seven vineyards in Pernand-Vergelesses have been promoted from basic village AOC to *premier cru*. Two of these are monopolies: Le Clos du Village (R Rapet & Fils) and Le Clos Berthier (Dubreuil-Fontaine). The remaining five have been regrouped under one name: Sous Frétille. The first-growth accolade applies to white wines only. Meanwhile, 10 ha of Ladoix, on the other side of the Corton hill, have been similarly upgraded. The *climats* are Les Gréchons (white wine only), Les Buis, En Naget, Le Bois Roussot, Les Hautes Mourottes, and Le Rognet.

ST-BRIS FINALLY GETS AOC STATUS

Retroactive to include the 2001 harvest, the VDQS of Sauvignon de St-Bris in the Yonne *département* has been elevated to *Appellation d'Origine Contrôlée*. This wine has been a VDQS since 1974 and covers an area of 895 ha in the *communes* of St-Bris, Chitry, Irancy, Quenne, and Vincelottes, although only 100 or so hectares are currently in production. With promotion comes a tightening up: maximum yield down from 60 to 58 hectoliters per hectare (hl/ha) (plus *Plafond Limité de Classement* or PLC), minimum alcohol up to 10 percent from 9.5 percent.

FIRST *PREMIERS CRUS* IN MARSANNAY?

Growers in Marsannay have begun to lobby the Institut National des Appellations d'Origine (INAO) to have their vineyards resurveyed with the object of promoting some to *premier cru*. The wines of this village were elevated from simple Bourgogne to AOC Marsannay in 1986.

AMERICANS BUY INTO BURGUNDY

The old established, and old-fashioned (in the best sense of the word), firm of Camille Giroud was sold in the spring of 2002 to a consortium of US investors led by Joe Wender and his wife Ann Colgin (of Napa cult-winery fame). The deal included the substantial stocks, the brand, and the winery, but not Giroud's own vineyards (just 1.5 ha). The small range of 2001 red wines was impressive in cask in December 2002.

LOUIS-MICHEL LIGER-BELAIR TAKES THE HELM AT LIGER-BELAIR

The 2002 vintage marks the first year when all the vines and winemaking of the Domaine Vicomte de Liger-Belair became the responsibility of the young Louis-Michel Liger-Belair. Previously, Régis Forey had looked after the land and fermented La Romanée and the Vosne-Romanée Aux Reignots, and Maison Bouchard Père & Fils had been responsible for the *élevage* and marketing. The marketing arrangement with Bouchard will continue for a couple of years, at least for part of the crop. So, caveat emptor: two versions of each wine could be marketed as of the 2002 vintage. Let us hope they resolve this anomaly soon.

NEW BROOM AT CHÂTEAU

Etienne de Montille of Volnay's Domaine Hubert de Montille became manager in January 2002 of the 21.5-ha Château de Puligny-Montrachet, which belongs to the Crédit Foncier de France, owners in Bordeaux *inter alia* of Château Beauregard (Pomerol) and Château Bastor-Lamontagne (Sauternes). The 2001 wines remain disappointing. We can expect to see this long-time underachiever pull its socks up in 2002.

GIRARDIN ACQUIRES HENRI CLERC AND RELOCATES TO MEURSAULT

Rising merchant Vincent Girardin, having outgrown his premises in Santenay, has moved to new premises in Meursault. At the same time, he has taken over on leasehold the 25-ha Domaine Henri Clerc. This will give Girardin three *grands crus* (Bienvenues, Bâtard, Chevalier-Montrachet; Échezeaux; and Clos de Vougeot) and six *premiers crus*.

GROWTH FOR JADOT IN BEAUJOLAIS

Five years after acquiring the Château des Jacques (Moulin-à-Vent) from the Thorin family, Maison Louis Jadot

Grapevine

- **Domaine Albert Morot** of Beaune has two additions to its portfolio, hitherto young vines not sold under the domaine name: Beaune Premier Cru Aigrots (both red and white).

- **Dominique Gallois** of Gevrey-Chambertin now offers Les Petits Cazetiers and Combe aux Moines separately. Previously these were vinified together and labeled simply *premier cru* without any indication of *climat*. Only Gallois and his cousin Philippe Naddef in Fixin offer wine from Les Petits Cazetiers, Gevrey-Chambertin's smallest *premier cru* (just 0.45 ha).

- **Domaine Jacques-Frédéric Mugnier** of Chambolle-Musigny will take back the lease (and monopoly) of Nuits-St-Georges Premier Cru Clos de la Maréchale from Maison Faiveley as of the 2004 vintage.

- **Domaine Arlaud Père & Fils**, recently located in Nuits-St-Georges, will move back to Morey-St-Denis in 2003.

has purchased the 35-ha Morgon Château de Bellevue from Prince Liévin. Bellevue's splendid vaulted cellar holds 350 casks, while the gardens are historically protected, containing a number of rare tree species.

HOSPICES DE BEAUNE: DECREASING RELEVANCE

Burgundy's once-pivotal auction is held on the third Sunday of November, and in 2002 it contained 691 pièces of wine, 111 of them white, from the latest harvest. Having increased in 2000, prices fell in 2001 and fell again at the latest auction. Prices were down by 8 percent, despite the generally acknowledged success of the 2002 vintage. Increasingly, these days, prices at the Hospices auction reflect neither the quality of the crop nor the current economic situation. Nor do they have much effect on prices current elsewhere in Burgundy.

USA: BURGUNDY IN THE DOLDRUMS

With California wineries awash with wine, and these wines being disposed of at any price dealers can get, Burgundian importers are finding it hard to get retailers to give space on their shelves for 2000s and 2001s. The problem is exacerbated by some American wine journals' reluctance to go and sample these vintages. They have been dismissed as poor without having been tasted. However, this erroneous judgment will eventually benefit US consumers as unsold lots are disposed of at bargain prices.

VIN DE MERDE

A small French magazine called Lyon Mag has been ordered to pay €350,000 worth of financial damages to Beaujolais producers for describing their wine as vin de merde. That translates as "shit wine" or "crap wine"—take your pick. However, this description was not the assessment of Lyon Mag per se, but a quote from François Mauss. The wine critic had been interviewed by a reporter from Lyon Mag about the revelation that 100,000 hectoliters of Beaujolais had to be distilled in 2001. Mauss blamed it on the craze for Beaujolais Nouveau, which is rushed to market barely two months after the harvest. He claimed that it was "not proper wine, but rather a sort of lightly fermented and alcoholic fruit juice," and that producers ignored all warning signs that consumers were no longer willing to buy such a product. Even though Lyon Mag balanced Mauss's unkindly comments with those of a Beaujolais representative defending the wine, 60-plus trade organizations were sufficiently incensed to sue the magazine. Interestingly, this was not for libel, but under a rarely used French law that protects products from being denigrated. If Beaujolais producers were worried about their reputation before the court case, it has been dealt an even more severe blow by the worldwide coverage of 'The Shit Wine Case,' the damages for which threaten to put the employee-owned Lyon Mag out of business.

Opinion:
Burgundy must yield to quality

The maximum permitted basic yield in Burgundy ranges from 35 hl/ha
for red wines in most of the *grand cru* vineyards to 60 hl/ha for
Bourgogne Blanc and Bourgogne Aligoté. On top of this is the
Plafond Limité de Classement (PLC), where growers can apply for an
excess (usually 20 percent). Effectively this means that yields can
range from 42 hl/ha to 72 hl/ha. This is too much. The Burgundian
grape varieties, especially the Pinot Noir, but also the Chardonnay, are
low-yielding. Diminishing returns rapidly set in with overproduction.
Above the basic yield (*rendement de base*), the wine rapidly becomes
weak in substance, without the sugar, the acidity, or the extract to
give them interest, let alone the potential to age gracefully in bottle.
There are some winemaking techniques—concentrating, bleeding,
chaptalization, acidification—that can be used to try to rectify
overproduction, but these will not result in anything better than
the mediocre. You cannot make a good wine out of a dilute must.
Moreover, if you have too large a crop, not only will it have difficulty
ripening properly, but the skins will be thin and prone to rot.

Practising restraint

With today's disease-resistant strains, every vine in the vineyard
fully productive, and increasing control over nature, growers need
to restrain the vine harder than ever to keep the harvest within
reasonable limits. The time to do this is at pruning time during the
winter, and from when the vine buds in April until just after the
flowering in June. The only point of green harvesting later is to
eliminate late-developing bunches, to ensure the whole crop is
evenly ripe, and to prevent clusters from being too close together,
which will encourage rot. Green harvesting in August and September
will not concentrate the eventual wine.

Critics of Burgundy in the past have thundered against practices
such as blending with south-of-France wine, overchaptalization,
overfining and filtering, overextraction, and the use of too much
new oak. Now it is time for the authorities to step in and force
growers to reduce the harvest. The maximum yields should be
changed to the following:

	Recommended hl/ha, inc. 20% PLC	Current hl/ha, inc. 20% PLC
GRAND CRU, RED	38	42
GRAND CRU, WHITE	42	48
PREMIER CRU, RED	42	48
PREMIER CRU, WHITE	45	54
VILLAGE WINE, RED	45	48
VILLAGE WINE, WHITE	48	54
CHABLIS, GRAND CRU	45	54
CHABLIS, PREMIER CRU	48	60
CHABLIS, VILLAGE WINE	54	60
POUILLY-FUISSÉ & SATELLITES	50	54
MACÔN BLANC VILLAGES	54	60
THE REST, AND THE GENERICS	Up to 72	No change

The name of good taste

All AOC wines have to be tasted and approved. This tasting "for the label" takes place early after the harvest. In Burgundy, this is normally before the wine has finished its malolactic fermentation. While quality does come into it, the most important issue at stake is a wine's typicity, plus its stability and fault-free condition as determined by chemical analysis. Moreover, the tasters are local oenologists, growers, merchants, and brokers, all or some of whom might have a vested interest. What expressly is not tasted, however, is the finished product. If the AOC is to be taken seriously, all wines should be subject to further tasting approval after bottling.

Furthermore, every bottling should be examined. Some wines, particularly those that are produced in larger volumes, have the same label but are bottled on a different date and can even come from different batches. Growers and merchants who fail this more meaningful AOC test too regularly should be fined as well as have their wines withdrawn from the market.

Vintage Report

Advance report on the latest harvest

2002

What already seems clear is that this is a very successful vintage in both red and white from the Mâconnais northward. In contrast to the rest of France to the south, it was a very dry summer indeed, though not conspicuously warm. Providentially, it was a small harvest. The early September weather was inauspicious, but from September 10 the skies cleared, the sun came out, and a north wind dried up and concentrated the fruit. It was even warm.

For Chablis, 2002 is the second great vintage after 2000. In the Côte de Beaune and the Côte Chalonnaise, growers are delighted with the whites. The reds were produced from small bunches of small berries with thick skins, concentrated juice, and high natural acidity: "the color of 1990, the acidity of 1996, and the sumptuous fruit of 1999," said one grower, "plus splendid intensity." Once again, as in 2000 and 2001, these red wines look like they will be at their best at the northern end of the Côte de Nuits. Save your pennies.

Updates on the previous five vintages

2001

Vintage rating: 75 (Red: 80, White: 70)

Unlike 1999, but similar to 2000, the health of the fruit of the average- to large-sized 2001 harvest gave cause for concern, making it vital to sort through and eliminate the unripe and rotten. The vintage is quite good, but variable, for whites. The quality at merchant level differs considerably between their own-domaine wines and those made from bought-in grapes and wines, while the best growers' wines are more than competent, yet lack real backbone, intensity, and definition. These are wines for the short term. They are better—or at least more consistent—in Meursault than Puligny-Montrachet and Chassagne-Montrachet; best of all in Corton-Charlemagne. The red wines are better than the whites, except in Volnay (due to hail). Quality gets progressively better as you journey north. The wines have fresh, pure fruit, balanced by good acidity, are medium- to medium-full bodied, and have soft, ripe tannins. The Pommards and Cortons are more civilized than usual. In the Côte de Nuits, the best wines come from Nuits-St-Georges and, especially, Gevrey-Chambertin. In between, in Vosne-Romanée particularly, some wines are a bit too soft. Drink the whites from 2005 for the better village examples, a year or two later for the *premiers crus*, a year or two later still for the *grands crus*. Drink village reds from 2005 (southern Côte de Beaune) to 2008 (Gevrey-Chambertin), with the same two-year and four-year delay for the better wines. Almost every British buyer was in the area in November 2002, when I was there sampling the red 2001s. Most had arrived just a little suspicious of the 2001s. Most left much more encouraged. The best of the Côte de Nuits reds should not be ignored. They are very representative of their origins.

2000

Vintage rating: *76 (Red: 70, White: 81)*

With the exception of a miserably cold July, 2000 was a warm and sunny year, and this led to an early, average- to large-sized harvest. Just as it began, the weather changed; and though it cleared up later, this had a material effect on the wines. The white grapes could be gathered relatively unscathed and in general are as good as—and in some cellars in Meursault, better than—1999. In contrast to 1999, quality here is better and more consistent than in Puligny or Chassagne. The better wines have depth and grip and will last well. Village wines will be ready from 2005/2006, *premiers crus* two years later, *grands crus* from 2009/2010.

The reds are soft, juicy, and for the most part very pleasant, especially to drink early—along the lines of the whites, above—but not serious. They get progressively better as one journeys north from Santenay, and are best of all in Gevrey-Chambertin.

1999

Vintage rating: *88 (Red: 90, White: 85)*

A heaven-sent vintage, not only fine quality in both colors, but huge in quantity. After a fine summer, the harvest was early and the fruit so healthy that in most cases no sorting was necessary. The red wines are fullish; show sumptuous, ripe, pure, concentrated fruit; and have ripe tannins and a very long complex finish—the vintage of the decade. The best will not begin to come around until 2008 or so. Indeed, the vintage as a whole will probably go into its shell in a while and not show very well for a few years. The whites are richer than the 2001s, but in some cases not as elegant. I find them best in Chassagne-Montrachet, and the most variable in Meursault. Both reds and whites of the Côte Chalonnaise are also fine, but it is 2000 that is the greater vintage in Chablis.

1998

Vintage rating: *78 (Red: 83, White: 73)*

This was a small and very good vintage for red wines, though some have somewhat dry tannins, and the wines are currently a bit adolescent. Gevrey-Chambertin is the most variable of the main villages. Drink the best from 2005 onward. Frost at Easter reduced the size of the crop, its depredation being most felt in the Meursault *premiers crus*. As a result, this is the most variable village for white wines. These, in any case, do not have the flair of the reds. The majority are now ready.

1997

Vintage rating: *74 (Red: 75, White: 73)*

An unusually hot September accelerated the progress toward maturity without giving the tannic elements time to form a firm base in the wines of this small vintage. The result is red wines with abundant ripe fruit, but in many cases lacking acidity and backbone. They are maturing fast; drink them soon. The northern Côte de Nuits (Gevrey-Chambertin, Marsannay) is the least consistent part of the Côte d'Or. The white wines are merely quite good, but better in Meursault than in 1998. They should also now be drunk. Wines from farther south may now be showing some age.

GREATEST WINE PRODUCERS

1. Domaine de la Romanée-Conti
2. Domaine Leroy
3. Domaine Comte Georges de Vogüé
4. Domaine Armand Rousseau
5. Les Héritiers du Comtes Lafon
6. Domaine Anne Gros
7. Domaine Jean Grivot
8. Maison Louis Jadot
9. Domaine Leflaive
10. Domaine Ramonet

FASTEST-IMPROVING PRODUCERS

1. Maison Nicolas Potel
2. Domaine Bertagna
3. Chanson Père & Fils
4. Domaine Prince Florent de Mérôde
5. Domaine Jean & Jean-Louis Trapet
6. Domaine Lucien Jacob
7. Domaine Gilles Remoriquet
8. Domaine Alain Michelot
9. Domaine Hervé & Cyprien Arlaud
10. Domaine Gilles Bouton

NEW UP-AND-COMING PRODUCERS

1. Domaine Bruno Lorenzon
2. Domaine Saint-Jacques
3. Domaine Arnaud Ente
4. Domaine David Duband
5. Domaine Michèle & Patrice Rion
6. Domaine de la Vougeraie
7. Domaine du Vicomte Liger-Belair
8. Domaine Vincent Dancer
9. Domaine François & Vincent Jouard
10. Domaine Martelet de Cherisey

BEST-VALUE PRODUCERS

1. Maison Louis Jadot
2. Domaine Saumaize-Michelin
3. Domaine Mathias
4. Domaine Bruno Lorenzon
5. Domaine Saint-Jacques
6. Domaine A & P Villaine
7. Domaine Lucien Muzard & Fils
8. Domaine Vincent Girardin
9. Domaine Jean-Marc Pavelot
10. Domaine Marc Colin & Fils

Note: Maison Louis Jadot for its Moulin à Vent, Château des Jacques, and Domaine Vincent Girardin for its Santenay Rouge and Santenay Blanc

GREATEST-QUALITY WINES

1. **La Tâche 1999** Domaine de la Romanée-Conti (€115)
2. **Richebourg 1999** Domaine Anne Gros (€110)
3. **Charmes-Chambertin 1999** Denis Bachelet (€50)
4. **Meursault Perrières 2000** Domaine Jean-François Coche-Dury (€45)
5. **Chevalier-Montrachet La Cabotte 2000** Maison Bouchard Père & Fils (€55)

1. **Chambertin 1990** Domaine Armand Rousseau (€110)
2. **Richebourg 1990** Domaine Jean Gros (€115)
3. **Clos de Vougeot 1985** Domaine Jean Gros (€80)
4. **Chassagne-Montrachet Grandes Ruchottes 1995** Domaine Ramonet (€60)
5. **Meursault Perrières 1995** Domaine des Comtes Lafon (€75)

Note: I have divided these wines into those for keeping (first five) and those for drinking (second five). The Chassagne-Montrachet Grandes Ruchottes is white.

BEST BARGAINS

1 **Mercurey Rouge Les Champs Martin Cuvée Caroline 1999**
Domaine Bruno Lorenzon (€16)

2 **Rully Blanc Clos Saint-Jacques 2001** Domaine Saint-Jacques (€10)

3 **Rully Blanc 1er Cru Les Pucelle 2000**
Domaine Jacquesson (€12)

4 **Savigny-Lès-Beaune La Dominode 1999**
Domaine Jean-Marc Pavelot (€15)

5 **Santenay Les Gravières Vieilles Vignes 1999**
Domaine Vincent Girardin (€13.50)

6 **Volnay Vendanges Sélectionnées 1998**
Domaine Michel Lafarge (€18)

7 **Bourgogne Rouge Les Bons Bâtons 1997** Domaine Michèle & Patrice Rion (€7.50)

8 **Mâcon-Prissé En Chailloux 2000** Domaine Thibert (€7.50)

9 **Chablis Grande Réserve du Domaine Vieilles Vignes 2000**
Domaine Pascal Bouchard (€10)

10 **Saint-Aubin Les Murgers des Dents de Chien 1999**
Domaine Hubert Lamy (€10)

MOST EXCITING OR UNUSUAL FINDS

1 **Bourgogne Blanc Cuvée Oligocène 2000**
Domaine Patrick Javillier (€8)
This is a generic wine from soil exactly the same as that found in Meursault, and it tastes like it, too.

2 **Bourgogne Blanc Côtes d'Auxerre 2000** Domaine Christine & Pascal Sorin (€6)
The Côtes d'Auxerre is a neatly made white from hitherto-forgotten wine country on the outskirts of Chablis.

3 **Bourgogne Chitry Blanc 2000**
Domaine Fontaine de la Vierge (€6)
As with the Côtes d'Auxerre, the Chitry is a notable white from the outskirts of Chablis.

4 **Bourgogne Pinot Noir 1999**
Domaine Michel Lafarge (€7.50)
Lafarge's Bourgogne Rouge is from vines just 33 ft (10 m) from AOC Volnay and rather better than the vast majority of Volnay village wines from other producers.

5 **Bourgogne Rouge 1999**
Domaine Ghislaine Barthod (€7.50) *This wine is from the wrong side of the road for the village appellation but is from soils similar to that of Chambolle-Musigny itself.*

6 **Bourgogne Rouge 1999**
Domaine Denis Mortet (€7.50)
Mortet's Bourgogne Rouge is from Daix, in the hinterland north of Dijon.

7 **Mâcon-Milly-Lamartine Clos du Four 2001** Comtes Lafon (€12) *This Mâcon-Lamartine Clos du Four is truly great Mâcon from the greatest white-wine domaine of the Côte d'Or. This the second vintage managed by Dominique Lafon from start to finish, and it is even better than the 2000.*

8 **Nuits-St-Georges Clos de L'Arlot Blanc 2000**
Domaine de l'Arlot (€32)
Clos de L'Arlot Blanc is a rare white wine from the Côte de Nuits: enjoy its individuality.

9 **Santenay Blanc Beaurepaire 2000** Domaine Vincent Girardin (€12) *This Santenay Blanc is also quite rare and good value, too.*

10 **Morey-St-Denis Blanc 1999**
Les Monts-Luisants (€30)
This Morey-Saint-Denis Blanc is largely from very old Aligoté and no malolactic. Unique!

Champagne

Tom Stevenson

Without doubt, the biggest news involving Champagne over the past 12 months has been the severe frost that has halved the potential crop in 2003.

TOM STEVENSON

In the worst climatic catastrophe since 1985, temperatures plummeted as low as 14°F (−10°C) for a three-day period in April, when the warmest temperature logged was 26.6°F (−3°C), but that accompanied an even more dangerous freezing fog. Chardonnay received the most damage, with an estimated 80 percent crop loss. Pinot Noir followed with a 50 percent loss, and Meunier, the widest-planted and most hardy variety, suffered between 30 and 40 percent loss. Unusually, the frost also hit high up the slopes, affecting many of the very best sites. All hopes are on the second buds, although many possess a very low number of embryo grapes, especially for Chardonnay, and it takes a very special year (such as 1989) to actually ripen a second harvest. Some growers on the Côtes des Blancs are predicting an average 2003 crop of about 5,500 kilograms per hectare (kg/ha). To put this into perspective, this is a district that easily averages 20,000 kg, with 30–40,000 kg not uncommon in a generous harvest, despite the fact that 13,000 kg is the absolute theoretical

TOM STEVENSON has specialized in champagne for almost 25 years. *Champagne* (Sotheby's Publications, 1986) was the first wine book to win four awards, and it quickly established Tom's credentials as a leading expert in this field. In 1998, his *Christie's World Encyclopedia of Champagne & Sparkling Wine* (Absolute Press) made history by being the only wine book ever to warrant a leader in any national newspaper (*The* [UK]*Guardian*), when it published a 17th-century document proving beyond doubt that the English used a second fermentation to convert still wine into sparkling at least six years before Dom Pérignon even set foot in the Abbey of Hautvillers. Tom's annual champagne masterclass for Christie's is always a sellout.

maximum, and even though 10,500 kg has been the officially declared yield in recent years.

Some villages, like Chouilly and Cuis, still looked like a desert one month later, while surrounding vineyards were sprouting with green color. The Petite Montagne, Ardre Valley, and Aube seem to be the least affected. Inexplicably, some vineyards that were not even touched by frost will also produce a relatively small harvest. In the Marne Valley, for example, the Meunier will probably yield a maximum of just 9,000 kg. As Benoît Marguet-Bonnerave of Champagnes Marguet-Bonnerave and Launois Père & Fils candidly admitted, "This is probably Nature's way of making us pay for overcropping the vines in 1999, 2000, and 2001."

Grapevine

• **Although grape prices** have been rising steadily over recent years, it is well known inside Champagne that Pierre Martin (see Double Whammy, below) single-handedly pushed up prices in 2002 by paying whatever it took to secure supplies over and above his own vineyards and contracted growers. Other buyers were miffed, but he did nothing wrong. Until, that is, he did not pay the growers. So everyone ended up paying above the market value except for the one guy who inflated the price.

• **Pierre Martin**, ex-chairman and CEO of La Financière Martin, which owned Champagnes Bricout and Delbeck, was charged with fraud, fraudulent bankruptcy, and breach of trust in April 2003. The group's financial director, Louis Fariello, and Epernay-based wine broker Luc Lhermitte were also charged. The charges surround the sale of Bricout and Delbeck's €185-million turnover from the sales of *vins sur lattes* (see *Sur Lattes* Transparency, at right). A well-placed source informed me that this involved speculation on a massive scale (6.2 million bottles, compared to the group's annual sales of less than 2 million). It seems that Philippe Baijot of Champagne Chanoine was the first to pull the rug from beneath Martin, even though he was someone he had long done business with. Martin allegedly telephoned Tony Rasselet at the cooperative Champagne H Blin to buy a large volume of champagne. Apparently, he would pay him at the end of the month, but could he have the bottles immediately? They have done business before, so no problem. Then he telephones Baijot and offers him a large volume of bottles at a price he could not refuse. The bottles would be with him by the end of the month, but to do the deal, could he have immediate payment? No problem. Martin pockets the money from Rasselet and Baijot nevers sees a bottle. When Opson-Schneider took over, it found the company had not been able to meet its payments for two months. On 24 April, Bricout and Delbeck filed for bankruptcy, with estimated liabilities of €100 million.

• **The European Commission** has given the go-ahead for Champagne Taittinger and its subsidiaries (including Bouvet-Ladubay, the Envergure and Concorde hotel groups, Baccarat crystal-ware, and Annick Goutal perfumes) to be jointly owned by Compagnie Nationale à Portefeuille, a financial holding company controlled by the Belgian baron Albert Frère and the Taittinger family, previously the sole owners. Albert Frère is also on the board of LVMH.

SUR LATTES TRANSPARENCY

The big frost might have been the most public story, but it was not the most important. By far the most significant event took place in March 2003, when the UMC (Union des Maisons de Champagne) unanimously agreed to ban all *sur lattes* transactions among *négociants* as from 1 January 2004. *Sur lattes* is an innocent name that has been coined for a far-from-innocent practice: the deceitful, but entirely legal, procedure by which a Champagne house purchases champagne made by another producer (house, grower, or cooperative), which is then disgorged and the Champagne house's own famous label slapped on. The stage of production at which most of these purchases are made is when the wine has been through its second fermentation but has not undergone *remuage*. It will be ageing on yeast lees and stacked horizontally (traditionally separated by lathes, hence *sur lattes*). So does this mean that at long last we can be sure what champagne we will be drinking, and if so, when will this be? Sadly the answers are no, and quite some time. The houses wanted an outright ban, but this was bitterly opposed by the cooperatives and growers. They did, however, agree to a certain transparency whereby any *sur lattes* champagnes must be identified on the label, albeit in small print, as 'Distribué par…' (rather than the 'Elaboré par…' in current use). So keep your eyes peeled for the tell-tale 'Distribué', which will tell you that the champagne in the bottle was not actually made by the name writ large on the label. As to when: well, it applies to wines as from the 2003 harvest, which as non-vintage could theoretically be on the market by April 2005, although realistically not likely before autumn 2006.

GETTING TOUGH IN THE VINEYARD

Of all those responsible for overcropping, the part-time growers who sell just grapes, not wine, are probably the worst offenders, yet even these might have seen the light. As part of its initiative to revalue AOCs throughout France, INAO (Institut National des Appellations d'Origine) has formed 'work committees' to visit the vineyards, to detect any aberrations. Essentially, but not exclusively, they will be looking for signs of over-production, and if found, they will tell the grower (depending on the time of year) to prune, green-harvest, or thin the bunches. Later in the year, the grower could have his entire crop declassified if he has not done as requested. In future years, such an offender might not be given the opportunity to rectify any over-cropping and could have his entire crop carted off for distillation for inadequate pruning.

CIVC SHOT MISSES FOOT

In March 2003, the CIVC (Comité Interprofessionnel du Vin de Champagne) pulled a series of advertisements slated for inclusion in major US newspapers, such as *The New York Times* and *The Washington Post*. The advertisements were supposed to put across the unique nature of the Champagne region and name, in support of EU negotiations to phase out the misleading use of semi-generic names (including Chablis, Sherry, Chianti, Cheddar, Stilton, and others) in the USA. With French opposition to the war against Saddam's regime in Iraq, the CIVC felt that there was too much anti-French feeling in the USA for the campaign to be effective. Indeed, it was thought that it could well backfire on them. This would have been the third time that the CIVC had shot itself in the foot in a bid to protect its name, having previously banned *méthode champenoise* globally (while Champagne houses produced and sold Champaña in South America), and looked a gift-horse in the mouth when the late Jack Davies of Schramsberg offered to convert from 'Champagne' to 'Champagne-style' in the USA.

THE POMMERY AFFAIR

Champagne Pommery was sold by LVMH to Vranken Monopole (since renamed Vranken Pommery) in June 2002 for a sum believed to be in the order of €150–180 million. The deal included some of the deepest cellars in Champagne, the wacky edifice above, and plenty of stocks, but just 20 out of 307 ha that LVMH acquired when it purchased Pommery in 1990. Some pundits believe that Pommery will now be repositioned at a lower price to facilitate the mass-market sales necessary to pay back Paul Vranken's debt. However, while it is true that he wants Pommery to sell more bottles, he does not want the brand to drop in price.

Although some *Champenois* resent this Belgian upstart owning one of their greatest institutions, the view from outside is quite clear: it is Vranken's greatest masterstroke. He bought Pommery at the bottom of the market, unlike Marne et Champagne, which notoriously purchased Lanson at the top of the market and has been struggling ever since. Although sales inevitably sunk after the millennium blip, they were about to rise, and Vranken saw this. Thus he knew that Pommery would soon be worth at least $50 million more than he paid, and indeed it is. Furthermore, Pommery sells at a significant premium compared to other Vranken brands, and this increased the group's profit margin overnight. The only smarter thing that Vranken could do now is to put Pommery's winemaker, Thierry Gasco, in overall charge of all Vranken winemaking operations.

ALL CHANGE

New winemakers over the past 12 months of so include Jean-Philippe Moulin, who took over from François Barot at Ruinart; Eric Lebel, who is now in charge at Krug following Henri Krug's retirement (although Henri will still be involved in the *assemblage,* as his father was following his retirement); Régis Camus, who assumed the mantle at C&P Heidsieck, following the untimely death of maestro blender Daniel Thibault; Jean-Baptiste Lecaillon, who followed Michel Pansu at Roederer; Thierry Garnier replaced Norbert Thiébert at Philipponnat; Monique Charpentier, who took over from Alan Parentheon at Mercier; and Georges Blanck succeeded Dominique Fourmon at Möet & Chandon. Patrick Laforest is due to take over from Gérard Liot at Bollinger.

Opinion:
Vintage nonsense

Disgorging to order is as traditional in Champagne today as bottling to order once was in Bordeaux. The *Bordelais* realized that the bottle variation this created was harming them and stopped the practice as long ago as the 1950s, but half a century later the *Champenois* still have no idea of the ramifications of their actions. Many critics are reluctant to describe a specific vintage champagne because when tasted it might be rich and toasty, yet, by the time their words are in print, a new shipment could have arrived and the recommended wine would now be fresh and crisp. Now perhaps readers realize why champagnes are rarely reviewed in *The Wine Advocate*. It is not because Robert Parker does not like champagne. Every year he publishes a list of 60-odd champagnes, all rated, many over 90 points, but with not a single word of description. I do not blame him. If the *Champenois* want the attention of Parker and others, they must ensure the wines these critics taste are the same as those their readers buy, and the only way to achieve that is to disgorge each vintage *cuvée* in one session.

Stagnated appellation

How long will it take the *Champenois* to realize that their single-wine AOC must go? It is ludicrous that this appellation does not distinguish, for example, between a *premier prix* with a fantasy name and Krug Clos du Mesnil. The dangers of clinging on to such an inappropriate appellation should have been blindingly obvious by 1999. That was the year that Bollinger launched its Charter of Ethics and Quality, which, in turn, prompted other producers to adopt myriad back labels guaranteeing quality criteria superior to those of the AOC itself. What better evidence that the criteria laid down by Appellations Champagne Contrôlee are inadequate than their own efforts to say so on the very bottles they sell?

Clamp down on sponge vineyards

There are several variations on the theme, but essentially these are vineyards that have been purchased in lower-classified areas, and ultimately go unpicked while the owners harvest double the official yield in their *grand* and *premier cru* vineyards. This illegal activity should be stopped.

Vintage Report

Advance report on the latest harvest

2002

I have seen miracle vintages before, but this takes the cake! It was a dry year, but with higher-than-normal rain in August. At first, this benefited the vines, but it poured down so hard in the last week of August that rot set in immediately and the grapes struggled to ripen. With September historically a wet month in Champagne, and the last four Septembers very wet indeed, growers feared the worst, expecting the harvest to be at least as bad as 2001; but the rain suddenly stopped and the vines basked in a dry period, especially in the last two weeks of the month. The grapes gained weight until September 5, and the rot disappeared one week later. Then something extremely rare for Champagne occurred: the crop started to shrivel and concentrate on the vine, reducing the yield by an amazing 30–40 percent. The last two weeks of September and the first week of October were unforgettably dry and sunny. This is doubtlessly a vintage year and a very special one too, though it will be a difficult year to rate because of its peculiarities. Tasting the *vins clairs*, it definitely seemed to be a Pinot Noir year, with Aÿ-Champagne the most successful village. There are some fine Chardonnays, but in general they are less impressively structured and lack acidity. Not that the Pinot Noirs are overblessed with acidity. Low acidity is a feature of this vintage. Not as low as 1999, but the lowest bar that in more than 25 years, and the pH is the third-highest in 16 years (after 1999 and 2000). The *passerillage*, however, has endowed these wines with the highest natural-alcohol level since 1990, and that was the highest since 1959. In structure, these wines fall somewhere between 1976 and 1989, leaning closer to the former in terms of concentration, but nearer to the latter's slightly better acidity. Then there is the *passerillage*. This will be the hallmark of the 2002 vintage, but precisely how it expresses itself is something we will not start to understand for at least another five years.

Updates on the previous five vintages

2001

Vintage rating: *35*

Dilute, insipid, and unripe. Anyone who declares this vintage needs their head examined.

2000

Vintage rating: *80*

Virtually vintage-quality ripeness, but more of a good non-vintage year, although there are a lot of *Champenois* who believe that 2000 is a magical number, so we can expect more declarations from this year than it really deserves. However, good, even great, champagne can be made in almost any year if the selection is strict enough, and with so many 2000s likely to be marketed, there should be plenty of good bottles to pick from. Some special wines, like Clos des Goisses, will be great.

1999

Vintage rating: *80*

Vintage-quality ripeness, but the worst acidity and pH levels Champagne has seen for a couple of decades. Some very good champagnes will no doubt be made through strict selection, but with fewer producers likely to declare, the number will probably be much lower than for 2000.

1998

Vintage rating: *85*

The 1998s and 1997s are not dissimilar to the 1993s and 1992s respectively, which means this vintage is in theory not quite as good as 1997; but although the 1993s were not supposed to be as good as the 1992s, they turned out to be better in the end. Indeed, some of the 1998s are already quite impressive, and a number of *Champenois* winemakers rate this vintage above the 1997s, so the underdog could triumph once again.

1997

Vintage rating: *85*

In theory, this vintage should have a definite edge over 1998, but it is not yet clear whether that is how it will pan out. However, there should be some very good champagnes produced in both vintages.

GREATEST WINE PRODUCERS

1. Krug
2. Pol Roger
3. Billecart-Salmon
4. Roederer
5. Bollinger
6. Deutz
7. Jacquesson
8. Gosset
9. Pierre Gimonnet
10. Vilmart

FASTEST-IMPROVING PRODUCERS

1. Mumm
2. Bollinger
3. Duval-Leroy
4. Bruno Paillard
5. Pannier
6. Mailly Grand Cru
7. Philipponnat
8. Vve Devaux
9. Moët & Chandon
10. Vilmart

NEW UP-AND-COMING PRODUCERS

1. Henri Giraud
2. Serge Mathieu
3. Fluteau
4. Bruno Paillard
5. Audoin de Dampierre

BEST-VALUE PRODUCERS

1. Charles Heidsieck
2. Serge Mathieu
3. Henri Mandois
4. Duval-Leroy
5. Alfred Gratien
6. Bruno Paillard
7. Lanson

8. Roederer
9. Drappier
10. Paul Déthune

GREATEST-QUALITY WINES

1. **Vieilles Vignes Françaises 1996** Bollinger (€295)
2. **Brut 1990** Krug (€150)
3. **Dom Pérignon Rosé 1992** Moët & Chandon (€310)
4. **Blanc de Blancs 1995** Salon (€160)
5. **Cuvée William Rosé 1996** Deutz (€130)
6. **Vintage Réserve 1996** Pol Roger (€44)
7. **Celebris 1995** Gosset (€68)
8. **Clos des Goisses 1991** Philipponnat (€90)
9. **Grand Sendrée 1996** Drappier (€27.50)
10. **Mis en Cave NV 1997** Charles Heidsieck (€25)

BEST BARGAINS

1. **Mis en Cave NV 1997** Charles Heidsieck (€25)
2. **Cuvée Victor Mandois 1996** Henri Mandois (€19)
3. **Brut Cazanova NV** Charles de Cazanove (€20)
4. **Club des Viticulteurs 1996** Goutorbe (€17.99)
5. **Princesse des Thunes NV** Paul Déthune (€22)
6. **Grand Sendrée 1996** Drappier (€27.50)
7. **La Cuvée Grand Siècle** Laurent Perrier (€70)
8. **Blanc de Blancs 1998** Duval-Leroy (€23)
9. **Brut 1996** Mailly Grand Cru (€25)
10. **Comtes de Champagne Blanc de Blancs 1995** Taittinger (€85)

MOST EXCITING OR UNUSUAL FINDS

1 Krug 1981 Collection (€320)
One of Krug's greatest-ever vintages, rereleased after more than 20 years.

2 Grand Cru, Fût de Chêne Brut 1993 Henri Giraud (€165)
Extremely rich, exquisite fruit. Not all overoaked, although the oak is indeed noticeable.

3 Dom Pérignon Rosé 1992 Moët & Chandon (€310)
Pure wild strawberries.

4 Mis en Cave NV 1997 Charles Heidsieck (€25)
The greatest-quality champagne sold at the best-value price, with an amazing consistency of style, including rich fruit and a touch of vanilla, although it never sees so much as a splinter of wood. All cuvées recommended, but the Mis en Cave 1997 is based on 60 percent 1996 and will cellar beautifully.

5 NV Cuvée aux 6 Cépages Moutard (€22.50)
Includes three other little-known Champagne varieties: Pinot Blanc and the ancient, obscure Arbane and Petit Meslier.

6 Verzy 1995 Nicolas Feuillatte (€30)
The best of Feuillatte's four mono-cru champagnes, the concept of which is the most innovative of any Champenois cooperative to date. The quality of all four wines is also of a considerably higher standard than Nicolas Feuillatte's norm.

7 Les Sarments d'Aÿ NV Moët & Chandon (€55)
The best of Moët's recently launched trilogy of single-vineyard champagnes, although the terroir concept is marred by the blending of more than one year.

8 Cuvée No 2 Trilogy 1996 Paul Déthune (€50)
The very best of three mystery cuvées sold together (€150). Your mission, should you be prepared to undertake it, is to decide the composition. Answers are provided on a scroll.

9 La Terre 1996 Mailly Grand Cru (€53)
All of this cooperative's 1996s are stunning, but this just beats Les Echansons, L'Intemporelle, and the standard brut vintage.

10 Blanc de Blancs Biodynamique 1998 Duval-Leroy (€26)
One of two blanc de blancs from this vintage that were vinified separately in barriques, both very good (see Best Bargains), neither the slightest bit oaky, but the biodynamic version is a tad racier.

Grapevine

• **In April 2002,** Henkell & Trocken purchased Gratien & Meyer and Alfred Gratien, thus one of Champagne's most traditional producers (fermentation in wood, hand riddling, corks used instead of crown-caps, and manual disgorgement) is now owned by a Sekt factory!

• **Champagne's chefs de cave** and oenologues are setting up a library of 30 growths of champagne. The idea is that every year base wines considered to be representative of these villages will be bottled with just enough sugar and yeast to create a slight *pétillance* and will be laid down for future reference.

• **The Piper and Charles Heidsieck** brands render about 3 percent profitability, which is far too low for shareholder satisfaction. Rumors are rife – yet again – that these Champagne houses are up for sale.

Alsace

Tom Stevenson

The hottest topic of debate is the increasing sweetness of Alsace wines, hitherto known for their dry style.

TOM STEVENSON

This situation has arisen because all the best producers, including many of the names most commonly encountered on export shelves, have dramatically cut their yields, particularly in the *grand cru* vineyards. Reduced yields produce higher must weights, and in sun-blessed Alsace this soon leads to a choice between overalcoholic wines or significant amounts of residual sugar. However, the *grands crus* are not so much sun-blessed as sun-traps, and lowering yields there has increased must weights to the point where, even at 15 per cent ABV, the wines have so much residual sugar that they are really quite sweet. Gewurztraminer and Tokay-Pinot Gris frequently contain residual sugar of 30–40 grams per litre (g/l), with 50 g/l or more not unusual. Zind-Humbrecht's Gewurztraminer 2001 Clos Windsbuhl, for example, weighs in at 35 g/l, while its Pinot Gris 2001 Heimbourg has 50 g/l and the Pinot Gris 2001 Clos Windsbuhl no less than 70 g/l, yet none of these wines is classified as a Vendange Tardive (VT). The pursuit of ever-richer late-harvest wines by lowering yields even further only exacerbates the problem, particularly as the best places to grow grapes for such wines are, of course, the *grands crus*. The sweetest style, Sélections de Grains Nobles (SGN), often has more sugar left after fermentation than some Sauternes have before fermentation! Furthermore, there are vast volumes of generic wine that are harvested with a potential alcohol of 11–12 per cent and chaptalized 1–2 per cent,

TOM STEVENSON specializes in Champagne, but he is equally passionate about Alsace. In 1987, he was elected a *confrère oenophile* of the Conférie St-Etienne, when he was the sole person to correctly identified a 50-year-old wine made from Sylvaner. In 1994, his 600-page tome *The Wines of Alsace* (Faber & Faber, 1993) won the Veuve Clicquot Book of the Year award in the USA.

yet end up with 10 grams of sugar per litre when Riesling, and considerably more for other varieties. In other words, they are sweetened by sugar, not the natural residual sweetness of the grapes. The producers of these wines are not only threatening the formerly dry-wine image of Alsace, but are abusing the spirit, if not the letter, of the law that allows chaptalization (*see* Opinion).

Fair play?

Between June and October (but mostly July and August), there are many traditional fêtes and fairs where you can cram in lots of tasting. These festivities celebrate particular grapes, specific styles, and new wines, mixed up with all sorts of local customs and cuisine. The big one is the regional Wine Fair in Colmar, a 10-day event during the week of 15 August (in 2003, for example, this was 10–19 August). Others you might like to coincide your visit with include the Winegrowers' Fair at Voegtlinshoffen (last weekend in June), the Wine Cellar Fair at Pfaffenheim (second weekend in July), the Pinot Noir Fair in Rodern (third weekend in July), the Grand Cru Wine Fair at Eguisheim (third Friday evening in July), the Gewurztraminer Fair at Bergheim (first weekend in August), the Art, Wine, Foie Gras, Folklore Fair at Epfig (first weekend in August), the Crazy Crémant Weekend at Cleebourg (first weekend in August), and the Klevener Wine Fair at Heiligenstein (second weekend in August).

Au Crocodile demoted

There are three Michelin three-star restaurants in Alsace, which is more than can be found in any other region of France with the singular exception of Paris. And three would seem to be its limit. Unless, of course, it was pure coincidence that Strasbourg's Au Crocodile got bumped down to two stars in 2002, the same year that L'Arnsbourg in Untermuhlthal received its third star. If it appears that the number of Michelin-starred restaurants has grown over the years, it has done so at a glacial rate. There is, no doubt, some notion that there should be only so many three-star restaurants, which is not such a bad idea if Michelin is to keep its elitist status. However, it must be hell for the likes of Au Crocodile's Emile Jung, who is still one of the best chefs in Alsace. As far as I am concerned, he definitely has not dropped his standards. In fact, his *Foie de Canard poêlé aux Pommes* is better than anything of a similar nature I have ever had in any three-star restaurant anywhere.

Opinion:
Understanding the *grands crus*

If the trade and media are to understand the *grands crus*, then CIVA (Conseil Interprofessionnel des Vins d'Alsace) must initiate the process. At annual tastings in major export markets, the *grand cru* wines are found, higgledy-piggledy, by this variety and that, on a producer-by-producer basis. The result is not so much confusion as pandemonium. The only way to discern the differences between *grands crus* is to focus on one grape variety at a time, and, since Riesling is the most sensitive to *terroir*, CIVA should start with that. Sugar masks the finer differences, so no SGN, no VT, and none of the sweeter *grands crus*. Just dry and off-dry styles, set up as a stand-alone tasting, *grand cru* by *grand cru*, with the wines within each *grand cru* lined up in order of residual sweetness, even though there should not be any that are actually sweet. The next year Muscat, followed by Tokay-Pinot Gris, and finally Gewurztraminer, then back to Riesling and so on. This should have started long ago, but better late than never.

Ban residual sugar in chaptalized wine

If a wine has to be chaptalized, it should be dry (residual sugar of less than 5 g/l would be a generous limit). This would not prevent anyone from selling wine with residual sweetness, but any such sweetness should be the natural product of the grapes harvested. Everyone I spoke to about this proposal told me it was both necessary and workable.

Dry cure

It should be obligatory to mention a dry-wine designation on all wines that contain less than 5 grams of sugar per litre. Wines with 5–10 g/l should also be obliged to use this designation if they contain a sufficient acidity to make them taste dry. However, it would be counterproductive to extend this concept to sweeter wines, whether through terms like *demi-sec*, numbered dry-sweetness scales, or the actual sugar and acidity reading on every bottle. This would only confuse the issue further, possibly 'banalizing' the great, naturally sweet wines of Alsace in the process. All the consumer needs is a simple solution to his/her dilemma: which Alsace wines are dry? The problem is not a complex one: consumers need to be confident that the wine purchased or ordered in a restaurant is going to be dry. With an obligatory dry-wine designation, the consumer would know that all wines not so designated will have some sweetness, after which VT will be truly sweet, while SGN will be intensely sweet.

Vintage Report

Advance report on the latest harvest

2002

Flowering went smoothly and swiftly, with a large, early harvest expected, but the vines suffered from alternating periods of very hot and damp weather during the summer, giving rise to fears of rot. Those who green-harvested in July avoided excessive problems, but those who left it until September to thin out excess bunches did too little, too late to do any good. Furthermore, those who harvested their main crop in the first two weeks of October and held back until November before picking their late-harvest wines beat the weather and should be rewarded with good quality. Riesling probably fared best. Some extraordinary SGN has been produced.

Updates on the previous five vintages

2001

Vintage rating: *89 (Red: 88, White: 90)*

Most growers rate 2000 over 2001, but size is not everything, and this vintage has the finesse and freshness of fruit that is missing from most of the 2000 bruisers. The hallmark of the 2001 vintage is a spontaneous malolactic that endowed so many of the wines with a special balance. You hardly notice the malolactic in the wines. It is just a creaminess on the finish, more textural than taste, and certainly nothing that can be picked up on the nose. Although I am an avid fan of non-malolactic Alsace wine, this particular phenomenon left the fruit crystal clear, with nice, crisp acidity.

2000

Vintage rating: *85 (Red: 90, White: 80)*

A generally overrated, oversized vintage, but with a few stunning nuggets. Lesser varieties, such as Sylvaner and Pinot Blanc, made delicious drinking in their first flush of life but have tired. The classic varieties lack finesse, although some exceptional VT was made. Excellent reds should have been made, but many were either overextracted or heavily oaked.

1999

Vintage rating: *80 (Red: 80, White: 80)*

Another easy-drinking vintage that has tired by now.

1998

Vintage rating: *84 (Red: 80, White: 88)*

My favourite vintage for current drinking, particularly for Riesling. Not great longevity, but a very good medium-term developer.

1997

Vintage rating: *87 (Red: 80, White: 95)*

Better than the foul-smelling 1996s and the delightful 1995s. However, this super-ripe vintage produced classic VT wines in such volume that many standard bottlings were of an equally sweet style. Those actually labelled VT are virtually SGN level, whereas the SGNs are simply stunning. Gewurztraminer and Tokay-Pinot Gris stand out.

Grapevine

• **When the authorities** finally made up their minds, deciding that Chardonnay should not be allowed in an AOC Alsace blend, Zind-Humbrecht was forced to sell the wine Z001 as *vin de table*. The funny thing is that the maximum permitted yield for *vin de table* is 90 hectolitres per hectare (hl/ha) as opposed to 100 hl/ha for the superior Alsace appellation, and chaptalization is banned. No wonder the French wine regime is in such a mess!

• **Rumours are rife** that Kuentz-Bas is up for sale, in name at least – there are conflicting reports about the stock, and the buildings are definitely not part of any proposed deal. Problems stem from a fallout between the two cousins, the French Christian Bas and German Jacques Weber. This culminated in Christian firing Jacques, who had been the winemaker for 20 years and owned one third of the firm's vineyards. Those vines are now being cultivated by Paul Zinck, and the Kuentz-Bas brand could go to a cooperative. Sad.

• **The 50th anniversary** of the Alsace Wine Route took place in March 2003, when 438 wine cellars opened their doors to welcome visitors.

• **According to Christophe Ehrhart,** the vineyard manager at JosMeyer, most Alsace producers will be biodynamic by 2005. In February 2003, he estimated that 70 per cent would be members of the Biodivin certifying organization, while 30 per cent would belong to the stricter Demeter. Biodivin is working on an extension of its principles to fully embrace the wine-making process, which could pave the way for 'organic wine' as opposed to the current situation where winemakers can only claim 'wine made from organically grown grapes'.

GREATEST WINE PRODUCERS

1. Domaine Zind-Humbrecht
2. Domaine Weinbach
3. Trimbach (Réserve and above)
4. Marcel Deiss
5. René Muré
6. Domaine André Kientzler
7. Domaine Ostertag
8. Hugel & Fils (Jubilée and above)
9. Léon Beyer (Réserve and above)
10. JosMeyer

FASTEST-IMPROVING PRODUCERS

1. JosMeyer
2. Jean Becker
3. Hugel & Fils
4. Domaine Ostertag
5. Domaine Lucien Albrecht
6. Domaine Paul Blanck

NEW UP-AND-COMING PRODUCER

1. J-P & J-F Becker
   (Jean Becker's organic range)

BEST-VALUE PRODUCERS

1. JosMeyer
2. Jean Becker
3. Domaine Lucien Albrecht
4. René Muré
5. Rolly Gassmann
6. Schoffit
7. Domaine Meyer-Fonné
8. Jean-Luc Mader
9. Domaine Paul Blanck
10. Hugel & Fils

GREATEST-QUALITY WINES

1. **Riesling 1997** Clos Ste-Hune (€130)
2. **Riesling Herrenweg 2001**
   Domaine Zind-Humbrecht (€23.60)
3. **Jubilée Riesling 1990**
   Hugel & Fils (€25)
4. **Riesling Cuvée Frédéric Emile 1999** Domaine Trimbach (€25.20)
5. **Muscat Goldert 2001**
   Domaine Zind-Humbrecht (€26.40)
6. **Riesling Brand 1998**
   Domaine Zind-Humbrecht (€47.10)
7. **Gewurztraminer Seigneurs de Ribeauvillé 1999**
   Domaine Trimbach (€19.30)
8. **Gewurztraminer Clos Windsbuhl 1997**
   Domaine Zind-Humbrecht (€48)
9. **Tokay-Pinot Gris Comtes d'Eguisheim 1985**
   Léon Beyer (€50)
10. **Riesling Grand Cru Pfingstberg Clos Schild 2001**
    Domaine Lucien Albrecht (€28)

BEST BARGAINS

1. **Riesling Gueberschwihr 2001**
   Domaine Zind-Humbrecht (€17.10)
2. **Riesling d'Epfig 2001**
   Domaine Ostertag (€12.10)
3. **Riesling Grand Cru Pfingstberg 2001**
   Domaine Lucien Albrecht (€12.50)
4. **Riesling Lerchenberg 2001**
   J-P & J-F Becker (€8.85)
5. **Riesling Grand Cru Kirchberg de Barr 2001** Domaine Stoeffler (€8.90)
6. **Tokay-Pinot Gris 2001**
   J-P & J-F Becker (€11.15)
7. **Tokay-Pinot Gris 2001**
   Hugel Tradition (€12.84)
8. **Pinot Auxerrois Vielles Vignes 2001**
   Domaine Paul Blanck (€10.21)
9. **Gewurztraminer Folastrie 2001** JosMeyer (€12.10)
10. **Riesling Grand Cru Vorbourg 2001** René Muré (€14.85)

MOST EXCITING OR UNUSUAL FINDS

1 **Riesling Brand 1998** Domaine Zind-Humbrecht (€47.10) *A wine of such elegance and purity of Riesling fruit that I defy anyone to guess its alcohol level under blind conditions (14.8 per cent!).*

2 **Zind Z001** Domaine Zind-Humbrecht (€16.09) *A luscious, effectively dry blend of 50 per cent Auxerrois, 35 per cent Chardonnay, and 15 per cent Pinot Blanc. Because this blend contains Chardonnay, it cannot claim AOC Alsace status and is thus sold as a vin de table, which does not allow a specific vintage on the label. However, it does not take a genius to figure out what Z001 stands for, or that the next NV will be numbered Z002, and so on.*

3 **Pinot Noir Burlenberg 2000** Marcel Deiss (€25) *The best red Alsace wine currently available from the most eccentric winemaker in the region, who has used a heavy Burgundian-style bottle, following special dispensation – at long last – for Pinot Noir.*

4 **Pinot Noir Réserve 2001** Domaine Weinbach (€13.50) *The second-best red Alsace wine currently available, and amazing value for a little Faller magic.*

5 **Riesling Heissenberg** Domaine Ostertag (€19.10) *This opulent, exotic, truly dry Riesling with its beautifully focused fruit proves that even this grape can be fermented successfully in barriques.*

6 **Riesling 2001** Hugel & Fils (€10.02) *This ripe, peachy Riesling with excellent acidity demonstrates a huge, relatively recent, improvement in Hugel's bottom-rung range.*

7 **Sylvaner Rouge 2001** JosMeyer (€8.50) *Lip-smacking fruit from a red-skinned Sylvaner variant.*

8 **Gewurztraminer Comtes d'Eguisheim 2000** Léon Beyer (€20.80) *Not my favourite vintage, but this demonstrates that power and elegance can be harmonious. Atypically off-dry for Beyer.*

9 **Riesling Vin de Glace 1985** Domaine Lucien Albrecht (€53) *A glimpse of the recent past come back to haunt me. I was dismissive of this wine in The Wines of Alsace, but it has a classic honey Riesling and reflects an era when wines were fermented as far as possible.*

10 **Riesling Rangen 1999** Domaine Zind-Humbrecht (€57) *I am not even sure that I like this wine, but its specifity of terroir is so overwhelming that I could not ignore it. The powerful, peaty, brulée character is so reminiscent of the hot, sun-baked, steep Rangen slope that you can almost taste its hard, unforgiving volcanic soil.*

Grapevine

• **Every September,** CIVA runs a two-day English-language course on the wines of Alsace – it is in French for the rest of the year. Contact Laurence Wipff at The School of Alsace Wines (phone +33 389 201620, email: civa@civa.fr) for more information.

• **A new book on Alsace,** *Les Grands Crus d'Alsace* (Editions Serpenoise, 2002), written by Serge Dubs in association with Denis Ritzenthaler, who writes for *L'Alsace*, is a must for French-speaking Alsace enthusiasts.

Loire Valley

Antoine Gerbelle

One weekend in June 2002, saboteurs broke into Rémy Pannier's premises in Chacé, near Saumur, and maliciously emptied the contents of 13 vats down the drain into the River Thouet.

ANTOINE GERBELLE

In excess of 300,000 liters of red, white, and rosé wine was lost, and it was assumed that this was the work of someone with a grudge against the company. However, the police investigation did not result in any arrests. "This is a hard blow for Rémy Pannier," said director Michel Boulaire. "Much of the wine we can re-source, but the domaine wines and those from Pouilly cannot be replaced." Boulaire has since left Rémy Pannier for the Val d'Orbieu, in the south of France, and the new director is Bernard Jacob. Rémy Pannier had been losing money since 2000, and in 2001 it was purchased together with its subsidiaries, Ackerman-Laurance and De Neuville, by Alliance Loire, which was formed by seven cooperatives of the Loire Valley (Saumur, Chinon, Bourgueil, Vouvray, Coteaux of Vendômois, and two in Nantes). This cooperative combo was created to offer the broadest possible range of Loire wines and to capitalize on the savings that could be made by centralizing the ordering, invoicing, and distribution of its seven cooperative partners. Alliance Loire was structured to distribute some 15 million bottles for a sales turnover of €35 million, but Rémy Pannier itself had a turnover of €47 million in 2001 on 30 million bottles in 30 different countries.

ANTOINE GERBELLE is a journalist and author of guides specializing in the wines of France, including *Wine Roads of France* and *Wine and Vineyards of Character and Charm in France*. He also contributes to the prestigious *La Revue du Vin de France* and is coauthor of the *Guide des Meilleurs Vins à Petits Prix*, the third edition of which will be published in September 2003.

Fizzical awakening

Blanc Foussy was taken over in 2002 by its minority shareholder, the German firm Underberg, which formerly held 40 percent of the stock against 60 percent held by Austrian sparkling-wine producer Schlumberger. Underberg wants Blanc Foussy to double its sales within the next three years by consolidating its position on the French market. Blanc Foussy produces 1 million bottles annually under the appellations of Touraine, Vouvray, and Crémant de Loire. The new owners have invested €150,000 in renovating the cellars of St-Roch in Rochecorbon, which boast 1.8 miles (3 km) of troglodyte galleries. They should be open to visitors by the summer of 2004.

Filliatreau moves into Chinon

Stéphane Filliatreau, the nephew of Paul Filliatreau, one of the most famous names of Saumur-Champigny, has purchased two vineyards totaling 15 hectares (ha) in Chinon: Moulin des Sablons and Clos La Ville au Maire. After 10 years in Chile, Filliatreau returned to the Loire in May 2000, moving into the Château du Petit-Thouars at St-Germain-sur-Vienne in Indre-et-Loire, which he manages and where he now makes wines under his own label.

Touraine-Azay-le-Rideau to double in size

The small appellation of Touraine-Azay-le-Rideau is due to grow by more than 50 percent in 2003. A mere score of growers produce white and rosé wines from a 60-ha patch of vines, but this will swell to almost 100 ha due to the purchase of the Domaine de l'Aulée by Chinon-based Jean-Pierre Crespin, who wishes to produce Touraine-Azay-le-Rideau on a 37-ha vineyard. Previously, this domaine, the largest property in Azay-le-Rideau, had not asserted its right to the appellation. Its former proprietors, the Lallier family, used to own Champagne Deutz and traditionally exported its entire production in the form of must to Germany, where it was blended into Sekt under the Geldermann label.

Since the death of Gaston Huet…

In April 2002, everyone knew that the succession within the Huet family would be difficult. The rumor at press time is that this prestigious 40-ha estate, with its impressive stock of old vintages, will be officially sold to Anthony Hwang. An American businessman of Filipino origin, Hwang is based in New York and already owns the Királyudvar winery in Hungary (managed by the legendary Tokaj winemaker István Szepsy). An arrangement has been made with Huet's son-in-law, Noël Pinguet, who has managed Domaine Huet for more than 20 years. Pinguet, who set up the biodynamic culture of Huet's vines in 1990, will remain in charge of the vineyard, applying the same quality objectives for at least the next eight years.

Vintage Report

Advance report on the latest harvest

2002

Sauvignons are quite ripe, the Muscadets of rare exception, and there are great dry Chenins. The Chenin is even better than in 1996, with excellent structure for aging. The reds, which are healthy, solid, and lively, are either equal to the 1996s or slightly lower in quality. Their limiting factor is, sometimes, reduced potential longevity, yet they are better than the average quality of reds produced farther south in France. With very little noble rot, sweet wines are uncommon, but some rare examples are better than the 1996s. However, some very good *demi-sec* wines were made.

Updates on the previous five vintages

2001

Vintage rating: 90 (Red: 90, White: 89)

The dry whites, Chenin and Sauvignon, are better than in 2000, but not as exceptional as the 2002s, and they should be drunk up. The Pinot Noir of Sancerre et al. are extremely average, as indeed are the Cabernet Franc, most of which should be consumed between 2003 and 2009. Generally, Bourgueil and Chinon will outlive Saumur-Champigny and St-Nicolas de Bourgueil. As for sweet wines with noble rot, this is the best year since 1997 in Anjou and Touraine. However, the greatest successes are in Coteaux du Layon and Quart de Chaume.

2000

Vintage rating: 87 (Red: 88, White: 85)

Both the Cabernet Franc and Pinot Noir reds are ready to drink, in a soft style with gentle blackberry fruit. They look like the 1997s, but with more freshness of fruit. The whites are more heterogeneous, with Savennières (for Chenin) and Sancerre (for Sauvignon) the greatest successes.

1999

Vintage rating: 76 (Red: 73, White: 79)

A poor-quality year, with reds and dry whites at best fruity, but more often diluted and precocious. Only a handful of growers succeeded in producing wines of exceptional standard. Even more difficult for sweet white wines.

1998

Vintage rating: 82 (Red: 82, White: 82)

A large harvest of average quality, due to a lack of sun at the end of the summer. Apart from rare exceptions, this year did not provide wines of any longevity in red or white, dry or sweet (which were spoiled by gray rot). The most successful wines were simple and best enjoyed young.

1997

Vintage rating: 91 (Red: 89, White: 92)

A very ripe vintage that produced both reds and whites of a rounded, warm, and inviting character. With little acid, however, the great majority should be drunk up by now. It was, though, a truly great year for the sweet wines, which reached an exceptional level of natural sugar and should age beautifully for 30 years or more.

Grapevine

• **François Chidaine,** a producer of excellent Montlouis, took over the vineyard and the winemaking of Clos Baudoin, the 12-ha Vouvray vineyard, in 2002. Prince Philippe Poniatowski, owner of this historic domaine, signed a compromise-of-sale agreement with his American importer, which leaves Chidaine free to exploit Clos Baudoin.

• The *négociants* Pierre Chainier (Amboise) and Donatien Bahuaud (Nantes) merged two years ago and have now been joined by Luneau Vineyards. Luneau contributes 160 ha of vineyards in Anjou-Saumur and Muscadet to the partnership, which now sells over 13 million bottles.

• **Jacky Blot,** owner of the Domaine de la Taille aux Loups in Montlouis and Vouvray, has bought a vineyard in Bourgueil. The first four wines from the 2002 vintage will be released under the name of Domaine de la Butte.

• **Following the bankruptcy** of the Caves St-Florent in Angers, with a liability of €11–12 million, and of Besnard & Co in Tours, some growers have lost more than €100,000 each.

GREATEST WINE PRODUCERS

1. Domaine Didier Dagueneau (Pouilly Fumé)
2. Domaine de la Coulée de Serrant (Savennières)
3. Domaine Huet (Vouvray)
4. Clos Rougeard (Saumur-Champigny)
5. Domaine Alphonse Mellot (Sancerre)
6. Domaine Yannick Amirault (Bourgueil & St-Nicolas de Bourgueil)
7. Domaine du Clos Naudin (Vouvray)
8. Domaine Philippe Alliet (Chinon)
9. Domaine de la Sansonnière (Anjou & Bonnezeaux)
10. Domaine des Baumard (Savennières & Coteaux du Layon)

FASTEST-IMPROVING PRODUCERS

1. Domaine des Roches Neuves (Saumur-Champigny)
2. Château Pierre Bise (Anjou)
3. Domaine François Chidaine (Montlouis)
4. Château de Villeneuve (Saumur-Champigny & Saumur)
5. Domaine de Bellivière (Jasnières & Coteaux du Loir)
6. Domaine Vincent Pinard (Sancerre)
7. Domaine de l'Ecu (Muscadet de Sèvre-et-Maine)
8. Domaine Henry Pellé (Menetou-Salon)
9. Domaine Pierre Soulez (Savennières)
10. Château du Hureau (Saumur-Champigny & Saumur)

NEW UP-AND-COMING PRODUCERS

1. Château Yvonne (Saumur-Champigny & Saumur)
2. Domaine du Collier (Saumur)
3. Domaine Richard Leroy (Anjou & Coteaux du Layon)
4. Domaine du Roy René (Anjou & Coteaux du Layon)
5. Domaine de la Butte (Bourgueil)
6. Laurent Chatenay (Montlouis)
7. Vignobles des Bois Vaudons (Touraine)
8. Domaine Robert et François Crochet (Sancerre)
9. Domaine des Chesnaies (Anjou & Coteaux du Layon)
10. Domaine St-Nicolas (Fiefs Vendéens)

BEST-VALUE PRODUCERS

1. Domaine Didier Dagueneau (Pouilly Fumé)
2. Domaine Alphonse Mellot (Sancerre)
3. Domaine de la Coulée de Serrant (Savennières)
4. Domaine Huet (Vouvray)
5. Domaine de la Sansonnière (Anjou & Bonnezeaux)
6. Clos Rougeard (Saumur-Champigny)
7. Domaine Philippe Alliet (Chinon)
8. Domaine Yannick Amirault (Bourgueil & St-Nicolas de Bourgueil)
9. Domaine du Clos Naudin (Vouvray)
10. Château de Fesle (Bonnezeaux)

GREATEST-QUALITY WINES

1. **Sancerre Rouge Génération XIX 2000** Domaine Alphonse Mellot (€33)
2. **Savennières Coulée de Serrant 2001** Domaine de la Coulée de Serrant (€40)
3. **Bourgueil La Petite Cave 2001** Domaine Yannick Amirault (€12.50)
4. **Chinon Vieilles Vignes 2001** Domaine Philippe Alliet (€11.50)
5. **Bonnezeaux Noble Sélection 2001** Domaine des Grandes Vignes (€25)

6 **Vouvray Sec le Mont 2001** Domaine Huet (€10.40)

7 **Coteaux du Layon Champ du Cygne 2001** Domaine des Sablonettes (€22)

8 **Chinon La Croix Boissée 2001** Domaine Bernard Baudry (€13.10)

9 **Saumur-Champigny Lisagathe 2001** Château du Hureau (€13)

10 **Saumur-Champigny Marginale 2001** Domaine des Roches Neuves (€16.80)

BEST BARGAINS

1 **Muscadet de Sèvre-et-Maine Expression d'Orthogneiss 2001** Domaine de l'Ecu (€5.20)

2 **Coteaux du Layon Terra Vitis Sélection 2001** Domaine des Grandes Vignes (€15)

3 **Touraine Rouge Ad Vitam 2002** Domaine Michaud (€4.50)

4 **Saumur Rouge, Clos de la Renière 2001** Domaine de la Renière (€5.20)

5 **Saumur Rouge 2001** Domaine de Château Gaillard (€4.90)

6 **Anjou Gamay 2002** Château de Putille (€3.40)

7 **Bourgueil Domaine 2002** Domaine des Ouches (€4.60)

8 **Montlouis Sec Les Lumens 2002** Domaine Levasseur Alex Mathur (€6)

9 **Chinon Prestige 2002** Domaine Charles Pain (€4.80)

10 **Touraine Sauvignon Cristal 2002** Paul Buisse (€4.50)

MOST EXCITING OR UNUSUAL FINDS

1 **Anjou Blanc Vignes Françaises 2001** Domaine de la Sansonnière (€80) *Ungrafted Chenin vinified without sulfur, this is the model of a rising generation of biodynamic producers.*

2 **Coteaux du Layon Sélection de Grains Nobles 1999** Domaine Delesvaux (€28) *This beautiful sweet wine proves what can be accomplished from a draconian selection in a very difficult year.*

3 **Anjou La Chapelle 2002** Vignobles Germain (€11.50) *From a Bonnezeaux vineyard of great finesse, this wine has been vinified for the first time in a dry style.*

4 **Touraine Sauvignon l'Arpent des Vaudons 2002** Vignobles des Bois Vaudons (€3.90) *Top Touraine Sauvignon from the younger generation, this wine sells at one-third the price of a basic Sancerre.*

5 **Vouvray Dilettante 2001** Domaine Breton (€11) *An idea of how Vouvray was 100 years ago, when it was bottled early and drunk in the spring: sweet, fresh, and a little cloudy.*

6 **Coteaux du Loir Rosé Verre d'Été 2002** Domaine Le Brisseau (€9.50) *An anti-rosé made in an anti-modern way, bottled without sulfur or filtration.*

7 **Muscadet de Sèvre-et-Maine Etiquette Blanche 2002** Château de la Bidière (€6) *A selection of old vines, late-harvested and vinified in barrel. The result is reminiscent of a dry Jurançon.*

8 **Fiefs Vendéens Rouge Le Poiré 2001** Domaine St-Nicolas (€20) *Made from Négrette, usually found much farther south.*

9 **PN 1328 2001** Ampelidae, Vin de Pays de la Vienne (€15) *Only the best Pinot Noir of Sancerre outshine this beautiful red wine from one of the region's most underrated vineyard areas.*

10 **Clos Roche Blanche 2001** Touraine Rouge Cot (€7) *Made from pure Cot, a vigorous and well-colored wine.*

Rhône Valley

Thierry Desseauve

The most ambitious new venture of the past few years is that of Les Vins de Vienne, a company created by three young wine growers from Condrieu: Pierre Gaillard, Yves Cuilleron, and François Villard.

THIERRY DESSEAUVE

Their mutual understanding, combined with a taste for risk-taking and a willingness to walk a financial tightrope, keeps bearing fruit. Without neglecting their own domaines, which are among the best in Côte Rôtie, Condrieu, and St-Joseph, they have created a trading company that now sells fine-quality wines from both the northern and southern Rhône, including particularly delicious examples from Visan and Châteauneuf-du-Pape. Yet the trio's fame really lies elsewhere: the resurrection of the long-neglected wines of Seyssuel.

Gaillard, Cuilleron, and Villard set about the titanic task of bringing back to life the most ancient vineyards of this village on the left bank of the Rhône. These are vineyards of antiquity that were mentioned by Pliny, but that have been in a state of complete dereliction since World War I and the phylloxera epidemic. They stand above the highway and Vienne on very steep and windy hillsides that are extremely difficult to work. The current wines took their names from the Gallo-Roman origins of their vineyards: Sotanum for the Syrah and Tabarnum for Viognier. There are now 11 hectares (ha) of vines but, after the stunning success of Sotanum 2000 and Tabarnum 2001, other producers might well follow

THIERRY DESSEAUVE is the publisher of *La Revue du Vin de France*, the most influential wine magazine in France and Belgium. He is coauthor with Michel Bettane of the annual *Classement des Vins de France*, the world's most respected buyer's guide to the best French wines. Thierry also writes on wine for the French newspaper *Le Figaro*.

their lead and bring more of this ancient *vignoble* back to life. Michel Chapoutier and Louis Chèze have already planted some parcels.

Guigal coup

Buying wine properties is rare in the northern Rhône, so it was a real master stroke when Marcel Guigal purchased the two other major domaines of the region. First Guigal acquired Domaine Jean-Louis Grippat, the quintessential producer of St-Joseph (most notably the Vignes de l'Hospice de Tournon) and owner of a very good parcel of white Hermitage. Then Guigal swooped on Domaine de Vallouit, which owns parcels of older vines in Côte Rôtie and Hermitage. The first consequence of these transactions is the creation of a super-premium St-Joseph, which will be called St-Joseph de St-Joseph and, of course, the addition to the range of a white Hermitage.

New St-Joseph for Jean-Louis Chave

After several years of meticulous and passionate work, Jean-Louis Chave, the most famous producer of Hermitage, has totally recreated a vineyard of St-Joseph on a wonderfully exposed, steep, south-facing slope. All the old terraces have been rebuilt traditionally, without cement, and the vines planted are from massale rather than clonal selection. The first vintage will be 2003, and you do not have to be a clairvoyant to realize that this new Chave creation will rapidly become a cult wine.

Back to Beaucastel

Having created WineandCo.com, the most important wine-selling website in France, Marc Perrin sold it to LVMH and Millésima in 2001, before it had made a single centime, and has now gone back to the family business, Vignobles Perrin, which owns Château de Beaucastel and Vieille Ferme.

Annus horribilis

Terrible storms caused dramatic flooding in the southern Rhône at the end of September 2002. Many vineyards and several cellars were completely flooded for several days, especially in the Vaucluse *département*.

Opinion:
Need for consultants

Too many producers in the Rhône Valley have only a vague notion of oenology; thus, they not only fail to extract the best quality inherent in the grapes they grow, but also make bad wines. There is too much systematic addition of tartaric acid in the south. Poor hygiene is widespread in some cellars, which harbor bacteria such as *Brettanomyces* with its animal aromas. Oxidation is frequently found, as are dry tannins due to uncontrolled elaborations. And where we should see seamless oak, we all too often find an exaggerated woodiness. These faults go unrecognized by the winemakers, who not only lack the technical knowledge, but also develop cellar-palates (an inability to recognize one's own faults). Consultant oenologists are well known in Bordeaux but not very common in the Rhône Valley, except for Jean-Luc Colombo. The Rhône needs more Jean-Lucs!

Cooperatives must divide!

The cooperatives dominate much of the production in the southern Rhône. Too often, they make stereotyped wines, blending the production of meticulous, well-situated winemakers with others of lower quality. They should isolate their best wines, since this would give consumers a better choice. It would also raise their reputations and increase their profit margins.

Vintage Report

Advance report on the latest harvest

2002

Dramatic rainfalls have destroyed a large part of the harvest, especially in the Vaucluse region. In the north, the first tastings show an average vintage only.

Updates on the previous five vintages

2001

Vintage rating: *86 (North: 88–92, South: 80–85)*

A solid vintage in the north. Some wines are too acid and coarse in structure, but the best are powerful and long. In the south, the level is mixed, with some problems of dilution and tartness.

2000

Vintage rating: *88 (North: 85–90, South: 85–90)*

Good but supple wines, with a lot of fruitiness in both parts of the valley. Most of the wines will not age very long.

1999

Vintage rating: *92 (North: 85–95, South: 90–99)*

The vintage in the south is less powerful than 1998, but the balance of many Châteauneuf-du-Papes is superb. The wines are soft-structured and will age wonderfully in under 10 years. This is also a great year in the north, particularly for Côte Rôtie, which enjoyed its best vintage since 1990.

1998

Vintage rating: *92 (North: 85–90, South: 95–99)*

An excellent and very powerful vintage in the south, above all at Châteauneuf-du-Pape. The wines must be kept in the cellar for years!

A good, rather than great, year in the north, with some Hermitage wines not as impressive in bottle as they were during the first tasting from barrel.

1997

Vintage rating: *81 (North: 85–90, South: 70–80)*

The vintage is even weaker in the south than it was in 1996, but it is very interesting in the north. Many wines in the north are too soft-structured, but the best are very fine and elegant.

GREATEST WINE PRODUCERS

1. Jean-Louis Chave (Hermitage)
2. E Guigal
   (best *cuvées* of Côte Rôtie, Condrieu, Hermitage & St-Joseph)
3. Château de Beaucastel (Châteauneuf-du-Pape)
4. Tardieu-Laurent (Vieilles Vignes cuvées)
5. Paul Jaboulet (Hermitage la Chapelle)
6. M Chapoutier (Hermitage)
7. Réserve des Célestins (Châteauneuf-du-Pape)
8. Clos des Papes (Châteauneuf-du-Pape)
9. Château Rayas (Châteauneuf-du-Pape)
10. Domaine du Vieux Télégraphe (Châteauneuf-du-Pape)

FASTEST-IMPROVING PRODUCERS

1. Domaine Georges Vernay (Condrieu & Côte Rôtie)
2. Domaine de la Janasse (Châteauneuf-du-Pape)
3. Domaine de Marcoux (Châteauneuf-du-Pape)
4. Delas Frères (all northern Rhône)

5. Domaine Pierre Gaillard (Côte Rôtie & St-Joseph)
6. Domaine Gangloff (Côte Rôtie)
7. Domaine Pierre Coursodon (St-Joseph)
8. Domaine Lafond-Roc Epine (Lirac)
9. Domaine de la Tourade (Gigondas)
10. Domaine Bernard et Yann Chave (Crozes-Hermitage)

BEST-VALUE PRODUCERS

1. Cave des Vignerons d'Estézargues (Côtes du Rhône)
2. Domaine de la Réméjeanne (Côtes du Rhône)
3. Domaine Marcel Richaud (Côtes du Rhône villages)
4. Mas de Libian (Côtes du Rhône)
5. Domaine Rouge Garance (Côtes du Rhône villages)
6. Les Domaines Bernard (Côtes du Rhône)
7. Domaine Graillot (Crozes-Hermitage)
8. Château de l'Amarine (Costières de Nîmes)
9. Château Mas Neuf (Costières de Nîmes)
10. Domaine Brusset (Côtes du Rhône & Côtes du Ventoux)

GREATEST-QUALITY WINES

❶ **Côte Rôtie La Mouline 1999**
E Guigal (€310)

❷ **Hermitage 1999**
Jean-Louis Chave (€140)

❸ **Hermitage Blanc 2000**
Jean-Louis Chave (€60)

❹ **Côte Rôtie Vieilles Vignes 1999** Tardieu-Laurent (€100)

❺ **Côte Rôtie La Landonne 1999**
E Guigal (€310)

❻ **Châteauneuf-du-Pape Blanc Roussanne Vieilles Vignes 2000** Château de Beaucastel (€60)

❼ **Châteauneuf-du-Pape Cuvée Vieilles Vignes 1999**
Domaine de la Janasse (€37.50)

❽ **Côtes du Rhône Rasteau 2000**
Domaine Gourt de Mautens
(€20.50)

❾ **Cornas Les Ruchets 2000**
Domaine Jean-Luc Colombo (€45)

❿ **Condrieu Les Terrasses de l'Empire 2001**
Domaine Georges Vernay (€24)

BEST BARGAINS

❶ **Château Mourgues du Grès Terre d'Argence 2001**
Costières de Nîmes (€7.50)

❷ **Côtes du Rhône Villages 2000**
Domaine Rouge Garance (€10)

❸ **Côtes du Rhône Rasteau 1998**
Chapoutier (€8)

❹ **Les Vignerons d'Estézargues Côtes du Rhône 2000**
Domaine Pierredon (€3.80)

❺ **Côtes du Rhône Tradition 2001** Domaine du Sablas (€7.50)

❻ **Cave de Lourmarin-Cadenet 2001** Domaine de Gerbaud,
Côtes du Lubéron (€7)

❼ **Costières de Nîmes Tradition 2001**
Château Mas Neuf (€6.50)

❽ **Côtes du Ventoux Boudale 2001** Domaine Brusset (€3.70)

❾ **Domaine de la Verrière 2000**
Côtes du Ventoux (€3.70)

❿ **Côtes du Rhône Cairanne Vieilles Vignes 2000**
Domaine des Amadieu (€5.90)

MOST EXCITING OR UNUSUAL FINDS

❶ **Côte Rôtie La Brocard 2000**
Domaine François Villard (€36.59)
In just a few years, the gifted modernist François Villard put this cuvée at the top of Côte Rôtie.

❷ **Fleur de Crussol 2001**
Domaine Alain Voge, St-Péray (€9)
This is an impressive version of the finesse that the white wines of St-Péray can achieve.

❸ **La Syrare d'Alain Gallety 2000** Domaine A Gallety,
Côtes du Vivarais (€11)
A superb Syrah from a forgotten district of the Ardèche.

❹ **Côte Rôtie La Serène Noire 2001** Domaine Gangloff (€38)
Voluptuous and charming.

❺ **Crozes-Hermitage Blanc Le Rouvre 2001** Yann Chave (€13.70)
Son of Bernard Chave, Yann is very talented, as this powerful, well-balanced white wine shows.

Jura & Savoie

Wink Lorch

Since 1997, the biggest event in the region has been the *Percée du Vin Jaune*, which is held over a weekend in February at a different village each year.

WINK LORCH

In 2003, it was the turn of the beautiful old village of Arlay in the Côtes du Jura, with the focal point being the grand Château d'Arlay, owned by the Comte de Laguiche. A record-breaking 50,000 visitors attended, and it was said that there were more journalists than there were *vignerons* exhibiting—and there were over 60 of them!

The most serious part of the weekend is the *clavelinage*. Named after the distinctive 62-cl *clavelin* bottle used for *vin jaune*, the *clavelinage* is a tasting competition to find the best *vins jaunes*. This year, for the first time, the tasting was run under official EU competition rules and supervised by a representative from INAO (Institut National des Appellations d'Origine). Around 60 *vins jaunes* were submitted, mostly 1995s and 1996s, but with some going back to 1989, and all four appellations (Château-Chalon, Arbois, Côtes du Jura, and Etoile) were represented. A maximum of one-third of the entries may become *claveliné*, and in fact just 17 were given the award, including two from Henri Maire, the largest *négociant* in the area.

The most public event was the ceremony of the *percée* itself, which involves the symbolic opening of a barrel of *vin jaune* that has just been released after its statutory six years and three months of aging. Thousands of eager supporters of this strange wine were prepared to stand in the cold, listening

WINK LORCH is a wine writer and educator with a passion for the mountains and a chalet in the Haut-Savoie. She is chairman of the Association of Wine Educators and has contributed to several books, including Time-Life's *The Wine Guide*, *The Global Wine Encyclopedia*, and Le Cordon Bleu's *Wine Essentials*. Wink particularly enjoys enthusing about wines from vineyards in sight of snow-capped mountains, whether the Andes, the Alps, or the Jura. She divides her time between the UK and the French Alps.

to endless speeches while waiting to be served the first taste of the "new" vintage, which in 2003 was the 1996. On both afternoons, the village of Arlay thronged with people out to taste and buy the whole range of Jura wines directly from the producers participating in the event. Make a date for next year's celebration in the village of Cramans, on February 7–8, 2004.

Top sommelier champions small producers

Stéphane Planche, head sommelier of the Michelin two-star restaurant Jean-Paul Jeunet in Arbois and a great supporter of fine Jura wines, has opened a shop, Les Jardins de St-Vincent, in the center of Arbois. He sells a selection of Jura wines from a generally eclectic bunch of smaller producers who do not have their own retail outlets in Arbois, as so many of the large producers do. This should introduce a new style of Jura wine to a wider public.

New-style Savagnin

Increasing numbers of Savagnin white wines are being made using the non-traditional methods of aging in topped-off vats or barrels. While this might be the norm everywhere else in the world, it most certainly has not been in the Jura, where such wines are usually stored in part-filled vessels. This deliberate oxidation is intended to start off the Savagnin as potential *vin jaune*. Certain producers in Arbois have adopted the nontraditional approach for Chardonnay over many years, but it is a new direction for Savagnin. Most of these new Savagnin wines are bottled in a fresh style with plenty of lees contact. The result is a fresh but intense, tangy wine, not typical of old-style Jura, but a worthy addition to the myriad existing styles, and, of course, it offers a much wider appeal. Philippe Chatillon at Domaine de la Pinte has gone one step further with his Cuvée S, vinified and aged in new oak.

Savoie can't get no satisfaction

With the best Savoie estates always moaning about a lack of wine to sell, and often bottling too early in order to satisfy demand, this is one region of France that would love the freedom of the New World to expand its vineyards. Just 20 hectares (ha) of new vineyard plantings are authorized each year (a 1 percent expansion of the total Savoie vineyard area), and in the past few years some of this allocation has been used to replant hillside vineyards previously abandoned due to the difficulty of working them. Notable are the new plantings higher up the south-facing slope of the Marestel *cru* above the village of Jongieux, in sight of the Rhône River. Here, several Jongieux producers have just finished a project to plant a further 8 ha with the traditional Altesse (Roussette de Savoie) variety. Other steep slopes have been replanted in the Combe de Savoie area between Chignin and Fréterive, mainly with Mondeuse and some with Bergeron (Roussanne).

ANCIENT VINE VARIETIES PRESERVED

An experimental vineyard has been established at St-Jean de la Porte, in the Combe de Savoie, by the Comité Interprofessionnel. Various clones of traditional Savoie varieties have been planted, both those in current use and others that have all but disappeared. The first harvest will be microvinified in 2004. Meanwhile, the first vintages of two revived grape varieties have been launched. One is from a white-wine variety known in Savoie as Malvoisie, but generally thought to be the Veltliner Rouge. The other is from an ancient red-wine variety, the Persan, which was widely planted pre-phylloxera. Although both are thought to have a good future, the Persan seems to have the greater potential. Indeed, the Persan is likely to be responsible for the Savoie's first premium-priced *vin de pays*. The 2003 vintage should see this eagerly awaited varietal's revival under the Vin de Pays d'Allobrogie appellation from 5 ha of recently planted vines on a formerly abandoned slope at Cevins, in the Tarentaise valley. Mastermind of the project is Michel Grisard, the biodynamic producer of Domaine Prieuré Saint-Christophe. He is amazed by the ripeness levels being achieved there even from very young vines. The main red plantings are of the virtually unknown old Persan variety, for which Grisard has high hopes, and there is a selection of white varieties that may be used to make a late-harvest wine.

Grapevine

• **A new standard half-bottle shape** is being designed for the various *vin de paille* AOCs of the Jura. At present, there is a wide variety of bottle shapes in use.

• **Château-Chalon** is still awaiting a response from the INAO regarding its application to gain *grand cru* status. The Château-Chalon AOC covers Château-Chalon and four other villages.

• **Compulsory tasting** under the auspices of the INAO will soon come into force in order for Château-Chalon to attain its AOC status. The wines will be tasted before bottling, but after the obligatory six years of cask-aging. The vintage concerned will be the 1997, which may be sold only from January 2004. Although the producers are in general agreement, this is bound to cause some controversy, especially if wines are rejected. Those rejected may not be sold as *vin jaune*, but only as a simple white Côtes du Jura.

• **Late harvest** has arrived in Chignin, where several producers have launched late-harvest Chignin Bergerons, notably from the 2000 vintage.

• **Wild boars** became a menace at Chignin in 2001 and 2002. They came down from the forested hillsides to cause damage and reduced crops in some of the best vineyards used for the production of Chignin Bergeron and Mondeuse. Agreement is being sought with local hunting groups to control the situation.

• **Raymond Quenard** in Chignin is going into semi-retirement and has passed on some of his vineyards to his son Pascal, who runs a separate estate (Pascal et Annick Quenard) with his wife. Raymond Quenard, who sells to many of the best restaurants in the area, has retained just 2 ha of vines.

Opinion:
Jura red or rosé?

The confusion between reds and rosés on producers' lists is a problem to consumers, and it is exacerbated by the Comité Interprofessionnel's summer 2002 advertising campaign for Rosé du Jura. It stated *Si bon qu'il en rougit* (meaning "so good it blushes," with a pun on the word *rouge*). They then launched a confusing winter campaign for *rubis* to promote lighter reds. While these campaigns were widely derided by producers, many continue to list wines from the Poulsard grape under rosés despite the fact that they are vinified as red wines. The terms *corail* or *rubis* are used by a few producers. The region needs to decide to market all these wines simply as reds, even if they are light-colored.

Jaundiced quality

There are still too many producers not taking *vin jaune* production seriously enough and selling substandard products to the supermarkets at a discount. A good producer will, in a typical year, reject around 70 percent of his barrels of potential *vin jaune*, using it for white wine instead. The temptation to put substandard barrels through the statutory six years of aging in order to market at the considerably higher price achieved by *vin jaune* is great. The introduction of the *clavelinage* competition gives an incentive for producers to aim for higher quality, but the local INAO and individual appellation *syndicats* must be vigilant to preserve the integrity of the region's most important product in terms of reputation.

Savoie sugar levels

Maximum residual-sugar levels in Savoie whites are not specified in the appellation laws, resulting in a wide variation of styles. This can be a problem for wines from both Jacquère and Altesse (Roussette) varieties, since consumers do not know if they are getting very dry, dry, off-dry, or even medium-dry wine. For Jacquère (used in the making of Apremont, Abymes, Chignin, and Jongieux among other *crus*), the style should be dry, with around 2–4 grams of residual sugar per liter to balance the high acidity. The rather fuller-flavored, but equally acidic, Altesse can cope with up to 6 or 7 grams of sugar per liter, but there are still some producers making sweeter wines. With a gradual reduction of yields in Savoie, resulting in a greater concentration of fruit, there should be even less need to use residual sugar for balance. Drier styles certainly match local foods better than sweeter ones.

Could do better

The general quality of wines handled mainly by local *négociants* is still too low, bringing down the image of the area. The tourist market (principally the winter-sports visitor) is all too easy to satisfy with thin, acidic wines to wash down a fondue or *tartiflette*. The worst quality is to be found from the largest and best-known *crus* of Apremont and Abymes. The Comité Interprofessionnel has taken steps to improve this by invoking the INAO initiative to systematically check on yields in the vineyards at the *véraison* stage, by taking the new AOC *agrément* laws seriously, and by practicing random sampling in local shops and restaurants. But this is none too soon. With the French wine consumer becoming more demanding, Savoie needs to be very careful if it is to maximize its potential. The *négociants* should listen carefully to the views of proprietors of the leading quality estates.

Urgent review of labelling required

For any development of Jura wine sales beyond the traditional local market, an urgent review of labeling laws is essential. At present, many white Jura wines are labeled with the simple AOC (Arbois, Côtes du Jura, or Etoile), with no mention of grape variety or, even more importantly, style. This is a big problem, because many wines are still made in the traditional oxidized, or partly oxidized, style—aged under *voile* (a layer of yeast similar to *flor* and essential for *vin jaune* production). Others are made in the more conventional, fresher, Burgundian way of topping off barrels or vats completely. Some producers name the former style *typé* or *tradition* and the latter *floral*, but there is no agreed standard term and the two styles of wine taste completely different. Some producers do not state the grape variety, either, and the wine may be Chardonnay, Savagnin, or a blend of the two. Current appellation laws permit the naming of a single variety, but not a blend. No term will please all producers, but a solution must be found to eliminate the current confusion.

Straw law could be the last straw

The rules on *vin de paille* production need reviewing to give growers more flexibility. At present, *vin de paille* is required to have a minimum of 14.5 percent alcohol, and three years in oak. This limits the styles of wines that can be produced, and is forcing some, like Stéphane Tissot of Domaine André et Mireille Tissot, to produce a similar style of wine, but with lower alcohol and higher sugar level, outside the auspices of the appellation. The regulations must be changed if the appellation is to survive.

Côtes du Jura lost within its own appellation

Although smaller than the Arbois AOC, the Côtes du Jura AOC is much more diverse and spread over a vastly larger geographic area. The region needs to consider applying to the INAO for a system of *crus* or named villages to highlight the *terroir* differences.

Late harvest overdue

A *vendange tardive* designation should be allowed for Chignin Bergeron, since this would encourage more growers to aim for lower yields and increase the value of their production.

Save the grapes

There should be more flexibility for producers who want to plant old traditional varieties such as Persan, Mondeuse Blanche, or Veltliner Rouge (known locally as Malvoisie). At present, these so-called minor varieties are only allowed to represent up to 10 percent of any single vineyard holding. These old varieties should be preserved and encouraged, to give added value and interest to the wines of Savoie. Of these varieties, there is wide agreement that the Mondeuse is the most important red-wine variety for Savoie, and in the right conditions it can produce high-quality, age-worthy wines. However, more study is needed into the best ways of cultivating, vinifying, and aging Mondeuse. Styles are many, and the best producers are doing a good job; but many young producers are scared of using expensive oak barrels, for example, because not enough research has been done into oak's compatibility with Mondeuse.

Grapevine

• **There has been** a change of management for the vineyards of Château de Monterminod, which are planted exclusively with Altesse. Following the premature death of Gilbert Bouvet, the future of G & G Bouvet, which used to run the château's vineyards, is in question. Management has therefore passed to Jean Perrier et Fils, which continues to bottle Château de Monterminod as individual-estate wines and will soon be launching the fine 2000 vintage.

• **A new Maison du Vin** will be built at Apremont in 2004. As well as being a center for the various local official wine bodies, it will also act as a regional wine center, welcoming groups for tastings and other events.

Vintage Report

Advance report on the latest harvest

2002

Jura—After a difficult summer, the north wind dried the grapes at the end of August, and a period of fine weather in September and early October gave overall good quality, if not great quantity. Nearly all varieties showed both good natural ripeness and high acidity levels. This bodes well for *vin jaune* in the future. However, a mild December meant that many *vin de paille* producers were struggling to get the requisite degrees. Those who waited until the cold snap in January should have achieved the right results. A promising vintage.

Savoie—Three weeks of fine, warm weather, accompanied by a cold north wind in late September and early October, saved the harvest after a relatively cool and wet August. It was considerably better for the later varieties, Jacquère and Mondeuse. Mondeuse shows particular promise from the Combe de Savoie. Altesse suffered from rot in places and is varied, though there was some concentration on the vine in the *cru* Marestel, and very good wines might have been made. Overall, a varied but fairly good vintage, with low to average quantities, but nowhere near as successful as in the Jura.

Updates on the previous five vintages

2001

Vintage rating: *67 (Jura: 69, Savoie: 64)*

Jura—A generally difficult, fairly small, and variable vintage. Growers decided to declassify all Château-Chalon before the pre-harvest inspection due to slightly low degrees of both sugar and acidity. However, soon after, the weather improved and there should be some decent *vin jaune*, though not under the Château-Chalon AOC. For the rest of the wine styles, there is much variation, with only those who made a severe selection making potentially elegant and balanced Chardonnays and Savagnins.

Savoie—A difficult year for many, with some mildew and intermittent hailstorms in places reducing quantities. It was cool at the start of September. Better producers who carried out careful selection at the vine have produced reasonable wines across the board, but generally a medium-quality vintage for all varieties and especially difficult for reds.

2000

Vintage rating: *79 (Jura: 78, Savoie:81)*

Jura—A rather cool summer gave, in the end, a good-quality vintage overall, with attractive fruit characteristics, reasonable structure, but some lack of concentration, often due to high yields. Enjoy these wines before the 1999s.

Savoie—A good year overall, with good yields, too. There was concentrated Bergeron and Altesse, but a lack of weight and structure in Mondeuse has resulted in quick-maturing reds.

1999

Vintage rating: *84 (Jura: 87, Savoie:78)*

Jura—An extremely sunny year gave the highest sugar levels ever seen in most varieties, great fruit concentration, and good yields, too. There were excellent overall results, especially for Chardonnay. It may lack the high acidity for the real long-term aging.

Savoie—There was some variation, but overall a good year with both Roussette and Mondeuse capable of aging well.

1998

Vintage rating: *77 (Jura: 79, Savoie: 75)*

Jura—Though this year was spoiled by rain in September, most producers were able to harvest a reasonable, healthy crop. Somewhat light, but well-balanced wines overall.

Savoie—Difficult spring and summer weather conditions gave relatively light, early-drinking wines, although it is an overall decent vintage.

1997

Vintage rating: *83 (Jura: 81, Savoie: 85)*

Jura—This was a year with good ripeness levels, but somewhat low acidity levels. The *vins jaunes* that will be released in 2004 should be of reasonable, rounded quality, perhaps maturing faster than some years.

Savoie—A sunny year that gave very good, rich wines. It was especially successful for Mondeuse, and good structure for Roussette de Savoie, the best of which are lasting well.

GREATEST WINE PRODUCERS

Jura
1. Domaine André et Mireille Tissot
2. Domaine Labet Père et Fils
3. Domaine Rolet Père et Fils
4. Domaine Berthet-Bondet
5. Domaine Jacques Puffeney
6. Domaine Jacques Tissot
7. Domaine Baud Père et Fils

Savoie
1. Domaine Prieuré Saint-Christophe
2. Domaine Louis Magnin
3. Domaine Dupasquier

FASTEST-IMPROVING PRODUCERS

Jura
1. Frédéric Lornet
2. Domaine de la Pinte

Savoie
1. Jean-Pierre & Jean-François Quenard
2. Jean-Pierre & Philippe Grisard
3. Pascal et Annick Quenard

NEW UP-AND-COMING PRODUCERS

Jura
1. Domaine de la Renardière
2. Domaine Ganevat
3. Domaine de la Tournelle
4. Domaine Ligier Père et Fils

Savoie
1. Domaine St-Germain

BEST-VALUE PRODUCERS

Jura
1. Domaine Rolet Père et Fils
2. Château Béthanie, Fruitière Vinicole d'Arbois
3. Daniel Dugois

Savoie
1. Domaine Dupasquier
2. Edmond Jacquin et Fils
3. André & Michel Quenard
4. Domaine de l'Idylle
5. Jean Perrier et Fils (Sélection Gilbert Perrier range)
6. Domaine de Rocailles
7. Eugène Carrel et Fils

GREATEST-QUALITY WINES

According to Jean Macle, vin jaune needs 10 years in bottle (16+ years from the vintage) before reaching perfection, so the Château-Chalons and vins jaunes selected do need time. The Chardonnays can be drunk from now. Tissot's Les Bruyères has more oak than the others. The Savoie wines can be approached now, but will also age well for several years.

Jura
1. **Château-Chalon 1995**
   Jean Macle (€27)
2. **Château-Chalon 1996**
   Domaine Berthet-Bondet (€28)
3. **Côtes du Jura Chardonnay Les Varrons 2000**
   Domaine Labet Père et Fils (€11)
4. **Arbois Chardonnay Les Bruyères 2000** Domaine André et Mireille Tissot (€12.20)
5. **Arbois Vin Jaune 1994**
   Domaine Jacques Puffeney (€27)
6. **Côtes du Jura Chardonnay Fleur de Marne, La Bardette 1998** Domaine Labet Père et Fils (€10.70)

Savoie
1. **Roussette de Savoie 2000**
   Domaine Prieuré Saint-Christophe (€13)
2. **Vin de Savoie Mondeuse d'Arbin Vieilles Vignes 2000**
   Domaine Louis Magnin (€10)

❸ **Vin de Savoie Chignin Bergeron Vielles Vignes 2001** Jean-Pierre & Jean-François Quenard (€8)

❹ **Vin de Savoie Mondeuse Tradition 2001** Domaine Prieuré Saint-Christophe (€13)

BEST BARGAINS

The Jura selections are enjoyable now. From Savoie, the Apremont, Abymes, and Cruet should be drunk early. The rest will repay some ageing.

Jura

❶ **Arbois Chardonnay 2000** Domaine Rolet Père et Fils (€7)

❷ **Arbois Chardonnay Vieilles Vignes 2000** Fruitière Vinicole d'Arbois (€7)

❸ **Crémant du Jura Brut Prestige** Grand Frères (€6.60)

Savoie

❶ **Roussette de Savoie Marestel 2000** Domaine Dupasquier (€6.80)

❷ **Roussette de Savoie 2001** Edmond Jacquin et Fils (€4.70)

❸ **Vin de Savoie Chignin Bergeron Les Terrasses 2001** André & Michel Quenard (€7.80)

❹ **Vin de Savoie Cruet Vieilles Vignes 2001** Domaine de l'Idylle (€4.50)

❺ **Mondeuse d'Arbin, Graine de Terroir, Selection Gilbert Perrier 2001** Jean Perrier et Fils (€6.60)

❻ **Vin de Savoie Apremont Prestiges de Rocaille 2002** Pierre Boniface (€5)

❼ **Vin de Savoie Abymes 2002** Château de la Violette (€3.40)

MOST EXCITING OR UNUSUAL FINDS

Jura

❶ **Spirale Passerillé sur Paille 1998** Domaine André et Mireille Tissot (€24 per half-bottle) *Technically a partially fermented must with just 8.5 percent alcohol, but 300 grams of residual sugar per litre. Made as a vin de paille from Savagnin, Chardonnay, and Poulsard grapes, dried unusually on real straw in wooden boxes, this wine does not have the level of alcohol required by the appellation laws for vin de paille.*

❷ **Arbois Naturé 1999** Frédéric Lornet (€8.50) *Savagnin from a very ripe year, aged on lees in large wooden foudres for 18 months, kept meticulously topped up. Naturé is the old Jura name for Savagnin.*

❸ **Arbois-Pupillin Vendange Oublié 2001** Domaine de la Renardière (€8.50) *This is two thirds Chardonnay, one third Savagnin, harvested late and partly vinified in barrel, with a little new oak and then aged with the barrels fully topped up.*

❹ **Arbois Trousseau Cuvée Grevillière 1999** Daniel Dugois (€8) *From a year with plenty of sunshine, this is one of the few traditional Jura reds tasted this year that shows true ripeness. A real pleasure to drink.*

❺ **Arbois Savagnin Naturé 2000** Domaine Jacques Tissot (€10.40) *Another Savagnin made in a fresh, non-oxidative style.*

❻ **Arbois Savagnin Cuvée S 1999** Domaine de la Pinte (€25) *Probably the only Jura Savagnin that has been vinified and matured in 100 percent new*

oak barrels, fully topped up.
Made as top-level white Burgundy
might be.

**❼ Côtes du Jura Pinot Noir
Cuvée Julien Ganevat 2001**
Domaine Ganevat (€8.50) *Jean-
François Ganevat demonstrates
with this wine that, even from
the difficult 2001, it is possible to
make an elegant, but structured,
Pinot with a Burgundian
character of the best sort.*

**❽ Arbois Savagnin Fleur de
Savagnin 2000** Domaine de la
Tournelle (€10) *Pascal Clairet does
not enjoy making traditional
oxidized Savagnin as much as this
fresh style, which has had almost
two years in barrel, topped up.*

Savoie
**❶ Vin de Savoie Le Bergeron
d'Elisa 2000** Jean-Pierre & Jean-
François Quenard (€16 per half-
bottle) *The Bergeron, alias
Roussane, can achieve great
ripeness on the slopes of Chignin
in good years. Here the grapes
have been left to ripen late to
give a vendange tardive style.*

❷ Vin de Savoie Persan 2001
Jean-Pierre et Philippe Grisard
(€7.50) *From the rare red-grape
variety Persan, the structure and
fruit of this wine, from very young
vines in a difficult vintage, shows
why there is such a buzz of
excitement about its revival.*

Southwest France

Paul Strang

The emergence of yet another *vin de pays* in the south of France may not be the stuff of headlines, but the story behind this one is unusual.

PAUL STRANG

Until 1998, the Ariège region south of Toulouse, which extends to Andorra and the Pyrenees, was the only *département* in the Midi not making wine on a commercial basis. Although pockets of vineyards, notably near Varilhès and Pamiers, had escaped the phylloxera epidemic, the 20th century saw the gradual disappearance of vines from the landscape. This occurred as people moved into the towns, leaving the more organized vineyards of Gaillac and Fronton to grab the share of the market formerly enjoyed by Ariège. In 1990, only two farmers in the whole *département* had more than 1 hectare (ha) of vines.

In 1982, Christian Gerber, a Swiss businessman, found himself heir to the Domaine de Ribonnet, a splendid property just over the border in the Haute-Garonne and previously the home of well-to-do *Toulousains*. Wine of sorts had been made there in the past, but Gerber started from scratch, planting a huge number of grape varieties experimentally. He soon became famous for his eccentric *vins de cépage*: Roussanne, Marsanne, Viognier, Riesling, Nebbiolo... you name it, Gerber grew it.

He inspired a couple of compatriots, Monsieur and Madame Zeller, to buy a property to the south, over the border in Ariège, called Château de Lastronque. Another part of the jigsaw was a local institution, the Centre

PAUL STRANG is recognized as one of the leading experts on the wines of southern France, where he has had a home for over 40 years. He is the author of *Wines of South-West France* (Kyle Cathie, 1994), which was shortlisted for the Drink Book of the Year by the Glenfiddich Awards. Another book, *Take 5000 Eggs* (Kyle Cathie, 1994), deals with the markets, fêtes, and fairs of southern France, and was also shortlisted for Glenfiddich in 1997.

d'Aide par Travail, one of a number of such organizations devoted to providing a meaningful working life for handicapped people. The center had 6 ha of land, which it was prepared to plant with vines, and a good site for a second *chais de vinification*. Along came a fourth interested party, a Monsieur Philippe Babin, prepared to plant a 6-ha vineyard a little to the south. The four formed a group, each member retaining their land and vines, but pooling the costs of running the vineyards, operating out of the two *chais*, and marketing their wines together through a separate company. The initial costs were partly met by subscription from 700 local enthusiasts and friends.

The first plantations, all on soil that is more or less a calcareous clay, were in 1998: Cabernet Sauvignon, Cabernet Franc, Merlot, Syrah, and Tannat. The early efforts were used to pay "dividends" to the subscribers, but now there is enough Vin de Pays d'Ariège to put on the open market. Each partner may sell their wine under their own label (that is, Domaine de Ribonnet, Château de Lastronque, L'Association Pour Adultes et Jeunes Handicapés, and Philippe Babin) or under the group brand (Les Vignerons Ariègeois). The wines are very promising.

Alain-Dominique Perrin

The owner of Château Lagrézette is certainly a powerful figure in the Cahors wine trade. His top wine is priced like a product of Cartier, a company of which he happens to be the managing director. After several years of boat-rocking in this troubled appellation, Perrin appears to have overstretched himself. At a recent local growers meeting, his plans to wield a new broom to sweep clean the whole Cahors vineyard were greeted with such catcalls and insults that he walked out. One can understand the frustrations that a dynamic businessman might feel in such a situation; but Perrin is not the sort of person to take a back seat for long.

Between Bordeaux and Buzet

The buzz vineyard of the southwest at the moment is Côtes du Marmandais. The stir, or most of it, has been caused by the rise of Elian da Ros (Clos Bacqueys, Chante Coucou). But the whole appellation, as headed by the two dynamic cooperatives of Cocumont and Beaupuy and the excellent wines of Domaine des Geais, has been making steady, if unspectacular, progress for years. The style of the wines is poised, like the geographical situation of the vineyard, between Bordeaux and Buzet, but with the added peculiarity of the grape variety Abouriou, which is found only rarely in other southwestern wines.

Opinion:
Closed-shop policy

There is a tendency in some appellations for certain members of the tasting committees, who determine whether a wine is to be given its 'label' (that is, the right to use the appellation name), to deny newcomers or smaller growers the proper expression of their *terroir*. This can be part of a policy (declared or not) to influence the image of an area in the direction of the kind of wines that the great and the good are themselves producing. For example, Patrice Lescarret of Domaine de Causse-Marines, one of the leading lights of the younger growers in Gaillac, finds his pure, dry Mauzac denied its *agrément*, despite the fact that it is regularly starred in all the French wine magazines and the *Guide Hachette*. It seems that some people in Gaillac are trying to draw growers away from the traditional Mauzac grape, historically the mainstay of white Gaillac, toward Sauvignon Blanc (for example), which the powerbrokers happen to grow a lot of themselves. This results in a betrayal of the authentic Gaillac style that Patrice is trying to cultivate.

Teamwork required

Most of the producers in the southwest are small. The largest vineyard in Jurançon, for example, is just 36 ha, and that is substantially larger than the second-biggest. Individual growers find it hard to make an impact on the market and to get their wines known. Furthermore, they cannot supply supermarkets and the like because they simply do not have enough wine to fulfill the demands of the big chains.

On the other hand, the great attraction of wines from the southwest is the highly individual typicity of each of the different areas. This has been safe only in the hands of the growers who are dedicated to their *terroir*—not *négociants* such as Primo Palatum, whose Cahors tastes much the same as its Madiran or, indeed, the cooperatives, however well made their wines might be. The artisan growers must therefore try to work together to promote their appellations, to make their individual wines known to the public, and not be wary of investing their own interests with those of other like-minded producers. Such cooperation is very hard for individualists like the Gascons, but they have to understand that it is in their own interest.

Vintage Report

Advance report on the latest harvest

2002

The winter was cold and dry, bitter at times, with temperatures plummeting to 5°F (–15°C); but the spring was warm and the buds broke early. The growing process was slowed down by a cool, cloudy, and dry early summer. The flowering was uneven, causing some *millerandage*. Except for a little fine weather toward the end of August, it was wet and cool—sometimes cold—up to the third week in September, when an Indian summer set in. This bright, sunny weather arrived somewhat earlier in Bergerac, Madiran, Jurançon, Tursan, and Irouléguy, so there were regional variations in the rate of ripening, as well as in harvesting conditions. Yields were generally much smaller than normal, sometimes 30 percent down (Gaillac, for example). Growers in the far west are confident of good quality, while farther east the vintage was more difficult; although in Cahors, where Malbec and Tannat ripen late, the grapes benefited from the late burst of fine weather, and the quality is probably the highest for this extremely diverse region. Indeed, some Cahors producers experienced unexpectedly high alcohol levels and unusually early malolactic fermentations. In Fronton, the Négrette is an early grape, thus the quality may be only fair. In Gaillac, it was mixed, the dry whites and reds being more difficult than the sweet whites.

Updates on the previous five vintages

2001

Vintage rating: *88*

This was an excellent year, with drought conditions for most of the summer and ideal picking conditions. However, low acidity and high alcohol were sometimes a problem, so the wines may not keep as long as the 2000s.

2000

Vintage rating: *85*

It was generally a very good year, especially for the sweet whites of Jurançon, Monbazillac, Saussignac, and Gaillac. Reds have good balance and promising tannins.

1999

Vintage rating: *78*

This was a mixed vintage, especially in those areas of the deep southwest that were caught by August hail. (There was no Château d'Aydie in Madiran, for example.) There were few sweet wines from the Bergerac appellations. Elsewhere it was a fair to middling year.

1998

Vintage rating: *90*

This was an excellent year everywhere, with both reds and whites extremely successful. However, with the exception of oak-aged Jurançons, most dry whites will be past their best.

1997

Vintage rating: *70*

This was a wet year with terrible harvest conditions, particularly in Gaillac and Cahors. The wines are generally light, with Madiran showing attractively over the short and medium term. The sweet wines bucked the trend, especially where picking was delayed until November or later.

Grapevine

• **The growers in Coteaux du Quercy** are having to show extraordinary patience. Having graduated from *vin de pays* status to VDQS, they anticipated rapid promotion to AOC, but there has been nothing but silence from the Institut National des Appellations d'Origine (INAO). Some say this is just the usual bureaucratic delay, while others think that the "mafia" in Cahors is trying to block AOC for the Quercy growers, whom they see as a threat. Cahors includes some very powerful names...

• **The progression of Côtes Saint-Mont** from VDQS to AOC has stalled because the local cooperative accounts for more than 98 percent of the production.

GREATEST WINE PRODUCERS

1. Châteaux Montus and Bouscassé (Madiran)
2. Château Lamartine (Cahors)
3. Château du Cèdre (Cahors)
4. Tour des Gendres (Bergerac)
5. Clos des Verdots (Bergerac)
6. Domaine Cauhapé (Jurançon)
7. Clos de Gamot (Cahors)
8. Clos Bacqueys (Côtes du Marmandais)
9. Domaine de Berthoumieu (Madiran)
10. Domaine des Très-Cantous (Gaillac)

FASTEST-IMPROVING PRODUCERS

1. Domaine de Causse-Marines (Gaillac)
2. Château Les Miaudoux (Saussignac)
3. Château Plaisance (Fronton)
4. Domaine Bordenave (Jurançon)
5. Domaine Arretxea (Irouléguy)
6. Domaine de la Bérengeraie (Cahors)
7. Domaine Rotier (Gaillac)
8. Domaine Nigri (Jurançon)
9. Château de Masburel (Montravel)
10. Domaine Laffont (Madiran)

BEST-VALUE PRODUCERS

1. Les Producteurs Plaimont (Côtes de St-Mont)
2. Château Plaisance (Fronton)
3. Clos de Coutale (Cahors)
4. Domaine Pichard (Madiran)
5. Château Les Ifs (Cahors)
6. Domaine de Labarthe (Gaillac)
7. Les Vignerons Réunis des Côtes de Buzet (Buzet)
8. Domaine de Larroque (Gaillac)
9. Château Le Roc (Fronton)
10. Domaines Lapeyre and Guilhemas (Béarn)

GREATEST-QUALITY WINES

1. **Château Montus 1995** Madiran (€32)
2. **Cuvée Madame 1997** Château Tirecul-la-Gravière, Monbazillac (€65)
3. **Jurançon Quintessence du Petit Manseng 1990** Domaine Cauhapé (€50)
4. **Vignes Centenaires 1985** Clos de Gamot, Cahors (€20)
5. **Chapelle Lenclos 1996** Madiran (€15)
6. **La Gloire de Mon Père 1998** Tour des Gendres, Bergerac (€28)
7. **Clos des Verdots 1998** Bergerac (€25)
8. **Château d'Aydie 1995** Madiran (€15)
9. **Cuvée Particulière 1998** Château Lamartine, Cahors (€30)
10. **Clos d'Yvigne 1997** Saussignac (€25)

BEST BARGAINS

1. **Lo Sang del Païs 2001** Domaine du Cros, Marcillac (€4)
2. **Château Plaisance 2001** Côtes du Frontonnais (€6)
3. **Mauzac Vieilles Vignes 2001** Château Vigné-Lourac, Gaillac (€5)
4. **Château de Palme 2001** Fronton (€5)
5. **Château Miaudoux Bergerac Sec 2001** Saussignac (€5)
6. **Château de Fitère Tradition 1998** Madiran (€6)
7. **Coteaux de Glanes Vin de Pays du Lot Rouge 2002** Glanes (€4)
8. **Domaine Meinjarre 2000** Madiran (€6)
9. **Château Latuc 2000** Cahors (€6)
10. **Château de Sabazan Rouge 1998** Côtes de St-Mont (€8)

MOST EXCITING OR UNUSUAL FINDS

1 **Vin de Lune 2000** Clos Triguedina, Vin de Pays du Comté Tolosan (€15) *The only sweet wine produced in Cahors, and surprisingly, it is made from 100 percent Chenin Blanc.*

2 **Domaine des Très-Cantous Mauzac Nature NV** Gaillac (€7) *A sparkler made by méthode gaillacoise rather than the Champagne method.*

3 **Cabirol Rouge 1995** Domaine de Ribonnet, Vin de Pays du Comté Tolosan (€6) *An unusual blend of Bordeaux and southwest grape varieties grown on the slopes of the Lèze valley, south of Toulouse.*

4 **Andéréna 2001** Cave de Saint-Etienne-de-Baigorry, Irouléguy Blanc (€6) *White Irouléguy is harder to come by than the red or pink versions.*

5 **Prunelar 2002** Domaine des Très-Cantous, Vin de Table (€6) *Made from 100 percent Prunelar, a near-obsolete Gaillac grape.*

6 **Vin de Pays du Lot Blanc 2001** Château du Cèdre, Cahors (€8) *This pure Viognier is another of the few white wines produced in the Cahors area.*

7 **Rosette Moelleux 2001** Clos Romain, Bergerac (€5) *A style of wine that used to prevail in southwest France, but has become the victim of the modern taste for dry whites.*

8 **Grain de Folie 1998** Domaine de Causse-Marines, Gaillac Liquoreux (€5) *Sweet wines used to be the specialty of Gaillac, but they were never as sweet as this luscious 100 percent Mauzac.*

9 **The New Black Wine of Clos Triguedina 2001** Cahors (€12) *In the bad old days, when the 'thin' wines of Bordeaux needed beefing up with the wines from the interior, Cahors supplied a wine that was cooked to increase its concentration and then fortified with extra alcohol. Jean-Luc Baldès here attempts to recreate this historic wine.*

10 **Muscadelle Moelleux 2001** La Borie Vieille, Gaillac (€5) *This property was the first to attempt a 100 percent Muscadelle wine in Gaillac. Others have now used the grape to produce a more sumptuous style, but here the freshness and acidity of a less sugary style is preserved.*

Grapevine

• **The appellation of Irouléguy** as a whole is threatened by the possibility that a large quarry will be excavated in the heart of the AOC area. The local winemakers are—understandably enough—up in arms about it; however, there are not many of them. On the other hand, there is plenty of political pressure in support of the quarry project, which would provide many jobs in an area that needs them. It would be sad, though, if this eccentric little appellation were to disappear after all the dedication and hard work that has gone into reestablishing it.

• **The hitherto all-too-rare white** Irouléguy seems to have caught on as a cult wine. Made primarily from Gros Manseng, with a little Petit Manseng and some Petit Courbet to provide extra vivacity, this wine emerges, not surprisingly, rather similar to a dry Jurançon, although less flowery and with more zing.

Languedoc-Roussillon

Paul Strang

On 8 and 9 September 2002, catastrophic floods and storms struck the vineyards of the Gard, with producers near Sommières and over towards the Rhône Valley being particularly badly hit.

PAUL STRANG

Up to 23 in (60 cm) of rain fell in 24 hours, which—for some places—was more than the total average annual fall. There was widespread destruction of vineyards, cellars, plants, and stocks. More than 30,000 hectares (ha) of vines were flooded, with 7,000–8,000 ha totally destroyed. When winter set in, pruning had to be carried out as normal, without knowing whether the vines would ever bud again. The older vines, whose roots penetrate deeper into the soil, have, of course, survived the best, but many new plantings and their rootstock have been wiped out. In terms of the vintage, between 600,000 and 800,000 hectoliters (hl) have been lost. As usual, it is the smaller growers who have suffered worst. How are they to finance replanting their vineyards when there is so little financial return from their last vintage? Reduced in quantity and quality, the light but quaffable wine will be hard to sell. What there is had to be heavily chaptalized (two extra degrees were authorized), because the growers could not leave the grapes on the vines until their full maturity for fear of rot and disease. The quality AOC growers had a terrible year; they are said to have lost more than €16 million in all.

The farther west one goes, the less the impact from this severe weather. One grower wrote, "2002 started pretty badly, with 6 in (150 mm) [of rain] at the end of August and another 6 in on September 9.

PAUL STRANG is recognized as one of the leading experts on the wines of the south of France, where he has had a home for many years. His most recent book is *Languedoc-Roussillon: The Wines & Winemakers* (Mitchell Beazley, 2002).

There followed nearly two weeks of damp and heavy weather, with rot developing almost every day. Fortunately, we grow very few grapes on each plant and so were able to control the damage, though not able to pick the Syrah and Grenache with as much concentration as usual, although the balance and the fruit are there."

The ill wind may still have blown some good. Perhaps some inferior sites will not be replanted at all, which will help reduce overproduction in future years. Perhaps the emphasis on quality rather than quantity will be further reinforced. But meanwhile, there is huge personal hardship among those least able to bear it. This disaster will leave scars for years to come.

Garage d'or

Although the trend toward the production of *vins de garage* looks likely to continue, this may not do Languedoc-Roussillon much good, since its reputation for producing good-quality wines at relatively inexpensive prices has been the key to its success in recent times. However, the *garagistes* seem determined to push prices ever higher. Hervé Bizeul, for example, the talented winemaker at Domaine de Clos des Fées, sells the tiny production of a *cuvée* called Le Petit Sibérie for €200 a bottle—a grotesque price, exceeding that of a first-growth Médoc. But such is the demand for novelty and fashion on the French market that he can sell the wine easily, and *en primeur* at that. It is pretty good, but then it ought to be.

Grapevine

• **Combative Jean-Louis Denois** may have sold Domaine de l'Aigle in Limoux, but he is still making very good wine in the area, including a champagne lookalike from Chardonnay and Pinot Noir. This is not a Limoux, Crémant, or Blanquette, since Denois's vineyard has no Mauzac, a variety still compulsory for both Limoux appellations. (Its compulsory presence in the Crémant has been reduced from 60 percent to just 10 percent.)

• **Gérard Depardieu** has succeeded where Robert Mondavi failed: he has bought and planted 5 ha in Aniane, where Mondavi was refused permission, and now plans to expand his interests. Let us hope he is better at husbandry than Jean de Florette! Meanwhile, Mondavi, in a huff, sold his other interests in the Languedoc to the Coopérative Aiméry Sieur d'Arques in Limoux, which is working with Baron Philippe de Rothschild (lovely Sauvignon).

• **Other investors** who have bought more than 1,000 ha of vines between them in the south include the Dourthe family from Bordeaux, Eric Prisette from Rol Valentin in St-Emilion, and François Mitjavile from Tertre-Rôteboeuf. Jean-Michel Cazes (from Lynch-Bages) has bought Domaine de Vipur in the Minervois.

• **Gérard Bertrand,** already owner of Domaine Laville-Bertrou in Minervois and Domaines Villemajou and Cigalus in Corbières, has bought Domaine de l'Hospitalet in La Clape, making him an increasingly important player in the Aude.

Opinion:
Carry on Carignan

The authorities should stop discriminating against traditional grape varieties such as Carignan and Cinsault, although they should encourage strict control over yields from these vines in all AOC areas.

Lac des Vignes

There is not enough quality control at so many cooperatives and, as a result, they are flooding the market with indifferent wine. They are holding back the image of Languedoc-Roussillon to the detriment of the independent growers and the quality-conscious *négociants*. That quality is the key to success is demonstrated by the good coops such as Embres-et-Castelmaure (Corbières), Sieur d'Arques (Limoux), La Livinière and Le Progrès (Minervois), and Roquebrun and Berlou (St-Chinian).

More variety required

The Viognier grape should be admitted into all Languedoc-Roussillon white-wine appellations. It sits well alongside Roussanne and Marsanne, which are not only allowed, but positively encouraged. Viognier is better suited to many of the southern *terroirs* than Chardonnay and Sauvignon, for example. Experimentation with grape varieties not yet seen in the south should also be encouraged, rather than the reverse, which is the present, heavy-handed policy. Alsace cannot claim a monopoly over the Riesling and Traminer grapes, even if it might like to, yet growers such as Denois have been refused the right to plant such varieties in Languedoc by INAO (Institut National des Appellations d'Origine), a position that would be difficult to uphold under European law. There are other growers itching to have a go with Nebbiolo and Sangiovese, but these are not permitted even in *vins de pays*. These sunny grape varieties might turn out to be more successful than either Cabernet Sauvignon or Merlot, which – except in atypical *terroirs* such as Aniane – are not always the success they are cracked up to be.

Vintage Report

Advance report on the latest harvest

2002

An exceptionally dry winter was followed by an early, warm spring. The early summer months were dry, too, but often cool and gray. There was some rain in the first two weeks of July, but it would not have been enough to reduce the risk of water stress had the summer been as hot and dry as it usually is. As it turned out, the latter half of July and a great deal of August continued to be cool, and there was some rain. In early September, the heavens opened for a short spell, just as picking had started in some areas (see lead story); but suddenly there was an Indian summer, and from September 20 it was very warm and dry, with none of the usual equinoxial storms. The fine weather came too late for those specializing in early-maturing grape varieties (Muscat, Merlot, and so on) or with vineyards in the hotter areas on the plain and by the sea. Crops were below normal practically everywhere, as were natural sugar levels. Overall quality will be generally disappointing, although good wines will have been made by the better growers on the higher ground. Wines on the whole will be ready for drinking young. Tannins are unusually soft, but there is good acidity. It is a year for the intelligent cellar master; the rest will find it hard to sell their crop, particularly since there are still wines unsold from the earlier, better years. In Languedoc they say there are no bad vintages, just some that are better than others: 2002 will test whether this really is true.

Updates on the previous five vintages

2001

Vintage rating: *90*

Exceptional throughout the region. A heat-wave summer produced very ripe fruit (perhaps too ripe in those cases where it has been at the expense of acidity), good sugar levels, and plenty of natural concentration. Reds and whites were equally successful, though the production of white table wine in the region is very much a minority business (5 percent of the total or thereabouts). The quantity was down on 2000. Everywhere east of Béziers needed a good year to offset the floods of 1999 and the disasters of 2002. The best vintage since 1998, and some wines will be better than that.

2000

Vintage rating: 86

A very good, abundant year. The weather was cool until the middle of July, thereafter very hot—sometimes too much for the Syrah, which is liable to stress if allowed to dry out. There was an unusually large discrepancy between harvesting times in the hot seaside vineyards and the cooler properties on the *coteaux*—up to a month for the same grape varieties. There was some disparity in sugar levels, too, and the quality was more variable than in 2001. Notable successes in this vintage are Banyuls, Collioure, Fitou, St-Chinian, Faugères, and Pic-St-Loup.

1999

Vintage rating: 80

There were some disasters through wet harvest times in the east. The Costières are weak and watery, with some growers declassifying altogether, and Pic-St-Loup had some trouble. However, farther west there were many successes. The Aude had a particularly good year, Corbières and Minervois often making wines as good as, sometimes better than, 1998. In a variable year, it is difficult to give an overall high rating, although many producers surpass the 80 score with ease.

1998

Vintage rating: 90

It is hard to find a disappointing wine from this vintage, which was excellent just about everywhere. Long drought conditions favored most varieties, but overall it was a year for the traditional Carignan, Cinsault, and Grenache, rather than the so-called *améliorateurs,* such as Syrah and Mourvèdre, which sometimes did not produce the phenolic levels hoped for. There were plenty of drying winds throughout the season and ideal harvesting conditions. The wines will generally be at their peak in 2004, but the best will keep longer, especially those raised in new wood.

1997

Vintage rating: 72

An underrated year, sandwiched between several good vintages before and after. The wines are admittedly lighter and softer than in most years, but there is room in every cellar for good wines of this weight and style, where finesse and elegance can triumph over brute force. The wines were always for early drinking and should not generally be kept longer, although there are always exceptions, of course.

Grapevine

• **A burgeoning new area** high up in the hinterland of the Agly valley in Roussillon is called Fenouillèdes. Gauby is making wine up there in partnership with English owners; the Verhaeghe brothers from Cahors have purchased Domaine Marcevol at Arboussols; Chapoutier bought 100 ha at Latour-de-France (but has sold his holding in Banyuls); and Marjorie Gallet, a professor of oenology from Côte Rôtie, has bought up some 100-year-old Carignan vineyards.

• **There is widespread** opposition from the vignerons of Nizas (just north of Pézenas) to a threatened large-scale expansion of a local quarry. It is claimed that dust from the increased quarrying would interfere with the photosynthesis of vine leaves. No doubt California's Clos du Val, which owns Château de Nizas, will be in touch with its lawyers.

• **When not made from Muscat,** Rivesaltes can be seen as on the decline because of lack of public demand. Many growers are switching from producing

red *vins doux naturels* from their Grenache grapes to making red table wines, most notably at Mas Amiel, where there have recently been replantings with Syrah. Meanwhile, the heady, red *vins doux naturels* of Banyuls continue to enjoy their recent revival, due no doubt to the small band of passionately enthusiastic growers.

• **New AOCs** are in the pipeline for white St-Chenin and Augers, which until now have sold as Coteaux du Languedoc. In St-Chenin, sub-appellations will soon be granted to the northern areas of Roquebrun and Berlou.

• **Chantal Comte,** the *chatelaine* at La Tuilerie, Costières de Nîmes, has declared war on the wine authorities of the Rhône Valley, which have stopped her from using the word "Rhône" on her labels. She says she pays them her dues and is being discriminated against. She is a big player in the Costières de Nîmes, so we can be sure there is a good argument brewing here.

GREATEST WINE PRODUCERS

1. Domaine Gauby (Roussillon)
2. Domaine Canet-Valette (St-Chinian)
3. Domaine Sarda-Malet (Roussillon)
4. Domaine Ferrer Ribière (Roussillon)
5. Coopérative d'Embres et Castelmaure (Corbières)
6. Domaine du Mas Blanc (Banyuls)
7. Domaine de Clovallon (Coteaux du Languedoc)
8. Mas Champart (St-Chinian)
9. Château Puech-Haut (Coteaux du Languedoc)
10. Domaine G Moulinier (St-Chinian)

FASTEST-IMPROVING PRODUCERS

1. Mas de Périé (Coteaux du Languedoc)
2. Luc Lapeyre (Minervois)
3. Domaine du Clos des Fées (Roussillon)
4. Domaine Perdiguier (Coteaux du Languedoc)
5. Domaine St-Antonin (Faugères)
6. Domaine Borie la Vitarèle (St-Chinian)
7. Domaine Fontcaude (Coteaux du Languedoc)
8. Château Mansenoble (Corbières)
9. Château de Beaufort (Minervois)
10. Domaine du Grand Crès (Corbières)

NEW UP-AND-COMING PRODUCERS

1. Roc d'Anglade (Coteaux du Languedoc)
2. Clos de l'Anhel (Corbières)
3. Domaine de la Prose (Coteaux du Languedoc)
4. Domaine du Tabatau (St-Chinian)
5. Château des Auzines (Corbières)
6. Domaine Rimbert (St-Chinian)
7. Domaine d'Escourrou (Corbières)
8. Château la Voulte-Gasparets (Corbières)
9. Mas des Brousses (Coteaux du Languedoc)
10. Domaine Le Fort (Côtes de Malepère)

BEST-VALUE PRODUCERS

1. Château de la Liquière (Faugères)
2. Domaine la Tour Boisée (Minervois)
3. Château de Gourgazaud (Minervois)
4. Mas des Chimères (Coteaux du Languedoc)
5. Domaine Jean-Michel Alquier (Faugères)
6. Château de l'Euzière (Coteaux du Languedoc)
7. Château Pech-Redon (La Clape)
8. Domaine du Vieux Relais (Costières de Nîmes)
9. Domaine de l'Arjolle (Coteaux du Languedoc)
10. Coopérative Aimery Sieur d'Arques (Limoux)

GREATEST-QUALITY WINES

1. **Grand Vin Rouge 1988** Mas de Daumas Gassac (€30)
2. **Muntada 1999** Domaine Gauby (€30)
3. **Le Clôt de Taillelangue 1999** Le Casot des Mailloles (€20)
4. **La Grange des Pères Rouge 1998** (€30)
5. **Le Prieuré de St-Jean de Bébian Rouge 1998** (€28)
6. **Clos des Cistes 1995** Domaine Peyre Rose (€42)
7. **Terroir Mailloles Blanc 2001** Domaine Sarda-Malet (€20)
8. **Capitelle de Centeilles 2000** Clos des Centeilles (€20)
9. **Cuvée Nicolas 2000** Domaine de Barroubio, Muscat de St-Jean de Minervois (€32 per 50 cl)
10. **Léon Barral Rouge 2000** Domaine Léon Barral (€10)

BEST BARGAINS

❶ **Roque-Sestières Vieilles Vignes Blanc 2001** Corbières (€5)

❷ **Domaine de Limbardié Rouge Classique 2001** Coteaux de Murviel (€6)

❸ **Domaine du Météore Rouge Tradition 2001** Faugères (€5)

❹ **Château L'Etang des Colombes Rouge Tradition 2001** Corbières (€6)

❺ **Château Pech-Céleyran Blanc Classique 2001** Coteaux du Languedoc (€6)

❻ **Château Creissan Rouge Tradition 1998** St-Chinian (€6)

❼ **Domaine de Causserels Rouge Tradition 2000** Minervois (€5)

❽ **Château Viranel Rouge Tradition 2000** St-Chinian (€6)

❾ **Château Coupe-Roses Les Plots 2001** Minervois (€6)

❿ **Domaine de la Coste Merlette 2000** Coteaux du Languedoc (€7)

MOST EXCITING OR UNUSUAL FINDS

❶ **Lledoner Pelut 1998** Domaine de la Colombette, Coteaux du Libron (€11) *Perhaps the only example of a 100 percent varietal from this minority grape.*

❷ **Le Soula Blanc 2001** Domaine Gauby, Coteaux des Fenouillèdes (€12) *A blend of Marsanne, Roussanne, Grenache Blanc, Chenin Blanc, and Rolle, grown 1,600 ft (487 m) up in the hinterland of the Roussillon, at the head of the Agly valley. At this altitude, the result is an exciting freshness and vivacity that is rare in a southern French white wine.*

❸ **Terret Bourret 2001** Domaine Fontedicto, Côtes de Thongue (€8) *Rare white varietal of excellent quality from an ultra-bio producer in the volcanic hills near Caux.*

❹ **Grenache Vendanges Tardives 2000** Domaine Henry, St-Georges d'Orques (€15) *An unusual, unfortified, sweet red wine to be drunk either as an aperitif, with desserts, or possibly, blue cheese. This is a traditional style that has nearly disappeared.*

❺ **Passidore 1998** Domaine Belles, Pierres, Coteaux de Murviel (€15) *Another pure varietal, this time Petit Manseng, which is used here to make a Jurançon lookalike.*

❻ **Domaine Jean-Louis Denois Vin Mousseux NV** (€13) *Many would mistake this for authentic champagne. Made from Chardonnay and Pinot Noir, the quality is exceptional.*

❼ **La Vieille Bataille 2001** Le Mas d'Aimé, Grès de Montpellier (€11) *One of the best of an increasing number of pure Carignan wines, this demonstrates the bitter almond quality of the grape and the standard that can be reached when the vines are old and the yields curtailed.*

❽ **Château des Estanilles Prestige Rosé 2001** Faugères (€25) *Made entirely from Mourvèdre, this saigné rosé is fermented and aged in oak. Very pretty, stylish, and powerful: not for the uninitiated.*

❾ **Sauvignon 2001** Château Malviès-Guilhem, Côtes de Malepère (€25) *Unorthodox vendanges tardives of surprising quality, made only in the best years.*

❿ **Château la Condamine-Bertrand 2001** Clairette du Languedoc (€6) *In one of its two AOC areas, the Clairette grape is making an exciting revival, spurred on by new winemaking techniques designed to prevent its oxidation.*

Vins de Pays

Rosemary George MW

Increasingly today, *vins de pays* are becoming the focus for winemakers who are at odds with their local appellation.

ROSEMARY GEORGE MW

The most obvious example of this is Domaine de Trévallon, which is situated within the appellation of les Baux, but owner Eloi Durbach obstinately and rightly refuses to conform to regulations that would not allow Grenache Noir in his vineyards. Thus he sells his wines as Vin de Pays des Bouches du Rhône.

There are numerous other examples of nonconformity. Producers of appellation wines who wish to try their hand at the so-called international grape varieties must label those wines *vin de pays*, such as Domaine de Fontcaude's Cuvée Alouette, which is pure Merlot. Then there are producers who have chosen to concentrate on more traditional grape varieties, but in a way that is unacceptable to the INAO (Institut National des Appellations d'Origine). For this reason Marc Parcé's wines at Domaine de la Rectorie in Banyuls are *vins de pays*. Gérard Gauby's white wines have always been *vins de pays*, since his alcohol levels are invariably too high for the appellation Côtes du Roussillon; and from 2002 his red wines will also be Vin de Pays des Côtes Catalanes, in deference to the tiny amount of Cabernet Sauvignon in the blend. Sometimes it may be a question of typicity, with a wine exuding quality and character,

ROSEMARY GEORGE MW was lured into the wine trade by a glass of The Wine Society's champagne at a job interview. Realizing that secretarial work was not for her, she took the wine-trade exams, becoming one of the first women to qualify as a Master of Wine in 1979. She has been a freelance wine writer since 1981 and is the current chairman of the Circle of Wine Writers. Rosemary is the author of nine books, including *Chablis*, *French Country Wines*, *The Wines of New Zealand*, and *The Wines of the South of France*. Her next book, *Walking through the Vineyards of Tuscany*, is due for publication in spring 2004.

and therefore failing to conform to what the local tasting commission deems appropriate for the appellation. This is particularly so in the Midi, where appellations were usually created to suit the cooperative growers, who often had little inclination to work for quality, thereby defending mediocrity. It is perfectly possible to earn at least as much money for a *vin de pays* as for an appellation wine, as Mas de Daumas Gassac demonstrates.

Then there are those who produce mere *vin de table*, such as René Rostaing, the talented Côte Rôtie producer who also has vineyards of Viognier and Syrah just outside the appellations of Condrieu and Côte Rôtie. "If my wine cannot be an appellation, it shall be nothing, just *vin de table*," he says, although with the vintage deliberately and poorly disguised as a lot number. There is no doubt that *vins de pays* are benefiting from a creativity stemming from a sense of frustration with the appellation controls, providing a useful opt-out clause for those dissatisfied with the strictures of the appellation system. This shows in the sales figures. On the export market, *vins de pays* from Languedoc-Roussillon gained 10 percent in value and volume in the first 10 months of 2002, whereas the appellations from the same region dropped 10 percent in volume and 5 percent in value in the same period.

However, *vins de pays* do not allow for total liberty, as will be seen on the following pages. There are restrictions, with prohibited grape varieties and various other constraints. Nonetheless, *vins de pays* are the prime source of creativity within an overregulated French winemaking industry.

Grapevine

• **Vin de Pays des Gorges de l'Hérault** has been renamed Vin de Pays de St Guilhem-le-Désert after the enchanting 11th-century abbey in the hills above the Hérault valley.

• **The popular Cuvée Mythique** has been the flagship of Les Vignerons du Val d'Orbieu for several years, and there is now a white-wine blend of Chardonnay, Viognier, Marsanne, and Roussanne.

• **The all-embracing Vin de Pays** des Portes de la Méditerranée now includes wines from the island of Corsica, as well as the *départements* of Provence, the Ardèche, the Drôme, and the Hautes-Alpes. Usually *vin de pays* from Corsica goes under the evocative name of Vin de Pays de l'Ile de Beauté and rarely

travels farther than *le continent*, as Corsicans refer to mainland France. However, some of Antoine Arena's excellent wines do not conform to the regulations for white Patrimonio, particularly his late-harvest Vermentino, and are well worth seeking out *sur place*.

• **The large *négociant*** company Bessière, which is an important producer of *vins de pays*, was the victim of protesting wine growers when its warehouse in Mèze was set on fire one night in January 2002. The growers were protesting about French imports of foreign, mainly Italian, wine. Tanks were emptied too, but a new and improved plant was opened in September 2002, just in time to celebrate the company's 100th anniversary.

WINES SPIRITED AWAY

In sharp contrast to the oversupply situation of just 12 months ago, there now threatens to be a shortage of *vins de pays*. The distillation of a considerable quantity of unsold wine to make room for the 2002 harvest was followed, ironically and unexpectedly, by a small crop, due to bad weather over large expanses of the Midi. This inevitably means that prices will rise. There is also a strong demand for Sauvignon du Jardin de la France from the Loire, resulting in price rises, whereas Chardonnay and Chenin have proved less popular and have not enjoyed what has been described as "the New Zealand effect."

ANYONE FOR ANIANE?

Now that the dust has settled after Robert Mondavi's retreat from the Midi, there is no doubt that an enormous opportunity has been missed—and one likely never to be repeated. The Midi would have reaped untold benefits from the influence of an international name with the prestige of Mondavi, with a reputation for quality and not just quantity. Much is now being made of the moves of the actor Gérard Depardieu, who with his *Bordelais* partner Bernard Magrez is buying land near Aniane, in the same area as Mondavi's planned purchase. The mayor of Aniane who said *non* to Mondavi is purported to have

recognized that "we have learned from our mistakes." While most people are welcoming the popular actor with open arms, others are muttering that he has pushed up land prices by paying over the odds for his 2.2-hectare (ha) plot.

VINS DE FRANCE?

Discussion over the proposed countrywide Vin de Pays de France has ground to a halt, thanks to—they say—the political clout of the *syndicat* of the Vin de Pays d'Oc, which dominates the *vins de pays* market. There are fears that such an all-encompassing *vin de pays* might become a graveyard for bad appellation wines, but this could be offset by stricter criteria than ever for a *vin de pays*. If properly policed, such a *vin de pays* could allow for judicious interregional blending. Thus, a successful Sauvignon blend might contain wine from the Loire, Bordeaux, and the Midi, thereby making the most of France's often marginal climate, and allowing for maximum flexibility. There has been talk, too, of a Vin de Pays du Sud-Ouest, which could allow for some subtle blending of riper wines from the Midi with the more structured wines of the Gironde and surrounding vineyards. There is no doubt that the *Bordelais* would benefit the most. Indeed, cynics might ask whether this is what happens anyway. For the moment, however, regional rivalries have prevented any progress.

Opinion:
Tap route?

Irrigation is a "mute" point in the Midi. It is allowed for *vins de pays*, but not for appellation wines, and not during August, although that is when the inspectors go on vacation. If linked to strict controls on yields, why not allow it for both categories?

More nonsensical is the official attitude toward the numerous late-harvest wines of the Midi—not the *vins doux naturels*, but the late-picked wines that may be the result of raisined grapes or even—occasionally—of noble rot. The political clout of the Alsatians within the INAO is such that the term *vendange tardive* is effectively forbidden. Marc Benin of Domaine de Ravanès in the Coteaux de Murviel found himself in court and fined for labeling late-picked Ugni Blanc as *vendange tardive*. Currently the term *vendanges surmûries* is tolerated, and more often than not bottles bear the long-winded description: "*Moût partiellement fermenté, issu de vendanges passerillés.*" Do not be put off by the terminology; the wines are delicious, but clearly they need to be given some legal definition.

Grapevine

• **The large cooperative** group of Plaimont continues to dominate the market for Vin de Pays des Côtes de Gascogne and is taking the innovative step of bottling its key brand, Colombelle, with Stelvin capsules from the 2002 vintage.

• **The merger** between BRL Hardy, owners of Domaine de la Baume, outside Pézenas, with the American company Constellation Brands, Inc. will bring an American presence to the *vins de pays* market. Hitherto, the only American in the Midi was John Goelet, the owner of Clos du Val in the Napa Valley, who has bought the Coteaux du Languedoc estate Domaine de Nizas.

• **The Vin de Pays d'Oc** regulations allow for 31 possible grape varieties, of which 25 may be mentioned on the label. You may never find a pure Petit Verdot in Bordeaux, but one has been produced as a *vin de pays* for the 2002 vintage by the innovative Domaine Condamine Bertrand near Pézenas.

• **Zinfandel** is making its first appearance in the Languedoc, with Domaine de l'Arjolle in the Côtes de Thongue producing Cuvée Z for the first time in 2002.

GREATEST WINE PRODUCERS

1. Domaine de Trévallon (Bouches du Rhône)
2. Domaine Gauby (Côtes Catalanes)
3. Domaine de la Rectorie (Côte Vermeille)
4. Mas de Daumas Gassac (Hérault)
5. Domaine la Grange des Pères (Hérault)
6. Château Routas (Var)
7. Domaine Vaquer (Catalan)
8. Domaine de l'Arjolle (Côtes de Thongue)
9. Domaines Grassa (Côtes de Gascogne)
10. Producteurs Plaimont (Côtes de Gascogne)

FASTEST-IMPROVING PRODUCERS

1. Domaine de Ravanès (Coteaux de Murviel)
2. Domaine de Magellan (Côtes de Thongue)
3. Domaine Belles Pierres (Oc)
4. Domaine Fontcaude (Oc)
5. Domaine d'Aupilhac (Mont Baudile)
6. Domaine de la Condamine l'Evêque (Côtes de Thongue)
7. Domaine la Croix Belle (Côtes de Thongue)
8. Domaine la Colombette (Coteaux du Libron)
9. Domaine la Grange des Quatre Sous (Oc)
10. Domaine de Triennes (Var)

NEW UP-AND-COMING PRODUCERS

Mas Amiel may already have a reputation for vin doux naturel, *but not for still wine; and René Rostaing is a highly rated Côte Rôtie producer, but new to* vin de table.

1. Domaine de Clovallon (Oc)
2. René Rostaing (Condrieu/Vin de Table)
3. Le Mas d'Aimé (Var)
4. Domaine Terre Megère (Oc)
5. Château de la Peyrade (Oc)
6. Les Chemins de Bassac (Côtes de Thongue)
7. Mas des Chimères (Coteaux de Salagou)
8. Jean-Louis Denois (Oc)
9. Mas Amiel (Côtes Catalanes)
10. Domaine la Capelle (Oc)

BEST-VALUE PRODUCERS

1. Domaine de la Baume (Oc)
2. Domaine de la Chevalière (Oc)
3. Domaine de Valmoissine (Gorges de Verdon)
4. Domaine Cazes (Côtes Catalanes)
5. Abbotts (Oc)
6. Guy Anderson (Oc)
7. Les Caves du Mont Tauch (Torgan)
8. Producteurs Plaimont (Côtes de Gascogne)
9. Les Vins Skalli Fortant de France (Oc)
10. Les Vignerons du Val d'Orbieu (Oc)

GREATEST-QUALITY WINES

1. **Domaine de Trévallon Rouge 2000** (€40)
2. **Domaine de Trévallon Blanc 1999** (€56)
3. **Mas de Daumas Gassac Blanc 2002** (€33)
4. **Mas de Daumas Gassac Rouge 2001** (€33)
5. **The Cabernet Sauvignon that Wild Boars Prefer 2000** Routas (€6.50)
6. **Le Merle aux Alouettes 1999** Domaine de Fontcaude (€30)

❼ **Domaine de la Grange des Pères Rouge 1999** (€45)

❽ **Grande Cuvée 2001** Jean-Louis Denois (€9.80)

❾ **Vieilles Vignes Blanc 2001** Domaine Gauby (€17)

❿ **Domaine de la Rectorie Rosé 2001** (€15.25)

BEST BARGAINS

❶ **Sauvignon Blanc 2002** Domaine de la Baume (€4.99)

❷ **Syrah 2001** Domaine de la Condamine l'Evêque (€6.50)

❸ **Viognier 2002** Domaine de la Baume (€4.99)

❹ **Pinot Noir 2000** Domaine de Valmoissine (€10)

❺ **Côtes de Gascogne Blanc 2002** Producteurs Plaimont (€3.10)

❻ **Sauvignon 2000** Les Vignerons Ardechois (€6.50)

❼ **Vins de Pays des Coteaux de Murviel 2001** Domaine de Limbardié (€7)

❽ **Blanc de Coupe Roses 2001** Vin de Pays des Côtes de Brian (€8)

❾ **Viognier 2001** Cante Perdrix, Vin de Pays de Cassan (€14)

❿ **Cuvée d'En Auger 2000** Domaine Perdiguier, Vin de Pays des Coteaux d'Ensérune (€12)

MOST EXCITING OR UNUSUAL FINDS

❶ **La Doyenne 2000** Le Mas d'Aimé, Vin de Table de France (€12) *From the much-decried Aramon grape, albeit grown on 100-year-old vines and blended with Grenache and Carignan.*

❷ **Le Ciste 2001** Domaine Laguerre, Vin de Pays des Pyrenées Orientales (€9) *The fruit of old Carignan and Grenache from a new Roussillon venture.*

❸ **Z de l'Arjolle 2001** Vin de Table de France (€11) *The first example of Zinfandel from the Midi.*

❹ **Les Lézardes "2000"** René Rostaing, Vin de Table Français Blanc (€15) *Ripe, unctuous Viognier, but from outside the vineyards of Condrieu. The label is not allowed to say Viognier, so perhaps you should take Lot 2000 to be vintage 2000, too?*

❺ **Les Pomarèdes Pinot Noir 2002** Domaine de Clovallon (€12) *This illustrates how good Pinot Noir can be in the Midi, when grown on cool, north-facing slopes.*

❻ **Chardonnay 2000** Dominique Laurent, Vin de Pays d'Oc (€11) *An elegant Chardonnay benefiting from a Burgundian hand.*

❼ **Sotanum 2000** Les Vins de Vienne, Vin de Pays des Collines Rhodaniennes (€28) *An exciting new joint venture between three recognized Rhône producers: Pierre Gaillard, Yves Cuilleron, and François Vieillard.*

❽ **Attitude Sauvignon Blanc 2002** Pascal Jolivet, Vin de Pays du Jardin de la France (€12) *Could be mistaken for Sancerre; the grapes are grown in Touraine and vinified in Sancerre, hence the declassification to a vin de pays.*

❾ **Muscat Grain d'Automne 2001** Domaine Barroubio, Vin de Pays d'Oc (€9 per 50cl) *Deliciously honeyed Muscat, without the fortification common in a vin doux naturel.*

❿ **Grenat 2001** Domaine de l'Aiguelière, Vin de Pays du Mont Baudile (€12) *This Grenat (pure Grenache Noir) has great depth of flavor for its variety.*

Germany

Michael Schmidt

The demand for dry German wine on the home market has been growing steadily for the past 20 years, reflecting the increasing recognition of wine's role as an accompaniment to food.

MICHAEL SCHMIDT

German consumers have taken a dim view of producers who are incapable or unwilling to supply the growing thirst for *trocken*. However, wines that were formerly light and sweet were often turned into thin, dry ones. With the reputation of German wines already tarnished by oceans of Liebfraumilch and the like, strong action had to be taken if the country was to avoid sliding any farther down the international wine order.

In July 2000, a new law was added to the much-maligned German wine legislation, providing an almost perfect solution to the quality issue of *trocken*-style wines. The designations of Classic and Selection were introduced to set higher standards for dry wines. As the top-drawer dry wine, Selection has to meet several stringent production criteria: yields are limited to 60 hectoliters per hectare; grapes must be handpicked; wines must come from a single variety, single vineyard, and single vintage; a minimum of 12.2 percent alcohol applies; and the residual sugar content must lie within the limits of the EU definition for dry wines. Selection wine must be made from traditional varieties prescribed by the regional authorities and cannot be released until September of the year following that of the harvest. The Classic-designation criteria are slightly less stringent, since this category identifies a range of sound dry wines for everyday drinking.

MICHAEL SCHMIDT runs his own wine school (www.wineschmidt.co.uk) in England. He has worked as a consultant on a number of publications, including assisting in the selection of recommended wines for the German chapter of *Sotheby's World Wine Encyclopedia* (Bullfinch, 1988) and *The New Sotheby's Wine Encyclopedia* (DK, 2001). Michael is a judge at the International Wine and Spirit Competition.

Just as the cat appeared to be in the bag, a small but very important faction of the German wine scene more or less withdrew its support for the Classic/Selection concept by deciding to set up a classification of its own. Although the VDP (Verband Deutscher Prädikatsweingüter), which represents just over 200 elite producers, agreed with many of the standards set by the top Selection designation, it was critical of the fact that no actual vineyard classification had taken place. The VDP's argument was that only top vineyards could consistently produce top wines, thus the very highest dry-wine designation should be reserved for the very best sites. In June 2002, the VDP announced a classification for all regions except the Ahr and Mosel-Saar-Ruwer. The Mosel-Saar-Ruwer joined the scheme in March 2003, albeit in a somewhat different format; the Ahr has so far voted unanimously not to adopt the concept.

The VDP classification is based on a three-tier system that rates wines primarily according to their provenance rather than original must weight (see box below). But what, apart from the classification of particular vineyards, are the differences in criteria between the highest dry-wine designation as defined by law (Selection) and by the VDP's (*Großes Gewächs et al*)? The band of grape varieties under the VDP system is much narrower and yields are restricted to 50 hl/ha instead of 60 hl/ha, but only *spätlese*, not *auslese*, must weights are required. One issue that the Mosel VDP has great reservations about is chaptalization. This practice has not been ruled out, but Mosel members feel that *Großes/Erstes Gewächs* is not something that should be taken for granted, and vintages not sufficiently supported

---

VDP Classification

1. *Großes Gewächs* (great growth), *Erstes Gewächs* (first growth—Rheingau only), and *Erste Lage* (first site—Mosel-Saar-Ruwer only) are reserved for wines from the most highly rated vineyards. Only *auslese*, *beerenauslese*, *trockenbeerenauslese*, or *eiswein prädikate* are allowed, except in the Mosel-Saar-Ruwer, where *kabinett*, *spätlese prädikate*, and various other designations may also be used. When not qualified by any *prädikat*, *Großes Gewächs* must be a dry wine made from grapes with a minimum *spätlese* must weight. All *Großes/Erstes Gewächs* and *Erste Lage* wines must be hand-harvested to a maximum yield of 50 hl/ha, subjected to a VDP taste test, and cannot be released until September of the year following that of the harvest (two years for red wines).

2. *Klassifizierter Lagenwein* (wine from a classified site) is restricted to wines from classified vineyards that impart site-specific traits, with a maximum yield of 65 hl/ha.

3. *Gutswein und Ortswein* (estate wine and commune wine) is applicable to wines observing the VDP's general standards, which include viticultural methods adhering to strict controls, regular inspection of vineyards, higher must weights than those prescribed by law, and a maximum yield of 75 hl/ha.

by Mother Nature should not be allowed to claim *Großes Gewächs* status. Food for thought, perhaps? And not just for German *grand cru* estates, either. The VDP does not allow any method of must concentration for its great growths and, of even greater importance, it has dispensed with the use of *grosslage* and *bereich* designations, which only serve to mislead the public.

However, the VDP is a private body, and its vineyard classification is not endorsed by German wine law, hence its various designations may not be referred to on the front label. The design of a special bottle in combination with the display of the VDP logo of a stylized eagle and cluster of grapes on the neck capsule and main label will enable consumers to recognize these great-growth wines, but any references to their classification are restricted to the back label.

There can be no doubt that the VDP's internal quality regime represents a milestone in the effort to reclaim the good name of German wine, and that its vineyard classification helps sort the wheat from the chaff, but there are two major criticisms. First, it undermines the validity of the general wine law's Selection designation as a means of identifying Germany's elite of dry wines. A simple solution to this problem would be the simultaneous use of both designations. Let's have *Großes Gewächs* by any means, but where's the harm in using the Selection designation for dry wines at the same time? As an obvious compromise, the wine law could permit the use of the term *Großes Gewächs* on the label in exchange for the association's commitment to displaying the Selection mark. Second, a weakness of the VDP's classification is that its regional boards could not even agree on a single term for great growth, let alone its criteria. At a time when consumers need a greater clarity and focus of labeling, the *crème de la crème* of German wine have merely added to their state of confusion.

Grapevine

• In 2002, **Hedwig and Klaus Keller** of Flörsheim-Dalsheim, in the Rheinhessen, won a gold medal for a record 21st time at the Deutsche Landwirtschaftsgesellschaft annual awards for those estates that have shown the most consistent overall performance.

• At the **2001 annual auction** of VDP wines, a 1994 *trockenbeerenauslese* from the top-ranking Saar estate Egon Müller fetched a record 3,000. Only 24 bottles of this rare wine have come onto the market.

• The **prominent position** of Müller-Catoir among Germany's elite of growers is undoubtedly attributable to the efforts of estate manager Hans-Günter Schwarz, whose retirement in 2002 after 41 years of service was crowned by the presentation of another masterpiece in the shape of the 2001 vintage. Celebrations were spoiled by a slight discord, though, when the decision to appoint an in-house successor was overturned by owner JH Catoir in favor of Martin Franzen, formerly of Baden estate Nägelsförst.

PRIMITIVO DISCOVERED IN GERMAN VINEYARDS

Two ampelographers from the wine research institute of Geilweilerhof in the Pfalz have made a number of exciting discoveries in some ancient vineyard blocks near Heidelberg, in the Baden region. They found 50 different varieties in an ancient plot of vines where some plants are up to 200 years old. A number of the varieties was previously thought extinct, while others had never been associated with Germany in the past. Most surprising, perhaps, was the discovery of Primitivo, better known as California's Zinfandel. Most relevant, however, has been the identification of the legendary Weiße Heunisch, which is credited with being an ancestor of a large number of today's noble vines, including Chardonnay and Riesling. Other finds include the Hungarian Mézes Fehér, the Austrian Roter Veltliner, and three representatives of the late-ripening Gelber Orleans. Used by their various owners mainly for the supply of table grapes and homemade wine, the mini-vineyards still feature all the traits of historic viticulture, including mixed cultivation of varieties, low bush training, and dense planting. The largest of the four sites consists of around 850 vines, while the smallest has just 100, and all are on their original roots.

DRYING UP

Only introduced in 2001, the Classic category of dry German wines doubled in volume in 2002. Originally mainly embraced by cooperatives and larger merchant–bottlers, the concept is now finding acceptance among smaller estates, which use the designation to restructure their range and take advantage of its positive reception by the consumer. More than 1,200 producers have already adopted the concept, and 2003 will probably see almost 200,000 hl, or around 2 percent of Germany's total output, sold as Classic wine. The maiden 2001 vintage of Selection, the top German dry wine, saw a tentative release of just 2,500 hl, but more than 10,000 hl were registered for 2002.

MOSEL MONSTER

Graacher Himmelreich and Wehlener Sonnenuhr are the names of two sites that raise the pulse of Riesling lovers the world over. However, like many other vineyards in their vicinity, they are under threat from an environmental monster that has yet to arrive but appears unstoppable. Those who have seen images of the beast report that it is 1 mile (1,700 m) long, 515 ft (157 m) high, and has 11 legs. If its masters get their wish, it will find its home in the area between Zeltingen and Ürzig, terrorizing thousands of locals with its foul smells and intolerable noise. Most people living in the area fear the effects of an enormous road-construction project designed to provide a direct, fast connection between the Eifel and the Hunsrück regions. In addition to a mile-long bridge, the state government of Rheinland-Pfalz also plans an access tunnel through the hill forests that act as a wind shield for the vineyards of Ürzig. The engineers and politicians in their ivory towers are full of self-congratulatory enthusiasm for their vision of a high-speed, large-volume traffic link between the Belgium–Netherlands border areas and the Rhein-Main district. Surveys predicting devastating damage to nature and the environment, including irreversible changes to the microclimate and water tables of famous vineyards, have not been able to stop the momentum of this Frankenstein freeway. Perhaps the ever-escalating costs, last calculated at over €500 million, will?

THE GREAT FLOOD

August 2002 saw some of the greatest European floods in living memory. Most German wine regions escaped unharmed, but severe problems were reported by a handful of growers in the Elbe valley of Sachsen (Saxony). As the river broke its banks, four estates were completely flooded: Joachim Lehmann in Diessbar-Seusslitz, Jan Ulrich in Seusslitz, Vincenz Richter in Meissen,

and Klaus Zimmerling in Dresden-Pillnitz. Stocks of wine remained largely unaffected, but the water caused damage to buildings and equipment estimated at over €1 million.

GERMAN *BARRIQUE* WINES

The Deutsches Barrique Forum was established in 1990 and consists of growers with a common interest in utilizing *barriques* for wines made from Chardonnay, Weißburgunder, Spätburgunder, and various other red varieties. At a 2002 workshop in Bad Mergentheim, Professor Schulz of the wine institute of Wiesbaden-Geisenheim explained the importance of the choice of rootstock and high-density planting for production of small berries, which are most compatible with tannins and oak flavors. However, the true benefits of these measures could only be expected after the vines had achieved a certain root depth, requiring at least 15 years' growth.

Grapevine

• **Karl Heinz Johner** made history by taking the top prize in the coveted Spätburgunder category of *Vinum* magazine's 2001 Deutscher Rotweinpreis with a wine that had been concentrated by vacuum condensation. The former winemaker at Lamberhurst in England managed to fend off nonconcentrated opposition from top rivals such as Dr Wehrheim and Meyer-Näkel with his 1999 Baden Spätburgunder Qualitätswein SJ.

• **Despite all the talk** of great Riesling, the British still love cheap German plonk. In 2002, the UK remained the top export market for German wine, accounting for 20 percent of total production and almost half of all exports, yet it is way down the

league in terms of value. The average price of German wines imported into the UK was €1.17 per liter, compared to €3.03 per liter for those imported into the US.

• **Ralf Bengel,** formerly of Graf von Kanitz at Lorch, is the new head of the red-wine specialist Rheingau Staatsweingut Assmannshausen.

• **A loose alliance** of growers dedicated to the organic cause is to hold regular presentations for the specialist wine trade to promote its range of *Grosse Bioweine*. All estates are VDP members and include Graf von Kanitz (Rheingau), Heyl zu Herrnsheim (Rheinhessen), Wittmann (Rheinhessen), and Prinz zu Saim-Dalberg (Nahe).

Opinion:
Great wines must be natural

The top prize taken by Karl Heinz Johner for his vacuum condensation-assisted red wine (see Grapevine) raises important questions. Although EU law has permitted must concentration as an alternative to chaptalization for some years now, its use in Germany has been as recent as 1998 and restricted to a trial basis only. Johner's estate was, in fact, one of the chosen few to be allowed to experiment with various winemaking techniques involving reverse osmosis and vacuum condensation under strictly controlled conditions. However, the trail that his 1999 Baden Spätburgunder Qualitätswein SJ has blazed at one of the most prestigious events on the wine competition circuit only added to the demand that such technology should be available to all. With the competition results on one hand and EU acceptance on the other, it was almost impossible for the authorities to refuse, and in July 2002 the German wine law was adapted to give its official blessing to must concentration. But will this be good for German wine?

Having worked with both the vacuum distillation of must and removal of water molecules by high-pressure filtration, Johner is encouraged by the positive results and thinks that their application will benefit German wine in the long run. One important question is, however, will other producers employ these methods with the same conscientious approach or just see them as another technical aid to compensate for a lack of effort in the vineyard? If the latter happens to any degree, the perpetrators could be in for a shock, since Johner believes that only musts from ripe and healthy grapes can gain from concentration. If inadequate raw material is used, its shortcomings are more likely to be emphasized than disguised.

What great German wine requires is not more technology in the lab but prudent vineyard management with a minimum of intervention in the winery.

Vintage Report

Advance report on the latest harvest

2002

If only October had stuck to the script of a balmy Indian summer, we might have been in for another vintage of the century. But even the late rainy days of autumn could not prevent good to very good results in almost all 13 regions. Despite isolated frosts in a few areas of the Franken, Baden, Württemberg, and Pfalz, and some scattered hail in the Rheingau and Mosel, Germany generally enjoyed an even growing season with an almost perfect balance of sunny days and rainfall until the end of September. The ripeness level of grapes was 10–12 days ahead of normal when the autumn deluge arrived, thus most of the grapes for *QbAs* (Qualitätswein bestimmter Anbaugebiete) and *kabinetts* had already been picked. Growers going for premium-quality wines faced a nail-biting time, but lessons learned from the difficult 2000 vintage paid off. A green harvest at most estates had reduced the number of bunches by some 20 percent, giving rot very little opportunity to spread, and this preventive measure was aided by generally cool autumn temperatures. Growers who waited until early November to harvest selectively were rewarded with must weights between *auslese* and *trockenbeerenauslese* quality. Between 10 and 12 December, a widespread biting frost created ideal conditions for relatively copious quantities of *eiswein*. Must weights of the frozen nectar soared to 200 degrees *Oechsle* and higher in places.

Updates on the previous five vintages

2001

Vintage rating: 92

Favorable weather conditions until the end of August led to well-advanced degrees of ripeness, but hopes for an outstanding vintage were somewhat dampened by September rains. However, a sun-blessed October dispelled fears of rot, and the continuation of fine weather right into November rewarded patient growers with *auslese* grape material. The majority of the harvest total weighed in at *kabinett* level. Red-wine producers in the Ahr, Pfalz, Baden, and Württemberg reported an almost perfect balance of phenolic and sugar ripeness. The Rheingau was less fortunate, with severe hailstorms devastating some of the crop in October. One of the earliest harvests ever of frozen grapes for *eiswein* took place at a few sites in the Nahe on 11 November, though almost all other regions were more than adequately compensated by a big, five-day freeze in mid-December, producing must concentrations of up to and above 200 degrees *Oechsle*.

2000

Vintage rating: *70*

It may have been a miracle vintage in Bordeaux, but no such luck in Germany. Any expectations after an optimal cycle up to July were dashed by rainfall throughout the summer. Subsequent swelling and bursting of the grapes led to an early onset of rot in September, accelerating at a rate that defied the efforts of all but the most meticulous growers to salvage any healthy material. Only continuous removal of rotten bunches and severely selective hand-picking at the final stage produced a small number of fine wines, while the less-fussy mechanical harvesters stood every chance of devouring grapes already affected by acetic bacteria. An average of more than 100 hl/ha for the country's vineyards will not have advanced the cause of German wine.

1999

Vintage rating: *85*

The early harvesters of mass-production wines had to face the consequences of a rainy September, with diluted raw material more often than not affected by rot. Premium-quality growers who thinned their crop during the wet period benefited from a golden October. At the top end, there were excellent Rieslings in the Mosel, Rheingau, and Mittelrhein, and fine reds from almost all varieties.

1998

Vintage rating: *88*

Early flowering and an extremely hot August laid the foundation for high expectations, only to be spoiled by continuous autumn rainfall. The end result of this large harvest was surprisingly good, but only where the principles of strictly selective picking had been employed. Two periods of sustained frost allowed for fair quantities of *eiswein*. It was a large-volume harvest.

1997

Vintage rating: *90*

This was the year that nature took care of the preselection process—which had too often been shunned by the growers themselves—with spring frosts, rain during the flowering period, and hail in places, followed by a dry summer and warm autumn to push up the sugar levels. This led to a substantially reduced crop of almost perfectly healthy grapes. Outstanding wines, with only early October frosts spoiling the chance of 1997 being a vintage of the century.

Grapevine

• **Reds are no longer under the bed,** according to official figures from the Federal Office for Statistics. The size of Germany's vineyard area planted with red-wine varieties has grown from 22,057 ha in 1997 to 27,200 ha in 2000. Spätburgunder now accounts for 9,255 ha, followed by Portugieser with 5,026 ha and Dornfelder's 4,372 ha. The relative newcomer Regent has leapt from 70 ha to 449 ha. On the white scene, there is now clear daylight between Riesling at 22,117 ha and Müller-Thurgau at 20,223 ha.

• **Having encouraged growers** for years with financial incentives to grub up some of their vines, Brussels performed a swift EU-turn in 2002 with its plans to extend Europe's vineyards by 51,000 ha. Germany's allocation is 1,534 ha, which is to be divided proportionately between the 13 regions.

• **Businessman Achim Niederberger** has acquired a 70 percent share in the Deidesheim flagship estate of Bassermann-Jordan. The wife of the late Dr. Ludwig von Bassermann-Jordan still retains her 30 percent share, but daughter Gabriele decided to sell her interest in the business despite a recent return to form of this traditional domaine.

• **Rumor has it** that in the Nahe region, some of the grapes for the 2002 *eiswein* vintage were mechanically harvested. Could it be that this was material originally left on the vines to rot because of inferior quality? Keenly priced 2002 *eiswein* from the Nahe is not necessarily a bargain. Caveat emptor!

• **Little Red Riding Hood** is alive and well in former East Germany. One of the few state-owned cooperatives that survived the downfall of its former communist masters was the sparkling-wine manufacturer Rotkäppchen (Little Red Riding Hood) of Freyburg in Saale-Unstrut. Possibly tempted by the operation's strong presence in Eastern Europe, it was kept afloat by an injection of capital from spirits producer Eckes. Since then, Rotkäppchen has developed a strong appetite. In 2001, it swallowed Sekt producer Mumm with its Mumm, Jules Mumm, and MM brands. Still hungry for expansion in 2002, Rotkäppchen took over Geldermann, another Sekt producer with historic links to a *grande marque* champagne.

• **The state government** of Rheinland-Pfalz has decided to sell the Trier estate of the Friedrich-Wilhelm-Gymnasium Trust, which includes 30 ha of prestigious holdings in Graacher Himmelreich and Zeltinger Sonnenuhr.

GREATEST WINE PRODUCERS

1. Keller (Rheinhessen)
2. Müller-Catoir (Pfalz)
3. Joh. Jos. Prüm (Mosel)
4. Dr Loosen (Mosel)
5. Fritz Haag (Mosel)
6. Hermann Dönnhoff (Nahe)
7. Egon Müller-Scharzhof (Saar)
8. Ökonomierat Rebholz (Pfalz)
9. Meyer-Näkel (for red wines only, Ahr)
10. Rudolf Fürst (Franken)

FASTEST-IMPROVING PRODUCERS

1. A Christmann (Pfalz)
2. Dr Heger (Baden)
3. Wittmann (Rheinhessen)
4. Georg Breuer (Rheingau)
5. Markus Molitor (Mosel)
6. Dr Wehrheim (Pfalz)
7. Deutzerhof-Cossmann-Hehle (Ahr)
8. Kruger-Rumpf (Nahe)
9. Bernhard Huber (Baden)
10. Knipser (Pfalz)

NEW UP-AND-COMING PRODUCERS

1. Josef Leitz (Rheingau)
2. Andreas Laible (Baden)
3. Oskar Mathern (Nahe)
4. Gerhard Aldinger (Württemberg)
5. Reinhard und Beate Knebel (Mosel)
6. Salwey (Baden)
7. Didinger (Mittelrhein)
8. Bernhart (Pfalz)
9. Van Volxem (Saar)
10. Lützkendorf (Saale-Unstrut)

BEST-VALUE PRODUCERS

1. Müller-Catoir (Pfalz)
2. Reinhold und Cornelia Schneider (Baden)
3. Horst Sauer (Franken)
4. Didinger (Mittelrhein)
5. Weingart (Mittelrhein)
6. Bernhart (Pfalz)
7. Oskar Mathern (Nahe)
8. Freiherr von Gleichenstein (Baden)
9. Carl Loewen (Mosel)
10. Abril (Baden)

GREATEST-QUALITY WINES

1. **Nackenheimer Rothenberg Riesling Trockenbeerenauslese 2001** Gunderloch (€125 per half-bottle)
2. **Bopparder Hamm Feuerlay Riesling Eiswein 2001** Didinger (€36 per half-bottle)
3. **Dalsheimer Hubacker Riesling Auslese Goldkapsel 2001** Keller (€56 per half-bottle)
4. **Weingut Rudolf Fürst Frühburgunder Trocken "R" 1999** Bürgstadter Centgrafenberg (€54)
5. **Spätburgunder Trocken "R" 2000** Bernhard Huber (€33.23)
6. **Westhofener Morstein Riesling Trocken Großes Gewächs 2001** Wittmann (€20)
7. **Siebeldinger im Sonnenschein Weißer Burgunder Spätlese Trocken Großes Gewächs 2001** Ökonomierat Rebholz (€19)
8. **Haardter Mandelring Scheurebe Spätlese 2001** Müller-Catoir (€11)
9. **Homburger Kallmuth Silvaner Spätlese Trocken "Asphodill" 2001** Fürst Löwenstein (€15.50)
10. **Brauneberger Juffer-Sonnenuhr Riesling Kabinett 2002** Fritz Haag (€9.50)

BEST BARGAINS

① **Bopparder Hamm Feuerlay Riesling Beerenauslese 2001** Didinger (€18 per half-bottle)

② **Haardter Mandelring Scheurebe Spätlese 2001** Müller-Catoir (€11)

③ **Schweigener Sonnenuhr Gewürztraminer Trocken Selection 2001** G Beck (€8.10)

④ **Ruländer Spätlese Trocken "R" 2001** Reinhold und Cornelia Schneider (€10)

⑤ **Bopparder Hamm Feuerlay Riesling Spätlese Trocken 2001** Weingart (€6)

⑥ **Brauneberger Juffer Riesling Auslese 2001** Willi Haag (€7.40)

⑦ **Scherzinger Batzenberg Weißer Burgunder Spätlese Trocken 2001** Ernst Heinemann (€7.60)

⑧ **Schweigener Sonnenberg Spätburgunder Spätlese Trocken 2000** Bernhart (€9.70)

⑨ **Oberrotweiler Eichberg Spätburgunder Weißherbst Spätlese Trocken 2001** Salwey (€9.70)

⑩ **Michelbacher Steinberg Müller-Thurgau Qualitätswein Trocken 2001** Höfler (€4.70 per liter)

MOST EXCITING OR UNUSUAL FINDS

① **Ürziger Würzgarten Riesling Auslese 1992** Alfred Merkelbach (€5.50) *Still available in 2003 and at a bargain-basement price!*

② **Pinot Blanc de Noirs Brut 1993** Friedrich Becker (€14.50) *Mature Sekt impersonating classic vintage champagne.*

③ **Röttinger Feuerstein Silvaner Eiswein 2001** Hofmann (€23 per half-bottle) *Superb, complex eiswein from this underrated variety.*

④ **Ruländer Spätlese Trocken "R" 2001** Reinhold und Cornelia Schneider (€10) *Full-bodied Pinot Gris not compromised by barrique fashion.*

⑤ **Silvaner Qualitätswein Trocken "S" 2001** Wittmann (€12.50) *The myth of boring Silvaner dispelled.*

⑥ **Fellbacher Lämmler Lemberger Qualitätswein Trocken 2001** Gerhard Aldinger (€22.39) *A "show reserve" Lemberger, on the verge of world-class red.*

⑦ **Alfred C Portugieser Trocken 2001** Deutzerhof (€17) *This wine is to Portugieser what Moulin-à-Vent is to Gamay.*

⑧ **Pfaffenweiler Oberdürrenberg Gutedel Auslese "Primus" Trocken 2001** Winzergenossenschaft Pfaffenweiler (€7.60) *A table grape that excels, and it is a bargain, too!*

⑨ **Cuvée "S" Sauvignon Blanc Qualitätswein Trocken 2002** Gerhard Aldinger (€14.33) *A German Sauvignon Blanc to rival New Zealand and the Loire.*

⑩ **Regent Auslese Trocken Barrique 2000** Kuhnle (€18.50) *One of the many maligned German crosses coming good. And red!*

Northern Italy

Nicolas Belfrage MW & Franco Ziliani

The most important event to hit the northern Italian wine scene in the past 12 months is the combination of a very small 2002 vintage (the lowest for 50 years) following on the heels of a rather poor 2001 vintage.

NICOLAS BELFRAGE MW   FRANCO ZILIANI

There has also been a steep decline in the key German market, the almost equally steep descent of the US market (as the dollar falls), the euro rising, recession biting in, and the Iraq war. Combine this with the producers' reluctance to lower prices, and the Italian wine industry has all the necessary ingredients for a massive slump in sales. Some producers are so determined to keep their heads stuck firmly in the sand when faced with the economic facts that they not only fail to put prices down, but many are actually putting them up—"to keep up with inflation," they say! Never mind the market. Barolo, the north's most prestigious brew, is a case in point, with certain growers increasing the ante by 15 percent "because the 1999s released in

NICOLAS BELFRAGE MW was born in Los Angeles and raised in New York and England. He studied in Paris, Siena, and London, earning a degree at University College London in French and Italian. Nick has been specializing in Italian wines since the 1970s and became a Master of Wine in 1980, the first US citizen to do so. He is the author of the double award-winning *Life Beyond Lambrusco* (Sidgwick & Jackson, 1985), *Barolo to Valpolicella* (Mitchell Beazley, 1999), and *Brunello to Zibibbo* (Mitchell Beazley, 2001). Nick is a regular contributor to *Decanter* magazine and *Harpers Wine & Spirit Weekly*.

FRANCO ZILIANI is a freelance writer who has specialized in Italian wines since 1985. He is a regular contributor to the Italian periodicals *A Tavola*, *Merum*, *Go Wine*, and *AIS Lombardia News*, as well as the weekly magazine *Il Corriere Vinicolo*. He is responsible for the journalistic side of WineReport (www.winereport.com), a weekly e-zine exclusively dedicated to Italian wines, and is a regular contributor to *Harpers Wine & Spirit Weekly* and California magazine *Wine Business Monthly*.

2003 are the best ever." Maybe so, but will the public buy them? Perhaps the bubble has not quite burst as we go to press, but readers will certainly be reading about it by this time next year.

Soave Superiore becomes DOCG

At long last, Soave has managed to achieve DOCG status as of the 2002 vintage. To qualify as Soave Superiore DOCG, the wines will have to come from either the Classico zone or the hills just outside Classico (to be called Colli Scaligeri) and have a minimum alcohol level of 12 percent (compared to 10.5 percent for Soave DOC) and 12.5 percent for the Riserva, with a dry extract of at least 20 g/l (as opposed to 15 g/l). There must be a minimum of 70 percent Garganega plus Trebbiano di Soave, Pinot Bianco, or Chardonnay. Trebbiano Toscano is no longer permitted. Vineyards have to be planted to *guyot* or cordon spur instead of the traditional *pergola veronese*.

One DOC, two names!

The so-called lesser wines of Franciacorta, Italy's most famous sparkling wine zone in Lombardy, hitherto called Terre di Franciacorta Bianco (Chardonnay and Pinot Bianco) and Terre di Franciacorta Rosso (Cabernet Franc, Cabernet Sauvignon, Merlot, Nebbiolo and Barbera) will have the option of a new name: Curtefranca DOC, the ancient name for the zone. The aim is to avoid confusion with the name Franciacorta, reserved for the DOCG *méthode champenoise* sparkler. Among those who will use the new name are Ca' del Bosco of Erbusco, while Fratelli Berlucchi of Borgonato has opted to keep the old Terre di Franciacorta denomination.

Grapevine

• **Valpolicella** has launched a legal action against a Hong Kong firm that recently introduced a line of red and white wines called Yu-lin Valpolicella and Gold Valpolicella.

• **Sforzato, a** *passito* **wine** made from Nebbiolo grapes (known locally as Chiavennasca) grown on the slopes of Valtellina in northern Lombardy, has been elevated to DOCG, the third Lombard wine to achieve this status after Franciacorta and Valtellina Superiore.

• **Valtellina** has added a fifth subzone, Maroggia, to the existing subzones of Grumello, Inferno, Sassella, and Valgella.

• **Producers of Asti** and the non-sparkling Moscato d'Asti are building an "Encyclopedia of Asti" as part of their "global relaunch" plans, which aim to link the wine name with the zone name, establishing it as a *vin de terroir*.

• **Mario Schiopetto,** the man responsible for Friuli's fame as a white-wine producing area, died in April 2003, age 72, after a long battle with cancer. Owner of the eponymous estate in the hills of eastern Friuli, Schiopetto excelled at his craft, producing wines—whites, in particular— that brought the northeastern region of Friuli-Venezia Giulia into the limelight.

• **Bardolino Superiore becomes DOCG** with the 2001 vintage. Bardolino DOC may no longer be called *Superiore*.

ALBAROSSA: LATE DEVELOPER

Piemonte's Albarossa grape seems set to take off in the new DOC zones of Acqui Terme and Ovada, no less than 65 years after this variety was created by crossing Nebbiolo and Barbera. Although planted in barely 3 hectares (ha) today, it is hoped that Albarossa will prove a winner later in the present century. The Nebbiolo genes should provide the high tannins and subtle perfume, while the Barbera contributes high acidity and straightforward cherry fruit. First reports are encouraging, crediting the grape with considerable vigor, good affinity for the desired rootstock grafts, and good resistance to parasites. It buds late, flowers well, and has a medium-sized bunch with small berries that ripen late.

NEW ITALIAN 'PARKER'

Daniel Thomases, an American wine journalist who has lived in Florence for over 20 years and who is known for his coauthorship of the Veronelli guide as well as for his books and articles and his contributions to Jancis Robinson's *The Oxford Companion to Wine*, has been appointed by Robert Parker as the *Wine Advocate*'s taster for Italy.

FRANCIACORTA PINOT NOIR A WINNER

Despite being held in the undisputed capital of Italian Pinot Noir (Pinot Nero), the first edition of the Concorso del Pinot Nero at Egna, in the South Tyrol, threw up neither a South Tyrolean nor a Trentino winner, but one from Lombardy's Franciacorta.

Out of 56 examples from eight Italian provinces, the winner by a nose was Sebino IGT l'Arturo produced by Azienda Agricola Ronco Calino of Cazzago San Martino. In second place came the much more famous Sanct Valentin from the Cantina Produttori San Michele Appiano.

CABERNET SUSPECTS

One of the persistent rumors concerns the alleged Cabernetization of wines like Barolo and Barbaresco. It is certainly remarkable how many inky-black colors are coming through in these denominations, considering Nebbiolo is by nature a pale-colored variety. Of course, the inclusion of foreign elements in these supposedly 100 percent varietal wines is strictly illegal, so nobody will admit that they are doing it, even if they consider it the right thing to do from a quality standpoint. Wicked tongues have suggested that the advance of scientific techniques capable of identifying all ingredients of a given liquid was what persuaded one world-famous producer to switch from Barolo and Barbaresco DOCGs to Langhe Nebbiolo DOC, which allows a 15 percent boost from other grapes permitted in the growing zone, of which Cabernet is one.

USE YOUR SUGAR LOAF

Rumors are rife about the inclusion of refined sugar in chaptalized wines—perfectly legal in France, perfectly illegal in Italy. Rectified concentrated must (MCR) is supposed to be the only choice for boosting the sort of not-quite-ripe fruit that northern Italy is likely to produce four years out of 10.

Opinion:
Dreaded concentrator

Italians have learned a great deal from the French over the past 30 years. Most of it, especially at the beginning, was positive. But now, like the *Bordelais*, they are learning to resort in lesser vintages to the concentrator, with the result that wines are getting darker, more extractive, more impressive, but less drinkable, less elegant, and less reflective of those vintage variations that always used to be an integral aspect of the game of wine appreciation. Where the motive for winemaking is to churn out an acceptable product at an acceptable price, the system seems unobjectionable, desirable even; but to apply it in classic zones like Barolo, Barbaresco, Valpolicella, *et al.* seems to threaten the very diversity that is the essence of fine wine. No longer able to compete at the bottom end of the world market, Italy depends for future sales on its image of being able to offer—thanks to its many grape varieties, microclimates, and carefully preserved local customs—an amazing array of different aromas, tastes, and styles. The concentrator, as an equalizer of all things, should be regarded by fine-wine producers not as a gift, but as a Trojan horse.

Passing off?

Grandarella is a wine that has been made in Friuli by the illustrious Valpolicella firm of Masi, from Refosco, Carmenère, and Corvina grapes that have been dried on mats (or in fruit boxes, or hung up in long strands) according to techniques invented by Veronese growers literally thousands of years ago and sold for hundreds of years under the name Recioto (when sweet) or Amarone (when dry). Nothing wrong with that. But is it really in the interests of Valpolicella that the name and image of Amarone should be used to promote the wine, to the extent not only of packing it in an Amarone-style bottle, with an Amarone-style label, but actually mentioning Amarone (in connection with the producer) on the back label? Surely the *Champenois*, who have protected their fortune by vigorously protecting their exclusive name worldwide, would not dream of allowing a similar situation to occur.

Vintage Report

Advance report on the latest harvest

2002

The smallest Italian vintage for 50 years, 2002 was some 25 percent below the average for the previous five years. In the north, Piemonte was 25 percent down on 2001, Lombardy 20 percent down, Trentino-Alto Adige and Friuli-Venezia Giulia both 15 percent down, and Veneto a whopping 30 percent down. Quality-wise, the Italian Association of Oenologists and Oeno-technicians (Assoenologi) opined that it "can be considered good, but with extremely rare high points and many more mediocre ones." In Barolo, different growers had different estimations of the potential for the wines. Some, like Beppe Rinaldi and Teobaldo Cappellano, were declaring that the crop would have to be declassified, as happened in 1972. Others—like Giovanni Minetti of Fontanafredda, president of the Consorzio Barolo, Barbaresco, Langhe e Roero—speak of 2002 as a year capable of yielding up some pleasant surprises and in which it is up to the producers to show what they can do in adverse conditions. One only hopes this is not the first of seven lean years to follow, in biblical mode, seven fat years (1995–2001). In Veneto, the southern and eastern shores of Lake Garda (Lugana, Bardolino, Custoza, and western Valpolicella) took a hammering from August hail, with some growers losing their entire production. The president of the Consorzio Vini Valpolicella, Emilio Pedron, defines 2002 as a "difficult and delicate vintage" but believes that the final result for Valpolicella is still salvageable. One thing is sure: the 2002 Italian crop has already been written off by the pundits, and whether the wines are good or not—and some will be very good—consumers will be reluctant to buy. More than ever, the public should trust what they taste rather than what they read.

Updates on the previous five vintages

2001

Vintage rating: *92 (Red: 94, White: 90)*

The first year of the new millennium had points of excellence to rival those of the previous six. There were predictions of Barolos and Barbarescos at the highest quality levels, possibly capping the achievements of the previous six years. Other Piemontese wines were excellent, too, with Barberas and Dolcettos of great concentration and structure. Nebbiolo (Chiavennasca) in Valtellina was also splendid. Very good year, too, for the whites of Friuli and for the Soaves of Veneto, as well as for reds of Valpolicella.

2000

Vintage rating: *88 (Red: 90, White: 86)*

A very hot year more or less everywhere, giving rise to wines of great concentration and power, albeit lacking a bit in subtlety. An excellent year for the Pinot Neros of Alto Adige, but also very good for the aromatic varieties, Sauvignon and Gewürztraminer, throughout the northeast. In Alba, Barolo, Barbaresco, and Barbera recorded the sixth excellent vintage in a row, the previous historical record being a mere three (1988, 1989, and 1990). The Amarones of Valpolicella enjoyed ideal conditions in the post-harvest drying period, thus we can expect some superb wines.

1999

Vintage rating: *98 (Red: 100, White: 96)*

An extraordinary year in the classic Alba zone (Barolo, Barbaresco, Barbera, and Dolcetto). The Barolos are seen by some to be superior to the great 1996s, on a par with 1989 and 1982, which are legendary. Excellent year in Friuli too, with white wines of particular elegance and freshness. In Valpolicella, a few problems with rain at vintage time, but the wines are still very good.

1998

Vintage rating: *83 (Red: 81, White: 85)*

A good, if not great, year. Wines of real elegance and balance were made in Piemonte. Barolos and Barbarescos in some cases are better than the 1997s, at least for drinkability. Rain during picking caused problems in Valpolicella, but the wines turned out to be more than respectable. A good year for whites.

1997

Vintage rating: *90 (Red: 94, White: 85)*

This has been exalted by pundits as the most magical year, but it is a view that has not been entirely maintained since. Weather conditions were perfect throughout the season and till the end of the harvest, and Barolos and Barbarescos are full of fruit, but perhaps just a touch jammy. Similarly in Valpolicella, where Amarones of great power were made, and in Valtellina. White wines tended to be a little fat and lacking in freshness.

GREATEST WINE PRODUCERS

1. Bruno Giacosa (Barolo & Barbaresco)
2. Giacomo Conterno (Barolo)
3. Angelo Gaja (Barolo & Barbaresco)
4. Roberto Voerzio (Barolo)
5. Allegrini (Valpolicella)
6. Lis Neris (Isonzo del Friuli)
7. Tenuta San Leonardo (Trentino)
8. Borgo del Tiglio (Colli Orientali del Friuli)
9. Leonildo Pieropan (Soave)
10. Cantina Produttori San Michele Appiano (Alto Adige)

FASTEST-IMPROVING PRODUCERS

1. Tommaso Bussola (Valpolicella)
2. Conterno Fantino (Barolo)
3. GD Vajra (Barolo)
4. Foradori (Trentino)
5. Massolino (Barolo)
6. Ca' Rugate (Valpolicella)
7. Pra (Soave)
8. Coffele (Soave)
9. Tenuta Mazzolino (Oltrepò Pavese)
10. Il Mosnel (Franciacorta)

NEW UP-AND-COMING PRODUCERS

1. Enzo Boglietti (Barolo)
2. Eraldo Viberti (Barolo)
3. Claudio Viviani (Valpolicella)
4. Cesconi (Trentino)
5. Poderi Colla (Piemonte)
6. Ascheri (Piemonte)
7. Matijaz Tercic (Friuli)
8. Le Fracce (Oltrepò Pavese)
9. Zenato (Veneto)
10. Conte Loredan Gasparini Venegazzù (Veneto)

BEST-VALUE PRODUCERS

1. Araldica Vini Piemontesi (Piemonte)
2. Michele Castellani (Valpolicella)
3. La Riva dei Frati (Valdobbiadene)
4. Tiefenbrunner (Alto Adige)
5. Franz Haas (Alto Adige)
6. Gianni Voerzio (Barolo)
7. Camerano (Barolo)
8. Barale Fratelli (Barolo)
9. Cavallotto Fratelli (Barolo)
10. Produttori del Barbaresco (Barbaresco)

GREATEST-QUALITY WINES

1. **Barolo Falletto Riserva 1996** Bruno Giacosa (€100)
2. **Monfortino Barolo Riserva 1996** Giacomo Conterno (€100)
3. **Barolo 1998** Bartolo Mascarello (€50)
4. **Barolo Ginestra Vigna Casa Maté 1998** Elio Grasso (€45)
5. **Barolo La Serra 1998** Gianni Voerzio (€100)
6. **La Poja 1999** Allegrini (€50)
7. **Recioto Classico della Valpolicella TB 1999** Tommaso Bussola (€40)
8. **San Leonardo 1997** Tenuta San Leonardo (€45)
9. **Chardonnay Jurosa 2000** Lis Neris (€35)
10. **Franciacorta Cuvée Annamaria Clementi 1995** Ca' del Bosco (€65)

BEST BARGAINS

1. **Nebbiolo d'Alba 2000** Pio Cesare (€15)
2. **Langhe Nebbiolo 1999** Barale Fratelli (€15)
3. **Barbera d'Asti Rive 2000** Araldica Vini Piemontesi (€15)
4. **Barolo Serralunga 1998** Fontanafredda (€20)
5. **Barbaresco Rabajà 1999** Cascina Luisin (€25)

❻ Barbera d'Asti La Vignone 2000 Pico Maccario (€10)

❼ Soave Classico Superiore Ca' Visco 2001 Coffele (€20)

❽ Erbaluce di Caluso La Rustia 2001 Orsolani (€15)

❾ Alto Adige Pinot Nero 2000 Gottardi (€25)

❿ Valpolicella Classico 2001 Corte Rugolin (€15)

MOST EXCITING OR UNUSUAL FINDS

❶ Dolcetto d'Alba Tiglineri 2001 Enzo Boglietti (€15) *Dolcetto grapes from three separate vineyards: FossaTI in La Morra, GaGLIassi in Monforte, and CalciNERI in Sinio, hence the name. One of the few Dolcettos made to withstand the test of time, Tiglineri can be delicious 10 years on.*

❷ Verduno Pelaverga 2001 GB Burlotto (€15) *Verduno is a commune of Barolo with excellent crus; the Pelaverga is a rare grape variety, perhaps of French origin, that gives a delicious red wine with intense peppery and geranium-leaf aromas.*

❸ Freisa Kyé Barolo 1999 GD Vajra (€30) *A wine of marvelous spicy-peppery bouquet, a robust tannic structure, and crunchy fruit from a Piemontese variety that has almost become a rarity in the Alba Langhe (fewer than 10 producers).*

❹ Barbera d'Alba Vendemmia Tardiva Vigna Preda 1999 Barale Fratelli (€15) *An unusual Barbera d'Alba made from overripe grapes, this wine has a particularly dense aroma, a fullness of fruit, and a softness of structure that puts one in mind of Amarone or Valpolicella Ripasso.*

❺ Colli Tortonesi Timorasso Costa del Vento 2001 Vigneti Massa (€18) *Timorasso is a grape of even greater rarity in Piemonte, but it is now being rediscovered by various producers. However, Walter Massa has always carried the flag for Timorasso and continues to make the best version.*

❻ Nas-cetta Bianco 2001 Elvio Cogno (€15) *The Nas-cetta is a very obscure grape variety that has been saved from extinction by Cogno, who grows it today in the Barolo commune of Novello, where it produces a fascinating, nervy, dry white wine with an extremely delicate aroma and juicy fruit.*

❼ Valtellina Superiore Sassella Rocce Rosse Riserva 1995 Arturo Pelizzatti Perego (€25) *Great wines of the Nebbiolo are also produced in the mountainous Valtellina, vinified in large chestnut botti rather than barriques. Pelizzatti Perego's splendid, weighty wine would not be put to shame in a Barolo tasting. A masterpiece!*

❽ Sergio Rosso Veronese 1998 Michele Castellani (€15) *This is what you might call a light Amarone: the grapes are dried after picking, but only for a couple of months. The result is a wine with Amarone characteristics but more suitable for drinking with meals.*

❾ Lagrein Scuro Abtei Riserva 1999 Cantina Convento Muri Gries (€20) *One of a gathering number of obscure native grape varieties making a comeback this century.*

❿ Studio di Bianco 2001 Borgo del Tiglio (€30) *Nicola Manferrari tried different blends for several years (hence the name), and finally came up with a fascinating mix of Italian Tocai Friulano, German Riesling, and French Sauvignon Blanc.*

Central & Southern Italy

Nicolas Belfrage MW & Franco Ziliani

The diversification of business interests throughout Italy's wine industry is the most significant phenomenon of our time.

NICOLAS BELFRAGE MW   FRANCO ZILIANI

Where once, really not long ago, producers would stay on their own turf, be it in the classic zones of Tuscany, Veneto, Piemonte, or Lombardy, today they are extending their tentacles in various directions, generally southward, sometimes eastward or westward, rarely northward. The original examples include GIV (Gruppo Italiano Vini), Italy's largest wine-producing conglomerate, and Antinori expanding all over Tuscany and Umbria, into the north (an early and, as it turned out, rare exception) with the acquisition of Prunotto and, more recently, south with the purchase of several hundred hectares in two zones of Puglia. Other names actively engaged in extending their empires are Gaja of Piemonte (into Montalcino and, more recently, Bolgheri), Bellavista of Franciacorta in

NICOLAS BELFRAGE MW was born in Los Angeles and raised in New York and England. He studied in Paris, Siena, and London, earning a degree at University College London in French and Italian. Nick has been specializing in Italian wines since the 1970s and became a Master of Wine in 1980, the first US citizen to do so. He is the author of the double award-winning *Life Beyond Lambrusco* (Sidgwick & Jackson, 1985), *Barolo to Valpolicella* (Mitchell Beazley, 1999), and *Brunello to Zibibbo* (Mitchell Beazley, 2001). Nick is a regular contributor to *Decanter* magazine and *Harpers Wine & Spirit Weekly*.

FRANCO ZILIANI is a freelance writer who has specialized in Italian wines since 1985. He is a regular contributor to the Italian periodicals *A Tavola*, *Merum*, *Go Wine*, and *AIS Lombardia News*, as well as the weekly magazine *Il Corriere Vinicolo*. He is responsible for the journalistic side of WineReport (www.winereport.com), a weekly e-zine exclusively dedicated to Italian wines, and is a regular contributor to *Harpers Wine & Spirit Weekly* and California magazine *Wine Business Monthly*.

Lombardy (Suvereto in the Maremma), Zonin of Veneto (Sicily and elsewhere), Pasqua of Verona (Puglia and elsewhere), Avignonesi of Montepulciano in Tuscany (Puglia), not to mention the acquisitions of southerners themselves, such as Calatrasi of Sicily into Puglia (and Tunisia) and Feudi di San Gregorio into Puglia and Molise.

Meanwhile, numerous Tuscans in classic zones like Chianti, Montalcino, and Montepulciano have been buying vineyards in the Maremma and the new DOC zones of the region. Names include Frescobaldi (with Mondavi), Antinori, Biondi Santi, Fonterutoli, Querciabella, Cecchi, Poliziano, Barbi Colombini, Coltibuono, Rocca delle Macie, Terrabianca. All these and more are seeing the sunnier climes as the promised land, where grapes never have any trouble ripening and it is relatively easy to achieve the deep colors and high extract that win the lofty accolades from the make-or-break journalists. Not that this has anything to do with the markedly deeper colors and higher extracts that we have been seeing in the classic wines of late…

Grapevine

• **A special subzone of Montepulciano** d'Abruzzo called Colline Teramane will have DOCG status as of the 2003 harvest. The new wine will derive from some 100 hectares (ha) of vineyard spread over 30 communes of the province of Teramo at a yield of 66.5 hectoliters per hectare (hl/ha) as against the DOC's 77. Other stipulations are the use of at least 90 percent Montepulciano grapes and, most significantly, an interdiction on the use of the traditional Abruzzese form of training, the high tent or *tendone*.

• **Greco di Tufo,** made from the prestigious Greco grape variety, and Fiano d'Avellino, already known as among the best white varieties of Campania, if not indeed all of Italy, are to become DOCG. This will make Irpinia, in the province of Avellino, the only commune in Italy to boast three DOCGs (along with Taurasi).

• **While other appellations** consider DOCG to be the height of denominational distinction, the producers of Frascati have thrown out the possibility by a large majority. Only 104 votes were in favor of applying for DOCG out of a total of 1,300.

• **Foglia Tonda,** an ancient Sienese grape variety abandoned over a century ago, will join Sangiovese in the new DOC Orcia.

• **Rocca delle Macie,** the Chianti estate owned by the family of the late spaghetti-western producer Italo Zingarelli, has bought Fattoria Casamaria, in the Morellino di Scansano zone, for around €3 million.

• **Franco Biondi-Santi,** doyen of Brunello di Montalcino (his grandfather Ferruccio virtually invented the wine) announced that "this year we have decided not to make Brunello at the Tenuta Il Greppo." It is not unusual for Biondi-Santi to skip years for his Riserva, but to declassify the entire Brunello *normale* indicates just how far below par this vintage must be in his estimation.

• **Altesino,** one of the most famous Brunello producers, has been acquired by a syndicate headed by Elisabetta Angelini Gnudi, already owner of Altesino's neighbor Caparzo (50 ha) and of Borgo Scopeto in Chianti Classico (90 ha). According to rumor, Signora Gnudi spent over €20 million on the acquisition. The estate will remain separate from Caparzo and Borgo Scopeto, and will not change identity or philosophy.

BEST 1998 BRUNELLOS

Although 1998 was not considered a great year in Tuscany, it was far from a bad one, and the annual tasting in February 2003 (Brunello cannot be released until four years from January following the harvest) revealed just how remarkable the overall quality of this new vintage is. I did not taste all 120 wines present, but of those I did taste, the best (in order of the tasting sheet, not of merit) were Fuligni, Brunelli, Il Poggione, La Palazzetta, Lisini, Mastrojanni, Pian delle Vigne, Piancornello, Poggio Antico, Salicutti, Salvioni, San Carlo, Talenti, Val di Suga Vigna del Lago and Spuntali, Caparzo, Valdicava, Agostina Pieri, Baricci (star wine of the tasting), Caprili, and Casanova di Neri Tenuta Nuova. Best of those tasted was Baricci, followed by Salvioni and Valdicava.

HOW CLASSICO IS CHIANTI?

At the annual Chianti Classico tasting in February 2003 there was some surprise among hacks at the depth of color, vibrancy of fruit, and pungency of aromas characterizing some of the new wines present. Was 2002 not a bit of a washout? Was the Sangiovese not lacking in color and substance, low in grape sugar, and high in green tannins, while earlier-ripening grapes like Merlot, Cabernet, and Syrah had far fewer problems? Admittedly, Chianti Classico allows 20 percent of recommended or authorized grapes in the blend (for which read Merlot, Cabernet, and Syrah), but some of these wines seemed to be more like 20 percent Sangiovese. The explanation emerged when one producer pointed out that very little Super-Tuscan wine

Grapevine

• **GIV** is the largest wine producer in Italy, with a turnover of €45 million (2002) and exports to no fewer than 65 countries. Its latest enterprise, GIV Sud, took three years to establish and consists of three subsidiaries: Terre Degli Svevi in Basilicata, Castello Monaci in Salice Salentino in Puglia, and Rapitalà in Sicily, which together sold 2.8 million bottles in 2002. During 2003, GIV will investigate the possible benefits of transforming itself into a public company.

• **Eugenio Campolmi**, one of the leading lights of the Italian wine renaissance, passed away in July 2002 after a prolonged illness. He was one of the first to experiment with Syrah, resulting in his outstanding Scrio, while his recently released Macchiole is arguably the best Sangiovese-based wine from the trendy Tuscan coastal

vineyards of Maremma. Campolmi earned himself a reputation as not just a creative thinker, but a doer, a man of humor, seriousness, and absolute dependability. Considering his achievements, it is amazing to realize that Eugenio was only 41 when he died.

• **The Italian wine world** lost one of its most charismatic figures with the death of Salvatore Leone de Castris, age 77, in February 2003. De Castris was considered the father of modern Puglian wine, having developed Five Roses, the first Puglian rosé to be bottled, in 1943. More importantly, in the 1950s De Castris created Salice Salentino Riserva from the Negroamaro grape, which at the time was thought good only for blending with Chianti, Valpolicella, and other wines of the center and north.

would be made in 2002. What does his Super-Tuscan usually consist of? Well, Merlot, Cabernet, and Syrah, of course. Welcome to Bordeaux Classico Hermitage.

PASSITO WINE LAW

The Associazione Città del Vino (a national association of 500 local consortia) has established The National Foundation Center for Passito Wines to protect and promote wines made from grapes that have been semi-dried both on and off the vine. Its primary function is to protect the systems of drying (appassimento) via regulations not presently provided by either Italian or European wine laws. Although these are niche wines, there are as many as 110 IGT, DOC, and DOCG appellations providing for the production of vini passiti. Because the greatest failing of the current legislation is the confusion between passito wines and vini liquorosi, which are fortified wines, the Associazione Città del Vino has proposed a modification to the current law that will define passito wines as "those obtained exclusively from white or red grapes subjected to surmaturation (drying) by natural or artificial methods, dry or sweet, without the addition of alcohol."

CITTÀ DEL VINO GOES NATIVE

Another important Città del Vino initiative is to safeguard about 350 officially recognized ancient indigenous grape varieties. This was announced by the association's president, Paolo Saturnini, in a letter sent to the mayors of all Italian wine communes. In his letter, Saturnini asked for a list of the vines cultivated in their areas in order of importance, highlighting those under risk of disappearance, sounding out their availability to participate in and willingness to contribute funds to a recovery program. The data obtained will constitute the basis for ongoing research in viticultural and oenological circles into the problems of protecting the varieties identified.

TRACEABILITY OF WINE BY INTERNET

The era of traceability has arrived. Various consortia of producers have instituted a system whereby any consumer in the world will be able to trace a bottle of wine back to the vineyard or vineyards from which it originated simply by entering the lot number on his or her computer. The first areas affected will include producers of Verdicchio dei Castelli di Jesi, Verdicchio di Matelica, Vernaccia di Serrapetrona, Lacrima di Morro d'Alba, Colli Maceratesi, Rosso Conero, Esino, Vino Nobile di Montepulciano, Chianti Classico, Brunello di Montalcino, and several others in northern and central Italy. Consumers have only to enter the appropriate website and click on the right box to be able to see, for example, a full analysis of the wine they are drinking. "We will be ready by the end of the year," said Doriano Marchetti, president of the overseeing body. "It is a complex business, but we have had the enthusiastic collaboration of all the relevant professional organizations." The system is claimed as an Italian first, copied from no one.

NEW WINEMAKERS IN THE MARCHE

Terre Cortesi Moncaro and Umani Ronchi, two of the most important producers of the Marche, have new winemakers. The cooperative of Terre Cortesi Moncaro (with 830 members, 4 million bottles, controlling some 30 percent of Verdicchio dei Castelli di Jesi) has taken on the current superstar of Italian winemaker–consultants, Riccardo Cotarella. Cotarella, brother of Antinori technical chief Renzo, has a string of successes at high-profile Italian wineries to his name, from Piemonte to Sicily. Meanwhile Umani Ronchi, famous for its Rosso Conero Cumaro, the Super-Marche Pelago, and others too many to mention among a production of over 4 million bottles, has decided to entrust the difficult post-Tachis era (Giacomo Tachis, creator of Sassicaia and Tignanello, was for 10 years its consultant) to Beppe Caviola, a hitherto little-known winemaker with experience mainly in Piemonte. According to some, this was an odd choice, but for others it was explained by the fact that Caviola was Best Oenologist in the 2002 edition of the *Gambero Rosso* Italian wine guide.

SALENTO'S PRIMA DONNAS

Twenty-one producers of the Salento, the southern tip of Italy's heel, have created a new association called I Grandi Vini del Salento ("the Great Wines of the Salento"). The association includes several famous names from the north who have immigrated to the area in the past few years, including Antinori, Avignonesi, Giordano, GIV, Pasqua, and Zonin, plus a couple of locals who have helped to increase the quality of wines in the area over the past couple of decades, such as Cantele and Conti Zecca, but there are some surprising omissions. De Castris, Michele Calò, Rosa del Golfo, Accademia dei Racemi and all of the producers who follow the Puglian oenological consultant *par excellence*, Severino Garofano (Taurino, Candido, Vallone, Cantina Sociale di Copertino, Masseria Monaci) are not included. Was their exclusion deliberate? One famous traditionalist said that they had indeed been approached but had decided to adopt a wait-and-see posture. Another, perhaps more frank, commented that "it is a club of prima donnas, doesn't mean anything, and I am not interested."

MERLOT IN CAMPANIA

In July 2002, Italy's Ministry of Agriculture published a decree recognizing Merlot as an authorized variety for Campania. Funny thing is, the Merlot vines of one famous producer were already there, as was the wine. Indeed, the 2000 vintage of this wine has been widely hailed as one of southern Italy's greats, collecting a Tre Bicchieri award in the *Gambero Rosso* guide and scoring 94/100 in the Veronelli guide. Since the new law was not retroactive, one must ask how it is possible to plant, cultivate, harvest, vinify, bottle, and, above all, market a wine from an unauthorized variety. Perhaps this particular producer has diplomatic immunity or some other kind of immunity Campania-style…

Opinion:
Too much oak in wines

Sometimes producers get it right, and the oak is subsumed beneath the fruit, enhancing—not challenging—the essential wine. Too often, however, the vanilla or smoky-toasty notes stand out on their own, taking over the wine or rendering it unbalanced. Such wines may do well in blind tastings, but they are not normally a pleasure to drink.

Classics should remain classic

Blending, illicit or not, of inauthentic grape varieties in classic wines threatens to undermine the reputation of Italy's historically greatest wines. This is fine in Super-Tuscans and other IGTs, but not in DOCs and DOCGs. Typicity, after all, is what these appellations are supposed to protect.

Pandering to the pundits

Winemakers of any integrity should not pander to the taste of pundits who wield the stick and carrot of high–low marks, even if scores below 90 can be almost a death sentence for some top wines.

Silly prices

Italians are obsessed with their image—*bella figura* or *brutta figura*. They cannot stand looking inadequate in the eyes of their peers. So if one producer puts a ridiculously high price on his wine, another has to follow suit or look foolish. This is fine while things are hunky-dory and the market seems capable of absorbing practically anything, as prior to 9/11, but potentially disastrous when major markets like Germany and the US are in free-fall. The tag of being overpriced is hard to shake off. Ask the Californians.

Grapevine

• **Another of Italy's classic conundrums** is the alleged "Cabernetization" of Brunello di Montalcino. This supposedly 100 percent Sangiovese wine seems to depart subtly (or not so subtly) from the color and aroma expected of Sangiovese. Nobody is admitting anything, of course, but surely that claret character detected in some of the trendier brews is not all coming from too much French *barrique*?

• **One year after** 7.5 million bottles of Beaujolais had to be distilled as a result of falling sales of Nouveau, the success of Italian Novello continues to soar. Despite the smallest Italian crop in 50 years, the production of Novello grew by 10 percent in 2002 to 18.5 million bottles. Prices average €4.34, up some 6 percent on 2001. The best value still comes from Abruzzo.

Vintage Report

Advance report on the latest harvest

2002

In quantity terms, Le Marche was down 5 percent, Tuscany 10 percent, Sardinia 15 percent, Latium 20 percent, Sicily 25 percent, and, hardest-hit of all, Puglia was 30 percent short. Abruzzo and Campania managed to get away with no fall. Hail was less of a menace than it was in the north, but central Italy had even freakier weather, with tornados wrecking vineyards wholesale. In terms of quality, the situation of the center and south was similar to that of the north: truly heterogeneous. Carmignano, west of Florence, seems to have had an excellent crop, but few others in Tuscany did, and the Sangiovese generally fared poorly. Campania, Sicily, and Sardinia brought in, respectively, some Aglianico, Nero d'Avola, and Cannonau grapes that were capable of making surprise five-star wines. There were negative indications from Puglia, especially the Salento, where hail, frequent thunderstorms, and persistent humidity caused first widespread peronospera and later rot in Negroamaro and Primitivo vineyards, and the September rains were too much for many who had labored to save their grapes from disease.

Updates on the previous five vintages

2001

Vintage rating: *93 (Red: 93, White: 93)*

A good year virtually everywhere. Marginally better, perhaps, than 1997, although that vintage received much more hype. Perhaps 2001 was less anomalous than 1997, with wines more in the mainstream but at a higher-than-normal level, while 1997s in retrospect seem almost too ripe, too much of a good thing. In Chianti Classico the level was very good from the start, and the emerging wines confirm that it is a year of excellent aroma, concentration, and balance. In the south, Puglia and Sicily enjoyed ideal conditions. All in all, a very satisfactory outcome, for both whites and reds.

2000

Vintage rating: *86 (Red: 88, White: 82)*

A very hot year, with a dry summer, giving rise to wines that are concentrated and potent, but lacking in elegance, with a slightly baked character—especially in central Tuscany. In some places the vegetation was temporarily arrested by the heat, yielding alcoholic wines with unripe tannins. On the east coast and south, where the varieties are more used to coping with such conditions, everything went swimmingly. As a rule, though, better for reds than whites.

1999

Vintage rating: *77–83 (Red: 77–83, White: 77–83)*

An extraordinary year in Tuscany, probably the best of the decade despite the excellence of 1990 and 1997 (and which, on its own, would rate 97 points). Tuscan classics of wonderful balance, with depth of color, good but not excessive sugar levels, beautifully ripe tannins, and plenty of extract. Not so great, however, east of the Apennines, and down south, where—particularly in Puglia—rains arrived just at vintage time to wash away the promise.

1998

Vintage rating: *88 (Red: 88, White: 88)*

A good year, at first discounted because compromised by vintage-time rains in central Tuscany, but becoming more appreciated, with Chiantis of grace and balance rather than power, and Brunellos of surprising drinkability, without loss of character, compared with the 1997s and 1999s. Seen by some as the best year of the decade for the wines of the Tuscan Maremma (which, on its own, would rate 96 points). The east and south did well too. A good year for whites.

1997

Vintage rating: *92 (Red: 92, White: 90)*

Hailed as the vintage of the century, especially in Tuscany, where some great wines were made, even if some appear almost too packed with polyphenols and fruit. The pundits and the markets went ape—no vintage of Brunello has ever sold so fast at such high prices. Wines for laying down, but with plenty of sappy fruit for earlier drinking. Whites of structure did well too. Most places excelled. Only the Sicilians, who got some harvest rain, were disappointed.

GREATEST WINE PRODUCERS

1. Antinori, Florence (Tuscany)
2. Tenuta San Guido (Tuscany)
3. Fattoria di Felsina (Tuscany)
4. Castello di Ama (Tuscany)
5. Tenuta Il Poggione (Tuscany)
6. Poderi Boscarelli (Tuscany)
7. Arnaldo Caprai (Umbria)
8. Valentini (Abruzzo)
9. Argiolas (Sardinia)
10. Tasca d'Almerita (Sicily)

FASTEST-IMPROVING PRODUCERS

1. Querciabella (Tuscany)
2. Castello di Volpaia (Tuscany)
3. Tua Rita (Tuscany)
4. Tenuta di Capezzana (Tuscany)
5. Avignonesi (Tuscany)
6. Marramiero (Abruzzo)
7. Mastroberardino (Campania)
8. Librandi (Calabria)
9. Odoardi (Calabria)
10. Santadi (Sardinia)

NEW UP-AND-COMING PRODUCERS

1. Poggiopiano (Tuscany)
2. Podere Capaccia (Tuscany)
3. Podere Collelungo (Tuscany)
4. Castello di Bossi (Tuscany)
5. Salcheto (Tuscany)
6. Tenuta di Ghizzano (Tuscany)
7. Montepeloso (Tuscany)
8. Terre de Trinci (Umbria)
9. Cantina del Taburno (Campania)
10. Morganti (Sicily)

BEST-VALUE PRODUCERS

1. Selvapiana (Tuscany)
2. Falesco (Lazio)
3. Coroncino (Le Marche)
4. La Vite Monteschiavo (Le Marche)
5. Contesa di Rocco Pasetti (Abruzzo)
6. Lepore (Abruzzo)
7. Accademia dei Racemi (Puglia)
8. Masseria Monaci, Copertino (Puglia)
9. Valle dell'Asso (Puglia)
10. Settesoli (Sicily)

GREATEST-QUALITY WINES

1. **Brunello di Montalcino Riserva 1997** Il Poggione (€45)
2. **Fontalloro 1999** Fattoria di Felsina Berardenga (€50)
3. **Flaccianello della Pieve 1999** Fontodi (€50)
4. **Vino Nobile di Montepulciano Vigna del Nocio 2000** Poderi Boscarelli (€40)
5. **Messorio 1998** Le Macchiole (€70)
6. **Brunello di Montalcino 1998** Gianni Brunelli (€50)
7. **Montevetrano 2000** (€55)
8. **Graticciaia 1997** Agricole Vallone (€50)
9. **Faro Palari 2000** Palari (€35)
10. **Turriga 1998** Argiolas (€35)

BEST BARGAINS

1. **Chianti Classico Riserva 1999** Casa Sola (€20)
2. **Chianti Colli Fiorentini 2001** Malenchini (€15)
3. **Brunello di Montalcino 1998** Baricci (€35)
4. **Poderuccio 2000** Camigliano (€25)
5. **Morellino di Scansano 2000** Fattoria Le Pupille (€15)
6. **Verdicchio dei Castelli di Jesi Grestio 2001** Armando Zannotti (€10)
7. **Campi Flegrei Piedirosso 2000** Cantine Farro (€15)

8. **Vigna Flaminio Brindisi Rosso
2000** Agricole Vallone (€15)
9. **Savuto 2000** Odoardi (€15)
10. **Vermentino di Gallura Canayli
2001** Cantina di Gallura (€15)

MOST EXCITING OR UNUSUAL FINDS

1. **Palafreno 2000** Querciabella
(€25) *A blend of 55 percent
Merlot and 45 percent
Sangiovese from the heart
of Chianti Classico.*
2. **Chianti Classico Le Trame
1999** Podere le Boncie (€15)
*A wine of wonderfully feminine
intricacy and subtlety from
Giovanna Morganti, daughter of
the illustrious late Enzo Morganti
of San Felice, the vines of which
surround her tiny property.*
3. **Sacromonte 2000**
Castello di Potentino (€11)
*The pure and delicious fruit of
Sangiovese that has been vinified
without the use of barriques by
Charlotte Horton, a charming
English lady with a dilettante's
passion for perfection.*
4. **Nativo Verdicchio dei Castelli
di Jesi 2001** La Vite (€15)
*The grapes are left to shrivel
on the vine for up to 14 days
following the normal harvest and
the wine is left on fine lees in
tank for many months before
bottling unfiltered.*
5. **Vigna Adriana 2001** Castel de
Paolis (€15) *Frascati is supposed
to be made from Trebbiano or
Malvasia, with up to 10 percent
other authorized grapes, but this
one has no Trebbiano and in
excess of 10 percent Viognier!*
6. **Masseria Maime Negroamaro
Salento 2000** Tormaresca (€18)
Although Antinori has owned the
*Tormaresca properties in Puglia
for just five years, it has already
grabbed the Gambero Rosso's
coveted Tre Bicchieri award
with this wine, made from the
Negroamaro grape, rather
than the international varieties
on which competition wines
normally rely.*
7. **Puer Apuliae Nero di Troia
2000** Rivera (€17)
*Made entirely from the Uva di
Troia (or Nero di Troia) grape,
an ancient indigenous variety,
producing here a full red wine
of unusual elegance.*
8. **Magno Megonio 2000**
Librandi (€25)
*Nicodemo and Antonio Librandi
searched all over Calabria to find
native grape varieties of interest
and came up with Magliocco, an
ancient and extremely obscure
grape that has never made a
wine of any note until Magno
Megonio was vinified with all the
artistry of modern oenology.*
9. **Ischia Biancolella Tenuta
Frassitelli 2001**
Casa d'Ambra (€12)
*Grown on the splendid island of
Ischia, where the Biancolella grape
is rich in personality. It can be
perfumed, full of fruit, and express
a marvelous finesse if unblended
and vinified with great care, as this
great wine of terroir has been.*
10. **Gravina 2001**
Cantina Botromagno (€10)
*Made by the ubiquitous and
celebrated Severino Garofano
from local varieties Bianco
d'Alessano and Greco di Tufo,
plus Chardonnay. Probably
Puglia's best white wine.*

Spain

John Radford

It was becoming a little embarrassing that some of Spain's greatest wines could only be sold as *vino de mesa*, the Spanish equivalent of *vin de table*, or table wine.

JOHN RADFORD

This situation arose because they are not located within an established *Denominación de Origen* (DO), although they produce wines of a much higher quality than many that are. One Spanish region has, however, come up with a solution. In 2002, Castilla-La Mancha created the first two *pago* or single-estate DOs, and the repercussions could well set the Iberian cat among the EU pigeons.

Spain has 17 autonomous regions, each with the power to make its own laws regarding local matters, including agriculture. In 2000, the regional government in Castilla-La Mancha passed new wine laws establishing a region-wide *vino de la tierra* (VdlT), similar to the French regional *vin de pays*, for the whole of Castilla-La Mancha. At the same time, they added a clause allowing private estates of international reputation to apply for DO status in their own right, whether or not they were situated within approved DO regions. In 2001, an organization called Grandes Pagos de Castilla ("Great Estates of Castile") was formed, with nine member wine estates in Castilla-La Mancha and Castilla-León. All had built impressive international reputations, but only one was located within an official DO. They were all seen as candidates for a *pago* DO, and in 2002 two of them achieved this: the DO Dominio de Valdepusa in Malpica (a.k.a. Marqués de Griñón) and the DO Finca Elez in the VdlT Sierra de Alcaraz (a.k.a. Manuel Manzaneque).

JOHN RADFORD is a writer and broadcaster with 30 years' experience of the culture, landscapes, architecture, food, and wine of Spain. He is the author of *The New Spain* (Mitchell Beazley), which won four international awards in 1999. A new edition will be published in the spring of 2004.

For the record, Madrid has not been happy about this whole business, but has no power to overturn regional legislation concerning local matters. Indeed, since the creation of these two *pago* DOs there have been rumblings in other Spanish regions, where great estates would dearly love to shake off the iron hand of the local *consejo regulador* and go their own way. If this becomes a trend, how long will it be before other highly regarded wine estates elsewhere in the EU start to demand equal treatment?

Grapevine

• **Bodegas Guelbenzu** seceded from the DO Navarra in the summer of 2002. Unheard of as recently as 1992, this family-owned *bodega* is now labeling its wines as VdlT Ribera del Queiles. Guelbenzu's reasons for quitting the DO Navarra were that it wanted to maintain the integrity of its brand by using grapes from vineyards in other regions (including Aragón) when the vintage in Navarra was not of sufficient quality. Guelbenzu was elected a member of Grandes Pagos de Castilla in 2002.

• **A new VdlT called Bajo Ebro** was created in 2002. This comprises VdlTs Andalucía, Castilla-León, Galicia, Castilla-La Mancha, and Aragón. These VdlTs had been fighting for years to include La Rioja and Navarra in the VdlT Bajo Ebro, but there has been little interest so far, particularly from La Rioja.

• **The first red DO Rueda** appeared on the market in 2002 (from the 2001 vintage). It took a major change to the regulations to award DO status to these wines, which previously had to be sold under the VdlT Medina del Campo or as Vino de Mesa de Castilla-León. Permitted grapes are Tempranillo, Garnacha, Cabernet Sauvignon, and Merlot.

• **The new DO Montsant wines** also arrived in 2002 (from the 2001 vintage). This horseshoe-shaped DO fits around the foot of the hilly area occupied by the DO Priorato in the province of Tarragona. Originally classified as DO Tarragona-Falset, the new appellation produces a style of wine that falls between the rather bland lowland wines of the DO Tarragona and the hefty and expensive wines of the DO Priorato. Celler de Capçanes (a former cooperative) has made the most inroads into the export market so far.

• **González Byass** has invested in a project called Alto Zano in La Mancha, not far from Osborne's Solaz and Griñón's Dominio de Valdepusa—plainly the province of Toledo is better for growing grapes than anyone had thought. Alto Zano already has 100 hectares (ha) planted with Tempranillo, Cabernet Sauvignon, and Syrah. Whites are made from Verdejo and Chardonnay, but they are sourced from Castilla-León. The wines are labeled as *vino de la tierra* and are intended to retail on the UK market at £3.99 (*sin crianza*) and £4.99 (*crianza*).

• **A 12th-century Dominican monastery** on the outskirts of Salamanca has been restored by Arco-Bodegas Unidas. Called Hacienda Zorita, this is where Christopher Columbus allegedly stayed in 1491 on his way to discover America. The monastery is now a hotel and *crianza bodega*: the first of what is to be a series of Haciendas de España hotel-*bodegas* across Spain.

• **The trend for boutique wines** seems to be gathering momentum. Peter Sisseck (Hacienda Monasterio, Ribera del Duero), who established his credentials as an innovator with Dominio de Pingus in the mid-1990s, has just completed a consultancy project with Celler Mas Gil in Calonge, in the province of Girona. A Cabernet-Merlot-Syrah mix, the top wine, Clos d'Agon, is already commanding top prices in the US market, and there is a second wine, Clos Valmaña. Both are currently badged *vi de taula*. There will be more of these.

NEW SPANISH STARS

Predictions that Duero wines have peaked over the past few years appear to be premature. Land prices and planting rights in the DO Ribera del Duero continue to head toward the planet Mars, with seemingly no shortage of investors wanting a piece of the action. A side effect of this has focused the minds of many existing producers on the neighboring DO regions of Toro and Cigales. Vega Sicilia has invested in Toro, as has that company's former winemaker Mariano García, now of Bodegas Mauro. Other investors in Toro include Castilla la Vieja from Rueda, Riojanas and San Vicente/Sierra Cantábria from Rioja, and winemaking guru Telmo Rodríguez. Most of these will see their first mature vintages come to the market in 2003, and if rising land prices are the barometer of a region's success, this DO is poised for stardom. Developments in Cigales lag a little bit behind, with recent investment from such as Matarromera of Ribera del Duero and the ubiquitous Telmo Rodríguez. Expect to see some ready-for-sale new-generation Cigales wine from 2003 onward. Further north, in the DO Bierzo, another of Spain's young-turk winemakers, Álvaro Palacios, seems at last to have tamed the recalcitrant Mencía grape at Descendientes de J Palacios. But, at present, the only sign of further moves in that region has been a 100 percent Mencía of considerable potential from Bodegas Castro Ventosa. Another little-known area of Castilla-León is the VdlT Ribera del Arlanza. A very promising lightly oaked 2000 Tempranillo from this VdlT was shown by Bodega Palacio de Lerma at the London Spanish Wine Trade Fair in 2003, suggesting that this too may be an area to watch.

OTHER AREAS ON THE UP

Formerly obscure regions, including the Alpujarras in Granada and Almería, are starting to win converts. Indeed, there is a fair amount of activity in Andalucía generally. Ribera del Arlanza in Castilla-León is applying for DO status, but this has been ongoing for some years and may come to nothing. Elsewhere, Fermoselle-Arribes del Duero and Sierra de Alacaraz have also applied for promotion, although this may lapse, since the prime mover in each area (Griñón and Manzaneque, respectively) are now *pago* DOs in their own right. One new DO that has finally made it is Ribera del Júcar, centered on the village of Pozoamargo in the province of Cuenca (originally part of the DO La Mancha). This has existed since September 2001 as a legal entity, but only in January 2003 were the regulations finally formulated and a *consejo regulador* elected; thus the 2003 vintage will be its first. There are eight members within the new DO, though not all the *bodegas* within its boundaries have joined, some preferring the flexibility of being able to buy grapes from the wider region.

Aragón is in ascendancy. Expect to see some improvements from the southwestern Aragonés DOs of Campo de Borja, Calatayud, and Cariñena. These have long shown promise, but only sporadically has this been fulfilled.

However, August 2002 saw reforms to local regulations, which ought to make it easier to produce better wines from that year on. Calatayud in particular has been making great strides and, encouragingly, a lot of the best new work is being done in cooperative *bodegas* that in the past have been reluctant to change their ways. One of the best is the Coop San Alejandro, which is turning out some excellent wines at ridiculously low prices. Codorníu has a new project in the obscure VdlT Valle de la Cina, in the province of Huesca. Sooner or later other investors will realize that this part of Aragón is easily accessed by the *autopista* that links Bilbao, Rioja, Navarra, Lérida, and Barcelona, with all the attendant benefits, from trucking wine out, to busing potential export customers in.

RECENTLY CREATED APPELLATIONS

The following new DOs were harvested for the first time in 2002:
• Arabako Txakolina (or Chacolí de Álava) from País Vasco in Cantabria. This completes the local Txakoli canon, joining neighboring Getaria (or Guetaria) and Bizkaia (or Vizcaya). Not seen, so far, outside the region.
• Pla i Llevant de Mallorca from the eastern-central part of Mallorca, around Felanitx. Grapes include the usual Mallorquí suspects, plus Tempranillo, Chardonnay, Cabernet Sauvignon, and Merlot.
• Sierras de Málaga from Ronda in

Andalucía. High-altitude vineyards (2,500 ft/750 m) allow the production of unfortified wines in the hot, traditionally fortified wine region of Andalucía. Grapes are Chardonnay, Sauvignon, Cabernet Sauvignon, Merlot, Tempranillo, and Syrah. However, the only producer of note within this appellation is Principe Alfonso de Hohenlohe, who does not belong to the DO, since he grows grapes that are not permitted under its regulations, most notably Petit Verdot.
• Gran Canaria in the Canary Islands. This is a catch-all DO for most of the vineyards that were left out when the DO Monte de Lentiscal was created for an area of Gran Canaria in 1999. Very varied styles of wine made from all the usual Canary suspects in vineyards varying widely in altitude from 165 ft (50 m) to 4,265 ft (1,300 m).

Wines from new VdlT areas seen for the first time in 2002 and 2003 include:
• Norte de Granada (Andalucía), Granada Sud-Ouest (Andalucía), Terrazas de Gállego (Aragón), Valle de la Cinca (Aragón), Cangas (Asturias— the only wine-producing zone in this region), Eivissa (Ibiza, Balearic Islands), and La Gomera (Canary Islands—amid rumors that it has already been promoted to DO). Not all of these VdlTs have been ratified by AVIMES, the national association.

Opinion:
Oak maybe, but never for oak's sake

An eternal problem: wood. There seems to be an item of received wisdom that a wine with *crianza* on the label is worth €1 more than one without, and that one with *reserva* is worth at least €2 more. This leads to cask-aging of totally inappropriate wines, especially in big-quantity years when the wine may offer little more than fruit. This is the main reason I chose Valdelosfrailes 2000 (Cigales) and Neonato 2000 (Murrieta, Rioja) as two of my best buys of the year: they are pure Tempranillo, vinified fresh, full of fruit, with enough natural tannin to provide a crisp balance and some complexity, without oak dominating the palate. Too many *bodegas* are still aging wine in cask hoping that the oak will somehow revitalize the wine. Instead, of course, it just destroys whatever fragile fruit character the wine has.

Wood should be regularly inspected

The quality of wood used is another issue. Señorío de Sarría in Navarra boldly destroyed thousands of barrels in 2002, sending the wine they contained to the vinegar factory. This was a final admission, after some 10 years of chivvying, that they had a problem with fungal growth in the *bodega*. This is not unique to them and not a new problem either: in 1988 Tom Stevenson pointed out the same problem with Marqués de Riscal. Although fungal growth is not a widespread problem, dirty old wood is much more prevalent. Curiously, Rioja probably has more experience in the management of cask-aging for red wine than any other region in the world, yet it appears to be one of the worst offenders for failing to maintain its casks properly or renew them often enough.

Irrigation rules need tightening up

In contrast to oak, irrigation is a relatively new problem. It was formerly banned, but since the great drought of 1992–93 irrigation has been permitted on an experimental basis. Some *bodegas* are using drip irrigation or more scientifically based programs, such as PRD (see Viticulture), while others simply install lawn sprinklers and hope for the best. Still others insist that the perforated hoses along the base of the vine row are there purely for frost prevention and have nothing to do with irrigation at all! The more scientific methods can certainly deliver an impressive consistency of quality in variable years, especially in the southern half of the country. There can be no argument, however, that the delivery of random or continuous quantities of water regardless of the needs of the vine should be banned completely.

Yields are too high

There is a real need to limit yields, to green-harvest effectively and, if necessary, more than once, well before the harvest. No one will ever forget the disastrous overproduction in Rioja in the 2000 vintage, after which the *consejo regulador* declassified thousands of hectoliters (hl) of watery wine, even though this left a similar quantity of equally poor quality in the system. This does the consumer and the wine region no favors. The yields need to be enforced rigorously if regions are to retain their integrity and reputation for quality. At the 2003 Spanish Wine Fair in London, for example, some of the greatest wines of Rioja and Ribera del Duero had been harvested at around 24–25 hl/ha, approximately half the permitted maximum. Perhaps that is why they are some of the greatest wines of those two regions?

Grapevine

• **Various Andalucían** *bodegas* that are well known in more traditional markets (notably Hidalgo in Sanlúcar de Barrameda and Alvear and Pérez Barquero in Montilla-Moriles) have been investing heavily in higher-altitude vineyards for the production of non-fortified wines from Syrah, Tempranillo, et al. No wine has yet been put on the market. González Byass has also planted a vineyard in the Arcos de la Frontera area, mainly Tempranillo and Syrah, but also with some Cabernet Sauvignon, Petit Verdot, and Malbec. The wines are, as yet, unnamed but will be labeled VdlT Andalucía.

• **Arco-Bodegas Unidas** continues its inexorable expansion with the completion of the new Durius *bodega* amid 30 ha of vines at what is being mooted as a future DO Alto Duero. This group already includes ownership of Berberana, Marqués de Monistrol, Lagunilla, Campo Burgo, Señorío de Urdaiz, Hispano-Argentinas, and 40 percent of Marqués de Griñón, and it is under the auspices of the latter that Bodega Durius has come to fruition. Arco's stated ambition is to make wine all the way along the River Duero, and it has consolidated this by buying a vineyard in the DO Ribera del Duero (Finca Abascal in Valbuena de Duero). Future plans include a project that will make wine in the DOC Douro

in Portugal. All these wines, whether Spanish or Portuguese, will carry the Marqués de Griñón Durius brand name.

• **The DO Priorato** has nominally been promoted to DOCa, making it only the second in Spain after Rioja. However, there is much confusion over when it will be displayed on the labels.

• **Look out for wines** from the regionwide DO Catalunya, which is being driven by Torres and in particular by the new range of wines made by Miguel Torres' daughter, Mireia Torres Maczassek. The DO reports acceptance by the markets to the tune of 31 million bottles in 2002, and the more relaxed rules of this DO suggest that we will be seeing more of these wines.

• **With the trend for boutique wines** at stratospheric prices, quite a few producers have been looking longingly at, say, a patch of 100-year-old Tempranillo vines and wondering whether to make a single-vineyard wine from it. This is all well and good, and some of these wines are excellent; but what happens to the mainstream wines into which those old-vine grapes used to go? Will they be sold as the same old wine at the same old price, even though their "heart" has been ripped out?

Vintage Report

Advance report on the latest harvest

2002

This year's harvest can be split roughly into a southwest/northeast divide, with the former having the better time of it. Picking started earliest in Catalunya because damp conditions had brought an attack of botrytis, particularly to Macabeo in the Baix-Penedès. Rain during the harvest did it no favors, extending the rot to Tempranillo and Merlot. The result was a much-reduced vintage of generally average quality, but those growers who managed to pick between the showers, and those north and west of Penedès, were much better off. La Mancha began harvesting in early September after a good ripening period, with the Malpica vineyards picking Syrah in the first week of the month, having reduced a potentially massive crop by green-harvesting in July and August, from a potential 125 hl/ha to a more manageable 62 hl/ha, amid predictions of very good wines. Rioja saw an overall 23 percent drop in quantity from 2001 after a rainy August, and up to half the crop in some areas (such as Cenicero) had to be discarded. Inevitably, producers who own their own vineyards and control all aspects of production with the utmost quality in mind were the ones who picked the healthiest fruit. In some of these cases, the quality will be a very good to excellent vintage. Despite bold talk from many *bodegas* about high quality, it seems likely that 2002 Rioja will be good to very good, rather than outstanding. In Ribera del Duero hopes are high for good to very good quality, with about 10 percent of wines achieving *gran reserva* status.

Updates on the previous five vintages

2001

Vintage rating: *90*

Excellent quality throughout Spain, with Rioja and Ribera del Duero showing particularly well, and La Mancha and Valdepeñas in the south making what may become some very long-lived wines. Good whites, too, particularly in Rías Baixas and Rueda, for early drinking.

2000

Vintage rating: *60–80*

Better in the south than the north. Rioja produced a vast, dilute, and unattractive vintage. Those *bodegas* that green-harvested and hand-selected made some good wines, but they were in the minority. Some of the better estates and Penedès fared better than most.

1999

Vintage rating: *70*

Generally a good, but not outstanding, year with a substantial minority of wines of *reserva* potential and a very few single-estate wines achieving very good quality. Some early-released *crianzas* have developed a rather prominent thread of acidity, but the few *reserva* wines that have been released show rather better.

1998

Vintage rating: *80–90*

A very good year in the north, with considerable potential for *reserva* quality and above in Rioja (even though it was the biggest vintage ever) and Ribera del Duero. Both of these are now showing well at *reserva* level, as are Valdepeñas and Penedès.

1997

Vintage rating: *60–70*

A difficult year in Rioja, with higher-altitude vineyards delivering healthy grapes, but many in the lowland areas having problems with rain during the summer. Ribera del Duero and Valdepeñas suffered much the same, with a disappointing vintage. Penedès did rather better.

GREATEST WINE PRODUCERS

1. Alejandro Fernández (Pesquera, Condado de Haza, El Vínculo)
2. Peter Sisseck (Hacienda Monasterio, Pingus, etc.)
3. Álvaro Palacios (L'Ermita, Finca Dofi, etc)
4. Vega Sicilia (Ribera del Duero)
5. Mariano García (Aalto, Mauro, Maurodos)
6. Telmo Rodríguez (Toro, etc)
7. Carlos Falcó (Marqués de Griñón, Durius, Dominio de Valdepusa)
8. Miguel Torres (Penedès)
9. Costers del Siurana (Priorato)
10. Contino (Rioja)

FASTEST-IMPROVING PRODUCERS

1. Osborne (Castilla)
2. Bodega Viña Bajoz (Toro)
3. Vinícola de Castilla (La Mancha)
4. Celler de Capçanes (Montsant)
5. Durius (Castilla-León)
6. Señorío de Sarría (Navarra)
7. Bodega Pirineos (Somontano)
8. Valdelosfrailes (Cigales)
9. Bodegas A Tapada (Valdeorras)
10. Principe Alfonso de Hohenlohe (Serranía de Ronda)

NEW UP-AND-COMING PRODUCERS

1. Ysios (Rioja)
2. Tarsus (Ribera del Duero)
3. Legaris (Ribera del Duero)
4. Luna Beberide (Castilla-León)
5. Estancia Piedra (Toro)
6. Torres (Catalunya by Mireia Torres Maczassek)
7. Dalcamp (Somontano)
8. Finca Sobreño (Toro)
9. Mustiguillo (Valencia)
10. Anima Negra (Baleares)

BEST-VALUE PRODUCERS

1. Coop Nuestra Señora del Rosario (La Mancha)
2. Bodegas Centro Españolas (La Mancha)
3. Bodegas San Alejandro Coop (Calatayud)
4. Bodegas Agapito Rico (Jumilla)
5. Viñas de Alange (Tierra de Barros)
6. Valdelosfrailes (Cigales)
7. Casa de la Ermita (Jumilla)
8. Comercial Vinícola del Nordest (Empordà-Costa Brava)
9. Bodegas E Mendoza (Alicante)
10. Martínez-Bujanda (Rioja)

GREATEST-QUALITY WINES

1. **Alenza 1996** Bodegas Condado de Haza (€50)
2. **Único 1989** Vega Sicilia (€120)
3. **Pingus 2000** Dominio de Pingus (€525)
4. **L'Ermita 1999** Álvaro Palacios (€200)
5. **Contino 1998** Viña del Olivo (€40)
6. **Malleolus de Valderramiro 2000** Bodegas Emilio Moro (€75)
7. **Finca Dofi 2000** Álvaro Palacios (€70)
8. **Marqués de Griñón Emeritvs 1999** Dominio de Valdepusa (€55)
9. **Grans Muralles 1998** Torres (€70)
10. **Artadi 2000** Viña El Pisón (€90)

BEST BARGAINS

1. **Joven Cigales 2000** Valdelosfrailes (€5)
2. **Altozano Tempranillo 2001** González Byass (€4.50)
3. **Monasterio de Santa Ana 2001** Casa de la Ermita (€4.50)
4. **Carchelo 2001** Bodegas Agapito Rico (€5)
5. **Palacio de Lerma Barrica 2000** Ribera del Arlanza (€5)

6 Solaz 2000 Osborne (€4)

7 Viñalange Roble 2001
Viñas de Alange (€2.50)

8 Tresantos Oinos 2001
Bodegas Viñas Zamoranos (€5)

9 Marqués de Nombrevilla Joven
2002 Bodegas San Alejandro
Coop (€2.50)

10 Torrelongares 2002
Covinca Coop (€2)

MOST EXCITING OR UNUSUAL FINDS

1 Bierzo 1999
Descendientes de J Palacios (€25)
*Álvaro Palacios has tamed the
difficult Mencía grape, at last.*

2 Neonato 2000 Marqués de
Murrieta (€9) *A great example
of what Rioja ought to do in
difficult vintages—excellent ripe
Tempranillo with minimal oak.*

3 Garnacha Centenaria 2002
Bodegas Aragonesas (€7) *Forty-
year-old vines give warmth, depth,
and spice at a budget price.*

4 Nerola 2000 Torres (€16)
*Made by Mireia Torres Maczassek,
the daughter of Miguel Torres, this
wine points the way for the
expanding DO Catalunya.*

5 La Legua Capricho 1999
Bodegas Emeterio Fernández (€10)
*Established as recently as
1997, this bodega in Cigales is
producing excellent wine from its
own grapes, under winemaker
Ricardo Sanz from Rueda.*

6 Expresión 2000
Bodegas San Alejandro (€12)
*This Calatayud cooperative has
made stunning strides in quality
in the past year, with wines that
are worth double the asking price.*

7 Petit Verdot 2000
Principe Alfonso de Hohenlohe (€8)
*The prince switched from blend
to varietal with the 2000 vintage,
and a big improvement in quality
was immediately noticeable.*

8 Aranzo Tinto Crianza 1997
Bodegas Huertas (€9)
*Another example of how the
Monastrell can turn out superb
wines when handled properly.*

9 Rozaleme 2001 Mustiguillo (€9)
*An astonishingly good wine,
fermented in oak vats by a tiny
bodega in the province of Valencia.*

10 Nuviana 2001 Cabernet
Sauvignon-Merlot (€6)
*A Codorníu project in Valle de la
Cinca, an obscure part of Aragón,
which starts to reveal the potential
of this region as a whole.*

Grapevine

• **Bodegas Beronia** in Rioja will be launching a new single-vineyard wine from a 20-ha vineyard of vines that average 30 years old, although at this stage it remains unnamed and may not reach the market for two more years. Elsewhere in Rioja, the trend should continue toward more individual, hand-crafted wines. This has been growing for the past five to seven years, and landmarks along the way have been wines with minimal oak (such as Primicia), wines supremely expressive of their *terroir* (Ysios, Allende), and wines from smaller plots (Contino Viña del Olivo, Marqués de Murrieta Capellanía).

• **Madrid** has been putting together a new national wine-regulatory regime for the past couple of years, and few, if any, DO regions are making any moves until they see what it contains. Rumors abound that it will be more flexible than the previous regulation, allow more experimentation, and encourage maverick winemakers, thereby heading off *pago* DOs (see lead article) at the pass.

Sherry

Julian Jeffs QC

Sherry country is an exciting place to be these days. In the last few years the old order has been stood on its head.

JULIAN JEFFS QC

In the past, big, old *bodegas* owned by the "Sherry aristocracy" supplied practically all the wine, much of it cheap and pretty dim. There were small shippers, too, of course, but they accounted for only a very minor part of the production. All of them were backed up by *almacenistas* (private stockholders), sometimes owned by people like doctors and lawyers, who were generally too small to be granted licenses to export, while a few bigger ones just did not want to be licensed, since they could sell all their wines to the shippers. One shipper, Lustau, developed a special market for small shipments of excellent Sherry labeled with the names of the *almacenistas* who supplied them. However, it is now much easier for the small houses to get shipping licenses and they are rapidly taking them up.

JULIAN JEFFS became a Gray's Inn barrister in 1958, attained Queen's Counsel in 1975, and retired from practice in 1991, although he continued as a Deputy High Court Judge until 1996. His love of Sherry began in 1956, when he was a Sherry shipper's assistant in Spain, and this led to a passion for writing when *Sherry* (Faber & Faber) was published in 1961. He began a two-year stint as editor of *Wine & Food* in 1965, the same year that Faber & Faber offered him the post of general editor for its radically new Wine Series. Over the next 40-some years he commissioned many of the most respected, long-lasting, definitive works on wine. He held this position until 2002, when Faber & Faber sold the Wine Series to Mitchell Beazley. Julian has been chairman (1970–72), vice president (1975–91) and president (1992–96) of the Circle of Wine Writers, winning the Glenfiddich Wine Writer award in 1974 and 1978. His books include *The Wines of Europe* (Faber & Faber, 1971), *The Little Dictionary of Drink* (Pelham, 1973), and *The Wines of Spain* (Faber & Faber).

To put this into perspective, it should be understood that Sherry sales peaked as long ago as 1979, going downhill just after there had been a lot of expansion based on optimistic projections of sales charts. At this point there were too many vineyards, too much stock, loans that could not be repaid, and, to cap this all, a steady decline in the price of Sherry. It was disastrous. Sherry became hard to sell, particularly at a profitable price. Part of this can be blamed on the caprice of fortune, but primarily it was caused by the terrible quality of cheap wines that had flooded the market, giving Sherry a bad name. Much the same was happening with German wine at the time.

Sherry is expensive to make; thus, as prices dropped, most of what was sold was sold at a loss. The shippers that did show a profit made it from their brandy sales. Most of the smaller shippers gradually disappeared, some were absorbed by the big names, while others simply went bankrupt. Now there appears to be the beginning of a renaissance. Sales have not materially increased, but the higher-priced wines are selling, and there is, at last, an understanding of and an appreciation for real quality. Shippers have finally realized that great Sherry is a great wine and, as such, should be sold in limited quantities. And, having been given the chance to taste the best that Sherry has to offer, there is a growing public recognition that it is indeed one the world's greatest wines. Because its reputation is on the rise, there is also a perception among informed consumers that Sherry is one of the last classic wines to be sold at bargain prices, even if they are on the increase.

If this has not penetrated the minds of multinationals, who seem to think only in terms of bulk and brands, some of the big family names have at least seen the light and are at the forefront of the new trade. The most conspicuous change is the arrival of boutique *bodegas*, selling fine wines to a discerning public. Some of these are ex-*almacenistas*, but others are entirely new creations, often belonging to members of the old Sherry dynasties, who have been displaced by takeovers and want to go back to their roots. In the old days, a *bodega* had to have stocks of 12,500 hectoliters (hl) in order to get an export license, but the figure has now been reduced to 500 hl, and this has opened the door of opportunity for many.

OLD SHERRY NOW OFFICIAL

The most important recent change has been the introduction of two new official designations: VOS and VORS. The former stands for *Vinum Optimum Signatum* or Very Old Sherry (minimum age of 20 years), the latter for *Vinum Optimum Rare Signatum* or Very Old Rare Sherry (minimum age 30 years). Either the abbreviation or the age may be used on the label. To qualify, a wine has to be analyzed and tasted, after which a minimum shipping quota must be laid down to ensure the quality is maintained. It is safe to say that any wine in either of these categories will be exceptionally good, but they only apply to Amontillado, Palo Cortado, and Oloroso. Why not Fino? Because a fino that is 20 years old will have turned into an Amontillado. Some wines that could well have the official classification are marketed without it, since the red tape involved is considerable and, if production is very small, not worth the effort. A VORS is, of course, older than a VOS, but it does not necessarily mean it is better. How old you drink your Sherry is a matter of personal taste, and some of the very old wines are not easy to approach: they can be wines for enthusiasts only. A further development in late 2002 saw new categories for 12-year-old and 15-year-old wines put in place.

VOS/VORS Certification

Those Sherries currently certified VOS and VORS are:

Barbadillo Amontillado Principe (VOS), Palo Cortado Obispo Gascón (VORS) Oloroso Cuco (VORS), Oloroso San Rafael (VORS)

Pilar Aranda Amontillado AD (VORS), Oloroso Alburejo (VORS)

Bodegas 501 Amontillado Miranda (VOS)

Bodegas Tradición Oloroso Tradición (VORS), Pedro Ximénez Tradición (VOS)

Dios Baco Amontillado Baco Imperial (VOS), Oloroso Baco Imperial (VORS)

Pedro Domecq Amontillado 51-1a (VORS), Palo Cortado Capuchino (VORS), Oloroso Sibarita (VORS), Pedro Ximénez Venerable (VORS)

José Estévez Oloroso Covadonga (VOS)

Garvey Oloroso 1780 (VORS), Pedro Ximénez 1780 (VORS)

Gil Luque Amontillado de Bandera (VORS), Palo Cortado de Bandera (VORS), Oloroso de Bandera (VORS), Pedro Ximénez de Bandera (VORS)

González Byass Amontillado del Duque (VORS), Palo Cortado Apóstoles (VORS), Oloroso Matúsalem (VORS), Pedro Ximénez Noë (VORS)

Emilio Hidalgo Palo Cortado Privilegio (VORS), Pedro Ximénez Santa Ana (VORS)

Emilio Lustau Amontillado VOS Lustau (VOS), Oloroso VORS Lustau (VORS)

Federico Paternina Oloroso Victoria Regina (VORS), Pedro Ximénez Vieja Solera (VORS)

Pedro Romero Amontillado Don Pedro Romero (VORS), Oloroso El Alamo (VORS) Palo Cortado Pedro Romero (VORS)

Sánchez Romate Amontillado La Sacristía (VORS), Oloroso La Sacristía (VORS), Pedro Ximénez La Sacristía (VOS)

Valdespino Amontillado Coliseo (VORS), Palo Cortado Cardenal (VORS), Oloroso Su Majestad (VORS)

Vinícola Hidalgo Amontillado Pastrana (VOS), Amontillado Viejo (VORS), Oloroso Viejo (VORS)

Williams & Humbert Amontillado Solera Especial (VORS), Palo Cortado Solera Especial (VOS), Pedro Ximénez Solera Especial (VOS).

EMILIO LUSTAU

Moving out of its rather cramped, if picturesque, premises by the city walls, Emilio Lustau has acquired the old Mackenzie and Misa *bodegas* from Harveys and turned them into a showpiece. Now there is plenty of room to help ensure its continued expansion. It still sells some of its famed *almacenista* Sherries but is now concentrating more on its own fine wines and has introduced single-cask Sherries in small runs of 600 bottles. Very good bottles they are, too.

PICASSO ON THE TILES

Bodegas Tradición is a name to watch. In 1998, Don Joaquín Rivero Valcarce, a descendant of the old Rivero Sherry family, bought the shell of an abandoned *bodega* on the Plaza Cordobeses, in the historic center of Jerez, and set about restoring it. He was joined by some friends, also from the old Jerez families, and together they aim to produce small quantities of the highest-possible-quality Sherry. They acquired old *soleras* from at least 20 companies and from these they have produced *soleras* providing a complete range of old Sherry styles, which will soon be put on the market. They have also laid down *añadas* from 1970 onward. The *bodega* contains Don Joaquín's collection of Spanish art, including a set of tiles painted by the eight-year-old Pablo Picasso.

DOMECQ IN ALL BUT NAME

When Allied bought Domecq, the family found itself, for the first time in nearly 300 years, without a *bodega*. One member has stayed on in the old firm, but most had to go and were bereft. Alvaro, though, was made of fighting stuff. He was not to be easily parted from Sherry, but he could not ship it under his own name, since that now belonged to Allied. Alvaro solved the dilemma in 1998 by buying an *almacenista*, Pilar Aranda, which dates from 1800. He was, in his own phrase, born again. And, with the trade depression, he had no difficulty in acquiring stocks of fine, mature wines. The quality is superb.

BEST *BODEGA*

José Estévez made his money out of glass for the manufacture of bottles, but being a true Jerezano, his love was wine. His first move was to buy the very reputable old established house of Real Tesoro and to build a fine new *bodega* on the edge of the city. Then he acquired the *soleras* of the excellent fino Tío Mateo, formerly a brand of Palomino & Vergara. In all this he showed that he was fully capable of keeping quality up. Then, in 2002, he bought AR Valdespino. This was the oldest and architecturally the most beautiful (in a small-scale way) of the Jerez *bodegas*, noted for wines of the very highest quality. The best of the old *bodega* buildings are likely to become a museum. The wines have been moved to the new *bodegas*, and the *capataz*, who was responsible for making the wines in the old *bodega*, has moved with them. The quality appears to be as good as ever, though it may well be that some of the prices will become more realistic.

Opinion:
Consejo Regulador should be stricter

The decline in popularity of Sherry can be blamed in part on the appalling quality of some of the cheap wines that have been shipped in recent years. The Consejo Regulador passes all the wines that are sold, and it does a good job in taking wines at random off bottling lines to compare with the control sample of the wine that it passed, but it would do a better job if it did not pass some of the poorer wines that are shipped.

Sweet-Sherry vineyards?

In the past, some of the sweetening wines used in the blending used to be made with the aid of invert sugar. This is a natural product that did no harm at all, but it is not allowed under EU regulations, so, as in other European wine-growing areas, "rectified" concentrated must (in Spanish *mosto concentrado rectificado*) has to be used instead. At present this comes from vineyards of little or no wine potential in the center of Spain. It would make more sense, surely, to grub up some of those vineyards and replant some of the excellent vineyards that lay fallow in Jerez, since this would give the Sherry industry scope for expansion when the demand rises again.

Grapevine

• **The shippers** in Sanlúcar de Barrameda realized that there was a potentially large domestic market and, being less oriented to export than those in the other two towns of Jerez de la Frontera and Puerto de Santa María, set out to conquer it. Their efforts began with the Feria de Abril in Sevilla (a week of dancing, horsemanship, and Manzanilla-drinking), and they had enormous success.

• **González Byass** has consolidated its position as the largest family-owned *bodega* in Jerez by purchasing Croft, noted for its bestselling Pale Cream Sherry. The vast Croft *bodega*, on the edge of the city, is still run independently, but some degree of integration will inevitably follow.

• **Sandeman Coprimar,** with its unique *soleras* of old Oloroso, has ceased being part of a multinational, having been bought by the Portuguese Sogrape company in 2002. In recent years, under Seagram, it had concentrated on exporting to the Continental markets, but changes will certainly come about and it is to be hoped that its fine wines will again be found on export shelves.

• **In 2002, the city of Jerez** awarded El Maestro Sierra a prize for quality and achievement. Founded in 1830, this used to be one of the oldest established of the *almacenistas*. It is now bottling its own wines, of excellent quality, and has been launched on the export markets. It also has the unique distinction of being run entirely by women.

• **Alas, the proud name** of Duff Gordon is no more! Long owned by Osborne, Duff Gordon has now been dissolved and the brand discontinued in all markets.

Vintage Report

For Sherry, vintage assessments per se are not particularly relevant because very little Sherry is vintaged, and that which is will not be released for 20 years or more. However, Sherry lovers should be interested to know how much Sherry has been topping up the various *soleras* in recent years, and whether the quality of these wines has been good or bad. Note that the maximum yield allowed for Sherry is 99 hectoliters per hectare (hl/ha).

Advance report on the latest harvest

2002

A yield of 64 hl/ha provided a total of 137,888 butts of new wine for all the Sherry *bodegas*. Quality: good maturity with a natural alcoholic strength of 11 percent.

Updates on the previous five vintages

2001

Vintage rating: *95*

A yield of 72 hl/ha provided a total of 152,102 butts of new wine for all the Sherry *bodegas*. Another early vintage. Quality: exceptional, the grapes had a perfect level of maturation.

2000

Vintage rating: *90*

A yield of 65 hl/ha provided a total of 135,524 butts of new wine for all the Sherry *bodegas*. One of the earliest vintages on record. Quality: very high.

1999

Vintage rating: *85*

A yield of 75 hl/ha provided a total of 157,525 butts of new wine. Rainfall: 9½ in (245 mm). Quality: good.

1998

Vintage rating: *85*

A yield of 73 hl/ha provided a total of 154,705 butts of new wine.
Rainfall: 27½ in (702 mm). Quality: good.

1997

Vintage rating: *85*

A yield of 85 hl/ha provided 179,989 butts of new wine. Rainfall: 36½ in
(927 mm). Quality: good.

GREATEST WINE PRODUCERS

1. González Byass/Croft
2. Bodegas Osborne
3. Emilio Lustau/Luís Caballero
4. José Estévez
   (Valdespino and Real Tesoro)
5. Bodegas Williams & Humbert, SL
6. Allied Domecq España
   (Domecq and Harvey)
7. Bodegas Barbadillo, SL
8. Vinícola Hidalgo y Cía
9. Sandeman Coprimar
10. Garvey/José de Soto

FASTEST-IMPROVING PRODUCERS

1. Delgado Zuleta
2. Díos Baco
3. Emilio Hidalgo
4. Herederos de Argüeso
5. Hijos de Rainera Pérez Marín
6. M Gil Luque
7. Pedro Romero
8. Sánchez Romate Hermanos

NEW UP-AND-COMING PRODUCERS

1. Bodegas 501 del Puerto
2. Bodegas J Ferris
3. Bodegas Pilar Aranda
4. Bodegas Tradición

5. Gaspar Florido Cano
6. Herederos de Argüeso
7. Juan Carlos Gutiérrez Colusía
8. M Gil Luque
9. Pilar Plá Pechovierto
   (El Maestro Sierra)
10. Torre Dama (Miguel Gómez)

BEST-VALUE PRODUCERS

1. Bodegas Williams & Humbert
2. Emilio Lustau
3. José Estévez
4. Wisdom & Warter

GREATEST-QUALITY WINES

1. **San León**
   Herederos de Argüeso (€5.20)
2. **Tío Pepe** González Byass (€5.90)
3. **Inocente** Valdespino (€6)
4. **Coquinero** Osborne (€5.60)
5. **Pastrana Manzanilla Pasada**
   Vinícola Hidalgo (€7.80)
6. **Del Duque Amontillado Muy Viejo** Aged 30 Years,
   González Byass (€32)
7. **1730 Palo Cortado**
   Pilar Aranda (€38.60)
8. **Oloroso Solera Especial Dry Sack** Williams & Humbert (€20)
9. **Matusalém** González Byass (€32)
10. **Solera 1842 Oloroso**
    Valdespino (€25)

BEST BARGAINS

1. **Matusalém** González Byass (€32)
2. **Bailén** Osborne (€9)
3. **Oloroso Seco Napoléon** Vinícola Hidalgo (€6)
4. **Amontillado Seco Napoléon** Vinícola Hidalgo (€6)
5. **Jerez Cortado** Vinícola Hidalgo (€17)
6. **Fino del Puerto** Gutierrez Colosía (€3.50)
7. **Manzanilla Las Medallas** Herederos de Argüeso (€3.50)
8. **Don Fino** Sandeman (€6.60)
9. **Fino Valdespino** (€4.27)
10. **Pedro Ximénez Viejo Napoléon** Vinícola Hidalgo (€8)

MOST EXCITING OR UNUSUAL FINDS

1. **El Maestro Sierra Amoroso** (€6.75) Once one of the most popular styles, it got rather debased and then fell out of favor. Although the word means "loving," the name is in fact derived from that of a vineyard that used to be noted for such wines. It is gently sweetened, which takes it into the dessert class, and is the perfect wine for a cold day.

2. **González Byass Viña AB** (€10) When the flor dies away as Fino ages, it passes into Amontillado but on the way has many of the virtues of both styles. This is a beautiful example.

3. **González Byass 1970 Añada Oloroso** (€85) Another fine vintage wine that, if slightly younger, is perfectly mature and bottled at its peak, showing the sheer majesty of a fine Oloroso.

4. **Vinícola Hidalgo Amontillado Viejo Pastrana** (€26) There are not many single-vineyard sherries, and this is one of them, kept apart because of its exceptional quality.

Amontillados from Sanlúcar are lighter and more delicate than those from Jerez or even from El Puerto, but its great maturity gives this one plenty of flavor.

5. **Lustau Moscatel Las Cruces** (€31) Moscatel is usually used for blending and has been rather eclipsed by the grander, sweeter Pedro Ximénez, but when fully mature it is a sweet wine of elegance and charm with a real Moscatel flavor.

6. **Lustau Old East India Sherry** (€17) The name is full of nostalgia. It used to be applied to wine matured by being shipped to the East Indies and back. This is no longer done, but the name is justly applied to a mature, sweet blend that gives a good idea of what our ancestors used to drink.

7. **Osborne Palo Cortado Abocado Solera P-D-P** (€95) Palo Cortado is generally bottled dry and shows remarkable subtlety, between an Amontillado and an Oloroso. Slightly sweetened, as this is, it can be a superb dessert wine— rare and wonderful.

8. **Sandeman Royal Esmeralda** (€25) Sandeman has changed the blend of this wine over the years. It used to be considerably sweetened but now it is dry and shows the great quality of the solera from which it is drawn.

9. **Valdespino Oloroso Solera Su Majestad** (€22) A magisterial old Oloroso, worthy of its royal title.

10. **Williams & Humbert Vintage Collection Palo Cortado 1962** (€250 estimated auction price) Vintage wines are very much the exception, but if left to develop without blending, Sherry can show remarkable flavor and complexity, especially Palo Cortado. No wine shows them better than this.

Portugal

Richard Mayson

The word 'crisis' has passed the lips of Portugal's winemakers over the past year almost as many times as wine has.

RICHARD MAYSON

Following a decade of continuous growth, Portugal has been plunged into a particularly virulent and challenging recession. The crisis began when it became clear that Portugal was set to become the first country in the euro zone to breach the economic criteria that is part and parcel of the EU's common currency. The socialist government of Antonio Guterres fell, to be replaced by a center-right coalition led by Jose Durão Barroso. When he took office in April 2002, the European Commission was threatening to fine Portugal and cut off much-needed EU funds unless he took drastic action to reduce the budget deficit. Since then, Durão Barroso, together with his "Iron Lady,'" finance minister Manuela Ferreira Leite, has slashed public spending with a vengeance. In the wine sector, generic promotion has felt the brunt, with the Port Wine Institute (IVP) and Portugal's Trade and Tourism Office (ICEP) experiencing budget cuts across the board. So far the fiscal crisis seems to have had a limited impact on the domestic market. Trophy wines like Barca Velha, Quinta do Vale Meão, Symington's Chryseia,

RICHARD MAYSON writes and lectures on wine, dividing his time between London, Portugal, and a family business in the Peak District. He speaks fluent Portuguese, having been brought up in Portugal, and is regarded as one of the most respected authorities on Port, Sherry, Madeira, and the wines of Spain and Portugal. His interest in the subject goes back to his college days, when he wrote a thesis on the microclimates of the vineyards of the Douro Valley. His books include *Portugal's Wines & Wine Makers* (Ebury Press, 1992), *Port and the Douro* (Faber & Faber, 1999), and his latest work, *The Wines and Vineyards of Portugal* (Mitchell Beazley), which was published in March 2003. He is currently preparing a second edition of *Port and the Douro*, a third edition of *Portugal's Wines & Wine Makers*, and a new book on the wines of Madeira.

Niepoort's Batuta, and Quinta do Monte d'Oiro from Estremadura are still trading at hugely inflated prices. A survey of the top wine retailers published in a Lisbon newspaper showed that Douro wines were faring particularly well, although sales of imported wine, especially champagne, had fallen sharply. However, sales of middle and lower-end Portuguese wine are more sluggish, and the cooperatives are holding large stocks of such wines, with few buyers. Sales of Vinho Verde are particularly depressed. The restaurant sector has fallen into recession, with two of Lisbon's top restaurants, Bacchus and Evaristo, closing their doors and others cutting menu prices. According to the Associacão de Restauracão e Similares de Portugal, restaurant turnover fell by 23 percent in the second half of 2003, while sales in cafés and *pastelarias* (cake shops) increased. Although the government deficit has now fallen below the requisite 3 percent, the effects of Portugal's deepest recession since joining the EU in 1986 do not bode well for the wine industry in 2003.

Grapevine

• **Vineyards on the Azorean island** of Pico are set to join those of the Alto Douro as Portugal's second viticultural UNESCO World Heritage Site. This unique checkerboard of vineyards, protected from the Atlantic westerlies by a network of low volcanic stone walls, has been under threat from development for some time. Now over 150 hectares (ha) of vineyard is to be protected along with a number of traditional *adegas* (wineries) making a fortified wine from Verdelho.

• **A futile battle** has been lost by the Comissão de Viticultura do Região dos Vinhos Verdes (CRVV), which tried to safeguard the name Alvarinho for Portugal. The CRVV contested the use of the name by California's Havens Wine Cellars, which recently launched a varietal wine under this name. The CRVV was told that although the name Vinho Verde was protected, Alvarinho is a recognized grape variety and could not be protected in the same way.

• **The wine department** at the University of Trás-os-Montes in Vila Real is in danger of closing due to a lack of

students. This would leave Portugal, a country with more vineyards than Australia and a higher percentage of its land under vines than France, without a center for education and research.

• **Quinta do Monte d'Oiro's** 1999 Homenagem a António Carqueijeiro was the outright winner in a head-to-head tasting of Spanish and Portuguese wines organized by wine magazines *Revista de Vinhos* in Lisbon and *Sibaratas* in Madrid. It is also the only Portuguese wine to be nominated among 22 Legendary Wines of the World at the Encuentro de Vinos Miticos del Mundo in Madrid in January 2003.

• **Caves Raposeira,** once Portugal's largest producer of sparkling wine by the traditional method, has been sold by Pernod-Ricard to former competitor Caves Murganheira. Raposeira, with cellars at Lamego, on the southern edge of the Douro region, used to belong to Seagram, but was sold to Pernod-Ricard in 2002 following the earlier sale of Sandeman to Sogrape for €100 million. Murganheira is now the largest producer by far of sparkling wine in Portugal.

SMART HOMOCLIMES

Australian viticulturist Richard Smart, who consults for a number of leading properties in Portugal, has been the talk of the trade after a presentation at Lisbon's Envoi trade fair in January 2003. On the basis that "Portugal has some of the finest grape varieties in the world" and that "in the future they will become popular in Australia as we begin to lose fascination with the international varieties," Smart compared the climatic characteristics of Portugal and Australia. Results from the Douro are particularly interesting. Smart compares the temperature profile of Pinhão, in the heart of the region, with Wagga Wagga, Yarrawonga, Wadonga, and Shepperton in Victoria, and Karnet in Western Australia and asks, "Are these Australia's best, best regions for fortified wines yet to be planted?" Perhaps the Portuguese should be asking similar questions about Shiraz, Semillon, and Verdelho.

GRAPE NAME CHANGE

The first wines bottled according to Portugal's internationally agreed list of grape varieties are from the 2002 vintage. The Port grape Touriga Francesa is now known as Touriga Franca, Castelão Francês (more commonly known in the past as Periquita or João de Santarém) is now officially Castelão, while Aragonez is the principal name for Tinta Roriz, Trincadeira for Tinta Amarela, Fernão Pires for Maria Gomes, and Sercial for Esgana Cão. The others remain as recognized synonyms. The Instituto da Vinha e do Vinho currently recognizes 341 different varieties growing in Portugal, the majority of which are indigenous.

Grapevine

• **The Caixa Geral de Depositos** has acquired an 18 percent stake in Portuvinus, owners of Companhia das Quintas and Caves Borlido. The bank's investment is required to fund future development, including the modernization of Caves Borlido's cellars at Sangalhos in Bairrada. Anyone who has experienced these wines onboard TAP–Air Portugal will agree that the work involved is not before time.

• **One of Portugal's** best-known brands, Mateus Rosé, has undergone its first makeover for 60 years. The flagon-shaped bottle, first inspired by the water flask used by Portuguese soldiers in World War I, has been given a new, slimmer look and labelling. The relaunch has been backed by the "Drink Pink" advertising campaign. Mateus Rosé is exported to 130 countries with sales totaling 20 million bottles.

• **Bruno Prats** (ex-owner of Château Cos d'Estournel) and the Symington family (owners of Dow, Graham, and Warre) have launched a new wine named Chryseia— Greek for Douro ("golden"). Following a few experimental lots in 1999, the 2000 Chryseia was launched in 2002. Using mainly Touriga Nacional and Touriga Francesa (or should that be Touriga Franca?), the wine is made by a Bordeaux-trained oenologist based in the Douro. To reinforce its *Bordelais* credentials, Chryseia was released exclusively on the Bordeaux market (only the second time that a non-French wine has been offered in this way).

• **Dino Ventura,** one of the founding partners of DFJ Vinhos, died suddenly in February 2003, at age 56. His loss will be felt by the wine trade in Portugal and the UK, where he built some of the bestselling brands of Portuguese wine.

Opinion:
Price–quality imbalance

The strong domestic market has produced all sorts of distortions over the past five years, the most evident of which has been Portugal's so-called trophy wines selling considerably cheaper on export markets than at home. Some worldly-wise producers freely admit that their wines could command higher prices at home but seek the long-term benefits of international exposure. The Symingtons' new prestige red, Chryseia, was initially sold in Portugal for a "reasonable" €37.50, but stocks from Bordeaux, where it was first launched, have been sucked back into the Portuguese market, where a bottle now fetches as much as €70. For the first time in my life, much of which has been spent in Portugal, I recently found myself opting for a Spanish wine from a hotel wine list in Lisbon. It was Torres Gran Coronas and was priced at just €12 a bottle compared to €50–70 for its closest Portuguese competitors. If the great wines of Portugal are to be recognized internationally, logic dictates that the majority must have a similar price-to-quality ratio as most other world-class wines. Should international travelers find the best Portuguese wines ridiculously overpriced in Portugal itself, they will not only fail to order those wines, the word will soon spread that the best Portugal has to offer are overpriced upstarts that do not warrant a second thought. It is understandable that producers are happy to charge whatever a market is willing to pay, but if that market is the home market and it is out of step with the rest of the world, then the gains are short-term and isolated. Producers should question what they have to gain from basking in isolated glory. In economically uncertain times, it is those producers that sell to the largest spread of markets that will be the most secure.

Vintage Report

Advance report on the latest harvest

2002

After one of the driest summers on record, many vineyards inland and south of the country were suffering from extreme stress. Barca d'Alva on Douro, by the Spanish border, registered just 2⅜ in (60 mm) of rain between the end of the previous harvest and the beginning of September 2002. Fortunately the summer passed without excessive heat, and in early September, after a little light rain, the grapes were generally in good condition. A fine vintage seemed to be in prospect, but with yields down by 15–20 percent on 2001. In the Ribatejo, Alentejo, and Douro Superior, picking began in early September, while growers in the rest of the country held off until the middle of the month. But Friday, September 13 lived up to its unlucky reputation when an unusually deep depression settled over the Iberian Peninsula and the rains did not let up for five days. Thin-skinned grapes like Trincadeira started to rot and, throughout the country, the vintage became a race against time. The unsettled weather continued into October, spelling disaster for Bairrada and Vinho Verde, where many growers watched grapes rot on the vine without even bothering to pick. Some excellent wines were made in the Douro by those who harvested early, and there are small quantities of good wine from the south. But for most producers, 2002 is a vintage they would rather forget.

Updates on the previous five vintages

2001

Vintage rating: *85*

With groundwater supplies replenished over winter and fine weather during flowering, the 2001 harvest produced a hefty crop, the largest since 1996, and seems to have matched quantity with quality. In the north an unusually cool and variable August led to uneven ripening, but warm weather in early September saved the day and some high sugar readings were recorded. In the Alentejo, torrential September rain brought sugar levels down, but Moreto (usually an insipid grape) was still harvested at a potential of 15 percent ABV.

2000

Vintage rating: *90*

Much of the flowering took place in adverse conditions, and by late May it looked as if 2000 would be the third small harvest in a row. However, unlike the two previous years, warm weather continued into October, allowing the harvest to take place throughout the country in near-perfect conditions. Bairrada, the Douro, and Dão produced some exceptional wines.

1999

Vintage rating: *70*

Poor weather conditions, including the remains of Hurricane Floyd, affected the north coast: Bairrada and much of Dão were particularly badly affected. Those areas inland and to the south where the grapes were picked before the rain made some excellent wines. It was a good year for the Castelão grape on the Setúbal Peninsula, but in the Douro, what looked like a miracle vintage was destroyed by rain at the last minute.

1998

Vintage rating: *60*

With reduced yields in the north of the country, 1998 looked set to produce minute quantities of potentially outstanding wines, following a period of unrelenting summer heat. However, just as picking began, rain swept in from the Atlantic. Grape sugars were diluted, and the old, interplanted vineyards of the Douro, Dão, Bairrada, and Vinho Verde were devastated by rot. The south fared much better, and good wines were made, albeit in small quantities, from the Ribatejo, Alentejo, and the Setúbal Peninsula.

1997

Vintage rating: *85*

It was an unusual year in Bairrada, where the Baga grape ripened to give wines with abnormally high levels of alcohol and supple tannins. Some excellent *garrafeiras* (the best since 1990) were bottled. The aging potential of these wines is enormous. However, 1997 was much less successful in Estremadura and Terras do Sado, although the Castelão grape in Alentejo produced small quantities of high-quality, well-balanced red wine.

GREATEST WINE PRODUCERS

1. Quinta do Vale Meão
2. Quinta do Monte d'Oiro
3. Niepoort
4. Sogrape
5. Prats & Symington
6. Luis Pato
7. Quinta do Crasto
8. Quinta do Roriz
9. Esporão
10. João Portugal Ramos

FASTEST-IMPROVING PRODUCERS

1. Borges & Irmão
2. Caves Alianca
3. Quinta do Carmo
4. Quinta de Cabriz
5. Real Companhia Velha
6. Quinta de Pancas
7. José Maria da Fonseca
8. Caves Dom Teodosio

NEW UP-AND-COMING PRODUCERS

1. Quinta do Vale Meão
2. Quinta do Monte d'Oiro
3. Quinta do Roriz
4. Lavradores de Feitoria
5. Bago de Touriga
6. Quinta do Vallado
7. Rui Reguinga
8. Quinta da Touriga
9. CARM (Casa Agricola Rui Madeira)

BEST-VALUE PRODUCERS

1. Adega Co-operativa de Pegoes
2. DFJ Vinhos
3. Dão Sul
4. Sogrape
5. JP Vinhos
6. Casa Santos Lima

7. Fiuza
8. Herdade do Esporão
9. José Maria da Fonseca
10. Venâncio da Costa Lima

GREATEST-QUALITY WINES

1. **Quinta do Vale Meão 2000** Douro (€65)
2. **Quinta do Monte d'Oiro 1999 Homenagem a António Carqueijeiro** (€100)
3. **Barca Velha 1995** Ferreira, Douro (€140)
4. **Batuta 2000** Niepoort, Douro (€125)
5. **Quinta do Crasto 2000** Vinha da Ponte, Douro (€80)
6. **D'Avilez Garrafeira 1998** Alentejo (€50)
7. **Chryseia 2000** Douro (€70)
8. **Quinta do Roriz Reserva 2000** Douro (€30)
9. **Quinta do Mouro 1999** Vinho Regional Alentejano (€25)
10. **Vinha Barrosa 2000** Luis Pato, Beiras (€30)

BEST BARGAINS

1. **Duque de Viseu 2000** Dão (€4.25)
2. **Evel Tinto 2000** Real Companhia Velha, Douro (€3)
3. **Quinta do Mouro 1999** Vinho Regional Alentejano (€25)
4. **Palha Canas Tinto 2000** Vinho Regional Estremadura (€3.50)
5. **Esporão Branco Reserva 2000** Alentejo (€8)
6. **Serras de Azeitão Tinto 2000** JP Vinhos (€2.50)
7. **Grão Vasco Tinto 2000** Dão (€2.75)
8. **Fonte de Nico Tinto 2002** Co-op de Pegoes, Terras do Sado (€2)

⑨ Muralhas de Moncão
Vinho Verde (€3)
⑩ Castelão Frances 2000
Venâncio da Costa Lima,
Terras do Sado (€2)

MOST EXCITING OR UNUSUAL FINDS

❶ Quinta do Monte d'Oiro 1999 Homenagem a António Carqueijeiro (€100)
A newcomer made by a man who is passionate about Syrah.

❷ Quinta do Mouro 1999
Vinho Regional Alentejano (€25)
A big, traditional Alentejano red from an old, low-yielding, dry-farmed vineyard, which in the days of irrigation is becoming increasingly rare.

❸ Quinta da Pellada Estágio Prolongado 2000 Dão (€20)
A powerful, concentrated red that has stood up well to prolonged aging in oak.

❹ Vinya 2002 José Maria da Fonseca (€10) *A new wine blending Syrah with the local Aragonez (Tinta Roriz).*

❺ Domingos Soares Franco Colecção Privada 2001 Touriga Franca (€17)
The Touriga Franca grape, a

staple of Port producers in the Douro, makes a wonderfully floral, well-structured red in Setúbal Peninsula.

❻ Muros de Melgaco 2001
Vinho Verde (€15)
Barrel-fermented Alvarinho, bottled without filtration after short aging on lees. Well made, but unusual and not to everyone's taste!

❼ Redoma Rosado 2000
Niepoort, Douro (€15)
From a country with no tradition for serious rosé, this full-bodied wine captures beautifully the scented fruit of the Douro.

❽ Quinta do Moledo 1999 Cabernet Sauvignon
VQPRD Madeira (€10)
A good attempt at making a varietal Cabernet on an island more usually associated with fortified wines.

❾ Casa da Vinha 2001 Vinha Biologica, Verdelho
VQPRD Madeira (€10)
An organic, unfortified Verdelho from Madeira: not just unusual, unique!

❿ Tinta Miuda 1998
JP Vinhos (€10)
A rare and successful example of Tinta Miuda, an underrated Estremadura grape thought to be the same as Rioja's Graciano.

Port & Madeira

Richard Mayson

When the Port trade was on its uppers in the 1970s, multinational companies rode like white knights and rescued a number of well-established family firms.

RICHARD MAYSON

After mergers, takeovers, and restructuring, Croft and Delaforce were acquired by UDV, Sandeman by Seagram, and Cockburn and Martinez by Allied Domecq. Even the Symingtons (owners of Dow, Graham, and Warre) relinquished 20 percent of their family firm to Pernod-Ricard in order to secure distribution. Now, with the notable exception of Allied, the multinationals have backed out, and a number of leading Port shippers believe their exodus reflects a general lack of confidence in the Port business. Global Port sales have fallen by the equivalent of 200,000 cases since 2000, when the industry shipped an all-time record of 10.63 million cases. The decline is greatest in the traditional volume markets of Belgium, Netherlands, Luxembourg, and France, while the premium markets are faring much better. The UK overtook Belgium in 2002 to become the fourth-largest market for Port. Sales of Port to the US grew by 20.3 percent in 2002 at an average price of €94 per case, compared to €51 for the UK and just €32 for France.

RICHARD MAYSON writes and lectures on wine, dividing his time between London, Portugal, and a family business in the Peak District. He speaks fluent Portuguese, having been brought up in Portugal, and is regarded as one of the most respected authorities on Port, Sherry, Madeira, and the wines of Spain and Portugal. His interest in the subject goes back to his college days, when he wrote a thesis on the microclimates of the vineyards of the Douro Valley. His books include *Portugal's Wines & Wine Makers* (Ebury Press, 1992), *Port and the Douro* (Faber & Faber, 1999), and his latest work, *The Wines and Vineyards of Portugal* (Mitchell Beazley), which was published in March 2003. He is currently preparing a second edition of *Port and the Douro*, a third edition of *Portugal's Wines & Wine Makers*, and a new book on the wines of Madeira.

Port: Long overdue reform of ailing institution

The long-running saga of the Casa do Douro (CD) took a new turn in November 2002, when the Portuguese government intervened to reform the institutions that govern both Port and Douro wine. The saga began in 1990 when the CD, which was then in charge of representing and regulating more than 30,000 growers in the Douro, bought 40 percent of the Port shipper Real Companhia Velha (better known as Royal Oporto). At the time this was thought to be tantamount to a referee turning player, and over the subsequent 12 years this deal has virtually bankrupted the CD. Under the proposed reform, a new body named the Instituto dos Vinho do Douro e Porto (IVDP) will be the sole organization responsible for Port and Douro wines, with an interprofessional council responsible for both the commercial and production (vineyard) sides of the business. Although the CD will keep and maintain the *cadastro* (register) of vineyard holdings in the Douro, it will be subject to independent audit by the IVDP. The CD will continue to represent growers on the interprofessional council. As part and parcel of the reform, the Portuguese government will settle the CD's debt using the CD's considerable stocks of wine as a guarantee. The government will negotiate the sale of these stocks to the commercial sector (probably through the IVDP) over an as-yet-undefined period of time. As part of the reform, the CD will no longer be able to buy stocks of wine for resale. In return for this, the CD will resume its participation in the affairs of Real Companhia Velha through its 40 percent holding.

Madeira: Must now be bottled

Since the start of 2002, the bulk shipment of Madeira is no longer allowed. All Madeira has to be exported in bottle, unless it has been denatured (seasoned) for culinary use or used for blending with other products (for example, as flavoring for schnapps). This has added considerably to the costs for Madeira's already-beleaguered shippers who, in the absence of any glass manufacturing on the island, have to import bottles from mainland Portugal before filling and re-exporting them. The shippers have faced up to this new challenge in different ways. The largest single producer of Madeira wine, Justino Henriques, has invested in new packaging. Most of the wine sold in France (the largest, albeit cheapest, market for Madeira) under the Cruz label is now shipped in lightweight 37.5-cl bubble packs that imitate the shape of a bottle. Two other leading shippers, the Madeira Wine Company and Henriques & Henriques, have launched new premium wines backed by high-profile marketing initiatives. Exports of Madeira have slumped in 2002 because the regional government had to step in to mop up excess stocks. The stock held by the government has now reached

1 million liters, representing about 20 percent of the volume of Madeira sold in 2001. It has also been a challenging time for hundreds of small growers, since shippers have cut their grape purchases by as much as half. It remains to be seen whether the suspension of bulk shipments will lead to a permanent drop in exports or whether volumes will recover once stocks of bulk wine shipped before the suspension have been depleted.

Port: The 2000 vintage declaration

All the major Port shippers and a growing number of single quintas declared the 2000 vintage during the spring and early summer of 2002. For most shippers this was only the 25th or 26th vintage declaration since 1900, indicating that Port is probably the last classic wine to adhere to the concept that a declaration of vintage is a declaration of superior quality. The shippers increased their opening prices by 7–10 percent on 1997 (the last declared vintage), and the top-tier wines were offered in the UK at around £390 a case in bond, and approximately $70 a bottle on the open market in the US.

Grapevine

• **Since 2002 the Port Wine Institute** has, for the first time, included so-called Reserve Ports in its Special Categories. This means that wines like Cockburn's Special Reserve, Warre's Warrior, Taylor's First Estate, and Fonseca Bin 27 will be classified as premium Ports, alongside LBV, Aged Tawnies, Colheitas, and Vintage.

• **Over 200,000 liters of Port** have been lost from a *balão* (vat) belonging to the Casa do Douro. The leak was detected in January 2003, when inspectors from the Port Wine Institute were valuing stocks as part of the government's refinancing project. The wine in question was a 1974 colheita, a year that was fortified with industrial alcohol, but was still on the books at €5,000 a pipe. The president of the Casa do Douro, Manuel Antonio dos Santos, emphatically denied suggestions of foul play.

• **A new official Port glass** designed by architect Alvaro Siza Vieira has been launched by the Port Wine Institute. The tulip-shaped bowl is similar to a standard tasting glass and is supported by a prismatic stem with an indentation for the thumb and a faceted base. It has had a mixed response from the Port trade.

• **Two of Portugal's** most prominent winemakers, Cristiano van Zeller (formerly owner of Quinta do Noval) and Domingos Soares Franco (vice president of José Maria da Fonseca) have set up a joint venture in the Douro. The first fruits of this partnership were released in 2002 with a 2000 Vintage Port and LBV and two Douro reds: Domini and Domini Plus.

• **The Vintage House Hotel** in Pinhão, opened in 1998, has been sold by Taylor's to the tour operator Douro Azul.

• **Much effort has** been concentrated in promoting Colheita Madeiras, a new category that allows a vintage-dated wine to be bottled at five years of age, as opposed to the minimum of 20 years for *frasqueira* or so-called vintage Madeira.

Opinion:
Casa do Farsico

The 13-year saga of the Casa do Douro has become as farcical as the most far-fetched soap opera, but no government seems to have the temerity to impose the deep structural reforms that the Port industry so urgently requires. In a country where governments have a four-year term and survive on political horse-trading and thin majorities, it seems that there is always too much political capital to be lost. Although the current reforms are a long-overdue step in the right direction, they do not go nearly far enough. "The Casa do Douro situation is tantamount to *Alice in Wonderland*," said one Port shipper, who asked not to be named. There is an overwhelming need for a root-and-branch reform of the institutions that govern the production of Port.

Grapevine

• **The Madeira Wine Institute** has been governed by the same president, Dr. Constantino Palma, since its creation in 1979. He has now retired, and a new board of directors has been installed, with Eng. Paulo Rodrigues, just 33 years old, the new president. His new vice presidents are Dr. João Nunes (31) and Enga. Conceicão Fernandes (31). This represents an important generational change for one of Portugal's most hidebound institutions.

• **The Madeira Wine Company,** owners of the Blandy, Cossart Gordon, Miles, and Leacock brands, has launched a radical new wine. Blandy's Alvada is made from a blend of Bual and Malvasia and is bottled in a 50-cl bottle (an increasingly popular format in Madeira) with a striking pink label. Alvada was inspired by the success of Warre's Otima, which is credited with revitalizing the 10-Year-Old Tawny category. The Madeira Wine Company is owned and managed by the Symington family in Oporto in partnership with the Blandy family in Funchal.

• **Luis Pereira,** winemaker at Henriques & Henriques, has won the Overall Fortified Winemaker Trophy in the 2002 International Wine Challenge. This is the first time Madeira has won this award. H&H also won the Madeira Trophy for the fifth time in seven years.

Vintage Report

Advance report on the latest harvest

2002

Port—After high hopes at the outset, the 2002 harvest proved to be a major disappointment for most Port producers. There had been very little rain throughout the previous winter, and the summer was dry, although fortunately without any of the extreme heat that burns the grapes on the vine. Rain in early September helped to swell the berries, and by early/mid-September the grapes were in near-perfect condition. Picking began in the Douro Superior on September 9 under clear skies, while those downstream held off for another week, when the weather broke and for most it became a stop-start vintage, picking between bouts of torrential rain. Growers who took a gamble by waiting for the weather to improve lost the bet as the rain continued, on and off, well into October. However, those who managed to pick before the rain set in have small quantities of good, possibly outstanding, wine. Although it is still too early to be certain, some producers in the Cima Corgo and Douro Superior should have sufficient quantity of high-quality wine to make a single *quinta* declaration early in 2004.

Madeira—This vintage saw a large production and particularly good-quality Tinta Negra on the south of the island, and excellent quality and large volumes of Bual in Calheta at the extreme west. Bual and Tinta Negra in the Campanario district in the southwest suffered from a difficult maturity due to persistent fog in the last four weeks or so before the vintage. Inconsistent Malmsey and Sercial. Verdelho was excellent, but limited in volume.

Updates on the previous five vintages

2001

Vintage rating: *85*

Port—After one of the wettest winters since records began, mild, humid conditions led to an early bud-burst in March. From April onward the weather cleared and only 4⅜ in (110 mm) of rain fell until the end of August. With flowering taking place under optimum conditions and the groundwater supplies thoroughly replenished, there was a large crop. Temperatures were uneven during August, but rain at the end of the month helped to swell the grapes prior to the harvest, which, for most, began on September 17. Some grapes, particularly Tinta Barroca, were overripe by this stage, with a potential 20 percent ABV on well-exposed slopes. Yields were up by 30 percent on 2000 in the A/B-grade vineyards. Overall, 2001 proved to be a useful year. A number of single *quintas* will undoubtedly produce some fine vintage Ports for drinking over the medium term, but in the wake of the universal declaration of 2000, it would be surprising if any shippers declared a full-fledged vintage.

Madeira—There was a big production of Tinta Negra, but the volume of Malmsey suffered due to *coulure* at flowering. Sercial and Verdelho from the northern vineyards suffered from particularly bad weather during flowering, which resulted in a greatly reduced vintage for these two varietals. Bual, by contrast, did not suffer as much as the others, and volumes were normal.

2000

Vintage rating: 95

Port—Low yields helped to make some wonderfully concentrated wines, perhaps not as overtly rich as the 1994s, but with more poise and harmony than 1997. A fine vintage combined with some truly excellent wines made for a universal declaration.

Madeira—There was good-quality Bual and Tinta Negra on the south and west of the island, and a very small crop of excellent-quality Verdelho from Camara de Lobos on the south of the island.

1999

Vintage rating: 75

Port—A potentially outstanding vintage became no more than good to mediocre, thanks to Hurricane Floyd. Nonetheless, small quantities of excellent wine were made by those who managed to avoid the rain, and a number of single *quinta* wines were declared.

Madeira—Not only was the general quality very high, but it was one of the largest crops of the last 10 years. Sercial and Bual were especially excellent.

1998

Vintage rating: 80

Port—Unsettled weather during the harvest took the shine off what could have been an outstanding vintage. Wines from a number of single *quintas* were declared, the best being from those upstream who, in general, managed to pick before the rains.

Madeira—A small vintage of good quality, particularly for Bual.

1997

Vintage rating: *90*

Port—Yields were down by as much as 40 percent on the previous year (a huge harvest), and this served to concentrate the musts. Nearly all the shippers saw fit to declare a vintage in the spring of 1999, marking up their prices by 30 percent on the 1994s. By no means as rich or opulent as the 1994s, or as harmonious as 2000, many 1997s have a somewhat hard, lean streak, although the best wines have tremendous color and power.

Madeira—A large vintage of very good general quality, especially for Verdelho and Malmsey, and Tinta Negra from southern vineyards. Bual was of good, but not exceptional, quality.

GREATEST WINE PRODUCERS

1 Fonseca (Port)
2 Quinta do Noval (Port)
3 Graham (Port)
4 Taylor (Port)
5 Henriques & Henriques (Madeira)
6 Niepoort (Port)
7 Dow (Port)
8 Warre (Port)
9 Blandy (Madeira)
10 Cockburn (Port)

FASTEST-IMPROVING PRODUCERS

1 Quinta do Noval (Port)
2 Pocas Junior (Port)
3 Croft (Port)
4 Madeira Wine Company (Madeira)
5 Real Companhia Velha (Port)

NEW UP-AND-COMING PRODUCERS

1 Quinta da Santa Eufemia (Port)
2 Quinta do Crasto (Port)
3 Quinta do Vale Dona Maria (Port)
4 Casal dos Jordoes (Port)
5 Van Zeller & Soares Franco (Port)

BEST-VALUE PRODUCERS

1 Smith Woodhouse (Port)
2 Martinez (Port)
3 Sandeman (Port)
4 Justino Henriques (Madeira)
5 Gould Campbell (Port)

GREATEST-QUALITY WINES

1. **Quinta do Noval Nacional 2000** (€1,750)
2. **Fonseca 2000 Vintage Port** (€100)
3. **Blandy's 1958 Bual** Bottled in 2002 (€99)
4. **Henriques & Henriques 15-Year-Old Verdelho** (€35)
5. **Graham's 2000 Vintage Port** (€100)
6. **Niepoort 2000 Vintage Port** (€100)
7. **Quinta do Bom Retiro, 20-Year-Old Tawny** Ramos Pinto (€40)
8. **Sandeman 20-Year-Old Tawny** (€40)
9. **Warre's Traditional1992 LBV** (€25)
10. **Taylor's Quinta de Vargellas 1987** (€50)

BEST BARGAINS

1. **Smith Woodhouse 2000 Vintage Port** (€75)
2. **Quinta do Vale 2000 Dona Maria** (€50)
3. **Martinez 1997 Vintage Port** (€90)
4. **Hutcheson 10-Year-Old Tawny** (€17)
5. **Henriques & Henriques 15-Year-Old Verdelho** (€35)
6. **Warre's Traditional 1992 LBV** (€25)
7. **Taylor's 1997 LBV** (€15)
8. **Graham's 1996 LBV** (€15)

MOST EXCITING OR UNUSUAL FINDS

Note: Including other Portuguese fortified wines.

1. **Blandy's Alvada 5-Year-Old Madeira** (€8) *A blend of Bual and Malvasia.*
2. **Quinta da Santa Eufemia 20-Year-Old Tawny** (€40)
3. **Churchill's Dry White Port** (€12)
4. **Blandy's 1976 Terrantez** (€70)
5. **Bastardinho de Azeitão** José Maria da Fonseca (€22 per half bottle) *Fortified wine from the Setúbal Peninsula.*
6. **Trilogia Setúbal** José Maria da Fonseca (€120) *A blend of the 1900, 1934, and 1965 vintages.*
7. **Blandy's Centennial Blend** (€45) *A 25-year-old blend of the best Blandy's Madeiras produced in the last century.*
8. **Champalimaud 1995 Vintage Port** (€40) *A vintage Port that is drier and less alcoholic than classic wines.*
9. **Kopke 1961 Colheita** (€100)
10. **Quinta de Bela Vista** Carcavelos (€130) *A blend of vintages from the 1940s, 1950s, and 1960s, bottled in 1990.*

Great Britain

Stephen Skelton

For over 30 years, 'English table wine' and 'Welsh table wine' have been the preferred labelling terms, despite the introduction of a regional appellation system for English and Welsh counties.

STEPHEN SKELTON

The main reason why growers prefer these terms is that they can be applied to wines of any quality without having to submit them for testing or tasting—something required for all quality and regional wines. That, however, is all due to change.

In an effort to tidy up the labeling regulations, the EU has decreed that English and Welsh wines must be subjected to testing and tasting because England and Wales are not separate countries, merely regions of the UK. Wines bearing a geographical area "smaller than the member state" must become quality or regional wines. During the process of reforming wine labeling, the EU Commission discovered—apparently to their amazement—that England and Wales were not actually separate member states!

Although it will mean some extra expense and form-filling, the United Kingdom Vineyards Association (UKVA) views the new labeling requirements as a positive move toward improving the overall quality of

STEPHEN SKELTON established the award-winning Tenterden Vineyards in 1977 and made wine there for 22 years. His wines have won the Gore-Browne Trophy for the Best UK Wine on three occasions, and he currently consults for Leeds Castle and Hush Heath (the latter of which is mentioned, thus asterisked, in the following report). Stephen has been a director of the United Kingdom Vineyards Association (UKVA) since 1982, and chairman since 1998. Having written on wine, winemaking, and viticulture since 1986, he published *The Vineyards of England* (Faber & Faber, 2001) in 1989. He rewrote and updated this work under the new title of *The Wines of Britain and Ireland* (Faber & Faber, 2001) and this won the André Simon Award in 2002.

all UK-grown wines. At present, the reputation of English and Welsh wines is sullied by growers who are able to label substandard wines with the words "England" and "Wales." But under the new arrangements, which apply to the 2003 vintage, all wines bearing the terms "England" or "Wales" will have to be tested and tasted to ensure a minimum level of quality. Increased quality criteria include higher natural alcoholic content and restricted vine varieties. The only alternative will be to label wines as UK table wine, a category that already exists, but has rarely been used. The drawback is that such wines cannot indicate the vintage, the variety, or the vineyard name, which is a serious drawback for anyone wishing to sell wine direct to the consumer.

English Wine Week

English Wine Week will be in its fifth year in 2004. It is fast becoming a firm fixture in the UK's wine calendar, with the number of vineyards taking part growing from 22 in 2000 to 45 in 2003. What is especially welcome is the fact that several of the vineyards listed are not generally open to the public, and this week is the only chance that lovers of English wine will get to see these operations at close hand. Such is the success of the open week that even the Welsh want to join in. Organizer Julia Trustram-Eve says that they are welcome to come on board, but since part of the financing for the week comes from a fund set apart for English projects (the Welsh have their own fund), any mention of Wales will be low-key. The next English Wine Week will be from May 29 to June 4, 2004; visit www.englishwineproducers.com for further details.

Grapevine

- **David Grey** is to build a winery at his Meopham Vineyards. Until now, Meopham wines have been made under contract at New Wave Wines at Tenterden, Davenport Vineyards in East Sussex, and Sedlescombe Organic near Hastings.

- **Major West Country producer** Three Choirs is grubbing up 1.5 acres of Müller-Thurgau and replanting with experimental Cabernet Sauvignon and Merlot under polythene tunnels. Although Three Choirs already makes a red wine using Pinot Noir, Rondo, Maréchal Foch, and Regent, winemaker Martyn Fowke is convinced that the two classic varieties will add class to his blend.

- **Vineyard to brew beer!** Three Choirs is building a boutique brewery. Known as Whittingtons, it will brew both ales and beers using local Herefordshire and Worcestershire hops. The first brew is to be in April 2003.

- **After three long conversion years,** East Sussex producer Davenport Vineyards has finally been granted full organic status by the Soil Association. From vintage 2003 all wines will be eligible to be labeled as "made from organically grown grapes."

- **With their first crop due in 2003,** Michael and Susan Thorpe of Purbeck Vineyard are busy building and equipping a winery.

ENGLISH AND WELSH WINE SERVED BY HMG

After strong lobbying by the UKVA, government ministers have at last taken the bait and started to insist that home-grown wines, both English and Welsh, are stocked in departmental fridges. Foremost among these is Margaret Beckett, the Secretary of State for DEFRA (the Department of the Environment, Farming and Rural Affairs), who now insists that English and Welsh wines be served whenever visitors, especially those from overseas, are entertained, and at all official functions and meetings where alcoholic refreshment is appropriate. This is a marked turnaround from earlier days, when ministers studiously avoided serving English and Welsh wines, preferring those from our European neighbors.

SPARKLING SUCCESS

Sparkling wines were once the Cinderella of the English and Welsh wine industry—seldom seen and then only on special occasions. Even though it was as long ago as 1978 that the imaginatively labeled Pilton Manor De Marsac Méthode Champenoise Brut won a medal at the UKVA's annual English Wine of the Year competition, their production has never been widespread. Now, however, the appearance of sparkling wines on the competition circuit is more than occasional—they positively litter the results page. In the 2002 competition, all three gold medals and 10 of the 14 silver medals went to bottle-fermented sparkling wines. Of the 29 sparklers entered, only two

failed to gain an award of some sort— surely a good indication of the overall level of quality in this category. Old hands such as John Leighton at Valley Vineyards with his Ascot and Heritage labels, New Wave Wines with their Epoch Brut, Bob Lindo from Camel Valley, Peter and Diana Andrews from Llanerch (one of the few Welsh vineyards to make the grade), and John Gibson from Bearsted, near Maidstone, all make medal-winning, bestselling sparkling wines.

WHEN DOES A HYBRID GRAPE VINE TURN INTO A VINIFERA?

The answer is, of course, when the Germans say so! After more than five years of negotiations with the UK government, English and Welsh wine growers have persuaded a skeptical DEFRA that a German decision about some new disease-resistant hybrid grape varieties is both valid and legal. Hybrid grape varieties have always been excluded from EU quality-wine schemes and confined to the lowest category of table wine. Anyone who knows the history will realize that the intention of this legislation was laudable at the time. By the 1930s, so many French vineyards had been planted with phylloxera-resistant hybrids that the country's reputation was in danger from the low-grade wines they produced. It was decided to discriminate against all hybrids. When the Common Market was formed, French wines reigned supreme and the AOC model was used as the basis of EEC's wine regime. Now, however, some would claim that the prejudice against hybrids is unfair. Why, they ask, should anyone be prevented from using hybrid grapes, particularly if the quality is good?

Furthermore, the percentage of non-vinifera "blood" is so small in the best and most recent German hybrids that some breeders considered them to be, for all intents and purposes, pure vinifera varieties. They hatched a clever scheme. Since the non-vinifera lineage in these new hybrids was so small and distant, and the only difference visible to the naked eye was that of better disease resistance, why not ask the Bundesortenamt (Federal Plant Patent Office) to investigate these interspecific crosses and see whether they could tell the difference? Thirteen of the new cultivars were thus presented. The Bundesortenamt did its best, looking into all aspects of leaf shape, tendril

characters, growth habits, grape shape, seed numbers, taste, and, of course, wine quality. Only resistance to disease was excluded from their tests. The answer was that there was no difference between these crosses and vinifera, and that with regard to the EU wine regulations these varieties were so like vinifera as to make no difference. UK growers, for whom four of the new varieties—Orion, Phoenix, Regent, and Rondo—are important additions to their variety lists, asked DEFRA to take the same stance. Eventually, after much cajoling and persuading, British officials were persuaded that the EU wine police would not clap them into the stocks, and as of February 2003 these four hybrids officially became vinifera varieties and therefore eligible for the production of English and Welsh quality wines.

Grapevine

- **A brand new 4-acre vineyard,** Hush Heath Manor*, was planted in spring 2002 near Cranbrook in Kent, and so good were the growing conditions that a small crop is expected in 2003. Owner Richard Balfour-Lynn has opted for the three classic champagne varieties.

- **Chilford Hall** vineyard and winery at Linton, near Cambridge, will celebrate its 30th vintage in 2004.

- **Following the purchase of Nyetimber,** the UK's premier sparkling-wine producer, new owner Andy Hill has appointed Plumpton-trained Peter Morgan to be his new winemaker. Stuart and Sandy Moss have finished their involvement after 10 incredibly successful vintages.

- **The UK's largest wine producer,** English Wines Group, had a storming

12 months. Owen Elias, who is responsible for brands such as New Wave Wines, Tenterden, Lamberhurst, Carr Taylor, Chapel Down, Epoch, and Curious Grape, was voted Winemaker of the Year at the 2002 UKVA competition. English Wines Group picked up 16 medals, almost 30 per cent of the total, disproving the adage that "big is not always best."

- **East Sussex's Battle Wine Estate** is celebrating its 20th anniversary by commissioning a brand-new winery and cellar-door sales facility.

- **Jersey's La Mare Vineyards** is expanding with an acre each of the reds Regent, Rondo, and Pinot Noir, together with experimental plantings of Cabernet Sauvignon, Merlot, and Viognier under polythene tunnels.

Opinion:
No sense

Why is it that still wines labeled as quality have to be tested and tasted, but sparkling wines labeled as quality do not? The answer, for what it is worth, is that the word "quality," when used for still wines, refers to such things as grape variety, natural alcoholic level, and analytical and tasting parameters. When applied to sparkling wine, though, the word "quality" merely defines its method of production. The UKVA thinks this is nonsense. Why should sparkling wines not be treated equally? Top sparkling-wine producer Mike Roberts at RidgeView Estate agrees. He thinks that sparkling wine needs the same sort of protection as still wine from low-grade, unpalatable sparkling wines that have not helped enhance the UK's reputation. DEFRA, which administers the labeling regulations in the UK, is considering ways in which all sparkling wines can be brought in line with their still-wine counterparts.

Come on the reds

Once it seemed white wines were pretty difficult to produce in the UK's benighted climate—now red wines are all the rage! What is going on? Is it the weather, the varieties, the growers, or the winemakers? Or perhaps all four? Although climatologists will point out that average temperatures have not risen enough to say that the southern UK climate is changing, there may well be subtle seasonal changes that are making it easier to ripen grapes. Nighttime temperatures during the key growing and ripening months of July–October appear to be warmer, suggesting that vineyards are not cooling down as much as they used to at night and are therefore easier to warm up in the day. What definitely has changed is the selection of Pinot Noir clones available to growers, and vines are often much more carefully selected in this respect. This has come about in part because makers of sparkling wines have had to look much more carefully into their clonal choices, and this has led red-wine makers to do the same. Another factor is that today's growers are much better versed in the techniques of pruning, canopy management, and disease control. This means that crops are better managed, with improved exposure and less fungal disease. The production of red wines, which for years accounted for only 6 percent of total UK production, has doubled in the last few years and looks set to double again when the results of the warm 2002 vintage are finally known.

Vintage Report

Advance report on the latest harvest

2002

After a dismal spring and early summer, when temperatures were low, disrupting the flowering in many vineyards, an Indian summer in the final three weeks of the harvest put some smiles on the growers' faces and sugar into their grapes. Even though the overall crop was smaller than average, the quality was exceptional, especially with the harder-to-ripen varieties, such as Chardonnay, and the successful red varieties: Pinot Noir, Rondo, Regent, and Dornfelder. Natural sugar levels, which usually languish at 7–9 percent, were well up into double figures in many cases. Several winemakers have made completely natural wines—that is, without chaptalization.

Updates on the previous five vintages

2001

Vintage rating: 79 (Red: 75, White: 82)

On balance, this was a very fair year. No spring frosts and a good flowering combined to produce a larger-than-average crop. Temperatures were higher in 2001 than for centuries, and this was reflected in an early harvest of clean, ripe grapes. Reds had more color than usual, and the generally tough-to-ripen varieties, such as Riesling and Pinot Blanc, did well. Chardonnay and Pinot Noir for sparkling wine put in a good performance, and this should be reflected in the quality of the wines.

2000

Vintage rating: 73 (Red: 70, White: 75)

This was a cooler-than-average year with a very wet harvest. Whites fared better than reds, and sparkling wines should be good. The best will keep, but the majority should be drunk within two years.

1999

Vintage rating: *77 (Red: 76, White: 77)*

Average yields and a warm summer helped most winemakers produce some interesting wines, especially with varieties such as Bacchus and Seyval Blanc. Harvesting conditions were fine and dry, allowing grapes to hang slightly longer than usual.

1998

Vintage rating: *81 (Red: 77, White: 85)*

Vineyards in the west of the country fared better than those in the east, which suffered from some spring frosts. Sugar and acid levels were average, and the specialist sparkling-wine growers reported ideal results. Varieties such as Bacchus and Schönburger produced very fresh, fruity wines with ideal acid/alcohol balance.

1997

Vintage rating: *80 (Red: 82, White: 77)*

One of the smallest harvests on record and generally of good quality. The autumn was warm, picking relatively early, thus the reds ripened well to produce good-colored wines. Bacchus was the best of the whites.

GREATEST WINE PRODUCERS

1. Nyetimber
2. RidgeView Estate
3. New Wave Wines
4. Valley Vineyards
5. Denbies
6. Three Choirs
7. Camel Valley
8. Wickham
9. Shawsgate
10. Beenleigh Manor

FASTEST-IMPROVING PRODUCERS

1. Barnsole
2. Great Stocks
3. Heart of England
4. Meopham
5. Beeches Hill

NEW UP-AND-COMING PRODUCERS

1. New Wave Wines
2. Three Choirs
3. RidgeView Estate
4. Camel Valley
5. Valley Vineyards

BEST-VALUE PRODUCERS

1. Davenport
2. Astley
3. Bearsted
4. Sharpham
5. Sandhurst
6. Biddenden
7. Nutbourne
8. Breaky Bottom
9. Mersea
10. Warden Abbey

GREATEST-QUALITY WINES

1. **Première Cuvée Blanc de Blancs 1995** Nyetimber (£22)
2. **Cuvée Merret Bloomsbury 1999** RidgeView Estate (£15.95)
3. **Cornwall Pinot Noir Sparkling 2001** Camel Valley (£19.95)
4. **Cuvée Merret Fitzrovia 2000** RidgeView Estate (£18.95)
5. **Vintage Brut 1997** Chapel Down (£9.99)
6. **Classic Cuvée 1995** Nyetimber (£21)
7. **Curious Grape Pinot Noir 2000** New Wave Wines (£12.99)
8. **Curious Grape Bacchus Reserve 2001** New Wave Wines (£8.99)
9. **Barrel Fermented Sharpham 2001** (£10.99)
10. **Fumé 1998** Valley Vineyards (£8.49)

BEST BARGAINS

1. **Curious Grape Bacchus 2001** New Wave Wines (£5.99)
2. **Heritage Rosé NV Sparkling Wine** Valley Vineyards (£7.99)
3. **Cornwall Brut 2000** Camel Valley (£14.95)
4. **Fumé 1998** Valley Vineyards (£8.49)
5. **Dry 2000** Tenterden Estate (£6.99)
6. **Vintage Brut 1997** Chapel Down (£9.99)

MOST EXCITING OR UNUSUAL FINDS

1. **Aluric de Norsehide Sparkling Wine 1999** Chilford Hundred (£14.95) *This full-bodied rosé sparkler is a touch on the demi-sec side, with good, fruity flavor and good length.*
2. **Rosé Sparkling Wine 1999** Chapel Down (£9.99) *This attractive pale pink wine has excellent balanced acidity and a long, fruit-filled finish.*
3. **Beenleigh Red 2000** Sharpham (£25) *Close your eyes and think of somewhere other than England. This is a serious red wine with good fruit definition, supple tannins, and good balance.*
4. **Atlantic Dry 2001** Camel Valley (£7.45) *Made from Schönburger, this is a delightful, fruity wine, with hints of peach and lychee. Ideal for summer evenings.*
5. **Vintage Brut 1997** Chapel Down (£9.99) *Despite its price, a really serious sparkling wine. Long on the finish, with a really fine, yeasty-lees character.*
6. **Curious Grape Ortega 2001** New Wave Wines (£6.99) *Although still young, with a lively, fresh acidity, this wine has good underlying fruit and well-balanced French oak, promising to develop into a magnificent wine.*
7. **Bacchus 2001** Sandhurst (£7.99) *Bacchus at its best: a full, fruit-filled nose, length on palate, with a finely balanced, crisp finish.*

Switzerland

Chandra Kurt

Two thirds of all Swiss wine comes from three cantons: the Valais, Vaud, and Geneva.

CHANDRA KURT

Much of the reputation of Swiss wine stands or falls on these three regions, and over the past two years they have received bad publicity because of their continued overproduction of a rather unspectacular quality of Chasselas. It has now reached the point where the selling of this simple white wine has become very difficult, especially since a new generation of Swiss consumers has taken to wines from the New World. As a result, growers are increasingly replacing their Chasselas with speciality or newly developed grape varieties. In the Valais, where Chasselas is known as Fendant, the 2002 crop from this variety was the smallest since 1957. Despite this, there was still too much Chasselas of a very ordinary quality, and the decrease reflects the fact that more growers in this canton are focusing on other grapes, often returning to the varieties for which Valais has historically been famous, such as Petit Arvigne, Amigne, Johannisberg, Cornalin, and Humagne Rouge. In the canton of Geneva, the grape that is currently showing favor with growers is Gamaret (Gamay x Reichensteiner), which is in line with the general trend toward red-wine varieties throughout Switzerland. In the 2002 harvest, almost 49 percent of the wine produced was red, and the proportion is likely to creep over the halfway mark. Two grape varieties that increase in quality each year are Syrah from the Valais and Merlot from Ticino.

CHANDRA KURT is the author of several wine books, including the bestselling annuals *Weinseller* and *The 1,000 Best Wines*. She is also a freelance wine writer who regularly contributes to several leading publications, including *Finanz und Wirtschaft* and *Schweizer Familie*.

Swiss champagne!

In July 2002, a group of 39 Swiss wine producers mounted a legal challenge in the European Court of Justice, demanding the right to label their non-sparkling white wine as champagne, after the name of their village near Lake Neuchâtel. The growers lost the right to their own name following an agreement reached between the Swiss government and the EU in 1999. "We want to fix the injustice committed against us," said Albert Banderet, the 90-year-old president of the wine-grower group fighting the case. The Swiss "champagne" producers contend that references to the name of the village date as far back as 885 AD and that growers in the village have been making wine since the 10th century. The village produces 280,000 bottles a year, and the loss of the name will cost the growers an estimated €770,000.

No move on Mövenpick

The whole trade was confused in 2002 when the rumor spread that one of the most successful wine shops was looking for a buyer. In addition to its retail chain, Mövenpick had its Caveaux wine bars and its entire wine division—including the wholesale distribution arm, which sells to hotels and restaurants—up for sale. The Australian Foster's group was mooted as a possible buyer, but Mövenpick scrapped its plans to sell in April 2003.

Government decisions

The Swiss government has finally accepted that the quality of mainstream wines (Chasselas, Riesling x Sylvaner, and Pinot Noir) has to increase. It has paid out more than 10 million Swiss francs to convert low-quality wine grapes into nonalcoholic grape juice as part of the fight against overproduction and mediocre quality.

Joint venture Rutishauser & Testuz

Two big traditional wine merchants, Weinkellerei Rutishauser of Scherzingen and J&P Testuz of Treytorrens, have launched a joint venture under the unsurprising name of Rutishauser & Testuz. More unexpected is the fact that companies from the German-speaking part of Switzerland and the French part could form such an alliance, their respective regions being famously unfriendly to one another.

Top Muscat from Valais

Hervé Fontannaz from the Cave La Tine Vétroz in Valais got a gold medal for his Muscat Chaleur d'Automne at the Confrontation Internationale des Meilleurs Muscats du Monde in Frontignan, France. Out of 186 Muscat wines entered, just 18 were awarded gold medals.

Opinion:
Cult status needed

Switzerland has a problem that denies its best wines the sort of international fame they truly deserve: no famous winemakers. Despite a lot of really great Swiss wines, there is no great personality who is able to act as an ambassador for the industry in general. The norm in Switzerland is to behave like everybody else, rather than be an individualist like Angelo Gaja or Robert Mondavi. Apart from Daniel Gantenbein in Fläsch, no Swiss winemaker has understood how to create a cult following for his or her wines, let alone realize the value of such fame. Even if every single wine in the country happened to be world-class in quality and available in the most limited of quantities, the image of Swiss wines would still be mediocre. Swiss wines need cult status, and to achieve that the industry needs its most talented winemakers to strut their stuff.

Vintage Report

2002

The quality varies from good to excellent, with wines that are more elegant than full-bodied. In some regions, the quantity dropped as much as 30 percent over 2001, which illustrates that a lot of growers are reducing quantity to increase quality. In Ticino, the year started very difficult, with a lot of rain in the summer and in September. The growers were resigned to harvesting a very poor crop; but the weather changed, and between September 27 and October 15, this canton enjoyed the longest good-weather period of the year. The Föhn (a warm and benevolent Alpine wind) helped to concentrate the grapes, and the result was a small vintage of very special quality. In east Switzerland, the famous Bündner Herrschaft region can always rely on the Föhn, and once again it saved the vintage. The red wines from top producers show a lot of color, fruit concentration, and ripe tannins. Regions that did not benefit from the Föhn included the cantons Schaffhausen and Thurgau, where growers who did not green-harvest or pick selectively have had problems with quality. In the Valais, the Chasselas was lighter in body than in 2001 and fresher. No problems with early-ripening grapes (Pinot Noir reached 100 *Oechsle* and Gamay 90), but the bad weather at the end of September was a problem for Petite Arvine, Amigne, Syrah, and Cornalin. Compared to the Valais, the harvest in the canton Vaud was almost perfect.

2001

Vintage rating: 92

A climatically difficult year produced a small crop of variable quality. In the Valais, the quality was very good indeed, while it was just average for the rest of the Romandie. It was excellent in Schaffhausen and the Grisons, too.

2000

Vintage rating: *98*

A large harvest of exceptional quality for both red and white wines in all parts of Switzerland. Those who called 1997 the vintage of the century have had to revise their judgment, because 2000 was even better! The very best wines came from the Grisons and Romandie.

1999

Vintage rating: *90*

A large harvest of variable quality. The Valais and Vaud both turned out good reds but average whites. The quality was very poor in Geneva, but very good in Italian-speaking Switzerland, and even better in east Switzerland and the Grisons.

1998

Vintage rating: *88*

French-speaking Switzerland showed the greatest differences in quality. Pinot Noir of the Valais was average to good, Gamay good, and white wines very good. The Vaud and Geneva had average-quality wines, while the Grisons ranged from good to excellent. In the Ticino, the quality was good, but not special.

1997

Vintage rating: *95*

A historic vintage due to difficult weather conditions, resulting in a tiny harvest of great quality, especially in the Valais, Ticino, and the Romandie. In terms of white wines, the quality is good to outstanding for Schaffhausen and the Valais. In the Ticino, it was the first DOC vintage with good to excellent quality, but there were also many average-quality wines. For some regions, it was the vintage of the century.

GREATEST WINE PRODUCERS

1. Daniel & Martha Gantenbein
2. Hans Ulrich Kesselring
3. Georg und Ruth Fromm
4. Jean-René Germanier
5. Adriano Kaufmann
6. Luigi Zanini
7. Werner Stucky
8. Daniel Huber
9. Christian Zündel
10. Charles et Jean-Michel Novelle

FASTEST-IMPROVING PRODUCERS

1. Domaine Grillette
2. Weingut Porta Rätia
3. Cave St-Mathieu
4. Baumann Weingut
5. Weinkellereien Volg
6. Guido Brivio
7. Domaine du Paradis
8. Anna Barbara von der Crone
9. Weingut Schmidheiny
10. Domaine de Balisiers

BEST-VALUE PRODUCERS

1. Provins
2. Weinkellereien Volg
3. Jean-René Germanier
4. Landolt Weine
5. Hans Ulrich Kesselring
6. La Cave de Genève
7. Henri Cruchon
8. Vins Rouvinez
9. Serge Roh
10. Philippoz Frères

GREATEST-QUALITY WINES

1. **Pinot Noir 2000** Daniel & Martha Gantenbein (SF 42)
2. **Rosso del Ticino 1999** Castello Luigi (SF 89)
3. **Ermitage Grain Noble 1999** Marie-Thérèse Chappaz (SF 39 per 50 cl)
4. **Cayas Syrah du Valais 2001** Jean-René Germanier (SF 39)
5. **Amigne de Vétroz 2001** André Fontannaz (SF 16)
6. **Malanser Pinot Noir Barrique 2000** Georg und Ruth Fromm (SF 19.50)
7. **Pinot Noir Auslese Nr 3 2000** Hans Ulrich Kesselring (SF 26)
8. **Conte di Luna 2000** Werner Stucky (SF 48)
9. **Montagna Magica 2000** Daniel Huber (SF 50.50)
10. **Chardonnay 2000** Daniel & Martha Gantenbein (SF 38)

BEST BARGAINS

1. **Truttiker Riesling x Sylvaner 2001** Familie Zahner (SF 12.20)
2. **Johannisberg 2001** Johanniterkellerei (SF 8.95)
3. **Buchberger Beerli 2001** Gebrüder Kümin (SF 12.40)
4. **Fläscher Riesling x Sylvaner 2001** Weingut Davaz (SF 14.50)
5. **Riesling x Sylvaner Chrachenfels 2001** Landolt Weine (SF 12.20)
6. **Chardonnay 2001** René Favre & Fils (SF 15.30)
7. **Fläscher Pinot Noir 2001** Jann Marugg (SF 16)
8. **Chasselas 2001** Association Viticole Yvorne (SF 14.20)
9. **Féchy Le Brez 2001** Domaine La Colombe (SF 12.80)
10. **Château de Châtagneréaz 2001** Schenk (SF 10.80)

MOST EXCITING OR UNUSUAL FINDS

1 **Heida Gletscherwein 2000** Chanton Weine (SF 22.80) *A very crisp, fresh wine from the highest vineyard in Europe.*

2 **Schiller 2001** Volg Weinkellereien (SF 16.90) *A traditional Swiss wine that has almost been forgotten.*

3 **Regent Cuvée Varietas 2001** Volg Weinkellereien (SF 14.80) *A good example of a very fashionable new variety that gives dark, fruity wine with a lot of texture.*

4 **Completer Barrique 2000** Peter und Rosi Hermann (SF 25) *A traditional wine from the Grisons. Because of its high acidity, it keeps for ages.*

5 **Mitis Amigne de Vétroz 2000** Jean-René Germanier (SF 20 per half-bottle) *The most famous Swiss sweet wine.*

6 **Paien 2000** Simon Maye & Fils (SF 32) *Another example of a wine made from concentrated, high-quality vines in the Valais.*

7 **Riesling 2000** Daniel & Martha Gantenbein (SF 28 per half-bottle) *After Pinot Noir and Chardonnay, the Gantenbeins came up with a Riesling. Top class.*

8 **Viognier 2001** Henri Cruchon (SF 20.50) *A wine that shows how beautifully Viognier can grow in Switzerland.*

9 **Gewürztraminer du Pays de Vaud 2000** Collection le Vin Vivant de Bernard Ravet, Caves Cidis (SF 11.10 per half-bottle) *A specialty from the Vaud, and one of the best Gewürztraminers from Switzerland.*

10 **Sauvignon Blanc Les Curiades 2001** Dupraz et Fils (SF 14.50) *Such freshness and typical fruit aroma gives this wine an international image. You would never guess it comes from Switzerland.*

Austria

Dr Philipp Blom

With 15 wine-growing regions and a plethora of officially sanctioned grape varieties, the current situation leaves even dedicated experts all but stranded.

DR PHILIPP BLOM

As a result, the introduction of a French-style appellation system to cut through the profusion of wines, especially for the export market, has caused a stir throughout many of Austria's wine regions. The country's largest wine-growing region, the Weinviertel, has just adopted an appellation system called Districtus Austria Controllatus (DAC). Known mainly for cheap tipple and Sekt base wines, the Weinviertel growers have their work cut out if they are to dig themselves out of the deepening economic hole that is the result of hitherto unchanging viticultural attitudes, but perhaps DAC will be the catalyst. The Weinviertel DAC wine is a Grüner Veltliner wine, and the appellation is awarded by a professional tasting panel on the basis of quality and typicity. A few exceptional producers, first and foremost Roman Pfaffl, have demonstrated that it is quite possible to make excellent wines in the Weinviertel. The big question is whether other regions will also adopt this system, effectively making it a nationwide restructuring of the wine law, or whether it will remain an isolated occurrence. Some regional committees set up to decide on the future of a DAC label in their region find it difficult to agree on operational points, while other regions, notably the Wachau, see no necessity for it at all. There is a strong danger of fragmentation, which would render DAC

DR PHILIPP BLOM was first introduced to Austrian wines in the 1990s, while studying in Vienna. He now lives in Paris and is the author of *The Wines of Austria* (Faber & Faber, 2000) and *To Have and to Hold: An Intimate History of Collecting* (Penguin, 2003). Philipp is a freelance journalist and writes on wine for *Wine & Spirits Magazine*, *Decanter*, *Vinaria*, and *FT Deutschland*.

just one more complicating factor. A rigorous simplification of the many regions and wine types, which would be the one really helpful means of increasing export, currently seems out of reach.

World beaters

A tasting in London caused national celebrations in Austria and has already passed into legend. The so-called Corso Tasting, named after the Vienna hotel where it was initially held, pitched some great international-name Chardonnays against top Austrian Chardonnays and Grüner Veltliners, which can, as has often been pointed out, develop in a fashion remarkably similar to the Burgundy grape. After initial criticisms about the wine choices, the blind tasting was repeated in London under the august auspices of, and with wines chosen by, Jancis Robinson and Tim Atkin. The wines awarded the highest places by the panel of professionals must have caused something of a collective intake of breath in the room as the results were revealed: seven of the top 10 were Austrian wines, with great Wachau and Kamptal growths (as well as some wines from Styria and the Burgenland) triumphing over great Burgundies and Californian Chardonnays. Tastings may never present more than an educated impression, but the placing of Austria's top-growth whites in this league was long overdue. The good news is that most of these wines still cost a fraction of what their illustrious competition is asking. Next: Great Rieslings?

Terraces

The disastrous rains in August 2002 caused the collapse of five hectares (ha) of the Wachau's terraced vineyards, when six months' worth of rain fell within one week, causing the waterlogged soil to burst through the often centuries-old walls after a build-up of immense pressure. Both the manual labor and the investment needed to restore the terraces are a great burden on many of the estates, some of which also have had to battle with submerged wineries and houses. The army and volunteers were brought in to help rebuild the terraces, which can only be achieved by manual labor on such steep hillsides.

Opinion:
Seeing red

Unfortunately, many producers of Austrian reds, egged on by journalists, have been seduced by a powerful, high-alcohol, high-oak garage style, which often covers up characteristics of *terroir* and vintage, while pushing up prices astronomically. Undrinkable super-premium wines with in excess of 14.5 percent alcohol and more new French oak than you can swing an ax at are no longer a rarity. Those pursuing such powerful wines in a climate that does not lend itself to the style will often resort to a whole battery of oenological improvements, from vacuum evaporation to intensified extraction methods. But if Austria's red wines are to follow its Rieslings and Grüner Veltliners in establishing themselves as world-class, their winemakers will have to alter their approach and craft wines in accordance with, not against, climatic conditions. This will take time because, unlike Austria's great white wines, its potentially great red wines cannot rely on centuries of tradition; consequently its red wine *terroirs* and grape varieties are less well understood. However, the potential is there, if only winemakers would concentrate on expressing what is possible in the vineyard, not the cellar. So far this potential of typicity has been achieved by Krutzler in South Burgenland, Ernst Triebaumer and Andreas Kollwentz in Neusiedlersee-Hügelland, and Juris-Stiegelmar in Neusiedlersee. These are the examples to follow.

Vintage Report

Advance report on the latest harvest

2002

This was a year that is unlikely to be forgotten soon in Austria. Almost-perfect growing conditions were spoiled in August, when the heavens opened and six months' worth of rain fell within just one week. Terraced vineyards collapsed and the Danube overflowed its banks, submerging the valley and low-lying vineyards and wineries in the worst flood conditions experienced for a century. Growers were still reeling from the damage when October brought more rain, causing considerable rot, added to which, cold temperatures did nothing to aid maturation of the few surviving healthy grapes. This forced producers to select with great rigor and in several sweeps through the vineyard, when harvesting could be restarted in November. Despite, or because of, this labor-intensive, nail-biting harvest, the grape quality was—amazingly—very good throughout Austria. In fact, 2002 is the most uniformly good vintage for red, white, and sweet wines since 1993. While the jury is still out on the very promising red and sweet wines, the best dry whites, particularly in Lower Austria, are of wonderful quality, especially the Grüner Veltliners and Rieslings, which have depth and a ringing purity of fruit.

Updates on the previous five vintages

2001

Vintage rating: 86 (White: 87, Red: 84, Sweet: 85)

The never-ending September rain (Vienna saw only four clear days in four weeks) made the harvest very work-intensive in order to sort out the healthy grapes. Two frosty periods in December, finally, allowed an icewine harvest. This is a year that vindicates conscientious vineyard work and good vinification, where wines marked by clarity and balance could be produced. The reds are less powerful than 2000, but possess more charm. A good crop of botrytis wines was harvested, too. Generally, these wines will evolve quite quickly.

2000

Vintage rating: *88 (White: 92, Red: 82, Sweet: 88)*

With little rain in November and above-average temperatures, the perfect conditions were created for a late harvest. This was an extraordinary vintage for red wines, with record must weights and dark colors, though too many growers let themselves be seduced into thinking they could produce competition-winning wines, when in fact it was not easy to balance the alcohol and tannins in the more concentrated wines. With their punch and body, this has been declared a great red-wine vintage, although I personally think that too many are too exaggerated. For white wines, this was an almost-perfect year, with big Grüner Veltliners and Rieslings in Lower Austria and Chardonnays in the Burgenland that were ideally suited for *barrique* treatment. Styrian growers also harvested wines of great concentration and harmony.

1999

Vintage rating: *92 (White: 96, Red: 88, Sweet: 90)*

This was a wonderful year for dry white and red wines. Red wines show good structure and deep fruit, with less tannin than the 2000s, which are usually rated even higher in Austria, although the best producers made beautifully balanced 1999 reds, especially with Blaufränkisch, Zweigelt, and Pinot Noir. White wines in Lower Austria reached great purity, equilibrium, and concentration, with less alcohol than 1998 but a more pronounced acidity than 2000. These are wines expressing varietal character and *terroir* to perfection, ideal for aging, but often already approachable. In the Wachau and the Kamptal, especially, this was a great year. Beautiful whites were also made in the Burgenland, where the Chardonnays in particular show beautiful fruit and often good integration of wood. Styria produced exceptionally deep and expressive Sauvignon Blancs and Morillons (Chardonnays).

1998

Vintage rating: *82 (White: 87, Red: 78, Sweet: 80)*

The grapes were almost too ripe, with high sugars and, as a result, too many wines from this vintage are very high in alcohol (up to 15 percent), low in acidity, and less clearly profiled than those of 1997.

1997

Vintage rating: 89 *(White: 92, Red: 85, Sweet: 90)*

This was indisputably the year of the great white wines, especially in Lower Austria and Styria. Red wines, too, made a major step forward in this year in terms of quality, style, and aging potential, with indigenous grape varieties such as Zweigelt and Blaufränkisch showing their true potential. This was particularly so around Lake Neusiedl and in the rest of the Burgenland, although some truly excellent Pinot Noirs were also produced. One of the greatest vintages of the century in Austria.

Grapevine

• **A discussion** that will not die down in Austria is cork taint, with growers convinced that they are getting the worst of international cork supplies, and up to 15 percent of bottles spoiled, despite buying from the best suppliers. After experimenting with plastic corks, the Kamptal grower Hannes Hirsch, who has strong ties to New Zealand, has now taken the step of bottling his top wines exclusively with screw caps. He may be the first of many.

• **One of Vienna's top growers,** Fritz Wieninger, has declared himself converted to the old local tradition of Gemischter Satz, in which various varietals are planted in the same vineyard, originally to spread risks and ensure reliable yields and average ripeness. He is now selling such a wine from a vineyard he has recently acquired and is very happy with the quality and distinctive taste of the wine. However, he candidly admits that the main problem with Gemischter Satz is replanting, since nobody seems to know the suitable proportions for the different varieties or where to plant them relative to one another.

• **Toni Bodenstein** of the Prager Winery has planted his new Ried Zwerithaler vineyard in the Wachau with 50-year-old Grüner Veltliner vines and has immediately made a great wine that is capable of challenging his more famous Ried Achleiten.

• **In May 2002,** the Austrian wine group Schlumberger bought the Wunderlich Rossbacher trademark from the Vienna-based firm of Wunderlich Austria Walser.

GREATEST WINE PRODUCERS

1. Alzinger
2. Bründlmayer
3. Franz Hirtzberger
4. Knoll
5. Kollwentz
6. Kracher
7. FX Pichler
8. Prager
9. Tement
10. E Triebaumer

FASTEST-IMPROVING PRODUCERS

1. Josef Gritsch
2. Ludwig Hiedler
3. Karl Lagler
4. Erich Macherndl
5. Franz Mittelbach
6. Franz Proidl
7. Engelbert Prieler
8. Undhof Salomon
9. Söllner
10. Johann Heinrich

NEW UP-AND-COMING PRODUCERS

1. Josef Bauer
2. Heribert Bayer
3. Günter Brandl
4. Walter Buchegger
5. Johann Donabaum
6. Josef Dockner
7. Meinhard Forstreiter
8. Toni Hartl
9. Alois Höllmüller
10. Bernhard Ott

BEST-VALUE PRODUCERS

1. Johann Bäuerl
2. Bründlmayer
3. Freie Weingärtner Wachau
4. Emmerich Knoll
5. Schloß Gobelsburg
6. Roman Pfaffl
7. Peter Schandl
8. Heidi Schröck
9. Ludwig Hiedler
10. Platzer

GREATEST-QUALITY WINES

1. **Grüner Veltliner Vinothekfüllung Smaragd 1990** Knoll (€45)
2. **Grüner Veltliner Kellerberg Smaragd 1995** FX Pichler (€50)
3. **Cuvée No 8 Zwischen den Seen 1995** Kracher (€50)
4. **Riesling Singerriedel 1995** Franz Hirtzberger (€45)
5. **Riesling Lyra 1997** Bründlmayer (€25)
6. **Chardonnay Tiglat 1997** Velich (€50)
7. **Riesling Steinertal 1997** Alzinger (€23)
8. **Morillon Zieregg 2000** Tement (€28)
9. **Blaufränkisch Perwolff 2000** Krutzler (€35)
10. **Riesling Wachstum Bodenstein 2002** Prager (€30)

BEST BARGAINS

1. **Grüner Veltliner Haidviertel 2002** Roman Pfaffl (€6.50)
2. **Grüner Veltliner Spitzer Point Federspiel 2001** Johann Donabaum (€6)
3. **Riesling Exklusiv Novemberlese 2001** Günter Brandl (€13.50)
4. **Riesling Alte Reben 2002** Hager (€7)
5. **Riesling Steinhaus 2001** Ludwig Hiedler (€10)
6. **Riesling Heiligenstein 2002** Schloß Gobelsburg (€12)

❼ Gelber Muskateller 2001
Meinhard Forstreiter (€6.80)

❽ Grüner Veltliner Rosenberg
2001 Bernhard Ott (€6.50)

❾ Grüner Veltliner Goldbühel
2002 Tanzer (€5.60)

❿ Ruster Ausbruch 1999
Seiler (€14)

MOST EXCITING OR UNUSUAL FINDS

❶ Gelber Muskateller 2001
Jäger (€10) *A dry, fruity, and elegant Gelber Muskateller with the mineral purity of the Wachau.*

❷ Riesling Rosengarten 2001
Josef Dockner (€10) *A young producer coming into his own with a strikingly delicate and floral Riesling.*

❸ Schilcher Standard 2002
Friedrich (€4.50) *You either love it or you hate it, but this is a very attractive example of a bracing rosé.*

❹ Schilcher Eiswein 2000
Jöbstl (€16) *It doesn't get any more unusual than this—a wine to defeat experts.*

❺ Ina'Mera 2000 Juris (€25) *This deep but beautifully balanced, finely structured red wine flies in the face of the current Burgenland fashion for blockbusters.*

❻ Gelber Muskateller Nussberg
2002 Gross (€9) *Another beautifully pure Gelber Muskateller—a much underrated specialty.*

❼ Riesling Beerenauslese 2000
Franz Hirtzberger (€40) *Wachau Riesling BA is always rare, and in Hirtzberger's hands it shows all the glory of the varietal.*

❽ Grüner Veltliner TBA 2001
Knoll (€50) *Knoll proves himself a master of TBA with this finely balanced wine, which explores new aromatic depths of Grüner Veltliner.*

❾ Gewürztraminer Auslese 2001
Minkowitsch (€9) *This is surely one of Austria's most beautiful dry aromatic wines. Finely spiced and smelling of roses.*

❿ Sauvignon Blanc Moarfeitl
Reserve 2000 Neumeister (€19) *Consistently underestimated, Neumeister proves its mastery with this rich, deeply concentrated Sauvignon.*

Eastern & Southeastern Europe

Caroline Gilby MW

Enlargement of the EU is the big story. Hungary, Slovenia, the Czech Republic, Slovakia, and Cyprus are the wine-producing countries that – subject to referendum – will be joining in 2004.

CAROLINE GILBY MW

Romania and Bulgaria are working toward the next round of expansion, probably in 2007, while Turkey hopes to start negotiations next year. EU membership will certainly provide a challenge to wine producers, who have, until now, been trading in comfortably protected domestic markets.

In Hungary, high demand for reds and limited quantities have allowed winemakers in areas like Villány to charge premium prices. These look difficult to sustain with the arrival of global competition, with the exception of the few who genuinely do make wines of international caliber. There has been some last-minute planting of vineyards before EU restrictions are imposed, and the Hungarian government has suddenly woken up to the opportunity to fully subsidize generic support for the industry until next year.

Some Hungarian producers see a positive side to joining the EU, since tougher regulations may force basic standards up. Many Slovenian producers are nervous about joining the EU because their cost of production is fairly high, and cheap Western European imports could provide serious competition on the domestic market. This is driving the

CAROLINE GILBY MW has a horticultural doctorate in plant tissue and was a senior wine buyer covering Eastern Europe for a major UK retail chain. She is now a freelance writer and independent consultant to the wine trade, including four years on the Wine Standards Board. Caroline also lectures WSET Diploma students on tasting technique, vinification, and wine handling, and judges at international wine shows.

private wineries to look for niche export opportunities— they would like to see themselves as the New Zealand of Europe.

The effect on other new member nations seems less dramatic. The Czech Republic and Slovakia already import a lot of EU wine, since both produce at levels well below their own domestic demand. Keo, the biggest Cypriot producer, is more pragmatic. While joining the EU may be a good trade opportunity, the company believes tourists will still demand local wine.

A couple of programs exist to provide funds to countries preparing for EU accession. Bulgaria is already benefiting from an agricultural and rural development program, which provides funding of some 50 percent for planting costs and winery equipment, although it does not provide money for grubbing up. Bulgaria is planning to replant around 8,200 hectares (ha) per year until 2006, and is talking of expanding to 190,000 ha while it is free to do so. However, preliminary estimates indicate only 150 ha were actually planted last year.

Romania seems desperate to show its wholesale adoption of EU standards and harmonizing legislation. Plans are in place to modernize 65,000 ha and uproot the poor-quality hybrids that cover nearly half of the existing 244,000 ha of vineyards. Where producers have managed to get hold of land, and have the funds, they are planting furiously in anticipation of EU restrictions. High-quality clones should give them a head start over more traditional areas of Europe. For Romania, a deal with the EU on mutual reduction of taxes will mean cheap imports from next year, and that may force some of the poorer producers out of business.

Grapevine

- **The Recas winery** in Romania has invested in a new underground cellar complex, temperature-controlled warehouse, and barrels. A 16-ha vineyard has been planted with new clones and 250 miles (400 km) of new trellising installed. The first vintage of new clone Pinot Noir has just been released.

- **Chateau Ruko** is a new 5-million-liter winery in Bulgaria's Iambol region. It was entirely designed and built through EU funds, and started operation in 2002.

- **Cricova-Acorex** in Moldova has converted 694 ha to organic production. The first certified vintage will be 2003.

- **Carl Reh** was the first Romanian winery to plant Shiraz, and the first vintage is 2002. Almost 80 ha of vines were planted in 2003 with imported clones and rootstock trials. Carl Reh is converting to organic production for its estate vineyards as from this year.

- **Renowned German producer** Egon Müller has just released his first wine from Slovakia, Château Belá Riesling 2001. For now, fruit comes from a neighboring grower, but the plan is to buy back the property's original vineyards.

DIVIDED THEY FALL

Post-communist reforms gave land back to the original owners, generally in tiny parcels. An estimated 100,000 growers in Bulgaria hold under 0.5 ha each, while Georgia shares 60,000 ha among 150,000 growers. In Romania, three quarters of the land is held privately, with average plots of under 1 ha, and 35,000 Slovenian owners average 0.4 ha each. New owners are rarely committed to managing the land properly, since each parcel is too small to provide a living, let alone pay for equipment and agrochemicals. This has resulted in a culture of very part-time farmers with city jobs, who do not want to sell their plot of heritage and their retirement hobby. To improve quality, however, commercial producers must be able to control their fruit. This means being able to buy or lease long-term, efficient, consolidated plots, something that is not easy to find. SERVE, the Bucharest-based wine producer, needs 145 contracts to lease just 28 ha of Romanian vines, and the Svischtov winery in Bulgaria has to deal with 600 owners in order to manage 228 ha of vines. Bulgaria has at least recognized that land fragmentation is a problem, but figures it is still 10–15 years away from completing a database that will allow landowners to be identified, even though this really needs to be tackled urgently. In Ukraine, the problem is less about fragmentation, more a lack of vertical integration. Its vineyards have remained cooperative-owned with primary winemaking nearby, but young wines are shipped off to outdated central facilities for malolactic and finishing. The privatization process is under way in Serbia and Montenegro; and with only 20 percent completed, the government at least has an opportunity to learn from other countries' mistakes.

Grapevine

- **Even in Tokaj,** the quality today reflects less than 65 percent of the potential of the best *terroir*. That's what top Tokaji winemaker István Szepsy thinks. He says there are too many big-bunch clones, while those vineyards that have been replanted with the best old selections are still too young.

- **Ernő Malya,** the winemaker at Budai, was named Winemaker of the Year 2002 by the Hungarian Wine Academy. **Nagyrede** was named Winery of the Year 2002.

- **István Szepsy and Anthony Hwang,** his partner in Királyudvar, have set up a new Tokaji winery in their children's names. The first vintage of Zemplen Ridge will be 2002, and the winery will concentrate on competitively priced five-*puttonyos aszú* wines and *szamorodni* wines of equivalent sweetness.

- **Russian winemaker MVZ** acquired Moldovan producer Calaras Divin in Calarasi for $3.7 million in February 2003.

- **Doluca** in Turkey is working with Australian-born, British-based consultant John Worontshak and the UK's Vinifera Wines on a project whose wine to be called Eurasia. There will be a red and a white, both made from blends of European and Asian varieties. The first vintage will be 2002, due for release later this year.

Opinion:
New Europe must reform quality

With global surpluses and the New World stealing market share in most wine-drinking nations, Eastern and Southeastern Europe must concentrate on quality and consistency to have any chance of survival. The region is often let down by inadequate fruit from elderly, poorly managed vineyards that were frequently planted for high-volume production. This problem is common in both the former communist nations and bulk shippers like Cyprus and Turkey. The producers in Eastern and Southeastern Europe see themselves as the New Europe, but they have no hope of matching the massive marketing spends of highly capitalized New World brands. If the wines of New Europe are to survive in the brave new world of an open EU market, their makers must overachieve on quality and provide it consistently, bottle after bottle.

What rot

In Tokaj, dry wines are a commercial and cash-flow necessity, since for most growers, 70–100 percent of their crop will not make *aszú* quality in any year. The challenge here is to change attitudes from managing wines for rot to understanding how to grow healthy fruit for dry wines.

Cut the bureaucracy

Paperwork in this part of the world is unnecessarily complicated, wasting time and resources that would be better spent on getting the vines and wines right. Phillip Cox at the Recas winery in Romania says he needs a truck to deliver the paperwork for employing casual labor for the harvest. Keeping up with the latest version of the ever-changing laws is also a burden, with the wine laws in Romania having changed no fewer than seven times in 2002. Bulgaria is no better: it can take over two years to set up a new business there. Hungary suffers from pointless bureaucracy, such as specifying the length of roots on new vines. Imported vines are too short and require special permits. The authorities need to dump the paper and focus on ways to help businesses compete on the international stage.

Must pull together

Few countries in the region succeed in presenting a united front to promote their wines. Working together does not seem to come easy to Slavic nations, although the Latin culture of Romania appears to be more cooperative. While there are some small organizations, like Tokaji Renaissance or Pannon Wine Guild in Hungary and the Wine Exporters and Producers Association (WEPA) or Dealul Mare Association in Romania, they represent barely a drop in the ocean. The wine industry must bring everyone into the fold; it is no good promoting a few icons if the country's image is let down by the many. At least Romania seems to have made a start with the recent formation of the Organizatia Nationala Interprofesionala Vitivinicola (ONIV), an interprofessional organization that represents wine interests across the industry. Tokaji is a good example of how a lack of unity can be damaging. Producers must come together to promote it as one of the world's truly great sweet wines, instead of indulging in self-defeating infighting over oxidative or reductive styles when there is a market for both.

Better money-management required

There has been a lack of investment in the Eastern European wine industry, but just as damaging has been the poor use of available funds. Expensive heavy-metal and state-of-the-art bottling lines have sprung up all over, and this year's potential white elephant in Bulgaria is bag-in-box lines. One source figures that 30–40 percent of Bulgarian wineries will install their own bag-in-box line this year. If the industry cooperated better, they could share such equipment. After 50 years of forced cooperative farming, Eastern European countries need to realize that cooperation is a different word and one that should not be avoided. Moldovan wineries have received over $60 million from the EU and World Bank, but spent most of it on bottling lines, instead of doing the vineyard groundwork.

Grapevine

- **French-based Belvedere Group** bought the Bulgarian Menada winery in Stara Zagora in September 2002 for an undisclosed price.

- **Boyar Estates in Bulgaria** has vinified the first Merlot grapes from its estate vineyards near Blueridge. These were planted with three imported French clones under the supervision of the Di Davidson consultancy. The wine will be a limited edition for the Bulgarian market.

- **The first-ever major generic tasting of Slovenian wine** was held in London in November 2002. Partly funded by the government, this was the first time it has supported private producers, since only cooperatives have received financial support in the past. There is still a major split between volume producers and the smaller private wineries that would like to establish Slovenia's reputation as a niche producer of high-quality wines.

- **Interest continues** in tracking the parents of Zinfandel after confirmation that the grape is genetically identical to the rare Croatian variety Crljenak.

- **The political situation in Serbia** and Montenegro stabilized in 2002, enabling exports to increase by 17 percent to 64,000 hectoliters, but the future looks less certain following the assassination of Prime Minister Djindjic in March 2003.

- **Slovakia agreed to adopt** EU wine law in June 2002 and is working on a vineyard register, since only registered producers will be able to trade within the EU after the country's accession in 2004.

Vintage Report

Advance report on the latest harvest

2002

This was a mixed year, ranging from outstanding in Romania's Transylvanian region to below average in areas such as northern Bulgaria and southeastern Romania, which were hit by heavy rains. In Hungary, the wines are very concentrated, with whites especially good and reds above average. Yield is down by 30 percent on average, but as much as 70 percent in some areas. In Tokaj, hopes for a great *aszú* vintage were dashed by some rain in October, but the wine is rated as very good, especially for fruit harvested early. In Romania, some reports suggest as much as 60 percent of the crop was rot-damaged around Murfatlar. However, most other areas are showing very good quality but heavily reduced yields due to drought at flowering, which caused poor fruit set and small berry size. In Dealul Mare, yields are only 30 percent of normal, and around Oprisor quantities are 50–60 percent down. In Bulgaria, summer rains with low temperatures affected sugar accumulation and kept acids high. Gamza was virtually wiped out, and many producers had to chaptalize in order to reach minimum alcohol levels. The vintage in neighboring Macedonia was also described as difficult and required careful selection. In Cyprus, quality was good, albeit low in quantity due to a green harvest imposed by the government to reduce yields. Summer rainfall also caused mildew around Paphos and Lemesos. Unusually, Turkey was hit by rain around harvest, which caught many growers unprepared, resulting in more rot and weather damage than normal. Ukraine produced promising reds, with good color and sugar levels around Odessa, which escaped rainfall during the vintage. In Moldova, 2002 was 17 percent down in volume and very good in quality. Slovenian production was down 20–30 percent because heavy rain after a warm June caused some rot in early whites. Overall, sugar levels were good and quality high.

Updates on the previous five vintages

2001

Vintage rating: *77 (Reds: 80, Whites: 75, Sweet: 75)*

Most Tokaji was poor, although some decent *aszú* wines have been made with ultra-careful selection. Elsewhere in Hungary, early-picked whites are above average, and there are some sound late-picked reds. In Romania, it was a good ripe year, while in Bulgaria some producers reported good wines, but many vines were drought-stressed, so their metabolism shut down and the grapes failed to ripen.

2000

Vintage rating: *85 (Reds: 85, Whites: 80, Sweet: 90)*

A long, hot, dry summer made for an excellent Tokaji vintage, with huge sugar levels and great flavors. It was a very good vintage across all of Hungary, with fully ripe fruit and high alcohol levels, but the wines are maturing quickly due to low acidity. It was also one of the finest recent vintages in Romania, showing ripe, healthy fruit, balanced acidity, and good keeping potential. It was a very good year in Bulgaria, too, with disease-free fruit and high sugars.

1999

Vintage rating: *87 (Reds: 85–90, Whites: 80, Sweet: 90)*

This is another classic Tokaji year, with highly concentrated *aszú* berries superbly balanced by intense fruit acids, combining aging potential with great elegance. A very good year for reds in Hungary and Romania, with uniformly ripe fruit, high sugars, and good acidity. Late frost damaged as much as 40 percent of the white crop in the southeast, and rain during harvest in some areas also affected whites. In Bulgaria, it was the international red-wine varieties, such as Cabernet and Merlot, that did best in this high-quality vintage.

1998

Vintage rating: *75 (Reds: 75, Whites: 75, Sweet: 75)*

It was a cooler and rainier summer than usual in Tokaj, bringing botrytis but not much shriveling, and limiting the quantities of *aszú* wines, which are lighter in body and more forward. Not an easy vintage across the rest of Hungary, which was very wet during the harvest, although early whites came in before the rain really set in and were the most acceptable of a generally disappointing crop. It was also a challenging vintage in Bulgaria, where the grapes did not ripen fully. In Romania, an extended drought resulted in very tannic, high-acid reds and small quantities.

1997

Vintage rating: 78
(Reds: 75–80, Whites: 70–80, Sweet: 70–90)

It was a very late season in Tokaj, with very little rain in September and hardly any development of botrytis, although pockets of *aszú* berries developed later in the season, and these were of outstanding quality (similar to 1993). Elsewhere in Hungary, it was an early harvest with very good to excellent results for both reds and whites. In Romania, the reds turned out well, with good sugar accumulation and fully ripe tannins, although they are very short on quantity. Some good quality in Bulgaria.

Grapevine

• **Hungary** assembled a committee of winemakers to start on developing a national wine strategy in 2003. Although it has already been criticized for lacking an overseas perspective, the committee is expected to reduce the number of wine regions from the current 22 to just 10.

• **Turkey's wine production** in 2002 went up to 48.5 million liters, and the industry now comprises 31 companies, with six that are state-owned and control 40 percent of the volume. Turkish ex-pats in Germany are the most important export market, taking nearly a third of exports.

• **Chris Cameron of Peppertree** in the Hunter Valley, Australia, plans to plant vines on the Gallipoli peninsula in Turkey overlooking Anzac Cove. His first wine will be a three-country white blend probably called PAX, made from wines from Australia, New Zealand, and Turkey, and due for release on Anzac Day 2004.

• **Bulgaria's wine lake** is drying up thanks to renewed sales to Russia and Poland. A new law has been passed requiring all wine producers to register, even if vinifying for home consumption only (which apparently accounts for as much as 60 percent of all wine output).

• **Reports from Hungary and Moldova** indicate that Italian companies have been buying up Pinot Gris in bulk, both as juice and wine, after the poor harvest in northern Italy.

• **Rumors are rife** that more Pinot Noir is produced in Romania than the official area of 1,750 hectares could possibly yield. Carl Reh subjects the Pinot Noir it purchases to anthocyanin testing, and claims to be 95 percent confident that it is the real thing.

• **Fraudulent Georgian wine** continues to be major problem in both the former Soviet Union and the US.

GREATEST WINE PRODUCERS

Tokaji
1. Szepsy
2. Királyudvar
3. Domaine de Disznókö
4. Royal Tokaji Wine Company
5. Oremus

Other wines
1. Attila Gere (Hungary)
2. Château Belá (Slovakia)
3. Edi Simčič (Slovenia)
4. Kupljen (whites only, Slovenia)
5. Movia (Slovenia)

BEST-VALUE PRODUCERS

1. Prahova Wine Cellars (reds only, Romania)
2. Vinarium Szekszárdi (Hungary)
3. Budai Winery (Hungary)
4. Hilltop Neszmély Winery (Hungary)
5. Carl Reh Winery (Romania)
6. Nagyréde Winery (Hungary)
7. Gyöngyös Estate (Hungary)
8. Chapel Hill (Balaton-Boglar Winery, Hungary)
9. Domaine Boyar (Schumen Winery, Bulgaria)
10. Binderer St Ursula (Macedonia)

FASTEST-IMPROVING PRODUCERS

1. Carl Reh Winery (Romania)
2. Prahova Wine Cellars (reds only, Romania)
3. Cricova-Acorex (Moldova)
4. Vinterra International (Romania)
5. Recas (Romania)
6. Budai Winery (Hungary)
7. Blueridge Winery (Bulgaria)
8. Domaine Boyar (Bulgaria)
9. Svischtov (Bulgaria)
10. SERVE (Romania)

NEW UP-AND-COMING PRODUCERS

1. Château Belá (Slovakia)
2. Tilia (Slovenia)
3. Sutor (Slovenia)
4. Batapaati (Hungary)
5. Crown Estates (dry whites only, Hungary)
6. Jeruzalem Ormož (Slovenia)
7. Vinska Klet Goriska Brda (Slovenia)
8. Chateau Vincent (Hungary)
9. Keo (Cyprus)
10. Sodap (Cyprus)

GREATEST-QUALITY WINES

Tokaji
1. **Tokaji Aszú 6 Puttonyos 1999** Szepsy (9,000 forints)
2. **Tokaji Cuvée 2000** Szepsy (11,900 forints)
3. **Royal Tokaji Aszú Essencia 1995** Royal Tokaji Wine Company (42,000 forints)
4. **Tokaji Cuvée 1999** Királyudvar (9,500 forints)
5. **Tokaji Aszú 6 Puttonyos 1999** Domaine de Disznókö (not released, estimated 9,000 forints)

Other wines
1. **Villány Cabernet Sauvignon Barrique 1999** Attila Gere (Hungary, 3,575 forints)
2. **Château Belá Riesling 2001** Egon Müller (Slovakia, 520 koruny)
3. **Extract of Styria 2001** Kupljen (Slovenia, 1,500 SIT)
4. **Duet Riserva 1999** Edi Simčič (Slovenia, 5,750 SIT)
5. **Merlot 1999** Tilia (Slovenia, 2,000 SIT)

BEST BARGAINS

❶ Cabernet Sauvignon 2000
Vinarium Szekszárdi
(Hungary, 1,075 forints)

❷ Pinot Grigio 2002
Budai Winery (Hungary, 825 forints)

❸ Dry Furmint 2002 Domaine de
Disznókö (Hungary, 1,160 forints)

**❹ Black Peak Cabernet Sauvignon
2000** Vinterra (Romania, 161,000 lei)

**❺ Limited Release Chardonnay
2002** River Route (Romania,
export only—£4.49–4.99 UK)

❻ Pinot Grigio/Chardonnay 2002
Riverview (Hungary, 1,000 forints)

**❼ Noble Late Harvest Furmint
1999** Oremus (Hungary,
1,500 forints per half-bottle)

❽ Merlot Rosé 2002 Riverview
(Romania, export only—£2.99 UK)

**❾ Mallia Estate Cabernet/
Vertzami 2001**
Keo (Cyprus, 5.12 Cyprus pounds)

❿ Chardonnay/Dimiat 2001
Blueridge Winery (Bulgaria, export
only—£3.99 UK)

MOST EXCITING OR UNUSUAL FINDS

❶ La Cetate Merlot 2000 Carl
Reh Winery (Romania, 180,000 lei)
*Intense chocolate and plum
Merlot showing what can be
done from a properly managed
single estate in Romania. The
2002 Shiraz from the same
estate looks even more exciting.*

❷ Pinot Noir Reserve 2000
Prahova Valley (Romania, 115,000
lei) *Ripe and velvety, my top wine
in a blind tasting against Pinot
Noirs from around the world—
some at twice the price.*

❸ Szekszárdi Cabernet Franc 2000
Vinarium (Hungary, 1,125 forints)
*Excellent-value Cabernet Franc
that can really stand up for itself.*

*Plenty of blackberry fruit, herbal
complexity, and a touch of oak.*

❹ Feteasca Neagra 2000 Vinterra
(Romania, 143,000 lei) *The native
"black maiden grape" may well
become Romania's signature
variety, with its dark plum and
dried cherry fruit, overlaid with
hints of chocolate and tobacco.*

❺ Albastrele Pinot Grigio 2002
Cricova-Acorex (Moldova, 31
Moldovan lei) *There is a touch of
Italian style in this fresh, ultra-
clean white.*

❻ Castle Island Hárslevelü 2002
Crown Estates (Hungary, 970
forints) *This new-wave dry wine
from Tokaj is fresh and aromatic,
with real lime-leaf notes and
a flinty, crisp palate. Even the
winemaker was surprised how
well this turned out!*

**❼ Special Reserve Sangiovese
1999** Prahova Valley (Romania,
170,000 lei) *Attractive tea leaves
and cherry fruit, with good acidity
and structure. Sangiovese is a rarity
in Romania, but this example is
riper than most Italians could
manage at the price.*

❽ Sauvignon Blanc 2002 Budai
Winery (Hungary, 963 forints)
*Fragrant, nettley, flinty Sauvignon
from a unique spot that is not far
from Budapest and noted for its
varietal purity and crisp acids.*

❾ Tamada Saperavi 1999 GWS
(Georgia, 15 lari) *Vibrant, fresh,
blackberry fruit backed up by
plenty of character and lively
acidity. The estate-grown version
due out later this year should be
worth watching for.*

❿ Ozel Kav White 1999 Doluca
(Turkey, 17 million Turkish lire) *The
native Narince grape has produced
a surprisingly fresh, zesty wine
with hints of ripe pear from Turkey's
most forward-thinking winery.*

Greece

Nico Manessis

Anything Greek is going to be in the spotlight for a short period, thanks to the unprecedented exposure of the Olympic Games in Athens next year; but is Greek wine capable of taking advantage of this? Probably not.

NICO MANESSIS

The shameful fact is that Greece has been dragging its feet in the public sector and is incapable of meeting the promotional needs of its emerging, vibrant wine-producing regions. Apathy rules in the Hellenic republic. There is no plan and no long-term commitment to support generically the Greek wine industry, which ranks 14th in the top 20 wine-producing nations. Indeed, the opposite has happened. Politics prompted the overnight closure several years ago of the Greek Wine Bureau in London. The closure was just one of several examples of half-baked ideas that are not well thought out and, subsequently, become counterproductive. Politically motivated and special-interest favors at government level have succeeded only in dampening winemakers' export-promotion efforts.

But there is hope, albeit on a much-reduced scale. The ensuing indignation prompted action by small breakaway groups like Ariston, an alliance of seven boutique-sized producers who have made an impression on the German market, despite a difficult economic climate. Road shows and tastings for the trade and press were held in key towns throughout Germany, and the reaction has been overwhelmingly positive. German

NICO MANESSIS is the author of *The Illustrated Greek Wine Book* (Olive Press, 2000) and the three editions of *The Greek Wine Guide* (Olive Press, 1994, 1995, 1996). He teaches at the Université du Vin, in France, and has been writing articles on the wines of his native Greece for more than 10 years. Nico is based in Geneva, where he is a member of the Académie Internationale du Vin.

consumers are at last recognizing that Greek wine can offer real-world quality and individuality. And this from a market awash with branded table-wine icons of the 1990s and retsina.

When the Olympic circus packs up and leaves town, what will the post-2004 future hold for Greek wine? It is a matter of speculation, of course, but the few privately funded promotional efforts planned prior to the Games should create an awareness of the improvements that have occurred over recent years. However, the odds are that the Greek authorities will mess up or miss out on this once-in-a-lifetime opportunity.

First Greek MW

At 32, Constantinos Lazarakis has become the first Greek-born Master of Wine, joining 240 other holders of the world's most prestigious wine qualification. Lazarakis's interest in wine started in Greece, where he honed his palate before receiving valuable international experience in London at Oddbins and the Conran restaurant empire. He now lives in Athens, working as buyer and marketing manager of a leading importer and distributor of fine wines. He has educationalist aspirations and would like to see more Masters of Wine in Greece—not to mention Master Sommeliers—to raise standards in the wine industry.

Grapevine

• **As of the 2003 vintage,** the important fledgling venture of Ktima Pavlides in Drama will be moving into a brand new winery adjacent to its 17-hectare (ha) vineyards, which are planted with a mix of indigenous and international varieties.

• **At Ktima Fountis in Naoussa,** oenologist Dimitris Ziannis is upping his game. After the very good 2000s, he had better-balanced, even more exceptional 2001s. This reflects a change of approach in the cellar, where vatting time is longer and, as a result, the wines have more flesh and color, yet are softer and have not lost the Gastras *terroir* or Xinomavro grape's attractive bite.

• **Quality at the Amynteon Cooperative** has received a major makeover. Production manager Kosmas Roufas has turned what used to be hard, old-fashioned wines into a modern, softer, fruitier style and now offers excellent value for the quality. All production is now bottled and reaches 750,000 bottles. New labels in the works include a *cuve close* sparkler.

• **The Boutari winery** at Skalani on the island of Crete, the country's most modern winery, has opened its doors to the public. From inception, its design has favored wine tourists, with a multimedia show, modern Cretan kitchen, and tasting facilities as some of the highlights.

• **Grape researcher** Haroula Spinthiropoulou continues his work at Vitro nurseries with the clonal selection of 300 indigenous grapes. He is also marking out the potential of the lesser-known grape varieties, thus saving them for future generations. He is helped by the Agricultural University of Athens, which now has its DNA identification programs up and running.

AMERICAN PREJUDICE A THING OF THE PAST

Is Greek wine the next thing to arrive on the US wine scene? Perhaps. Peter Franz of the influential *Washington Post* seems to think so, having dedicated his fourth column in 18 months to the subject. He even went as far as to state in March 2003, "I've received more favorable reader reactions to the Greek wines I recommended here than any others I've done in the past nine years." Not to be outdone, Pierre Rovani has been reviewing Greek wines for the *Wine Advocate* since 2001. This has had a measurable effect, too. One importer maintains that the new Greece is losing its ethnic market image. This is especially true with sommeliers and restaurateurs who are tuned in to the broader picture and are making ever-increasing listings.

MORE WINE ROUTES

The establishment of wine routes throughout Greece is finally becoming a reality. The project is moving forward, with healthy inter-regional competition beginning in earnest. Macedonia was the first to pioneer a wine route, which stimulated a friendly rivalry from the Peloponnesian wine routes and, from around the capital's remaining vineyards, the Attica wine routes. All three now have structured organizations with promotional programs and ad hoc events. Attica routes have gone a step further, capitalizing on the fact that many of the vineyards and wineries are situated around the international airport. At the terminal, a wine shop dispenses information about member wineries and affords the opportunity to buy bottles from the very vineyards you see as you fly in or out.

FIRST IN MORE WAYS THAN ONE

Bearing the first letter of the Greek alphabet and thus easy to remember, Ktima Alpha is the first vineyard-driven new venture in the sleepy Amynteon appellation of northwestern Macedonia. Vineyard consultant Stephanos Kountouras is using Australian-developed techniques, with regulated-deficit irrigation and canopy management being the two major areas on which he has concentrated. In 2001, Kountouras produced just a trickle of wine under the Alpha Estate label from the 42 ha he planted in 1997. As promising as it was, the quality was a mere shadow of the perfumed, seamless Syrah-Merlot he produced in 2002.

Opinion:
Foreigners wanted

There are countries with lower production costs—Argentina and Chile, to mention just two—but Greece is not geared for large-volume, low-price wines, and it would greatly benefit from foreign or joint ventures in the premium sector. Greece is, and will remain, a niche player, and there is unending potential for outside investment in the fabulously diverse *terroir*, varied microclimates, and no fewer than 300 indigenous grape varieties. One such area that comes to mind is Epirus, with its relatively cheap land, cooler climate, higher rainfall, and mountain setting. Epirus is the last frontier for top-quality Greek wine, and with an annual crop of graduates from the TEI University in Athens, there is plenty of gifted home-grown talent to pick from.

Indigenous grapes: the way forward

The invaders are slowly taking root. International varieties were first planted in 1963, but they now account for more than one in every 10 Greek vines. The usual culprits dominate: Sauvignon Blanc, Chardonnay, and Viognier for whites, and Cabernet Sauvignon, Merlot, and Syrah for reds. They were chosen in deference to outside demand from the 30-odd countries Greece exports to, in varietal form or as Greek-international blends. However, the way forward must lie with indigenous grape varieties. There are plenty to choose from (more than 300), and they cover a wide range: from the non-aromatic, severe, mineral character of Assyrtiko (arguably Greece's model white) to the subtle, insistent pear-drop Rhoditis, and on to the aromatic *blanc de gris* Moschofilero, which is distinguished by its high-acid grapey structure and rose-scented bergamot flavors. These are just three of the most widely planted, higher-profile cultivars. Two more rediscovered stars have joined the white-grape constellation: the aromatic Malagousia, dripping with citron and mint, and Lagorthi, the most recent addition, which has the advantage of naturally low alcohol (between 10.5 percent and 11 percent) combined with a sheer elegance that makes it the Greek answer to Riesling. There are more waiting in the wings.

Vintage Report

2002

There was rain and more rain, mostly at the wrong times, both before and during harvest. However, with such a fragmented vineyard and so many types of grapes picked at different dates, there are always exceptions. Cooler median temperatures and, in particular, unusually low nocturnal temperatures hugely benefited the earlier-harvested whites. Drama, Kavala, and Epanomi wines are all very good, vibrant, and fruity. Elsewhere, a contrast of extremes was the case. Santorini harvested a fraction of its usual tonnage. Naoussa was a washout, with unripeness and widespread rot. Nemea was a disaster, although a couple of higher-elevation vineyards produced healthy grapes, albeit in small amounts and with less color and body than normal. The unprecedented shortfall resulted in strong domestic demand for red wine, pushing up prices. Mantinia had little rot, good aroma, and satisfactory, if lower, levels of ripeness. Rhodes, the most eastern island vineyards, experienced the best vintage in years.

Updates on the previous five vintages

2001

Vintage rating: *89 (Red: 90, White: 89)*

Another very good vintage. Lower yields and higher acidities encouraged wines of notable quality in both colors. Crete, Cephalonia, and Santorini produced superb, crisp, dry whites. Attica vineyards equipped with drip irrigation excelled, following the previous year's heat wave, which had stressed Savatiano vines to their limits. Mantinia had one of its finest harvests, with a quantity and quality not seen since 1998. Standout reds are to be found everywhere. Naoussa wines are delicious, without the overripe jammy fruit found in the previous vintage. Those of Goumenissa are a little less ripe, though delicate. Nemea has produced atypical wines, the best of them characterized by an inspired combination of class and ethereal edge. Balanced Samos Muscats are a delight.

2000

Vintage rating: *90 (Red: 93, White: 88)*

A superlative vintage for red wines, with a rarely seen uniformity of healthy grapes in all regions. Some whites were at the limit of low acidity, but most were concentrated. Vineyards in Mantinia were generally stressed, causing an unusually rapid loss of aroma and fruit. Santorini came up with superb, *terroir*-driven, bone-dry whites, and Crete upped its white-wine profile significantly. In Drama, Merlots were somewhat over the top. Elsewhere, they are keepers. Without a doubt, it was one of the greatest Naoussa and Nemea harvests on record, the likes not seen since the 1994 and 1990. Some Naoussa single vineyards went for broke and harvested overripe, losing the character of their *terroir*. Phenolic maturity in Nemea was perfect. The wines are packed with fruit and the more structured top-notch labels will age up to 12 years. Amber Samos are a shade darker and duller on the palate, due to high temperatures and arid summer conditions.

1999

Vintage rating: *86 (Red: 85, White: 87)*

The quality was more inconsistent than poor. Santorini was mediocre, because this extreme microclimate was deprived of the cooling Meltemi north wind and experienced sporadic rot. Patras came up with good Rhoditis, illustrating that the eastern appellation's potential is being realized. In Mantinia, low levels of maturity confirmed that the 1998 crop was an impossible act to follow. The leading estate in Ilia produced a stunner from 120-year-old vines that could not have succeeded in a richer vintage. The traditional reds from Naoussa are delicately aromatic and will mature faster than those from 2000. Nemea wines are less good and not for aging. Here, the tables were turned for the lower-altitude valleys such as Gymno and Ancient Nemea, which had less-frequent harvest showers and have outperformed the better-rated, higher Koutsi vineyards. The Aegean islands of Samos and Limnos produced fragrant wines from Muscat Blanc à Petit Grains and Muscat of Alexandria respectively.

1998

Vintage rating: *89 (Red: 89, White: 88)*

This was a more-than-decent vintage, with good quantity and sound quality. The microclimates highlighted regional differences. Several appellations made exceptionally good wines. Mantinia scaled new heights with good ripeness levels and very floral wines. A drop in yields in Naoussa made for more-concentrated wines, following a series of mediocre harvests. In July, a week-long heat wave reduced berry size of Agiorgitiko in Nemea, resulting in ultra-smooth tannins in all vineyards. Weather during harvest was near-perfect with dry, warm conditions late into autumn, allowing late-ripening, high-altitude vines to fully mature.

1997

Vintage rating: *88 (Red: 87, White: 90)*

One of the cooler recent vintages. Flowering was later than usual, and the entire growing season remained behind schedule. Lower temperatures prevailed throughout the summer. Some whites are quite exceptional. In some regions they are a little austere—atypical, with malic acid present in grapes grown in the higher regions. Patras white wines were reminiscent of their Italian counterparts in the Friuli. In Macedonia, both Drama and Amynteon made highly aromatic whites. Mantinia whites were crisp and lean. A dry and warmer September and early October saved the red-grape vintage. Some red wines are lacking in grace, particularly Naoussa, though not in color. Nemea excelled and highlighted the appellation's *cru* potential, deep in color and loaded with fruit. Concentrated wines came from the lower-yield sloped vineyards. These will age for 8–10 years.

GREATEST WINE PRODUCERS

1. Ktima Gerovassiliou
2. Gaia Wines
3. Ktima Mercouri
4. Oenoforos
5. Tselepos
6. Ktima Katsaros
7. Parparoussis
8. Sigalas
9. Kostas Lazaridis
10. Samos Cooperative

FASTEST-IMPROVING PRODUCERS

1. Ktima Gerovassiliou
2. Skouras
3. Gentilini
4. Boutaris (Ktima Fantaxometoho)
5. Evharis

NEW UP-AND-COMING PRODUCERS

1. Biblia Hora
2. Ktima Pavlides

BEST-VALUE PRODUCERS

1. Oenoforos
2. Parparoussis
3. Creta Olympias
4. Ktima Mercouri
5. Ktima Voyatzi
6. Ktima Roxane Matsa
7. Emery
8. Samos Cooperative
9. Karydas
10. Tatsis Bros

GREATEST-QUALITY WINES

1. **Syrah 2001**
   Ktima Gerovassiliou (€15)
2. **Gaia Estate 2000**
   Gaia Wines (€18)
3. **Cava 1999** Ktima Mercouri (€11)
4. **Merlot Kokkinomylos 2000**
   Tselepos (€18)
5. **Chardonnay 2001**
   Antonopoulos (€16)
6. **Santorini Bareli 2001**
   Sigalas (€11.50)
7. **White 2002**
   Ktima Gerovassiliou (€8)
8. **Nemea Epilegmenos 1998**
   Parparoussis (€10)
9. **Rosé 2002** Biblia Hora (€7)
10. **Xerolithia 2002**
    Creta Olympias (€5.80)

BEST BARGAINS

1. **Nea Ghi 2002**
   Creta Olympias (€4.35)
2. **Zitsa 2002**
   Orion Zitsa Cooperative (€4.80)
3. **Athiri Vounoplagias 2002**
   Emery (€6)
4. **Samos Muscat Grand Cru 2001** Samos Cooperative (€6)
5. **Ta Dora Tou Dionysou 2002**
   Parparoussis (€6)
6. **Goumenissa 2000**
   Tatsis Bros (€6)
7. **Limnos Muscat Vin Doux Naturel NV**
   Limnos Cooperative (€6)
8. **Naoussa 2000** Karydas (€6.50)
9. **Malagousia Ktima Roxane 2000** Matsa (€7.50)
10. **Syrah 2001** Oenoforos (€15)

MOST EXCITING OR UNUSUAL FINDS

❶ Lagorthi 2002 Oenoforos (€9.50) *Feather-light elegance meets mineral terroir. Astonishing.*

❷ Malvasia 2001 Ktima Voyatzi (€10) *Aromatic floral nose, fat and honeyed aftertaste. A standout from all other aromatic whites on the scene.*

❸ Viognier 2001 Cuvée Eclectique Skouras (€18) *Concentrated varietal definition without the clumsy oaking of the past.*

❹ Gris de Noir 2001 Antonopoulos (€8 per 50 cl) *A cornucopia of rose-petal scents, with tropical fruit flavors in abundance. Dry.*

❺ Ktima Pavlides 2002 (€9) *Sauvignon Blanc and Assyrtiko create a wine of surprising depth from this important new venture in Drama.*

❻ Malagousia 2002 Ktima Gerovassiliou (€8) *A new star in the making from this consistently top-flight producer.*

❼ Syrah 2001 Gentilini (€17.50) *Organic grapes packed with young Syrah spice. Good now, even better after 2005.*

❽ Antaris 1999 Ktima Mercouri (€10) *East meets West in this unique Mediterranean blend of 55 percent Avgoustiatis and 45 percent Mourvèdre.*

❾ Gewurztraminer 2002 Tselepos (€9 per 50 cl) *The cool and wet 2002 vintage provided more flint-edged vibrancy than normal.*

❿ Ritinitis Nobilis 2001 Gaia Wines (€7.50) *Citrus and lavender. More popular in New York and London than in Athens.*

Lebanon

Michael Karam

Lebanon's modest stock within the wine community finally began to perform in 2003. The sector is enjoying a period of unprecedented growth, professionalism, and international interest.

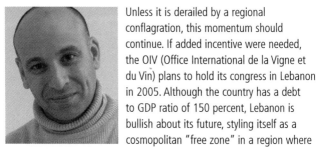

MICHAEL KARAM

Unless it is derailed by a regional conflagration, this momentum should continue. If added incentive were needed, the OIV (Office International de la Vigne et du Vin) plans to hold its congress in Lebanon in 2005. Although the country has a debt to GDP ratio of 150 percent, Lebanon is bullish about its future, styling itself as a cosmopolitan "free zone" in a region where East and West are gradually polarizing, and wine has an integral, albeit small, part to play.

The UVL (Union Vinicole Du Liban) was established as recently as 1997, and has often found it difficult to behave as an association, since the Lebanese are, by and large, a fractious and suspicious lot. However, at the LIWSF (London International Wine and Spirits Fair) in May 2003, five members—Ksara, Kefraya, Massaya, Wardy, and Clos St Thomas—presented a unified front to the wine world by gathering, for the first time, under the UVL banner. And to prove it was not a fluke, there was similar *esprit du corps* one month later at Le Vin Expo in Bordeaux.

New Lebanese wine law

Since its formation, the UVL has successfully lobbied for a new wine law, which was passed in 2000. Article 17 of the new law stipulates that a

MICHAEL KARAM has been reporting from Lebanon since 1992. He has written for *The Times* of London, *Sunday Express*, *Esquire*, and a host of regional publications, and is currently editor of *Executive*, a regional business monthly published in Beirut. Before that, he was a reporter and features editor on the *Beirut Daily Star*. He has written numerous articles on Lebanese wine.

national wine institute must be created. The UVL says this should be in operation by the end of 2003, with the help of EU funding. In collaboration with the government, the institute will be responsible for all areas of grape growing and wine production (viticulture, viniculture, legal issues, commercial concerns, quality control, and analysis), as well as the eventual foundation of a regime similar to, and inspired by, the French AOC system.

If it's Thursday, it must be the Bekaa

The UVL has created a wine route in its bid to capture a sliver of the lucrative wine-tourism market. Visitors are nothing new to Lebanese vineyards. Ksara, Lebanon's biggest producer, receives around 40,000 visitors each year, and has invested $100,000 on a *son et lumière*. However, Lebanon carries an added burden when it comes to wooing wine tourists. The number of non-Arab visitors dropped by 90 percent after the events of September 11, 2001. This situation has not been helped by a travel article in *The* (London) *Guardian*, in which the writer referred to the Bekaa as "the main stronghold of the Hizbullah terrorist group."

Today Beirut…

At $25 million or 6 million bottles, Lebanon's wine sector is virtually a cottage industry by global standards, but new wineries are opening at a rate of two per year, with a new generation of producers offering affordable, eye-catching wines. Local consumption is increasing, and it is due not only to the influence of new wines, but also to the returning diaspora, which has brought with it a modicum of Western ways.

… tomorrow the world?

Lebanese wineries exported 170,000 cases in 2002 for $6.5 million, an increase of 10 percent on 2000 in both volume and value, and double what it was six years ago. Lebanese wine enjoys a loyal customer base in France, the UK, Scandinavia, and Canada. However, many foreign wine drinkers still lack an awareness of Lebanese wine, and the country's dubious international image has not helped sell the idea of Lebanese wine to the average drinker. Even though consumption is increasing both at home and abroad, Lebanon lacks the economies of scale to compete with the New World giants, in terms of both volume and pricing. Lebanon needs at least 10 years to produce between 40 and 100 million bottles annually—planting a further 10,000 hectares (ha)—to be a genuine international player. The land is there. The Bekaa valley, once the preserve of hashish growers and the Syrian army, is ripe for a government-inspired—or private—campaign to plant vines; although many wine growers feel that expansion should only proceed if, as in France, there is demand.

EURO-MED AGREEMENT

Lebanon's signing of the Euro-Med Agreement in June 2002 will eventually make the country an open market for European wines. Fears have been expressed that the Euro-Med-inspired slashing of tariffs on imported wines (currently set at 70 percent) will be the kiss of death for Lebanese wine producers. Imported wines already have a 15 percent market share, and their consumption is increasing by 150 percent each year. These fears, however, may prove unfounded, since it is widely believed that the true value of the majority of imported wine is not declared. The evidence is already in the local supermarkets, such as Monoprix and Spinneys, where French, Italian, and New World products sell for the same price as Lebanese brands. "In effect, we are already competing with foreign wines as if they were paying no tax," said one local producer.

STANDARDS

By and large, the Lebanese wine growers are a pretty honest bunch. Basically, they have too much to lose, and any "incidents" that do occur will always be writ large, given the minute size of the sector. There have been scattered episodes of local producers pushing the ethical envelope—overharvesting, medal-sticker abuse, diluting, and misrepresentation—but these should be mopped up when the Lebanese Wine Institute finds its feet. Furthermore, the new law prohibits the import of foreign wine in bulk quantities, thwarting the ambitions of those who might be tempted to bottle their own and pass it off as Lebanese.

Grapevine

• **The legal battle** drags on between Château Kefraya and the new label Koroum de Kefraya. Michel de Bustros of Kefraya, one of Lebanon's biggest producers, contends that allowing Koroum to use the Kefraya name will cause confusion among wine buyers and could compromise a brand equity that he has worked hard to establish. Koroum's Bassim Rahal argues that Kefraya, like St-Emilion or Chianti, is a region and de Bustros has no rights to exclusivity. The first round went to Rahal, but de Bustros appealed, arguing that the Koroum grapes are not actually grown in the Kefraya area. Both sides are now engaged in out-of-court discussions in an attempt to reach a settlement. Whispers from the UVL say that Rahal may be prepared to bend on the issue of his brand name.

• **Bhamdoun** is known as a summer resort for Gulf Arabs escaping the heat, but this mountain town will soon be producing wine. Dental surgeon Dr. Fadi Gerges and Naji Boutros, a former Merrill Lynch executive, have declared their intention to put Bhamdoun on Lebanon's wine map. Gerges has invested over $1 million in his Clos de Cana winery, which has already been inspected by the UVL and had its membership approved. Having produced 120,000 bottles in 2002, Gerges expects to produce 500,000 bottles by 2004 and hopes the majority will be exported. Meanwhile, retired financier Naji Boutros has invested "a similar sum" to establish Chateau Belle-Vue, a winery he has named after his grandfather's hotel. Boutros hopes to produce 120,000 bottles by 2005, one year after his first proper harvest.

Opinion:
Boutique or bust

Any rampant growth could result in a loss of identity. Lebanon can carve out a very lucrative niche for its wine, not only by canny marketing, using all the fabulous images associated with its rich history, but also by producing wine with a distinctly Lebanese identity. Australia, Chile, and South Africa can get away with turning out correct but ultimately anonymous varietals because they have the production levels to fill the world's supermarket shelves; Lebanon does not. Low volume is not necessarily a handicap. Lebanon can compete if positioned correctly. There are very small wineries in the New World with reputations that punch way above their weight and that sell limited quantities abroad.

Generic campaign needed

New World wine producers have spent many years building up the profile of their winemaking capabilities through generic campaigns, and these brands are now reaping the rewards of exposure and consumer awareness. Lebanese winemakers have to understand the importance of PR and be prepared to work—and spend—to create the right image, if they wish to raise their profile.

Culture vultures

With a little imagination and vision, Lebanon's new wine route could be enhanced to encompass the country's cultural attractions. Wine tourists are by and large a civilized bunch, so why not give the wine route—which currently takes in only the vineyards—a modular itinerary, allowing for excursions to Lebanon's many stunning archaeological sites?

Religious dynamic

Lebanon's multisectarian makeup has meant that tensions are inevitable when it comes to winemaking and grape growing. Any long-term ambitions to exploit the Bekaa valley's wine-growing potential will have to contend with local religious sentiment, which is twitchy at the best of times. Apart from being the epicenter of Lebanon's wine industry, the Bekaa is also an Islamic stronghold, whose political representatives have to tread a fine line between maintaining religious integrity and being sensitive to the economic needs of local farmers. All the major wine growers are Christian, but many of the wineries in the Bekaa employ Muslim workers. Islamic leaders in Lebanon accept the country's multisectarian nature and will not let dogma obscure sound political judgment. A spokesman of one major group said that, in principle, the party does not approve of growing grapes for wine (or any other alcoholic drink), but it would not take action against those farmers who did so. In parliamentary votes involving alcohol, such as that on the 2000 wine law, Islamic MPs traditionally abstain, since it would be politically unwise to do otherwise. Farmers can make an almost guaranteed $0.50/kg growing wine grapes. By comparison, table grapes sell for less than $0.20/kg.

Grapevine

• **Serge Hochar,** the owner of Chateau Musar, has been nominated for the presidency of the OIV. Hochar believes he has a good chance of winning the June elections, especially given Lebanon's close ties with France and its wine industry. (Lebanon is a Francophile nation: Prime Minister Rafik Hariri is a personal friend of French President Jacques Chirac, and more Lebanese wine is exported to France than to any other country.)

• **Ksara,** Lebanon's biggest producer, has spent $350,000 lining 14 of its cement storage tanks with stainless steel. According to general manager Charles Ghostine, Ksara is the first Lebanese producer to use this relatively new process, which replaces epoxy resin.

• **One year after its launch,** Lebanon's new wine route has reportedly caught the eye of those nice people at Arblaster & Clarke. The prestigious London-based wine-tour operator is considering adding Lebanon to its itineraries; although, with regional tensions as they are, this is far from a done deal. Watch this space.

• **Massaya,** the Franco-Lebanese collaboration between the Ghosn brothers and Hubert de Boüard de Laforest (coproprietor of Château Angélus), Dominique Hébrard (former coproprietor of Château Cheval Blanc), and Daniel and Frédéric Brunier (of Domaine le Vieux Télégraphe), is now offering summer yoga retreats at the picturesque Bekaa winery. Tasting the winery's much-commended Silver and Gold selections is recommended, but optional.

Vintage Report

Advance report on the latest harvest

2002

The year was full of surprises. After four successive years of drought, there was a long, cold, rainy winter, and it lasted until June. A mild July and a hot August followed. The vines took longer than normal to ripen their grapes, and the harvest started one week late. The grapes of 2002 were characterized by having high levels of sugar, acidity, and tannin. The ripeness level varied from vineyard to vineyard, forcing wine growers to be selective in their picking. Fermentation went perfectly, but against all the odds was very slow—therefore much longer—and the wines have turned out to be much bigger, riper, and fuller than expected.

Updates on the previous five vintages

2001

Vintage rating: 85

According to Serge Hochar of Chateau Musar, 2001 was "a most bizarre year," with almost no rain and one of the earliest harvest dates in living memory. The crop was good, albeit 15 percent down, with ripe fruits but without much tannin or acidity. Fermentation progressed well, and the malolactic fermentation followed easily and naturally, as it did in 2000. The wines were easy and fruity, with good alcohol levels.

2000

Vintage rating: 85

The crop was healthy, although 15 percent down, with grapes that were sweet yet tannic, and with good acidity. Alcohol levels were higher than usual—almost the same as 1999. It was an easy harvest, and fermentation proceeded with hardly any problems. Malolactic fermentation followed its normal course. The wines were very well balanced, tannic, concentrated, and powerful.

1999

Vintage rating: *95*

An exceptional year. The grapes reached maximum maturity, with great all-around concentration, good acidity, and a high sugar level. These features were immediately apparent in the wine: very high alcohol, high acidity, and a lot of extract. The wines are highly concentrated; very rich, round, and full-bodied; with an exceptionally long finish. According to Serge Hochar, this was "really an exceptional year, perhaps the year of the millennium."

1998

Vintage rating: *80*

For no apparent reason, some grapes were quite mature, while others could have waited two more weeks. The crop was typical, both in quality and quantity; grapes were in good shape, with no problems or disease, and good to eat. Fermentation went smoothly but was quicker than usual. Results were good; 1998 was a very aromatic and fragrant year, but it lacked the body of 1997.

1997

Vintage rating: *90*

Perfect conditions allowed grapes to mature slowly but surely at a volume rarely achieved. Harvesting took place between September 15 and October 11 for the reds, and until October 21 for the whites. Harvesting was halted for four days from September 30 to October 3 due to rain. Fermentation continued at about the same pace at which the grapes had matured.

GREATEST WINE PRODUCER

1 Chateau Musar

FASTEST-IMPROVING PRODUCER

1 Ksara

NEW UP-AND-COMING PRODUCERS

1 Massaya
2 Domaine Wardy
3 Clos St Thomas

BEST-VALUE PRODUCER

1 Château Kefraya

GREATEST-QUALITY WINES

1 Chateau Musar 1988 (LL 60,000)
2 Chateau Musar 1994 (LL 24,000)
3 Chateau Musar 1991 (LL 34,000)
4 Chateau Musar 1996 (LL 22,000)
5 Chateau Musar 1995 (LL 26,000)
6 Comte de M 1998 Chateau Kefraya (LL 42,000)

BEST BARGAINS

1 Hochar Père et Fils 1999 (LL 14,000)
2 Selection 2001 Massaya (LL 14,000)
3 Reserve Du Couvent 2001 Ksara (LL 10,000)
4 Classic Rosé 2001 Massaya (LL 8,000)
5 Les Breteches 2001 Château Kefraya (LL 8,000)
6 Gris de Gris 2001 Ksara (LL 8,000)
7 Cabernet Sauvignon 2001 Domaine Wardy (LL 11,000)
8 Le Lacrima D'Oro 1995 Château Kefraya (LL 15,000)
9 Selection White 2000 Massaya (LL 13,000)
10 Chardonnay 2000 Ksara (LL 18,000)

MOST UNUSUAL AND EXCITING FINDS

1 Cuvée de Printemps 2001 Ksara (LL 8,000) *A fabulous, fruity summer red, best served chilled.*
2 Reserve 2001 Massaya (LL 20,000) *Full-bodied and pulpy, with notes of sandalwood and incense.*
3 Merlot 2000 Domaine Wardy (LL 11,000) *Great-value Merlot. Spicy, plumy, and smoky.*
4 Hochar Père et Fils 1999 (LL 14,000) Chateau Musar *The beginners' Musar. Woody and smoky, a taste of Mount Lebanon.*
5 Blanc de Blancs 2001 Château Kefraya (LL 12,000) *A blend of Chardonnay, Sauvignon Blanc, and Viognier. Lebanon's most popular white.*

Israel

Daniel Rogov

High-quality Israeli wines continue to make their appearance on the local and international markets.

DANIEL ROGOV

Unfortunately, in the last year, the greatest influences on both the wine industry and consumers have been the impact of the ongoing *Intifada* (the uprising of the Palestinians), the increasingly depressing economic situation that has resulted from it, and the fear of an impending outbreak of wider hostilities in the region. What this has meant is that, although wine consumption has held steady at about 7–8 liters per person annually, the present psychological and economic mood drives many consumers to seek out less expensive wines, often those imported from Europe, Australia, and South America.

During the preceding five-year period of growth and prosperity, wineries invested heavily in new equipment and in the planting of new vineyards, some with Sangiovese, Pinot Noir, and Syrah, which are exciting new varieties for the region. During this period, public awareness of wine increased dramatically. Today, however, with growing difficulty in selling their wines and a sudden glut of grapes from the new plantings, several major wineries are showing clear signs of economic distress.

Three satellites launched

Golan Heights Winery, Carmel Mizrachi, and Barkan Wineries are the three largest wineries in Israel, controlling nearly 80 percent of wine production and sales. All three companies have opened brand-new satellite wineries,

DANIEL ROGOV is the wine and restaurant critic for the Israeli daily newspaper *Haaretz* and the Israeli edition of the *International Herald Tribune*. He is a regular contributor to *Hugh Johnson's Pocket Wine Book* (Mitchell Beazley) and publishes wine and gastronomic reviews and articles on his Internet site, Rogov's Ramblings (www.stratsplace.com/rogov/home.html).

which, over the last 12 months, released their first products. Golan Heights Winery, with its facilities and many of its vineyards actually on the Golan Heights itself, has its Galil Mountain winery at Kibbutz Yiron, in the upper hills of northern Galilee. Carmel Mizrachi has Ramat Arad, a boutique winery and vineyards in the hills of the Negev Desert; while Barkan Wineries has opened Hulda Winery on the central plain of the country.

Mid-sized winery debuts

A new endeavor called Chateau Golan recently launched its first wines, which included a Cabernet Sauvignon, Merlot, and Cabernet–Merlot blend. First releases included over 100,000 bottles, and the winery has announced that it will triple production in the near future. The quality of the new wines is good, but the winery is encountering resistance on the local market because of what many perceive as very high prices.

Boutique banality

Although a handful of boutique wineries and *garagistes* are producing excellent and exciting wines, mini-wineries continue to multiply at a somewhat ridiculous pace. There are now over 90 in the country, 14 of which released their first wines in the past year. Many of those wineries are nothing more than the efforts of winemaking hobbyists who have decided that their wines are good enough to put on the market. Unfortunately, the quality of most so-called boutique wines being released is of no interest to even the least sophisticated consumers.

Grapevine

• **The second all-Israeli wine exposition** was held in Tel Aviv-Jaffa in March 2003, under the sponsorship of local food and wine magazine *Al ha Shulchan* (On the Table), and was even more successful than the first event. Nearly 12,000 visitors attended, even though it was held on the eve of the war in Iraq.

• **The first Viognier wine** made from grapes grown in the Shomron region is scheduled to be released by Binyamina Wineries. Barrel tastings reveal that the wine has definite potential; but when bottled, the wines are disappointing. However, the first Sangiovese from the Golan Heights Winery was such an immediate success that it sold out within days of its release.

• **Factions in the wine industry** are lobbying the Israeli parliament to reinstate draconic import duties in order to limit imports and thus protect Israeli wines.

• **Recent years** have seen a dramatic increase in the number of small importers. Because many of these mini-importers lack appropriate distribution systems, and because many of their wines are expensive, some are now trying to dump their stock on larger importer–distributors. Since 2002 was a difficult economic year, and predictions are that 2003 and 2004 will be even more trying, many of these small companies will probably be folding up their tents.

ZIV DRIVE

Carmel Mizrachi, the largest producer of wines in the country, recently appointed David Ziv as its new CEO. In the few months since he took the helm, Ziv has already undertaken a major reorganization of the winery's management. This included hiring the services of California-based consultant Peter Stern, formerly of the Golan Heights Winery, a move that was barred by the courts (see below). What Ziv needs to accomplish is to gain better control over the structure of what is now a bulky cooperative constituted of independent growers affiliated with the winery. He has to ensure reduced yields in the field and carry out his plan to shift the winery's interests from poor clones of Petite Sirah, Carignan, French Colombard, and Emerald Riesling to more ascendant varieties.

A CHANGE IS AS GOOD AS A REST!

After serving as the senior consultant to the Golan Heights Winery since its inception in 1983, California-based winemaker Peter Stern shifted sides at the end of 2001 and started consulting for Carmel Mizrachi. The Golan Heights demanded that Stern take a "cooling-off" period of several years, and in August 2002 convinced the Israeli court to issue an injunction forbidding Stern to give his consulting services to Carmel. This was contested by Stern, but the injunction was upheld by the Israeli Supreme Court in March 2003, barring Stern from Carmel Mizrachi until January 2004.

KOSHER BOUTIQUES

Reflecting their need to increase exports, several smaller wineries are now in the process of shifting from non-kosher to kosher production in the hope that this will woo a captive audience, especially in the United States. Included in this list are Castel and Tzora. This move should not have an impact on quality. Although there is a problem with *mevushal* wines (wines that used to be "cooked" but are now mostly flash-pasteurized at 185°F/85°C), there is no contradiction between the rules of *kashrut* (rules for keeping kosher) and those for producing fine wines. None of the wineries making the shift is planning on producing a *mevushal* wine.

SAFRA ON HOLD

Several years ago, one of Israel's wealthiest clans, the Safra family, invested large sums in the planting of vineyards; and speculation at that time had it that they planned to build a winery capable of producing up to 5 million bottles annually. The grapes from these vineyards are now sold to other wineries, and it is believed that the current grape glut (for which Safra is partly responsible) has led the family to lose interest in the wine industry and put their plans on hold.

Opinion:
Proper regulatory controls required

Since the country has no proper regulatory body and no valid appellation-control system, labeling and bottling procedures at some wineries are done in an unprofessional, even haphazard, manner. Wines continue to be bottled in batches—sometimes over a period of several months, sometimes over a period of a year or more—and there is no guarantee that even the same blend was used from batch to batch. In some cases, it is difficult to tell precisely what is in the bottle at all. A bottle labeled as Cabernet Sauvignon may at times have aromas and flavors that are remarkably similar to wines containing large amounts of Carignan or Argaman grapes.

New Israeli wine institute needed

Good Israeli wines are already noted for their quality, but what is missing is a central body that will ensure orderly growth and increased sales, both locally and abroad. Perhaps the most important step would be to replace the obsolete and ineffective Wine Institute with a new institute that could function via full-fledged wine laws. The new institute should act both as a proper regulatory body (with control over defining a proper appellation system as well as regulating bottling and labeling) and as an industry representative. Such a body should be structured so that it allows for the dissemination and promotion of Israeli wines, both locally and abroad. It should also have a public-relations function, publishing and distributing educational, promotional, and statistical materials; marketing and promoting Israeli wines abroad; and having a major presence at wine fairs and seminars. The new institute should conduct serious research on determining which grapes are best suited to different subregions within the country. No less important, such an institute should encourage an atmosphere of cooperation rather than distrust among local wineries.

The need for new varieties

Israeli wineries invested a lot of money in the 1980s, planting vineyards with Argaman, a locally produced Souzao–Carignan cross. That experiment was largely a fiasco, producing wines that lacked depth, tannins, flavor, or other charms. The time has come to uproot those vineyards and replace them with other grapes. However, these new plantations should go beyond the often-overplanted Cabernet Sauvignon, Merlot, Chardonnay, and Sauvignon Blanc, looking instead at varieties such as Viognier, Sangiovese, Nebbiolo, Pinot Noir, Syrah, and Canaiolo, all of which showed promise in experimental plantings.

Vintage Report

Advance report on the latest harvest

2002

In northern Galilee and on the Golan Heights, it was a good but not exciting year, with very warm weather in February and March, followed by a particularly cold spell in April and May, which stretched out the ripening season. This caused the harvest to be an extended, 15-week process, while rains during blooming had reduced yields by 15 percent. In the rest of the country, several prolonged hot spells scattered throughout the year caused sporadic but enormous damage, with some vineyards losing as much as 80 percent of their crop. Overall, 2002 will prove challenging to winemakers. Expect quite a few acceptable wines, but not many that will be appropriate for long-term cellaring.

Updates on the previous five vintages

2001

Vintage rating: 85

This was one of the earliest harvest years in recent history. Overall, it was a better year for reds than whites.

2000

Vintage rating: 89

Fortunately, the harvest was on schedule; torrential rains hit the area just after the picking. Had the crop been delayed, it would have been under the coldest and wettest conditions for the past quarter of a century. Whites and reds fared equally well during this good vintage.

1999

Vintage rating: *86*

An early bud break allowed the harvest to begin three weeks early, but cooler temperatures in mid-August, followed by a cold spell in September and October, prolonged the picking, which ended as late as mid-November. Good, long-lived reds and some excellent whites, especially from higher-altitude vineyards.

1998

Vintage rating: *85*

Hot weather continued until early October, when a cold snap hit, extending the harvest well into November. A better year for reds than for whites.

1997

Vintage rating: *90*

Most of the crop ripened two weeks late but, more to the point, harvest was very much at the same time among the different varieties, causing what one winemaker called "a hectic, compressed vintage." Despite the problems, the year produced quite a few excellent, long-lived reds, and was overall a very good year for whites.

Grapevine

• **Rumor has it** that the nation's largest producer of wine and spirits, Carmel Mizrachi, may be taken over by the Carlsberg–Coca-Cola conglomerate. Many speculate that such a buyout will have a positive effect, altering Carmel from an outmoded cooperative structure into a modern business, thus improving wine quality.

• **On a more positive note,** there is a good chance that Israeli kosher wines will increase their exports. At least one American firm, the Royal Wine Corporation, is making major moves to assist Israeli wineries in selling and distributing their wines in the United States.

GREATEST WINE PRODUCERS

1. Golan Heights Winery (Yarden, Gamla, Golan)
2. Castel
3. Margalit
4. Amphorae
5. Flam
6. Dalton
7. Soreq
8. Galil Mountain
9. Tzora
10. Recanati

BEST-VALUE PRODUCERS

1. Golan Heights Winery (Gamla, Golan)
2. Dalton
3. Galil Mountain
4. Flam
5. Amphorae
6. Recanati
7. Tishbi
8. Orna Chillag
9. Barkan
10. Tzora

FASTEST-IMPROVING PRODUCERS

1. Tishbi
2. Saslove Winery
3. Tabor
4. Sde Boker
5. Zauberman
6. Barkan
7. Mayshar
8. Sea Horse Winery
9. Gush Etzion
10. Deux Paysans

NEW UP-AND-COMING PRODUCERS

1. Alexander
2. Gustavo & Jo
3. Galil Mountain
4. Ramat Arad
5. Bazelet ha Golan
6. Orna Chillag
7. Zauberman
8. BenHaim
9. Chateau Golan
10. Bustan

GREATEST-QUALITY WINES

1. **Cabernet Sauvignon Reserve 2000** Flam (NIS 130)
2. **Merlot 1999** Bustan (NIS 145)
3. **Grand Vin Castel 1999** Castel (NIS 160)
4. **Merlot Reserve 2000** Flam (NIS 130)
5. **Cabernet Sauvignon Special Reserve 2000** Margalit (NIS 165)
6. **Cabernet Sauvignon, Alexander the Great 1999** Alexander (NIS 180)
7. **Cabernet Sauvignon 2000** Amphorae (NIS 130)
8. **Merlot 2000** Amphorae (NIS 110)
9. **"C" Blanc du Castel 2000** Castel (NIS 130)
10. **Yarden Cabernet Sauvignon 1999** Golan Heights Winery (NIS 95)

BEST BARGAINS

1. **Classico 2001** Flam (NIS 65)
2. **Rhyton 2000** Amphorae (NIS 100)
3. **Chardonnay Reserve 2001** Recanati (NIS 65)
4. **Pinot Noir 2001** Galil Mountain (NIS 55)

❺ **Cabernet Sauvignon Estate 2001** Tabor (NIS 67)

❻ **Moscato 2002** Golan Heights Winery (NIS 30)

❼ **Yarden Johannisberg Riesling 2001** Golan Heights Winery (NIS 48)

❽ **Merlot 2001** Galil Mountain (NIS 40)

❾ **Golan Chardonnay 2001** Golan Heights Winery (NIS 32)

❿ **Golan Cabernet Sauvignon 2001** Golan Heights Winery (NIS 42)

MOST EXCITING OR UNUSUAL FINDS

❶ **Cabernet Sauvignon Reserve 2000** Flam (NIS 130)
Well focused, well balanced, and with enviable structure, this deep-purple wine with medium to full body contains 10 percent Merlot. A wine so deep you feel you can get lost in it.

❷ **Merlot 2000** Margalit (NIS 125)
An unusual wine for Margalit, which is more famed for Cabernet than Merlot. Remarkably tannic for a Merlot, this full-bodied wine is rich and concentrated.

❸ **Cabernet Sauvignon Reserve 1999** Saslove Winery (NIS 125)
The best-ever release from this small winery. Dark, deep, and elegant, this is a very well-crafted, full-bodied wine.

❹ **HeightsWine 2001** Golan Heights Winery (NIS 90) *This honeyed Gewurztraminer dessert wine offers up an exquisite array of fruits. The name is a play on words of the English term icewine and its German equivalent, eiswein.*

❺ **Sauvignon Blanc Reserve 2001** Dalton (NIS 35) *This smooth, elegant, unoaked Sauvignon Blanc is perhaps the very best Sauvignon Blanc in Israel.*

❻ **Gamla Chardonnay 2000** Golan Heights Winery (NIS 45) *Medium- to full-bodied and with an exceptional array of aromas and flavors.*

❼ **Elul 2000** Sea Horse Winery (NIS 85) *From a very young boutique winery, this medium- to full-bodied blend of 70 percent Cabernet Sauvignon and 30 percent Syrah shows excellent balance between tannins, fruits, and wood.*

❽ **Yiron 2000** Galil Mountain (NIS 82) *This medium- to full-bodied blend of 60 percent Cabernet Sauvignon and 40 percent Merlot has smooth, well-integrated tannins and generous overtones of the small oak barrels in which it developed for 16 months.*

❾ **Cabernet Sauvignon Special Reserve 1999** Kerem Sde Boker Tishbi (NIS 145)
This is not so much earthy and herbal as distinctly marked by green olive and spice flavors, reflecting perhaps its origin in the heart of the Negev Desert.

❿ **Gamla Sangiovese 1999** Golan Heights Winery (NIS 60) *The first Sangiovese released in Israel, this wine contains 15 percent Cabernet Sauvignon, both varieties having been harvested in the northern part of the Golan Heights.*

South Africa

John Platter

Being the world's largest producer of Chenin Blanc was not, in the past, something that South Africans advertised much.

JOHN PLATTER

As recently as five years ago, farmers were lucky to earn R450 ($60) a ton for Chenin grapes, a small fraction of what growers could expect for Chardonnay. Chenin was common; it lacked class and was known locally as Steen. When Cape Wine Master Irina von Holdt, first chair of the Chenin Blanc Producers' Association, first punted Chenin as the white-wine face of the new South Africa, the consensus was that she might have been better advised to pour her energies into a less quixotic cause. However, by 2003, those farmers who had kept faith in their old vines were asking—and getting—R3,000 ($380) a ton, more than a six-fold increase. The grape's reputation has been reinvented. Chenin is one of South Africa's latest stars and now offers an opportunity to stake a national varietal claim. Styles are still varied, but wild yeast, barrel fermentation, and low cropping from old bush vines are making for serious, longer-lived wines that offer a counterpoint to the yards of Chardonnay and Sauvignon Blanc on wine lists. An oaked, natural yeast-fermented FMC 2001 Chenin has been priced by UK supermarket chain Waitrose at a previously unheard-of £15 ($25) a bottle. The Cape's top-echelon Chardonnays do not go much higher—and perhaps should not.

JOHN PLATTER A former foreign correspondent, John Platter grew and made wine in the Cape for 20 years before semi-retirement in 1997. In the early years, John and his wife Erica founded South Africa's bestselling wine guide, *John Platter's South African Wines*, which has been published every year since 1979. Most recently their visits to wine-producing countries all over the continent have been chronicled in their offbeat, award-winning travel-cum-wine book *Africa Uncorked* (Kyle Cathie, 2002).

There is now hardly a top producer who is not trying very hard with this grape, and the local *WINE* magazine's 2003 Chenin Blanc Challenge is now in its eighth year, drawing 93 entries, with a trip to the Loire for the winner.

South African *terroir*ists

As from the 2004 vintage, Cape growers will be permitted to name single-vineyard wines on their labels, a prestigious marketing tool long available to serious growers of top-end wines around the world but, hitherto, incredibly, prohibited here because it supposedly conflicted with the existing estate-wine regulations. Suddenly the obstacles have been cleared. Why not 10 years ago, growers ask, when the New World competition in California, Australia, and elsewhere was showing the way? Growers can now register designated vineyards prior to cropping—and there could even be some retroactive dispensation for 2003 wines. A new Distinctive Wine of Origin (DWO) label for "terrain-specific" wines should also begin appearing at the same time. Each of South Africa's 52 demarcated regions, districts, and wards can now recommend their own terrain-specific wine criteria, drawn up by growers and officials from the area.

Grapevine

• **Having built a vast new cellar** to meet the demand for his instant hit brands, Goats Do Roam, Goats Roti, and Goats d'Afrique, Fairview's Charles Back was wondering what to do about the cheeses (goat's and other) that he makes just across the road. They have been bursting out of their tasting premises. One idea led to another and architects, "not accountants," were summoned. In no time at all, a vast Fairview food–wine emporium was off the drawing board and under construction. Opening is scheduled for December 2003.

• **Giving a new twist** to the concept of a concrete jungle is a proposal by Warwick's Michael Ratcliffe, the radical, risk-taking, new Cape wine generation personified. He wants to plant vines and build a winery under an overpass in downtown Cape Town! The precise location is at the foot of the city's central Adderley Street, next to the new convention center. "We've done the soil and climate tests," Ratcliffe said, "and the vines would be fine."

• **Jabulani Ntshangase** of Thabani Wines is negotiating an historic deal with the Algerian wine industry, through the offices of Office Nationale de Commercialisation des Produits Viti-vinicole (ONCV), to produce an "all-African blend"—in a winery to be built halfway between Johannesburg and Durban.

• **South Africa's** most successful new mining mogul—ANC aristocrat, Robben Island ex-prisoner, and fellow Mandela inmate Tokyo Sexwale—has bought a wine farm in Franschhoek.

• **California's Silver Oak winery** and R&V are joining forces to make a Shiraz (in Stellenbosch) named Cirrus.

• **Alain Moueix of Pomerol,** cousin of the Pétrus proprietors, has just begun releasing his first wines from a 25-hectare (ha) property near False Bay in Somerset West, using evocative Xhosa names for his labels: Ingwe (meaning "leopard") and Amehlo ("eye").

AUSSIE–CAPE TIE-UP

It has been explored for years with various Aussie big movers, including the now-ailing Southcorp. But the announcement late in 2002 of, potentially, the country's biggest foreign joint wine venture has set local Jeremiahs wondering. With Australia's BRL Hardy and Stellenbosch Vineyards linking up, the question being asked is whether there will be enough Cape wine available at the right price and of the right quality to satisfy the new beast. BRL Hardy-SV is due to launch its Shamwari ("friendship" in Shona) brand in late 2003, having registered the name internationally. They will kick off with three wines, mainly in Europe: a Robertson Chardonnay and two Stellenbosch reds, a Cab-Merlot and a Shiraz, targeted at the €6.50 to €7.00 price points.

CAPE BLEND – A THORNY ISSUE

The Rhône and Bordeaux have their classic, region-specific blends. Shiraz and Cabernet have become partners as Australian as Bruce and Sheila. And Chianti has Chianti, of course. So what's a Cape blend? This was the category set in 1999 for the award every local winemaker wants to win— the Diners Club Winemaker of the Year. But the controversy that erupted when Hazendal Estate's Ronel Wiid triumphed with a Cabernet-Shiraz blend showed that the question had not been answered satisfactorily for at least one party—the Pinotage Producers' Association (PPA), a missionary society for South Africa's homemade grape (a 1925 crossing of

Pinot Noir and Cinsault). And it begged another: if a generally accepted Cape blend did not exist, should it not be invented? The PPA appointed a working group to investigate. Unsurprisingly, its report recommends that Pinotage—no less than 30 percent and no more than 70 percent – ought to be the nonnegotiable ingredient required to qualify a wine for "Cape Blend" status. (If it is not this actual label, the group advocated finding another name, à la California's Meritage.) Its preferred local partners should be Merlot and/or Cabernet Sauvignon/Franc. Among the other recommendations are a mandatory alcohol content of 12.5–14.5 percent, a minimum of nine months maturation in barrels (of which 25 percent should be new), and the use of a "unique" bottle based on the claret shape. However, producers like Jean Engelbrecht of Rust en Vrede (R&V), whose eponymous blend of Cabernet, Shiraz, and Merlot was the first SA red to make *Wine Spectator*'s Top 100 wines of the year, believes it would be "missing the ball altogether" to make Pinotage compulsory in a Cape blend.

SAUVIGNON FLYING THE FLAG

There are no blending or identity hangups to confuse the issue of the Cape's best Sauvignon Blancs. In the past year, the streams of visiting wine palates have become positively declamatory in judging Sauvignon as the country's top-performing variety. "The equal of anything from Sancerre, New Zealand, or California," wrote Matt Kramer in *Wine Spectator*. No other grape gets similar accolades. The Cape's finest Sauvignons come from a relatively small band of growers, many of them clustered around the coastlines: Steenberg, Vergelegen, Mulderbosch, Cape Point, Klein Constantia, Thelema, Neil Ellis, Jordan, and Bouchard Finlayson.

CALL IN THE CONSULTANTS

From an attitude of famous antipathy to home truths (from rotten politics to virused vineyards), the Cape winelands have done a huge U-turn in the past decade—no more paralyzing insularity, much more globalization. Help is being sought from Californian Phil Freese; New Zealanders Rod Easthope, Emma Williams, and Clive Hartnell; Italian Alberto Antonini; Germans Stefan Dorst, Bernd Philippi, and Bernhard Breuer; and Frenchmen Paul Pontallier, Michel Rolland, Alain Moueix, Paul Chatonnet, and Pierre Lurton. And those not prepared to go quite this far are calling in local specialists. There is now scarcely a cellar that does not employ a viticulturist, in-house or outsourced, like Aidan Morton, who was formerly full time at Thelema, but now freelances all over the place.

RELAUNCHING BACKSBERG

Rod Easthope, consulting in the Cape since 1996, has pruned his portfolio to take on the challenge of revitalizing the 300-ha, 1,000-ton Backsberg Estate at Paarl. This was once an industry innovator, producing the Cape's first barrel-fermented commercial Chardonnay in 1986, but the range has long since become "a bit flat," according to Easthope. Seen as a good-value icon, Backsberg's virtual relaunch is aimed at reclaiming a leadership role and notching up its price and quality profile.

HAVING A GO

Of the 50-some wineries that have opened their doors over the past year, the majority represent the old, rather than the completely new. Many farmers who have been long-time suppliers of grapes to co-ops or merchants are now keeping back a portion of their crop and venturing into the DIY market—with conspicuous success, too. A stunning example is Ridgeback, behind Paarl mountain. All the grapes previously went to Windmeul Coop, but the homemade Ridgeback 2001 Shiraz was instantly rated five stars by SA *Wine Guide* judges.

GIVE THE GREEN LIGHT

High international demand for organic wines has seen new green growth in the Cape. A striking example: the Du Preez family's Bon Cap winery, handling the fruit of the first internationally certified organic vineyards in the Robertson region, had to be built four times bigger than they planned, such was the clamor for wines long before a single grape had been picked. Hidden Valley and Upland (which even produces an organic brandy) are among other leading greens. A rich and extensive new source in the future will be up the Cape West coast, around Vredendal, where the climate is tailor-made for organic wine-growing.

NO DIVORCE

The Cape winelands were agog for much of 2002 over rumors about a major rift between Kanonkop's popular and famously forthright winemaker of 22 years, Beyers Truter, and the estate's owners, brothers Johann and Paul Krige. Truter recently moved off the estate to Beyerskloof, a smaller property in which he and the Kriges were partners. They say it is not really a rift or split, but Truter and Simon Halliday, the British-based merchant handling Beyerskloof and Kanonkop wines, have teamed up 50/50 to buy out the Kriges from Beyerskloof.

THE NEW INDUSTRY REGULATOR

For what was publicly touted as a "quantum leap," the launch in 2002 of the South African Wine and Brandy Company (SAWB) was a bit of a dud. SAWB encompasses the Cape's 4,500 registered growers, all the wine-industry unions and farm-labor committees, and every one of the industry's wholesalers under "one, overarching umbrella." This organization takes on many of the KWV's former functions, but attempts to broaden participation and, thereby, avoid much of the criticism that was levelled at the once all-powerful KWV. The KWV was a quasi-government body that ran the production end of the Cape wine industry for most of the 20th century, but it was the subject of a controversial privatization in 1997 after being stripped of these powers. Unlike the KWV, the SAWB will not actually be selling anything, its function being more akin to

Australia's similarly named Australian Wine & Brandy Corporation (AWBC); but in this capacity it does, of course, include the KWV. The SA wine industry's movers and shakers have made Australia their role model in more ways than one. Vision 20/20, an attempt to chart a cohesive industry strategy for the future, is a sort of me-too version of Australia's earlier Vision 2005, and one outcome of Vision 20/20 was, in fact, SAWB itself. Like AWBC, it too aims to coordinate generic marketing, technical research, human-resource development, and marketing intelligence. The only difference is that, being South Africa, the SAWBC is committed to "social and economic empowerment" on an industry-wide scale.

MOONLIGHTERS

More and more winemakers are branching out with their own labels— and with their employers' blessings. What previously was often regarded as disloyal and even grounds for dismissal—setting up alongside or even in open competition with the mother ship—is now an accepted occupational perk. Among the notable moonlighters are Chris Joubert, winemaker at Overgaauw, with his own-label Gilga Syrah, another five-star winner; Bruwer Raats, ex-Delaire, now consulting for Zorgvliet and Agusta with his own Raats Family Chenins; Teddy Hall of Kanu with his award-winning Rudera range (starring the Robusto Chenin); Niels Verburg of Beaumont with his Luddite label, showcasing Shiraz, a variety that also looms large in Nico van der Merwe's sideline-to-Saxenburg range.

THE POWER OF ONE

Cape winemakers have traditionally favored the safety-in-numbers approach, but more exceptions to the rule have surfaced recently. De Toren (new and small) offers just the one Fusion V blend from 1999 (Bordeaux-style blend), and Tony Mossop's Axe Hill (smaller) produces just the one Cape vintage Port style. Now one of the much-bigger boys is planning to go this route. Rust en Vrede's seven-year plan is to phase out its varietal wines to focus solely on R&V, the Cabernet-Shiraz-Merlot blend that has become the estate's signature wine.

THE *GARAGISTES*

The idea that lavish wineries are compulsory for impressive wines was consigned to the shredder long ago. Eben Sadie, a former winemaker at the overnight success story called Spice Route (now part of Charles Back's portfolio) is receiving much acclaim for his Columella, a Shiraz with a dab of Mourvèdre that he makes in a friend's garden "shack." Etienne le Riche moved from the comfort zone of Rustenberg into a disused tractor shed in the Jonkershoek Valley, Stellenbosch, and instantly turned out a fine Cabernet. Jean Daneel continues, from his boutique cellar in Franschhoek, to win the sort of awards he always used to when at Buitenverwachting and Morgenhof. Tom Lubbe (also ex-Spice Route) is making his Shiraz, The Observatory, in a small corner of an old railroad station in Cape Town. Tanja Beutler, the marketing dynamo for Hartenberg and a clutch of other Cape wine estates, makes Topaz wines in her backyard and garage, with partner (and Cape Wine Master) Clive Torr. Beutler is the driving force of a new Cape association of these and other *garagistes*.

SMART MONEY

Foreign investment continues to roll in, changing the Cape's traditional face:
• Scottish golf-resort owner Michael Johnston swallowed his neighbors in Devon Valley, Stellenbosch, recently, to expand Louisvale, his 26-ha spread.
• The owners of Cos d'Estournel sniffed about seriously in the Banhoek Valley (neighborhood of Thelema and Tokara) in the mountains behind Stellenbosch, before leaving the acquisition of Zorgvliet Farm to former President Steyn gold-mine proprietor Mac van der Merwe. He has presented it to his 20-something daughter and her husband De la Rey Blignaut, who helicopters in and out to huddle with consultant winemaker Bruwer Raats.
• Swiss artist and scion of a German aeronautical company, Christophe Dornier snapped up three farms in the so-called Golden Triangle (the slopes of the Helderberg closest to Stellenbosch) and built "not a cellar, but a contemporary work of the 21st century."
• A surgeon from Connecticut has bought Lievland Estate in Stellenbosch, across the road from Warwick.
• A bunch of boy wonders from London are aiming to make their Tulbagh Mountain label world-famous.
• California wine couple Phil Freese and Zelma Long make their Cape labels (Merlot, Cabernets Franc and Sauvignon, and Malbec) at Tokara, from fruit off a 30-ha spread at Paarl.

Opinion:
Black empowerment economically vital

The South African winelands remain very white indeed. Less than a score of the 4,500 registered wine farms and vineyards are black-owned or can boast any serious black equity. Wine "activist" Jabulani Ntshangase maintains that until black South Africans have a stake in vineyards and the wine market, they will not embrace wine. Domestic consumption declines relentlessly—by about 1.5 percent in 2002. South Africa ranks 33rd in world consumption tables, yet it is the world's eighth-largest producer. Bruce Jack of Flagstone Winery & Vineyards, among the most thoughtful of the young generation of South African wine producers, says: "The most important future trend in our industry will be black empowerment. It has to be. This is the last white, male, Afrikaans industry left in an environment where it is at best irritating, at worst an anathema, to the government. It is a very high-profile industry. It makes good money. It is growing. The reason the majority of players have not actively supported real black empowerment is not easy to determine. It's simplistic and inaccurate to assume the majority don't care about blacks. There's a dangerous, illogical, emotionally motivated obsession with land ownership. As anyone who has tried to make a living off the land knows, it can be financially crippling. Black empowerment needs to take place in the brand ownership, distribution, and retail levels if this industry is to thrive." Thabani Wines, owned by Jabulani Ntshangase, is the first (and "the only real," goes the claim) black-empowerment company in the wine industry. It started in 2002 with some notable orders from the US (Wal-Mart) and the UK (Waitrose), but it is the South African black market that could see Thabani really soar, says Ntshangase.

First black oenology graduate

However, it is when the graduation of someone like Mzokhona Mvemve becomes an unremarkable event that the post-apartheid transformation will be complete. In 2002, he became the first black African oenology graduate from Stellenbosch University—the only SA university offering oenology and viticulture degrees—sponsored by *négociant* wholesaler Cape Classics, where he is now a winemaker, making his first solo wines under the Indaba label. When asked how he would cope with all the inevitable publicity, Mvemve replied, "I'm not going to think about that too much." That is precisely the frame of mind the South African wine industry must strive for.

Vintage Report

Advance report on the latest harvest

2003

At 1.14 million tons, 2003 was well above the average of the past decade, which is welcome news for producers running low on stocks after two exceptional export years. Quality across the board was very good to outstanding. Generally a ripe, disease-free, dry, hot year with clean fruit— a typical Cape vintage. But many top growers reported unusually small berry size and thick, flavor-filled skins. There were some outstanding Cabernets and Sauvignon Blancs, with beautifully layered flavor profiles. A three-week hot spell from late February made for a rush of varieties ripening simultaneously. Those growers unable to handle big daily intakes ended up with flatter, high-alcohol wines of around 14.5 percent and more.

Updates on the previous five vintages

2002

Vintage rating: 86 (Red: 82, White: 89)

Patchy quality, with more moderate alcohols a plus point. As usual, however, the top estates seemed to produce fine top-end labels.

2001

Vintage rating: 86 (Red: 85, White: 87)

A lower-than-average crop, and a generally trouble-free, hot, and dry vintage. High alcohols and concentrated reds (the best sufficiently fruity to handle big tannins and alcohol). Should be a reasonably long-lived vintage.

2000

Vintage rating: 83 (Red: 80, White: 85)

Difficult and variable weather-wise, with generally softer acids. An uneven, spottier vintage, but reduced yield provided compensations in flavor intensity, where producers managed to gather before overripeness began flattening fruit profiles.

1999

Vintage rating: *79 (Red: 75, White: 83)*

This very warm year produced a large crop of big, juicy, accessible reds. Most were not for long cellaring, although many retained quite strident tannins. Typically a year when whites showed less excitement.

1998

Vintage rating: *79 (Red: 78, White: 79)*

A sustained, hot summer produced a smallish crop of full, dark, muscular reds. Whites could have done with finer, more complex flavors.

Grapevine

• **Not satisfied** with merely consulting for the local Rupert and Rothschild operation in Franschhoek, Michel Rolland has taken a stake in Hakuna Matata (Swahili for "no worries") in partnership with the Stellenbosch owners of Remhoogte, Murray and Juliette Boustred.

• **Rumor has it** that high-rollers GT Ferreira (Tokara, First National Bank), Michael Johnston (Louisvale, Carnoustie Golf Resort), and Dave King (Quoin Rock, multientrepreneur) are discussing a "bigger than big" winelands development.

• **David Finlayson of Glen Carlou** near Paarl—in which Donald Hess of California's Hess Collection has an interest—has bought vineyards opposite Morgenhof in Stellenbosch.

• **Bruce Jack's Flagstone Winery** has decamped from the Cape Town Waterfront to an old dynamite factory alongside the N2, near Somerset West.

• **The cool upland area** of Elgin is attracting some cool new customers. Ross Gower of Klein Constantia and Gyles Webb of Thelema are two recent big-name buyers joining the established Paul Cluver and Thandi in this once predominantly apple-orchard district.

• **Fashionable invaders** are also sweeping up the Hemel en Aarde Valley behind Hermanus: they include GT Ferreira of Tokara and—again— Gyles Webb.

• **Checking his ripening 2003** crop in Stellenbosch one morning, Victor Sperling discovered that thieves had beaten him to his prized Cabernet grapes in Delheim Wines' flagship Vera Cruz vineyard. "Two tons, through a big hole cut in the fence, overnight. They knew exactly what they were doing," he said. "This was well coordinated—they selected a hidden corner."

• **Montagu and Robertson** were declared national disaster areas after floods began on March 23, 2003, washing away vines, topsoil, and wine stocks. Van Loveren's cellar was flooded, causing R9 million of damage; Zandvliet lost vines and topsoil on 4 ha of vineyards; and Paul Hoffman of Bloupont in Montagu reported, "Not one fence is standing. We've lost all of our main pipelines for vineyard irrigation, which we installed only six months ago. And all our topsoil is gone, which is irreplaceable."

GREATEST WINE PRODUCERS

1. Vergelegen
2. Thelema
3. Rustenberg
4. Charles Back (Spice Route, Fairview)
5. Boekenhoutskloof
6. De Trafford
7. Jordan
8. Kanonkop
9. Rust en Vrede
10. L'Avenir

FASTEST-IMPROVING PRODUCERS

1. Graham Beck
2. Ken Forrester
3. Newton Johnson
4. Spier
5. Flagstone
6. Cederberg
7. Muratie
8. Kloovenburg
9. Vergenoegd
10. Du Preez Estate

NEW UP-AND-COMING PRODUCERS

1. Tokara
2. Kanu
3. Mont du Toit
4. Quoin Rock
5. Morgenster
6. Stark-Conde
7. Waterford
8. Durbanville Hills
9. Havana Hills
10. Diemersfontein Waterford

BEST-VALUE PRODUCERS

1. Villiera
2. Kaapzicht
3. Stellenbosch Vineyards (Genesis, Kumkani, and Welmoed ranges)
4. Eikendal
5. Neil Ellis Wines
6. Boland
7. Cape Bay
8. Darling Cellars
9. Avondale
10. Woolworths

GREATEST-QUALITY WINES

1. **Stellenbosch 1999** Vergelegen (R150)
2. **Sauvignon Blanc Reserve 2002** Vergelegen (R100)
3. **Vin de Constance 1997** Klein Constantia (R200)
4. **Merlot Reserve 1999** Thelema (R200)
5. **Rustenberg 1999** Peter Barlow (R175)
6. **Fusion V 2000** De Toren (R135)
7. **Estate Wine 1998** Rust en Vrede (R200)
8. **Solitude 2001** Fairview (R160)
9. **Cabernet 2000** Boekenhoutskloof (R120)
10. **Semillon 2002** Steenberg (R60)

BEST BARGAINS

1. **Homtini Shiraz 2000** Anthony de Jager (R75)
2. **Old Vines Red 2001** Brampton (R44)
3. **Merlot 2001** Jordan (R70)
4. **Cape Vintage Reserve 1998** JP Bredell (R90)
5. **Chenin Blanc 2002** Kanu (R30)
6. **Cathedral Cellar 1999 Merlot** KWV (R64)
7. **Chenin Blanc 2002** L'Avenir (R40)
8. **Groenekloof Sauvignon Blanc 2002** Neil Ellis Wines (R50)
9. **White Muscadel 2001** Nuy (R29.99)
10. **Sauvignon Blanc Reserve 2002** Steenberg (R75)

MOST EXCITING OR UNUSUAL FINDS

❶ Bouchard Finlayson Hannibal 2001 (R115) *Pinot Noir in the quirkiest of company (Sangiovese and Nebbiolo), but getting along famously.*

❷ Vin de Paille 2001 De Trafford (R120) *Cape pioneer of the vin de paille style from air-dried Chenin.*

❸ Chenin Blanc 2001 FMC (R200) *Ken Forrester and Martin Meinert are styling the Cape's most common grape with uncommon chic.*

❹ SMV 2001 Fairview (R116) *Rhône-style Shiraz, Mourvèdre, and Viognier blend made for California's Hospice de Rhône auction.*

❺ Viognier 2001 Fairview (R80) *Still rare in the Cape, and hailed by Jancis Robinson as one of the finest examples from the New World.*

❻ Green on Green Semillon 2001 Jack & Knox Winecraft (R70) *A good example of the current hectic search way off the beaten track for single-vineyard, old-vine gems.*

❼ Sauvignon Blanc 2002 Quoin Rock (R35) *The first vintage from a new Cape vineyard area, near Africa's most southerly point, Cape Agulhas.*

❽ Columella 2000 Sadie Family (R395) *Shiraz with a splash of Mourvèdre from ex-Spice Route star Eben Sadie, now flying solo between the Cape and Priorato in Spain.*

❾ Nebbiolo 2001 Steenberg (R68) *The first unblended Cape example of this variety. Oz Clarke pronounced it the best he had tasted outside Italy.*

❿ Infiniti Shiraz NV Stellenbosch Vineyards (R49.50) *Sparkling red Shiraz might be old hat to the Aussies, but it is new for South Africa.*

California

Dan Berger

California growers, responding to a shortage of grapes in 1995 and 1996, created a massive oversupply by extensive new plantings between 1997 and 2002.

DAN BERGER

In 1996, California had fewer than 350,000 acres of wine grapevines, but by 2001 this had risen to 570,000 acres. The result has been a massive lake of wine that wineries, wholesalers, and retailers are having difficulty disposing of, even though per capita consumption has risen significantly during the 1990s (from 2.0 to 2.7 gallons). This situation has been exacerbated by a worldwide surplus that has driven imported wine prices down, encouraging Americans to buy foreign wines rather than California wines. By the end of 2002, one bottle in every four sold in the United States was made overseas, and in the autumn of that year a thumping great harvest in California saw numerous vineyards go unpicked. Prices for many bulk wines plummeted, and the glut of wine resulted in deep discounting of the more modest-priced wines. At one point, a wine-crushing facility in California's central coast was offering 1,200 gallons of Chardonnay for free! The only hitch was that the taker had to haul it away, and haulage costs were higher than the juice could command.

In 2002, Trader Joe's, a small national chain of grocery stores, contracted with Bronco Wine Co, the largest vineyard owner in the state,

DAN BERGER is a wine writer syndicated by Creators Syndicate to newspapers around the world, and is publisher of *Berger's Vintage Experiences*, a weekly wine newsletter available only by subscription. A speaker at wine symposiums on topics such as wine marketing and public relations, he is also a judge at many wine competitions, including the New World International, San Francisco Fair, California State Fair, Los Angeles County Fair, West Coast, the International Wine Competition at Lubljiana, Concours Mondial in Brussels, and seven wine shows in Australia.

to market a range of varietal wines under the Charles F. Shaw label at $1.99 per bottle ($2.99 in other states due to wholesaler markups). These wines quickly became known as "Two Buck Chuck," as they flew out the door, with sales going from nowhere to 3 million cases in one year.

Meanwhile, California's fine-wine strategy in the 1990s to push its prices further upmarket came home to roost in the defining light of 9/11, as buyers dropped to lower price points, avoiding even well-known brands. By 2002, many merchants were wary of holding large amounts of high-priced wines, even those accorded cult status by powerful wine scribes.

Polarized industry

Wine diversity in California has taken a beating over the last decade as direct result of all the consolidation that has vested a huge portion of wine production in just a few hands. By "wine diversity," I mean the decline, if not outright abandonment, of such excellent alternative wines as Chenin Blanc, Petite Sirah, Riesling, Gewurztraminer, Muscat, French Colombard, Carignane, and a number of other grapes and style that once added depth and interest for the consumer. Larger wine companies prefer to have more limited portfolios, and now most major companies focus on Chardonnay, Cabernet Sauvignon, Sauvignon Blanc, Merlot, lesser amounts of Pinot Noir and Zinfandel, and a growing interest in Syrah. The result in 2002 is far fewer alternatives for the consumer, and a simpler "book" for wholesalers to deal with.

Grapevine

• **Francis Ford Coppola** has purchased vineyards from the famed JJ Cohn ranch for $400,000 per acre, setting an all-time record for American vineyard land sales.

• **PS I Love You** is the name of a trade group formed in September to support Petite Sirah, a superb grape for making dark-red aging wine. Click on to www.psiloveyou.org for details of events.

• **American restaurants** have suddenly discovered German Riesling and Austrian Grüner Veltliner. Sales of the two white wines were up dramatically in restaurants in 2002, partly as a result of reports of great vintages in Germany and a growing awareness that GV is a superb alternative to Chardonnay.

• **The price for Sauvignon Blanc** grapes in Napa Valley is expected to rise higher than that of Chardonnay in 2003, the first evidence that Chardonnay is far too heavily planted.

• **Justin Meyer,** one of California's greatest wine pioneers and the founder of Silver Oak Cellars, died in August 2002 after a lingering ailment. He was 63.

• **Dr. Curtis Ellison,** a Harvard University epidemiologist, was awarded the Wine Industry Integrity Award by the Lodi-Woodbridge Winegrape Commission, which annually honors an individual who has done most to further the cause of wine even though he personally has gained nothing from his own actions. Ellison has long publicly championed regular moderate consumption of wine as a path to better health—one of very few physicians who have been so vocal.

PRAISE FOR PINOT

The rise of Pinot Noir in California has clearly been one of the most dramatic news stories for wine lovers over the past few years, peaking in 2002 with the release of some spectacular 1999 wines. Pinot Noir was once looked down on as a poor-quality grape that made only thin, lifeless wine in California, but it has experienced phenomenal growth in statewide acreage, rising from just over 9,500 acres in 1996 to a staggering 25,000 acres in 2002. The top California regions for Pinot Noir remain Russian River Valley, Carneros, and Santa Barbara County, but in the past year or two, numerous successful subregions began to emerge and newer ones came on line. Sonoma Coast got the greatest media attention, its potential intriguing prognosticators the most, but the Santa Lucia Highlands, a long, narrow, cold region on the western edge of Monterey County's Salinas Valley, rapidly stole some of Sonoma Coast's thunder.

SYRAH SYNDROME

The discovery of Syrah led California growers into a frenzy of planting, which prompted literally dozens of upscale wineries to plunge into the Syrah game. Because they saw consumers paying $30–50 for Cabernet Sauvignon, they believed that the same consumer would pay $25 and $35 for Syrah, and thus began a test market for overpriced Syrah.

Hundreds of Syrahs hit the shelves at prices far in excess of the actual quality. In fact, lots of the wines seem indistinguishable from one another, with some of the best-value wines available around the $9 mark. Even $7 versions from some of the largest producers are not radically worse than the $35 wines. Meanwhile, some industry analysts are worried that there is a danger that appeal of Syrah could become so generic that it would leave the market wide open for great-value Aussie Shiraz to take over.

SUPREME COURT TO RULE ON POST-PROHIBITION FALLOUT

The one truly debilitating hangover from Prohibition is the way in which it was ended, with a stipulation that each of the 50 states had the right to determine how alcoholic beverages could be distributed within its borders. This means that California wine producers, who produce more that 90 percent of all US wine, must go through 51 different regulatory bodies (each state plus the District of Columbia) in order to sell their wines in the rest of the country. Moreover, the 21st amendment to the US Constitution that allowed wine, beer, and liquor to be sold again legally also permitted out-of-state wineries to sell in each state only if the wine goes through official channels, either a state-owned distribution system or a licensed wholesaler. This means that if the wholesalers decline to carry the products of a winery, that winery is prevented from selling to customers in the state in question. By 1995, it became clear that a consolidation of the wholesale tier in the United States had wiped out so many

many wholesalers that many small, family-owned California wineries were being shut out of numerous states. Some wineries began to ship wine across state lines direct to consumers who ordered over the phone or on the Internet, but this soon resulted in the states passing laws to make such an act a felony. Shipping companies complied, and numerous shipments of wine across state lines were destroyed, by either the shipping firms or the local authorities. By the mid-1990s, there were multiple legal challenges to the interstate shipping prohibitions, and in the late 1990s, various courts ruled that any barriers to trade among the various states violated the Commerce Clause of the Constitution. However, one ruling in 2001 by a Michigan judge ruled that the states do indeed have the right to erect trade barriers. This was a blow to the small winery, but that ruling was forcefully challenged just months later when a Texas judge admonished the Michigan judge for having failed to do his homework, arguing that the Commerce Clause takes precedence over a restriction of free trade between the states.

This acrimonious battle, which is a huge one for the wholesalers, is heading for a US Supreme Court decision, possibly as early as October 2004.

CORK PRODUCERS SCREWED

Cork taint became a huge issue in California in 2002, with a number of wine companies arguing that cork quality was still too variable for them.

Kendall-Jackson said it switched more than half of its 4.5 million case production over to synthetic corks in 2002. Toward the end of the year, the impact of Australia and New Zealand wineries putting screw caps on their finest, early-drinking wines had a huge impact on domestic producers. At least a dozen major wineries said (most of them privately) that they were testing the effects of screw caps, and one, Bonny Doon of Santa Cruz, said it would switch all of its house wines (blended, non-varietals) into Stelvin-sealed bottles. Meanwhile, many users of agglomerate corks were unable to resolve a cork-taint issue with one producer, and a number of lawsuits were filed after various wine companies claimed that the agglomerates gave all of their wines a tainted smell. Many of the suits were settled quietly out of court.

WHEELS OF FORTUNE

California wineries live in fear of the day George Louie pays them a visit. Louie is a wheelchair user who regularly visits businesses with public facilities. If he believes they fail to meet the standards imposed by the Americans with Disabilities Act (ADA), his affiliated organization, a nonprofit corporation called Americans with Disabilities Advocates, will file a lawsuit. He has already sued more than 700 California businesses, including 140 wineries, and it is believed that Louie is about to file more than 100 lawsuits against California wineries. The fact that Louie is very quickly willing to settle most cases out of court has led many to doubt his motives, but there is no question about his effectiveness: to bring themselves up to ADA compliance level, wineries have installed wheelchair ramps, lowered bars in their tasting rooms, removed gravel from walkways, and made many other modifications to accommodate disabled persons.

TOP-END CABERNETS TAKE A DIVE

Demand for some of the cult Cabernet Sauvignons of California appears to be waning, although the very top wines, like Screaming Eagle, make such a small amount of wine that the very wealthy who need some will always keep prices high. Prices for many such wines topped $100 a bottle over the past two years, and during the dot-com boom that created new millionaires almost overnight, those prices were no barrier to desire. But after the economic downturn, the bottom suddenly seemed to drop out of the almost unquenchable demand for the expensive wines, and soon many wine shops were left with inventories of high-priced Cabernets.

Grapevine

• **Zinfandel** has finally, formally, and scientifically been identified, according to Carole Meredith, a UC Davis researcher who has worked on the project for decades. Zinfandel, known as Primitivo in Italy, is in fact Crljenak Kastelanski (pronounced "sirl-yen-ack kastelanski") from the Dalmatian Coast. Meredith was aided in her DNA fingerprinting work by the University of Zagreb.

• **Bankruptcies and mergers** are anticipated in the wake of the long wine glut that has hurt a number of wineries. Already, two Sonoma County wineries have filed for bankruptcy, and the famous old Louis Martini Winery was purchased by the huge E&J Gallo.

• **The final big deal** of the last decade came when Canandaigua of New York acquired BRL Hardy of Australia, thus becoming the largest wine company in the world, surpassing E&J Gallo—the first time in five decades that the Modesto giant was second to anyone. The deal was significant in that Canandaigua now has a major Napa brand (Franciscan), a major Sonoma brand (Simi), a flood of bargain-priced brands, and an import line sure to soar now that its Australian brands have the power of a successful American wine company behind them.

• **In October 2002,** James Conaway, a Washington-based journalist, published a book called The Far Side of Eden. A stinging indictment of many vineyard practices in Napa Valley, Conaway portrays environmentalists in a very favorable light and winemakers and vineyard managers as uncaring louts who want to rape the land. Conaway is also editor of the official journal of the National Trust for Historic Preservation.

• **Only two** of all the large-sized wine companies remain in private hands—Kendall-Jackson and Trinchero (Sutter Home)—and of these, only the former has explored super-premium concepts with brands like Lokoya (high-end Napa Cab) and La Crema (Russian River Pinot Noir).

• **Despite the glut of wine,** the abandonment of about 3 percent of vineyards in California's hot Central Valley, combined with a reduced level of planting, has some analysts worried about a shortage of wine by 2006!

Opinion:
Too alcoholic

Intentional late picking has led to excessively high alcohol levels in so-called table wines. Notably, the average Zinfandel today is well over 14 percent ABV, with some of the most popular with new drinkers weighing in at 16 percent-plus. Chardonnay and Cabernet Sauvignon are becoming ridiculously massive. All this is due to the desire for high scores from alcohol-insensitive wine critics. The result is that varietal character has been compromised, and that weight and extract are now the key elements in a supposedly fine wine. Gone is any hope that delicacy will once again be rewarded. Winemakers should return to more reasonable alcoholic levels and concentrate on balance and finesse.

Too much malolactic and oak

Far too many wineries seek to make white wines with more "complexity" by putting them through full malolactic fermentation. The result is a compromise in varietal character, the acidity is stripped away, and flaccid, fruit-flavorless wine with generally more oak than is needed. No wonder many longtime wine drinkers are seeking Anything But Chardonnay (ABC) and finding more authentic alternatives such as Pinot Gris, although those wines (and Viognier) are also starting to be ruined by overzealous malolactic. Barrels remain the dominant flavoring element for top-level wines, with fruit becoming a secondary issue.

Acid comment

Too few California wineries understand or use ascorbic acid in their early-drinking white wines, thus many of these wines decline faster than they ought to.

Call for de-alcoholization

More wineries should adopt modern tools, such as reverse osmosis, to lower excessive alcohol levels. A slight dealcoholization can make a splendid, tasty wine.

Vintage Report

Advance report on the latest harvest

2002

The 2002 vintage in Northern California (Napa, Sonoma, Mendocino) was marked not so much by prolonged heat as by a series of shorter heat spells late in the season, which resulted in excessively high sugars in much of the crop. The heat spells occurred after a relatively cool summer, so the sugar accumulated fairly quickly. In some areas, there was a lot of fruit loss due to shriveling, except for those wineries that had the ability to hand-sort. Most red wines are probably going to be pretty concentrated, and winemakers may have to deal with high alcohol levels. Some predict an awkwardness in many wines. White grapes, however, may have survived better, since the slightly cooler summer left Chardonnay, Sauvignon Blanc, and Pinot Gris with good acid levels. Since these grapes were harvested before the series of heat spells could set in, it could be a very good vintage for these varieties.

Updates on the previous five vintages

2001

Vintage rating: 94

A warm summer followed by a cooling trend in September brought acids back up. Some fruit was harvested early, leading to better acidity structure.

2000

Vintage rating: 87

An El Niño vintage. Flavors for most grapes were satisfactory, but many reds lack body and richness unless harvested very late, although the later flavors were a little contrived. Unlike 1998, time does not appear to be helping them. Just an average year, with certain wineries doing better by making severe selections.

1999

Vintage rating: 99

The best reds were startlingly complex early, with bright fruit acids, and the wines had near-perfect structure. Perhaps a better vintage than the vaunted 1997s, many of which appear to be aging quite quickly.

1998

Vintage rating: *90*

Another El Niño vintage. Ripening was not bad, but early on the wines seemed to lack depth. Early reports were negative, but many winemakers made splendid blending decisions, and the vintage turned out to be a lot better than early reports.

1997

Vintage rating: *90*

Harvesting of the Cabernet began two to three weeks later than normal, with high sugars and good acid levels. Early on, the wines were roundly praised as wines equal to the exciting 1994s and the bold 1991s. However, in the past few years, the wines seem fast-evolving, and the vintage may not have been as good as first thought.

GREATEST WINE PRODUCERS

1. Navarro
2. Joseph Phelps
3. Stag's Leap Wine Cellars
4. Gary Farrell
5. Au Bon Climat
6. Etude
7. Ridge Vineyards
8. Spottswoode
9. Gundlach Bundschu
10. Robert Mondavi

FASTEST-IMPROVING PRODUCERS

1. Gallo of Sonoma
2. Charles Krug
3. Gloria Ferrer
4. Trentadue
5. Niebaum-Coppola
6. Morgan
7. White Oak
8. Rutz
9. Firestone
10. Jekel

NEW UP-AND-COMING PRODUCERS

1. Dutton-Goldfield
2. Domaine Alfred
3. Terra Valentine
4. Lynmar
5. La Crema
6. Rios-Lovell
7. Artesa
8. Brewer-Clifton
9. Atalon/Lokoya
10. Clos Pepe

BEST-VALUE PRODUCERS

1. Forest Glen
2. Fetzer Vineyards
3. Sutter Home Vineyards

4 Turning Leaf
5 Bogle
6 McManis
7 Barefoot
8 Hess Select
9 Canyon Road
10 Delicato

GREATEST-QUALITY WINES

1 **Insignia 1999** Joseph Phelps Napa Valley ($125)
2 **Navarro Gewurztraminer 2001** Anderson Valley ($14)
3 **La Reve 1996** Domaine Carneros ($40)
4 **Gary Farrell Pinot Noir 1999** Rochioli Vineyard ($60)
5 **Cluster Select Gewurztraminer 2000** Navarro ($39)
6 **Chardonnay 2001** Stony Hill Napa Valley ($27)
7 **Knox Alexander Pinot Noir 2000** Au Bon Climat ($40)
8 **Monte Bello Cabernet Sauvignon 1999** Ridge Vineyards ($100)
9 **Syrah 2000** Dutton-Goldfield ($35)
10 **Cabernet Sauvignon 1998** Staglin Family ($80)

BEST BARGAINS

1 **Sauvignon Blanc 2002** Geyser Peak California ($10)
2 **Shiraz 2001** Delicato California ($7)
3 **Pinot Noir Reserve 2001** ForestVille ($9)
4 **REDS 2000** Laurel Glen ($9)
5 **Syrah 2001** McManis ($9)
6 **Dancing Bull Zinfandel 2000** Rancho Zabaco ($9)
7 **Sauvignon Blanc 2002** Canyon Road ($8)
8 **Pinot Gris 2002** Sutter Home Vineyards ($7)
9 **Chenin Blanc 2001** Husch ($8)
10 **Chateau La Paws 2001** Rosenblum Cellars ($9)

MOST EXCITING OR UNUSUAL FINDS

1 **Le Mistral 2000** Joseph Phelps ($25) *A fruit-driven, Rhône-style red wine that uses a superb infusion of cool-climate, low-yielding Grenache. A great and complex wine. The 1999 was even better.*
2 **Grenache 1999** Philip Staley ($18) *Cool-climate Grenache fruit with a penetrating aroma of cranberries.*
3 **Grenache Blanc 2001** Beckmen ($20) *A limited-production wine of ethereal fruit qualities.*
4 **Rose of Pinot Noir 2002** Iron Horse ($12) *What great pink wine is all about, with sufficient acidity to make the wine food-friendly, but structured to work well as an apéritif on a hot day.*
5 **Sparkling Shiraz 1997** Geyser Peak ($25) *A rare treat, with big, bold plum/pepper flavors and sufficient sugar to allow it to work with chocolate.*
6 **Freisa Con Fresa NV** Bonny Doon ($18) *Flowery, fizzy, and sweet enough to stand as a dessert on its own.*
7 **Teroldego 2000** Il Podere dell'Olivos ($20) *Deeply flavored red wine with an exotic fruit note.*
8 **Bouteille Call NV** (Syrah Port with Raspberry Wine) Bonny Doon ($22) *A sort of concocted wine, but nevertheless tasty and entirely for fun.*
9 **Trousseau Gris 2001** Fanucchi ($20) *A nearly lost grape variety treated with respect and barrel fermentation.*
10 **Chardonnay NV** Black Box Wines ($25 per 3-liter bag-in-box) *A Napa Valley Chardonnay that sells for the equivalent of barely $6 per bottle. Such a non-stuffy way to market Chardonnay, particularly for Napa.*

Pacific Northwest

Paul Gregutt

After two decades at the helm of Stimson Lane, Allen Shoup has a new project centred in Washington state that seems destined to attract considerable attention from around the world.

PAUL GREGUTT

Named Long Shadows Vintners, the partnership will build a consortium of six ultra-premium wineries, each headed by a well-known winemaker from outside the Northwest. First to sign up for Shoup's vintner "Dream Team" are two Napa Valley superstars—Quintessa's Agustin Huneeus and Dunn Vineyard's Randy Dunn. Joining them will be Michel Rolland of Le Bon Pasteur in Bordeaux. At least three more winemakers are due to be named within the year, most likely coming from Australia, Italy, and Germany. Long Shadows vineyard sites are being selected, with the first crush for at least three of the wineries coming in the fall of 2003. Each winery will aim to produce a single "best of type" wine under a boutique label, using Washington grapes. Expect the first wines to be released in 2005, at prices ranging from $40 to $90.

New AVAs

The rush to create new AVAs (American Viticultural Areas) or appellations is a sure sign that a region is maturing and its wine growers are gaining confidence in the individual *terroirs*. In 2001, Red Mountain became Washington's latest AVA, located on the southeastern flank of the Yakima Valley AVA. With just 700 acres planted and a dozen wineries in situ, it is also the smallest by far. At the same time, it is arguably the most important AVA, since it is these vineyards that provide grapes to many of Washington's

PAUL GREGUTT lives in Seattle and is the author of *Northwest Wines* (Sasquatch Books, 1994). He is the wine columnist for *The Seattle Times* and regularly contributes to *Wine Enthusiast* and *Seattle Homes & Lifestyle*.

most prestigious boutique wineries, such as Andrew Will, Betz Family, Cadence, DeLille, Januik, Matthews, McCrea, and Quilceda Creek. The next Washington AVA likely to gain approval will be the Horse Heaven Hills. Proposed in the summer of 2002, this large area west of the Walla Walla Valley AVA is home to several of Washington's largest vineyards. This is Merlot country, with Chalone's Canoe Ridge and Stimson Lane's Columbia Crest vineyards located at its core. Also in the application phase is a proposed Columbia River Gorge AVA, covering vineyards west of the Horse Heaven Hills, either side of the Columbia River. It will soon be joined by several more, including a Wahluke Slope AVA, encompassing some of Washington's warmest sites on a high plateau in the Vantage-Othello area, between the Columbia River and the Saddle Mountains.

Even more ambitious plans are under way in Oregon, where producers in the northern Willamette Valley petitioned for six new AVAs in 2002. If approved, these will double the total number of AVAs in the state. The six proposed AVAs are Chehalem Mountains, Eola Hills, McMinnville Foothills, Red Hills of Dundee, Ribbon Ridge, and Yamhill-Carlton District. However, several AVAs have hit snags over their proposed names. The proposed Eola Hills AVA, for example. If approved, Eola Hills Wine Cellars, which has been making wines since 1986, would suddenly be required to source 95 percent of its fruit from the Eola Hills AVA. Applicants had hoped that they would be allowed to 'grandfather' in any wineries which had names that coincided with the AVA names, but it now appears that this won't happen. The approval process for new AVAs can easily stretch to two years or longer, but consumers will benefit by knowing not only where the grapes were grown, but what style a given region has become known for. In the long run, these fine-tuned appellations will help to map the Pacific Northwest wine country in a far more precise and meaningful way.

Grapevine

• **Oregon's WillaKenzie Estate** has named Thibaud Mandet as its new winemaker. He replaces founding winemaker Laurent Montalieu, who left to pursue his own venture. Mandet, a native of Auvergne, France, had been Montalieu's assistant since joining WillaKenzie in 2000. He began his winemaking career in Bordeaux and holds a graduate degree in Oenology from the Faculté d'Oenologie de Bordeaux.

• With ripples from the worldwide grape glut affecting even the low-yielding vineyards of Pinot country, Hatcher Wineworks has introduced a *négociant*-styled $19 Oregon Pinot Noir—named A to Z— blended from several top sites; 2001 is the first vintage. Hatcher Wineworks is a "virtual" winery operating out of several Yamhill facilities.

• **Dunham Cellars,** another of Walla Walla's best boutiques, has officially merged with sister winery Trey Marie. Initially, Trey Marie was a joint venture between the Dunham and David Syre families, but now both families will be partners in both wineries.

Opinion:
Independence good for Oregon

The Oregon Wine Advisory Board (OWAB), which has operated under the governance of the Oregon State Department of Agriculture for many years, is sponsoring legislation that would, at long last, grant it complete independence. Though the official stance is that the proposals are not sweeping changes, clearly the wine growers and winemakers of Oregon have been casting a jealous eye to the north, to the independently run and wildly successful Washington Wine Commission, whose nonstop promotional tours and tastings bring Washington wines to the attention of consumers around the globe. Hopefully, OWAB can reorganize and elevate its own efforts to a comparable level. Unfortunately, the isolated, stubbornly anarchistic bent of some of Oregon's winemakers makes any change, however positive, difficult to implement.

Grapevine

• **Gary Andrus,** cofounder of Napa's Pine Ridge and Oregon's Archery Summit wineries, which he lost during a well-publicized divorce, has returned to Oregon to start a boutique winery in the Willamette Valley. He recently acquired the 40-acre, $1.75-million Lion Valley Vineyards in Cornelius, southwest of Portland, and made his 2002 wines from purchased fruit. A new label will be announced by the autumn of 2003.

• At a pair of blind taste-offs in New York City and Chicago in early 2003, the Washington Wine Commission put up four of the state's best red wines against two of the best wines from Napa (Mondavi Reserve Cabernet and Caymus) and two of the best Bordeaux (Mouton and Palmer). All eight wines came from the 1999 vintage, generally considered excellent in all three regions. The tasters, comprised of media and wine trade, were asked to rank the wines in order of preference. When the votes were tallied, Washington wines took the top four spots in New York and the top three in Chicago one month later. Most impressively, the average retail price of the Washington wines was just $35, while the average retail price of the four competitors was $104. The first and second columns below are the results in New York and Chicago, respectively.

1 1 Columbia Crest 1999 Reserve Cabernet Sauvignon ($28)

2 3 Kiona 1999 Estate Bottled Cabernet Sauvignon, Red Mountain ($35)

3 2 L'Ecole No 41 1999 Apogee, Pepper Bridge Vineyard ($42)

4 6 Chateau Ste Michelle 1999 Reserve Cabernet Sauvignon ($34)

5 7 Caymus 1999 Cabernet Sauvignon ($70)

6 4 Robert Mondavi 1999 Reserve Cabernet Sauvignon ($125)

7 5 Château Palmer 1999 Margaux ($76)

8 8 Château Mouton Rothschild 1999 Pauillac ($145)

Vintage Report

2002

Washington—For the fifth consecutive year, Washington wine growers feel they have hit a viticultural home run. Despite weird spring weather that hammered Walla Walla vineyards with 3 in (75 mm) of snow in early May, and a heat spike in mid-July that fried some vines and badly stressed others, everything ended well. Crop-thinning and perfect autumn weather brought in a generous crop that has high sugars, high acidity, and high extract, much like the splendid 1999s. It looks to be a very good year for white wines and a great year for the reds, particularly Cabernet and Syrah. As an added bonus, a freeze on Halloween night allowed some winemakers to make icewines.

Oregon—Touch and go from the beginning. A cold, wet spring got things off to a slow start in the northern Willamette Valley. In southern Oregon, a summer heat spike adversely affected some vineyards, while drought and isolated hail storms damaged others. Heavy rains hit parts of the Willamette Valley as harvest was getting under way in early October. Some wineries chose to pick before the storms hit; those patient enough to wait the rains out were greeted with warm, sunny weather throughout the rest of the month. Overall, 2002 seems destined to be a vintage with considerable variation.

Updates on the previous five vintages

2001

Vintage rating:
88 (Washington: 90, Oregon: 86–89)

Washington—Extremely hot summer temperatures ripened some cooler sites quite early, and harvest began early, on 1 September. The hot weather finally backed off and picking extended well into November, making this both one of the earliest and latest harvests on record. It was also the largest crop on record. The wines are lush, forward, and fruit-driven. Syrahs may be the best of the reds, while the white wines are unusually ripe and tropical for cool, crisp Washington.

Oregon—Extensive green-harvest and exhaustive sorting at crush paid off for those who did the work, with wines that are showing clean brilliant fruit and great elegance. For too many wineries, however, the 2001s are soft, forward, and simple.

2000

Vintage rating:
90 (Washington: 89, Oregon: 91)
Washington—Merlots and some Cabernets from favored sites are the standouts, along with some careful Rieslings. The reds are very dark and tannic, although they lack the structured concentration of the 1999s. The whites are fresh and crisp, with clean, ripe fruit flavors.
Oregon—A magic vintage, the third in a row for Oregon. The ripening was so uniform that many wineries were buried in grapes as everything came in at once. The Pinots show loads of fruit, with lovely blackberry and cherry notes, as well as smooth tannins and no bitterness.

1999

Vintage rating:
95 (Washington: 96, Oregon: 94)
Washington—The blue skies and warm daytime weather, coupled with significant temperature drops at night, created virtually perfect conditions for ripening grapes, with deep colors, intense flavors, and remarkable acid levels in abundance. The top reds show astonishing depth, power, muscle, and structure, making this a superb vintage for the cellar.
Oregon—Growers dropped up to half their fruit in order to get loads to manageable ripening levels; and with warm, sunny

weather finally arriving in September, the strategy paid off, resulting in a miracle vintage with an exceptionally long hang time. Chardonnays are concentrated, even unctuous (particularly those from Dijon clones), while the Pinots are fine, ripe, and beautifully structured for aging.

1998

Vintage rating:
92 (Washington: 91, Oregon: 93)
Washington—This year was especially notable for the spectacular, consistently warm summer weather, which promoted full, even ripening across the state. Both reds and whites came out loaded with ripe, lush flavors, although most of these wines were definitely for early drinking, since many are already past their prime. The lesson learned in 1998 is that, in some years at least, Washington fruit can get just as jammy and ultra-ripe as anything from California.
Oregon—Dramatically reduced yields and a dry harvest brought in good fruit, with lush, ripe flavors.

1997

Vintage rating:
86 (Washington: 87, Oregon: 84)
Washington—After the disastrous freeze that wiped out a big chunk of the 1996 harvest, many Washington vineyards put out a large crop of evenly ripened fruit.

Most of the wines were flavorful and fruit-forward. In some cooler sites, the red grapes failed to ripen enough to overcome traces of stemmy, green tannins.

Oregon—Huge crop loads forced growers to green-harvest up to one third of their fruit, but heavy rains at harvest only created more problems. Tannic, lean wines were the result, with some vineyards experiencing unwanted rot as well.

GREATEST WINE PRODUCERS

1. Quilceda Creek Vintners
2. Andrew Will
3. Beaux Frères
4. Leonetti Cellar
5. DeLille Cellars
6. Chateau Ste Michelle (single-vineyard wines)
7. Domaine Drouhin Oregon
8. Ken Wright Cellars
9. Columbia Crest
10. Woodward Canyon

FASTEST-IMPROVING PRODUCERS

1. Barnard Griffin
2. Kiona Vineyards Winery
3. Woodward Canyon
4. Caterina
5. Argyle
6. Camaraderie Cellars
7. Kestrel Vintners
8. King Estate
9. L'Ecole No 41
10. Bookwalter

NEW UP-AND-COMING PRODUCERS

1. Betz Family
2. Januik
3. Cadence
4. Sineann
5. Penner-Ash Wine Cellars
6. Rulo
7. Patricia Green Cellars
8. Lemelson Vineyards
9. Cayuse Vineyards
10. Walla Walla Vintners

BEST-VALUE PRODUCERS

1. Columbia Crest
2. Waterbrook
3. Hedges Cellars
4. Firesteed Cellars
5. Snoqualmie Vineyards
6. Hogue Cellars
7. Randall Harris
8. Bridgeview Vineyards
9. Covey Run
10. Stone Wolf

GREATEST-QUALITY WINES

1. **Cabernet Sauvignon 2000** Quilceda Creek Vintners ($75)
2. **Père de Famille Cabernet Sauvignon 2000** Betz Family ($45)
3. **Sorella 2000** Andrew Will ($50)
4. **Pinot Noir Louise 2000** Domaine Drouhin Oregon ($75)
5. **Tapteil Vineyard Red Table Wine 2000** Cadence ($35)
6. **Merlot 1999** Northstar ($50)
7. **Chardonnay Cold Creek Vineyard 2001** Januik ($30)
8. **Reserve Cabernet Sauvignon 1999** Kiona Vineyards Winery ($30)
9. **Pinot Noir 2001** Beaux Frères ($58)
10. **Single Berry Select Riesling 2000** Chateau Ste Michelle/ Dr Loosen ($200 per half-bottle)

BEST BARGAINS

1. **Grand Estates Chardonnay 2001** Columbia Crest ($10)
2. **Cabernet Sauvignon 1999** Waterbrook ($15)
3. **CMS Red Wine 2001** Hedges ($12)
4. **Merlot 2001** Randall Harris ($10)
5. **Chardonnay 2000** Covey Run ($8)
6. **White Riesling 2002** Kiona Vineyards Winery ($6)
7. **Pinot Noir 2001** Firesteed ($10)
8. **Sauvignon Blanc 2001** Chateau Ste Michelle ($10)
9. **Merlot 2000** Barnard Griffin ($13)
10. **Dry Riesling 2002** Washington Hills ($6)

MOST EXCITING OR UNUSUAL FINDS

1. **Tempranillo 2000** Abacela ($22) *Abacela has led the way with this varietal in the Pacific Northwest, finding the perfect growing conditions in central Oregon.*
2. **Ciel du Cheval Syrah 2001** McCrea ($50) *The unbeatable combination of a sensational Red Mountain vineyard and the winemaking genius of Doug McCrea, who has pioneered Syrah in Washington state.*
3. **Old Vine Zinfandel 2001** Sineann ($36) *Who knew Zinfandel this ripe and jammy could grow in the Pacific Northwest?*
4. **Single Berry Select Riesling 2000** Chateau Ste Michelle/ Dr Loosen ($200) *A stunning collaboration between Ernst Loosen and Erik Olsen.*
5. **Cailloux Vineyard Viognier 2002** Cayuse ($30) *Christophe Baron had the vision to find a rock-strewn Rhône vineyard hidden in Walla Walla apple country.*
6. **Sangiovese 2000** Leonetti Cellar ($50) *The lush, oaky Leonetti style dresses up Washington Sangiovese in a whole new way.*
7. **Arneis 2002** Ponzi ($18) *Yet again, a brilliant idea brilliantly executed.*
8. **Barbera 2001** Columbia Winery ($20) *This winery has produced so many firsts over the past 25 years, and here is yet another!*
9. **Pinot Blanc 2001** WillaKenzie Estate ($16) *Who needs Chardonnay when Oregon can make Pinot Blanc this vibrant and fresh?*
10. **Dolcetto 2001** Abacela ($19) *The Tempranillo is stunning, but the Dolcetto is simply delicious, in a forward, friendly, and immensely flavourful style.*

Grapevine

- The 2001 vintage heralds a philosophical about turn at the Andrew Will Winery. Its winemaker Chris Camarda has pioneered vineyard-designated Cabernets and Merlots, frequently showcasing the state's top vineyards ahead of his peers. As from the 2001 vintage, however, he has abandoned his single-vineyard varietals (up to five different Cabs and an equal number of Merlots) in favor of a much smaller number of carefully blended wines.

- Among the rarest of Oregon wines have been Pinots from the Goldschmidt vineyard, belonging to former Oregon Governor Neil Goldschmidt and his wife. Following their purchase in 1998 of a historic property in the Dundee Hills, the couple sold a few grapes to Adelsheim, Patti Green, and Rex Hill, while they focused on replanting and expanding the vineyard. Now they are ready to release the first wines under their own label. Their winemaker is the talented Lynn Penner-Ash, formerly at Rex Hill and now making wines under her own label as well as the Goldschmidts'. The first few hundred cases of the still-unnamed Goldschmidt wines are expected to hit the market in the summer of 2003.

Atlantic Northeast

Sandra Silfven

Though Americans generally can carry wine across state lines, most cannot order wines to be shipped to them from retailers or wineries in other states.

SANDRA SILFVEN

This issue, which is all about wholesalers staying in business and state governments collecting taxes, is a hot topic in the entire country, but it is at boiling point in the east. Gradually, the states are chipping away at antiquated laws dating back to the end of Prohibition in 1933: Virginia has dropped its shipping restrictions and New York is likely to be next. There is ongoing legal action in other eastern states, too. Recently, even the US government has helped with a loophole in the Homeland Security Act that lets air travelers ship wine home. Shipping is important because it enables small wineries to expand their customer base and gain wider recognition. King Ferry Winery in the Finger Lakes, one of the leaders in the drive to free the grapes in New York, has a list of 10,000 out-of-state customers who want to buy its wine. Owner Peter Saltonstall says his business will increase by 10 percent if direct shipping is made legal. At publication date, West Virginia and Virginia are the only states in this region where wineries are free to ship directly to consumers in states with reciprocal legislation. (Rhode Island and Connecticut allow limited shipping, but their laws are fraught with restrictions.) That leaves a vast region stretching from New England, south to Maryland, and across to Pennsylvania, Ohio, Michigan, and Indiana, with more than 400 wineries forced to operate at a great

SANDRA SILFVEN is wine writer at *The Detroit News* and produces the *Michigan Wine Report* for Detroit News Online at www.detnews.com/wine. Assisting her in tasting wines were Madeline Triffon MS (Master Sommelier) and sommeliers Richard Rubel and Jeff Zimmerman. Special thanks go to Sally Linton, Jill Ditmire, Donna Csolak, Mark Chien, Hudson Cattell, Linda Jones McKee, Jim Trezise, Tom Payette, Michelle Widner, Donniella Winchell, and Jenny Engle for their assistance.

disadvantage. Sure, they can take a cut in profits and distribute their products through a wholesaler, but most wholesalers are not interested in small, regional American wineries.

Patricia Kluge storms Virginia

London-raised Patricia Kluge (pronounced klu-gee) does things in a large way at her new 1,200-acre Kluge Estate in central Virginia, just 7 miles (11 km) from Thomas Jefferson's home, Monticello. Bordeaux specialist Michel Rolland is consulting winemaker; noted Virginia vintner Gabriele Rausse is senior winemaker for red wines; and Emmanuel Fourny from France will oversee sparkling production. The David Easton–designed Kluge Estate Farm Shop will be run by Tom Thornton, former CEO of Dean & Deluca. Providing food there will be pastry chef Serge Torres and Dan Shannon, formerly of the Charlie Palmer Group. Kluge Estate's first release, 2000 New World Red, is sold exclusively at the winery and at Morrell & Co in New York for $495. (It comes in a box designed by David Linley, which may explain the price.)

Drinking Band

In Charlottesville, Virginia, pop star Dave Matthews (of the Dave Matthews Band) has excited locals with three single-vineyard Chardonnays, a single-vineyard Merlot, and a Meritage from his Blenheim Vineyards. Matthews's longtime chum and managing partner–winemaker Brad McCarthy, who has spent 15 years as a winemaker in Virginia and California, is responsible for the wines. The new state-of-the-art, gravity-flow winery has no tasting room and is not open to the public, but the wines are available in nearby wine shops and restaurants, along with select stores in Florida and New York.

Long Island vineyard given the chop

Leslie Alexander, owner of the Houston Rockets basketball team, shut down his infant winery in Cutchogue, on the North Fork of Long Island. Known as B&L Farms, the property had its third leafing of Bordeaux varieties, but the quality of the wine did not satisfy Alexander, who said he will sell his 177 acres, 32 of which are planted in vinifera.

Rhode Island whites

Sakonnet Vineyards, the winery that has attracted so many famous chefs and wine lovers to wine festivals in the smallest US state, Rhode Island, is up for sale. "We brought the operation to a level where we are ready to turn it over to somebody who has fresh ideas, fresh money, a fresh outlook. I am 70 years old," said owner Earl Samson. Recently, Samson and his wife Susan hired Dr. Christian Butzke, extension oenologist at the University of California at Davis, to be the new director of winemaking.

WORD GAMES

Bottles of Long Island Duck Walk Vineyards Merlot rarely migrate out of state, but the mighty Duckhorn Vineyards in Napa Valley cites marketplace confusion over the use of the word "duck," and is suing. In Michigan, Leelanau is the name of a sparsely populated northern peninsula, county, and American Viticultural Area (AVA). Yet Leelanau Wine Cellars, one of the state's bigger wineries, was able to trademark it, then sued boutique winery Chateau de Leelanau for infringement. First, the judge sided with the big winery and ordered the smaller one to change its name and strike out the word Leelanau on every label, sign, and brochure. It did. Six months later, the judge reversed his ruling!

ASIAN LADYBUGS

Researchers are testing ways to best deal with Asian ladybugs, which tainted wines in Ohio and other eastern states in the 2001 vintage, but not in 2002. So far, the treatment of choice is applications of Aza-Direct, an insect repellent that is legal for grapes, even organic vines. The problem occurred when the beetles were introduced to the US to kill aphids on a variety of crops, especially soybeans, and then developed a passion for grapes. At harvest, they were swept up by mechanical picking machines, and when crushed, emitted a sticky, yellow liquid that imparted a cooked spinach/rancid peanut butter character to wine. "The aroma threshold would be the same as for TCA," said Roland Riesen, the research director at the Lake Erie Enology Research Center at Youngstown State University in Ohio. Tests have found that a single beetle can taint one liter of wine.

WINE SPA

A 4,000-acre land-development project near Williamsburg in southeastern Virginia, called The Farms of New Kent, will have retirement villages, estate houses, a golf course, a winery, and a spa. Consulting winemaker Tom Payette will oversee production, according to Pete Johns, one of the partners. Fifteen acres of vinifera vines are in the ground, with the first crush planned for 2004.

KEY INDUSTRY FIGURES PASS AWAY

The Finger Lakes said goodbye to Ed Dalrymple, 77, a partner in Glenora Wine Cellars, Logan Ridge, and Knapp Vineyards; Jerry Hazlitt, 64, of Hazlitt 1852 Vineyards; and John Rose, 52, president of Heron Hill Winery. Elsewhere, the Atlantic Northeast lost Cortlandt Parker, 80, who published the *New England*, *Finger Lakes*, *Long Island*, and *Virginia Wine Gazettes* with wife Nancy Knowles Parker. Ben Sparks, still known as "Junior" at the ripe old age of 84, was the unofficial spokesman for Indiana wines and the vintner who helped found the Indiana Winegrowers Guild in 1975. John Crouch, 55, was cofounder of Allegro Vineyards in Brogue, Pennsylvania. Last, but by no means least, Jean Leducq, 82, who was a partner in Prince Michel Winery, Virginia, and gave 100 percent of the profits of Prince Michel, Rapidan River, and Madison wines to the Leducq Foundation to fund international cardiovascular research.

Opinion:
Get real

The east needs to quit experimenting with varieties that cannot consistently endure harsh winters, ripen well, or meet international standards. (Cabernet Sauvignon is a tough one.) The obvious varieties to grow are Chardonnay for sparkling and still wines, Riesling, Pinot Gris, and Cabernet Franc. Everybody wants to do Pinot Noir, but not everybody can or should. The benchmarks are out there, and smart consumers know if a wine is for real or a lame pretender. Whether it is Pinot Noir or Merlot, most consumers will not accept dry reds with vegetal flavors, hard acids, and green tannins. Comparing wines to those of more-recognized regions or making wines in a style to imitate them is risky if quality is not part of the equation. Too much oak, especially new American barrels, can overpower underripe fruit. What is wrong with used French oak? Or no oak? Also, the temptation to ferment a sparkling wine or still wine such as Riesling to austere levels of dryness can strip it of appeal.

Authenticity

Some vintners corrupt the regional character by buying juice from outside the state to make price-sensitive wines and pass them off as local.

Cannot see the trees for the wood

What is the point of long product lines that telegraph no specialty, or multiple-label designs that suggest no distinctive identity? Quality is not the overriding issue it used to be, but the various wine regions in the Atlantic Northeast need to figure out their own specialty, then market it aggressively, rather than muddy the waters with dozens of lesser wines. Clearly, Riesling and sparkling wines are proven winners and have consumer appeal in all styles. Why not organize a Riesling summit, like Oregon puts on with Pinot Noir? The spicy, dry Gewurztraminers are coming on strong, too, and are unlike any grown in the rest of the US. The Atlantic Northeast faces a two-part challenge: first, in the vineyard, to identify the best clonal selections and put them on appropriate rootstocks that suit the soils, and then cast a hawk's eye on vine vigor, trellis type, and crop estimates. "Errors in the vineyard have held back the industry," said David Miller, winemaker at St. Julian in Michigan, who sets rigid standards for his growers. Second, the region needs to broadcast the styles and strengths of its best wines to other states and the national media. Do not think that recognition in the region is enough. New York wineries took a road show to COPIA: The American Center for Wine, Food & the Arts in Napa Valley, which opened many eyes to the quality in the east. The northeast needs a good blast of confidence, too. If more quality-oriented regional wineries had the courage to make a statement by charging a high price for a deserving specialty, the respect meter might go up.

Grapevine

• **Wölffer Estate** on Long Island released the area's first $100 wine—the 2000 Premier Cru Merlot made from select berries harvested at 1.5 tons per acre, and presented in a 4.3-lb (2-kg) bottle. "I want to break the prejudice against East Coast wine," said winemaker Roman Roth. "A wine has to be really perfect to sell at this level."

• **Husband-and-wife team** Gary Crump and Gloria Priam opened Priam Vineyards in Colchester, Connecticut. Crump has been key in writing legislation to ease state constraints on the wine industry. His latest coup: a law allowing Connecticut wineries to sell each other's wines in their tasting rooms.

• **Oliver Winery,** Indiana's oldest and largest winery, in the south-central part of the state, is even larger since the construction of a $1.5-million winemaking facility, which triples winemaking capacity to more than 250,000 cases. Tourist appeal has grown, too, with the planting of a one-acre demonstration vineyard.

• **Chaddsford Winery,** a force in southeastern Pennsylvania, marked its 20th year with a complete revamping—new equipment, remodeled tasting room, three new retail stores, and a new label design.

• **There is talk** that growers in New England are tired of the all-encompassing appellation name of "Southeastern New England" and want to change it to something more descriptive of the geographic area. This AVA covers coastal sections of Connecticut, Massachusetts, and Rhode Island.

• **Quality-oriented Ohio vintners,** weary of the pop wine image they have from boaters' destinations on Lake Erie, are considering setting up a quality-alliance program.

• **Coeditor and copublisher** of *Wine East* magazine Linda Jones McKee and her husband, wine consultant Richard Carey, opened the Tamanend Winery in Lancaster, Pennsylvania, which makes red wines only. Tamanend is the name of the American Indian chief who signed a treaty with William Penn to establish a colony there in the early 1680s, and Carey's family is related to Penn.

• **The granting of a Seneca Lake AVA** in New York seems certain, according to Beverly Stamp of Lakewood Vineyard, who led the campaign. The new appellation would cover almost 4,000 acres of vineyards and more than 30 wineries.

Vintage Report

Advance report on the latest harvest

2002

Adversity builds character and, with a few exceptions, that was the story of 2002. Higher-than-normal temperatures and lower-than-normal moisture led to a spectacular vintage in most areas. According to Doug Welsch, who owns Fenn Valley Vineyards in southwest Michigan, "All we had to do after picking was add yeast and stand back." Warm weather in April caused an early bud-break throughout much of the northeast, leaving flowers vulnerable to a late frost in May. This was devastating for some growers, but just a natural crop-thinner for others. Powdery mildew caught the Finger Lakes by surprise and slashed Chardonnay production. Fox Run dropped 80 percent of its fruit on the ground. But disease and pests were mostly rare. The ladybug problem that plagued Ohio, Michigan, and neighboring states in 2001 made no encore. On the Atlantic seaboard, vineyard manager Joetta Kirk of Sakonnet in Rhode Island had a roller-coaster ride, but her Gewurztraminer showed well. An early cold snap in November enabled many wineries throughout the region to make icewines. In general, yields were down a little, but flavors were described as rich and intense for whites, concentrated with balanced acids for reds. There was much excitement over Pinot Noir. In general terms, only 2001 has produced better whites, and the reds are a match to that exceptional vintage.

Updates on the previous five vintages

2001

Vintage rating: *93 (Red: 92, White: 94)*

Except for New Jersey, which was deluged with rain at harvest, this was a thrilling vintage for the quality of both reds and whites. Rieslings had high acids, and Pinot Noirs showed spicy, upfront fruit. The only blot on 2001's copybook was the invasion of Asian ladybugs, which tainted some wines in Ohio.

2000

Vintage rating: *78 (Red: 72, White: 84)*

Except for New York, this was a difficult vintage for most states, with cool weather, rains, and hurricanes. Jim Law of Linden Vineyards in Virginia described it as "awful." Chardonnay and Riesling showed the best; reds were underripe and diluted.

1999

Vintage rating: *90 (Red: 92, White: 88)*

Except for Connecticut, which was soaked by late rains, most states had a long, hot, dry season that led to exceptionally ripe, highly concentrated Cabernet Franc, Pinot Noir, and Merlot. Whites lacked some of their typical crispness and aging ability.

1998

Vintage rating: *91 (Red: 95, White: 88)*

This El Niño vintage brought the northeast springlike weather in February, which led to a long, hot season that produced wines with exceptional ripeness and unusual tropical notes. It was something new for most wineries, which went on to produce some pretty atypical wines: reds that were lush and concentrated, whites that were fuller, richer, and had less acidity. Rieslings lacked their usual racy acidity.

1997

Vintage rating: *81 (Red: 78, White: 84)*

The winter was hard, and the summer uniformly cool and wet across the northeast, leaving winemakers thinking they were doomed. But in October there was an Indian summer, which ripened the Rieslings and Chardonnays, leaving many observers calling it the "miracle vintage." Reds, though, were a washout.

GREATEST WINE PRODUCERS

1. Wölffer Estate (New York)
2. Lenz Winery (New York)
3. Pellegrini Vineyards (New York)
4. Dr. Konstantin Frank's Vinifera Wine Cellars (New York)
5. Red Newt Cellars (New York)
6. Barboursville Vineyards (Virginia)
7. Bedell Cellars (New York)
8. L. Mawby Vineyards (Michigan)
9. Markko Vineyard (Ohio)
10. Sharpe Hill Vineyard (Connecticut)

FASTEST-IMPROVING PRODUCERS

1. Chateau LaFayette Reneau (New York)
2. St. Julian Winery (Michigan)
3. Oliver Winery (Indiana)
4. Clover Hill Vineyards & Winery (Pennsylvania)
5. Lakewood Vineyards (New York)
6. Huber Winery (Indiana)
7. Oakencroft Vineyard & Winery (Virginia)
8. Alba Vineyard (New Jersey)
9. Heron Hill Winery (New York)
10. Pindar Vineyards (Pennsylvania)

NEW UP-AND-COMING PRODUCERS

1. Standing Stone Vineyards (New York)
2. Breaux Vineyards (Virginia)
3. Chrysalis Vineyards (Virginia)
4. Anthony Road Wine Company (New York)
5. Winery at Black Star Farms (Michigan)
6. Bel Lago Vineyard and Winery (Michigan)
7. Blenheim Vineyards (Virginia)
8. Troutman Vineyards (Ohio)
9. Martha Clara Vineyards (New York)
10. Bellview Winery (New Jersey)

BEST-VALUE PRODUCERS

1. Lamoreaux Landing Wine Cellars (New York)
2. Peninsula Cellars (Michigan)
3. Sakonnet Vineyards & Winery (Rhode Island)
4. Boordy Vineyards (Maryland)
5. Fox Run Vineyards (New York)
6. King Ferry Winery/Treleaven Wines (New York)
7. Horton Vineyards (Virginia)
8. Shade Mountain Vineyards (Pennsylvania)
9. Good Harbor Vineyards (Michigan)
10. Bellview Winery (New Jersey)

GREATEST-QUALITY WINES

1. **Premier Cru Merlot 2000** Wölffer Estate, New York ($100)
2. **Old Vines Merlot 1997** Lenz Winery, New York ($55)
3. **Vintner's Pride Encore 1998** Pellegrini Vineyards, New York ($28.99)
4. **Johannisberg Riesling Reserve 2001** Dr. Konstantin Frank Vinifera Wine Cellars, New York ($24.95)
5. **Gewurztraminer Reserve 2001** Red Newt Cellars, New York ($24.50)
6. **Cupola 1999** Bedell Cellars, New York ($27.50)
7. **Brut 1998** Bel Lago Vineyard & Winery, Michigan ($18.99)
8. **A Capella Riesling Ice Wine 2000** Winery at Black Star Farms, Michigan ($79.50)
9. **Octagon Virginia Red Table Wine 1999** Barboursville Vineyards, Virginia ($30)
10. **Vidal Ice 2001** [sic] Standing Stone Vineyards, New York ($22.99)

BEST BARGAINS

1. **Chardonnay 2000** Fox Run Vineyards, New York ($9.99)
2. **Chardonnay 2001** Raftshol Vineyards, Michigan ($7)
3. **Semi-Dry Riesling 2001** King Ferry/Treleaven, New York ($10.49)
4. **Dry Riesling 2001** Lakewood Vineyards, New York ($10.99)
5. **White Label Chardonnay 2001** Lenz Winery, New York ($11)
6. **Chardonnay Vineyard Reserve 2000** Sharpe Hill Vineyard, Connecticut ($15.99)
7. **Edelzwicker 2001** Chateau Grand Traverse, Michigan ($9.99)
8. **Pinot Gris 2001** Chalet Debonné, Ohio ($10.99)
9. **Salmon Run Pinot Noir 2001** Dr. Konstantin Frank's Vinifera Wine Cellars, New York ($12.95)
10. **Pinot Grigio 2002** Mount Nittany, Pennsylvania ($12.99)

MOST EXCITING OR UNUSUAL FINDS

1. **Mille 1997** L. Mawby Vineyards, Michigan ($30) *A new release of Larry Mawby's top-of-the-line vintage sparkler. Nicely knitted flavors flaunt a bright, creamy core supported by ripe acidity.*
2. **Sparkling Viognier NV** Horton Vineyards, Virginia ($25) *Dennis Horton planted the first Viognier in Virginia in 1990, and look where he has taken it now.*
3. **Heritage 1999** Huber Winery, Indiana ($39.95) *This dry red blend of Chambourcin, Cabernet Sauvignon, and Cabernet Franc shows how well a hybrid can marry with vinifera.*
4. **Nebbiolo Reserve 1999** Barboursville Vineyards, Virginia ($34) *Even in Virginia, if you are owned by Zonin, you find out if you can grow classic Italian varieties, and do it if you can!*
5. **Cuvée RJR, Brut NV** Westport Rivers Winery, Southeastern New England ($19.95) *This bubbly can stand on a world stage.*
6. **Tarula Vineyard Syrah 2001** Valley Vineyards Estate, Ohio ($22) *This is the first commercial release of Syrah from the state of Ohio.*
7. **Fumé Vidal 2000** Sakonnet Vineyards & Winery, Southeastern New England ($10.95) *Vidal does not have to be sweet. This wine is 100 percent barrel-fermented in new and used French and American oak.*
8. **Braganini Riesling Reserve 2001** St. Julian Winery, Michigan ($15) *Bravo to St. Julian Winery's first reserve.*
9. **Gewurztraminer 2001** Lamoreaux Landing Wine Cellars, New York ($12.99) *This wine proves how expressive Gewurztraminer can be in western New York.*
10. **Dry Riesling 2001** Alba Vineyard, New Jersey ($12.99) *This is a strong player for a winery better known for reds.*

Other US States

Doug Frost MW

A landmark was reached in 2002, when every state in the USA held a winery within its borders.

DOUG FROST MW

The last, recalcitrant state, North Dakota, saw the opening of Pointe of View Winery, which will rely upon fruits such as apples, chokecherries, and rhubarb for its wines. But fruit wineries are the exception. There are nearly 400 wineries within the 30 states covered by this report, and most of the wines made are from grapes. Some of them are genuinely excellent. For the majority of these wineries, it is the front-door traffic that will provide all but a small fraction of their revenue. A successful winery such as Kansas's HolyField Winery can see as much as 95 percent of its sales from visitors. The national retail chains are little interested in the pioneering work required to promote wines from unknown US areas, but this parochial attitude conceals an advantage for wineries outside the well-known, coastal vineyard regions. Regional pride, local media, and plain old curiosity offer small wineries opportunities unavailable to large-scale wine areas. Texans consume virtually all of Texas's great output of over a million gallons a year. Approximately 1.5 million people visited the wineries of Missouri in 2002, many of them stopping to shop. The regional wine business, fueled by wine tourism, is growing, and the US is not wanting for entrepreneurs willing to take a chance to create a new winery. The winery lifestyle, if for no other reason, attracts many new investors.

DOUG FROST MW is the author of two wine books, including *On Wine* (Rizzoli International Publications, 2001). He is one of only three people in the world to hold the titles of both Master Sommelier and Master of Wine.

State governments coming round

The road to creating a winery in some of these states is very bumpy. There are continued hostilities toward the alcohol industry in some states, such as Utah and Ohio, while in numerous other states, such as Kansas and Tennessee, state authorities provide no support for local wineries. It is illegal for a Minnesota winery to list its wines and prices on the Web, and of the nearly 30 Texas wineries bonded between 1975 and 1989, 60 percent of them no longer exist. However, most of even these states are beginning to make things easier for what is, after all, a growing and substantial source of tax revenue. Only in Utah has there been a recent winery closure and talk of more. Minnesota's legislature has just teamed up with the Wineries Association to open a new research facility to fuel success of viticulture in its extremely marginal climate. A new South Dakota law gives residents access to purchase wines that have been unavailable through normal retail channels, and laws are loosening in other states, too. For nearly every state covered by this report, the work has only just begun, while in a few the movement away from the traditional hybrid grapes and toward classic vinifera varieties has been ongoing for at least a decade. In Texas, the reliance on the tried-and-tested grapes of more moderate American climes (Chardonnay, Cabernet Sauvignon, and Merlot, for example) has begun to give way to varieties that many in the state believe to be better suited to local conditions, thus plantings of Syrah, Tempranillo, and Sangiovese are increasing.

Grapevine

• **There will be a flood of new AVAs** over the next several years. The system favors sparsely populated areas, where it is easier to secure a majority approval from a few rural growers than among many in a more populous area. New AVAs will soon be found in many states, including Colorado, Texas, New Mexico, and perhaps even Idaho. Davis Mountain AVA in Texas and Yadkin Valley AVA in North Carolina are just two examples. At 1.4 million acres, Yadkin Valley hardly suggests a selective sense of soil or climate, but that remains typical of most of America's new AVAs.

• **A new grape,** Valiant, is catching on but has yet to prove itself. Developed from a wild grapevine found in Montana crossed with another native variety, Fredonia, it is a winter-hardy grape that is grown in New York state. As critical as winter-hardiness is in northern-plains states, this and similar grapes (Beta, Bluebell, Elvira, Swenson) have yet to yield even moderate-quality wine.

• **The Asian ladybug** is a seemingly benign, even cute, insect that has concentrated in the Niagara Peninsula and Pennsylvania, but there are also infestations in Ohio and Minnesota, making wine growers from Illinois to Missouri and Georgia nervously check their clusters each summer for signs. If the bug infests a vineyard, there is no easy answer, and the smell and taste of rancid peanut butter that these darling bugs impart is not an ideal organoleptic characteristic of any wine. Pheromone research continues.

Opinion:
Seduced by the wrong varieties

The lure of the siren vinifera wine continues. The best wines in Idaho, Wisconsin, Colorado, Texas, North Carolina, and Georgia are made from vinifera vines. States such as Texas, which formerly succeeded with hybrid vines, have abandoned them for vinifera such as Merlot, Chardonnay, and Viognier. However, other states that might be better advised to stay with hybrids cannot resist the song either. Despite all the good work that is being done, lack of imagination in varietal selection will continue to dog the best efforts of most of the wineries of these regions. Chardonnay and Cabernet Sauvignon should give way to grapes many describe as hot-climate grapes. Market forces are turning the growers' attention to Syrah in many states, yet the Syrah's performance is lackluster in unrelieved hot climates. Grenache is far more forgiving, as are other lesser-known Rhône, Italian, and Spanish varieties. Growers in states bearing more marginal climates for viticulture should think very carefully before jumping from hybrids to vinifera—not to have second thoughts, but to be sure their choice of which vinifera varieties to plant is the most appropriate one. And for those growers who realistically should not gamble beyond hybrids, at least not at the current level of technology, it is up to the wine writers, stewards, and retailers to be more responsible about hybrids. These people are the gatekeepers of the industry, but there is a snooty element that offers resistance to hybrid-labeled wines. Most American consumers do not know Chardonel (Chardonnay x Seyval) from Chardonnay, but they could be encouraged to try the former.

Purchased grapes

Too many wineries are dependent upon grapes purchased from the West Coast. Indeed, the Alcohol and Tobacco Tax and Trade Bureau (TTB; formerly ATF) has fined some wineries for blending California juice into their wines without proper disclosure. One pioneering Missouri winemaker was forced to sell his stake in his own winery after being caught blending non-Missouri wines into his Missouri-labeled wines. The temptation is still too great for many to avoid, and new wineries are particularly susceptible to this sign of terminal insecurity. New wineries often have no other source of juice when their own vines are too young to bear fruit, yet their bankers expect them to generate revenues. And California's ever-cheaper gallons of unsold wine will provide an ever-more-tempting solution to wineries in the middle states looking for quality wines from their young and poorly sited vineyards.

Vintage Report

Selected highlights only. Vintage ratings would not be meaningful for such a vast and diverse area

2002

Idaho had another warm and sunny year, its harvest having finished before the first week of October was over. The reds are a bit high in alcohol, but the whites show nearly ideal balance. Ripening was as uniform as the previous three vintages. Missouri's white grapes were all very clean coming in, but the aromatics are not as intense as in 2000, with the exception of some pretty Chardonels. The reds are intense and concentrated. For New Mexico, this was yet another drought year. The wines will likely show good concentration as a result. Georgia was a victim of the same excessive rains that hit the rest of the Atlantic coast, including the Carolinas, but some parts of Georgia were actually short of moisture. All vineyards were cooler than normal, and the wines are a mixed bag, particularly the reds, although whites generally have good aromas. Texas saw cooler temperatures and more rain than normal.

2001

Good quality in Idaho, where the white wines are even crisper than usual and the reds show nice balance and length. Some lovely white wines were made in this vintage in Missouri, although the Vignoles was difficult. The reds are a bit stingy, but some Nortons are delightful. This was year four of the drought, and forest fires raged throughout much of the state.

2000

Idaho wines are ripe with very good acidity and offer better longevity than the 2001s or the 1999s. Missouri's wines are as balanced as any in the last four years, with some Nortons the best ever, and it was another good year in New Mexico.

1999

A fairly small harvest in Idaho, but the wines show elegance and are really supple and rich. Missouri experienced a challenging year, yet the wines have solid fruit and structure. It was a very good vintage for many in New Mexico, the second drought year in a row.

1998

Idaho's wines have pronounced acidity, but alcohols are a bit high for some. Rainstorms hammered many Missouri wineries, yet some of the reds are pretty, even charming, although they are the exceptions. A good year for some in New Mexico, but too short and hot for some wines, which lack balance.

1997

Idaho is a bit uneven, even though the harvest suggested otherwise. Flavors have not developed as well as initially hoped. Missouri's harvest was uneven, and its wines will not last much longer.

GREATEST WINE PRODUCERS

1. Stone Hill Winery (Missouri)
2. Vickers Vineyards (Idaho)
3. Gruet (New Mexico)
4. Tiger Mountain Vineyards (Georgia)
5. Flat Creek Vineyards (Texas)
6. Becker Family Vineyards (Texas)
7. St James Winery (Missouri)
8. Creekstone Vineyards (from Habersham Winery) (Georgia)
9. Callaghan Vineyards (Arizona)
10. Cap★Rock Winery (Texas)

FASTEST-IMPROVING PRODUCERS

1. Callaghan Vineyards (Arizona)
2. Mountain Spirit Winery (Colorado)
3. HolyField (Kansas)
4. Becker Family Vineyards (Texas)
5. Messina Hof (Texas)
6. St James Winery (Missouri)
7. Cap★Rock Winery (Texas)
8. Alamosa Wine Cellars (Texas)
9. Wollersheim (Wisconsin)
10. Cottonwood Canyon (Colorado)

NEW UP-AND-COMING PRODUCERS

1. HolyField (Kansas)
2. Tiger Mountain Vineyards (Georgia)
3. Flat Creek Vineyards (Texas)
4. Adam Puchta (Missouri)
5. La Dolce Vita (Missouri)
6. Mountain Spirit Winery (Colorado)

7. Dry Comal Creek (Texas)
8. Plum Creek (Colorado)
9. Pend d'Oreille (Idaho)
10. Sawtooth Winery (Idaho)

BEST-VALUE PRODUCERS

1. HolyField (Kansas)
2. Adam Puchta (Missouri)
3. Cedar Creek (Wisconsin)
4. Arthur Vineyards (Nebraska)
5. Stone Bluff (Oklahoma)
6. Cuthills Cellars (Nebraska)
7. Alexis Bailly (Minnesota)
8. Hermannhof (Missouri)
9. Dry Comal Creek (Texas)
10. Wollersheim (Wisconsin)

GREATEST-QUALITY WINES

1. **Norton 2000** Stone Hill Winery, Missouri ($18)
2. **Chardonnay 2000** Vickers Vineyards, Idaho ($15)
3. **Blanc de Blanc Sparkling Wine 1999** Gruet, New Mexico ($22)
4. **Touriga Nacional 1999** Tiger Mountain Vineyards, Georgia ($25)
5. **Travis Peak Select Moscato d'Arancio 2002** Flat Creek, Texas ($13 per 50 cl)
6. **Late Harvest Vignoles 2001** St James, Missouri ($17)
7. **Late Harvest Vignoles 2001** HolyField, Kansas ($13 per half-bottle)

❽ **Norton Port 2000** Stone Hill Winery, Missouri ($20 per 50 cl)
❾ **Creekstone Viognier 2001** Blackstone Vineyards, Georgia ($20)
❿ **El Guapo 2000** Alamosa Wine Cellars, Texas ($18)

BEST BARGAINS

❶ **Seyval Blanc 2001** HolyField, Kansas ($10)
❷ **Cream Sherry** Stone Hill Winery, Missouri ($15)
❸ **Chateau Deux Fleuves Chardonnay 2000** Two Rivers, Colorado ($13)
❹ **Prairie Blush 2002** Wollersheim, Wisconsin ($7.50)
❺ **Vignoles 2001** Hermannhof, Missouri ($14)
❻ **Augusta Cynthiana 2001** Missouri ($15)
❼ **Maréchal Foch Reserve 2000** Tabor Home, Iowa ($13)
❽ **Traminette 2002** Cuthills Cellars George Spencer, Nebraska ($10)
❾ **Chardonel 2001** Alto Vineyards, Illinois ($12)
❿ **Riesling 2002** Shelton, North Carolina ($9)

MOST EXCITING OR UNUSUAL FINDS

❶ **Gewurztraminer 2001** Carlson, Colorado ($10) *If the high elevations of western Colorado can produce such a nicely balanced and perfumed version of this grape, then there is fascinating potential in many places in the western US.*
❷ **Viognier 2001** Alamosa Wine Cellars, Texas ($16) *The delightful aromatics of the Viognier grape are in no way muted by the challenges of Texas wine growing. The wine is short but promising.*
❸ **Pinot Grigio 2001** Cedar Creek, Wisconsin ($11) *A pity this is not a Wisconsin-grown wine, but the trip from the Pacific Northwest did not do the grapes a great deal of harm. Clean, bright, green and red apple notes throughout.*
❹ **Norton 1999** St James Winery, Missouri ($14) *A slightly meatier version of Norton, but with the same chocolate and blueberry flavours that the best wines from this variety exhibit.*
❺ **Mountain Spirit Winery Duet 2000** Colorado ($18) *This is 80 percent Viognier and 20 percent Chardonnay, with intriguing elements in the nose, mouth, and finish, which might go unspoken in California, but it is truly symbiotic.*
❻ **Chardonel 2001** Les Bourgeois, Missouri ($19) *The best Chardonel to date from the middle US, this is crisp and clean, like apple slices, but with soft peach and citrus elements in the finish.*
❼ **French Colombard 2002** Dry Comal Creek, Texas ($15) *As nice a version of this often-bland grape as anything America has produced since the Carmenet French Colombards of the 1990s.*
❽ **Padres 2001** Callaghan Vineyards, Arizona ($35) *A 70 percent Tempranillo and 30 percent Petite Sirah. More integrated and seamless than these two disparate grapes might suggest. Rich and balanced.*
❾ **Tannat 1999** Tiger Mountain Vineyards, Georgia ($23) *The tough character of this grape as seen in southwestern France is nowhere in sight. Instead it is fruity, herbal-tinged, and well structured.*
❿ **Riesling 2002** Shelton, North Carolina ($9) *This Riesling is never going to compare favorably against the best of Finger Lakes' Riesling, but it is soft and only barely sweet.*

Canada

Tony Aspler

The late summer and autumn of 2001 saw an unusual phenomenon – an infestation of Asian ladybugs across northeastern North America.

TONY ASPLER

As a defense mechanism, these insects secrete an orange fluid containing various methoxypyrazines, which smell like old peanut shells. The pests took residence in the vineyards and either sprayed the bunches as the harvesters approached or were crushed with the berries. As a result, this aroma was detectable in about 20 percent of wines from Ontario's 2001 vintage. In lighter concentrations, the aroma is grassy and green-pepper-like, similar to Sauvignon Blanc or Cabernet Franc; but at higher levels it can mask the characteristics of other varietals. In 2002, the Ontario wine industry withheld 1 million liters of 2001-vintage red and white wine (out of a total production of 40 million liters) found to have the aroma.

TONY ASPLER is the most widely read wine writer in Canada. He was the wine columnist for *The Toronto Star* for 21 years and has authored 11 books on wine and food, including *Vintage Canada*, *The Wine Lover's Companion*, *The Wine Lover Cooks*, and *Travels with My Corkscrew*. Tony's latest book is *Canadian Wine for Dummies*. Tony is a member of the North American advisory board for the Masters of Wine, creator of the annual Ontario Wine Awards competition, and a director of the Independent Wine & Spirit Trust. He is also a director of The Canadian Wine Library and serves on the wine selection committee for Air Canada. At the Niagara Grape & Wine Festival 2000, Tony was presented with the Royal Bank Business Citizen of the Year award. Tony also writes fiction, including a collection of wine murder mysteries featuring the itinerant wine writer-cum-detective Ezra Brant: *Blood Is Thicker than Beaujolais*, *The Beast of Barbaresco*, and *Death on the Douro*. He is currently working on *Nightmare in Napa Valley*. Tony Aspler's website can be found at www.tonyaspler.com

British Columbia sells out

The 2002 season saw a significant increase in the number of wine tourists, particularly in the far southern part of the Okanagan Valley, where a number of smaller wineries sold out of current releases for the first time. Previously, the tide of Canadian and international visitors arriving from the coast and prairie provinces filled the Okanagan as far south as Okanagan Falls. With the increased prominence of the award-winning wines being grown in the southern Okanagan, and an agglomeration of destination wineries, a much larger number of visitors continued south of Penticton to experience this unique desert growing area, effectively opening up the entire Okanagan wine region.

Vincor expands

Canada's largest winery, Vincor International, got bigger in 2002, when the company acquired Goundrey Wines in Western Australia for C$53.7 million. This purchase is part of an aggressive strategy by Vincor's president and CEO Donald Triggs to create a billion-dollar company within five years. Vincor is already closing in on the $500-million mark, owning RH Phillips in California and Hogue Cellars in Washington state, while its Canadian subsidiaries include Inniskillin Wines in Ontario, Sumac Ridge and Hawthorne Mountain in British Columbia, as well as its own Jackson-Triggs label, making it the fourth-largest wine group in North America.

Grapevine

- **At least five** of the 100-plus wineries in Ontario are rumored to be up for sale, including the icewine specialist Royal de Maria.

- **The Mission Hill Family Estate** winery in the Okanagan Valley was refurbished in 2002. Proprietor Anthony von Mandl spent C$35 million redesigning the property and purchasing more vineyards. The results are so spectacular that it rates as one of the 10 most beautiful wineries in the world.

- **Le Clos Jordan winery** in Ontario, a joint venture between Vincor and Boisset, was unveiled in the summer of 2002. It was designed by the renowned Canadian architect Frank Gehry, who created the Guggenheim Museum in Bilbao and the Rock 'n' Roll Museum in Seattle, and remodeled Marques de Riscal in Rioja. The dramatic roof looks like a low cloud or a lemon meringue pie. It is expected to be completed in 2005.

- **Canada** will soon have a new QVA wine region, Prince Edward County, located between Toronto and Kingston, in eastern Ontario. Almost entirely surrounded by water at the eastern end of Lake Ontario, Prince Edward County has some 400 acres of vines, the oldest planted just eight years ago, and three wineries: Waupoos Estate (the only estate winery, so far), The County Cider Company, and Peddelston Wines, with two more to open in 2003 (Chadsey's Cairn and Robert Thomas Estate).

FIRST NATIVE CANADIAN WINERY

On September 13, 2003, in British Columbia, the sound of drums heralded Chief Clarence Louis of the Osoyoos Indian Band as he cut a ceremonial rope of green sage to open Nk'Mip, North America's first aboriginal-owned and operated winery. Green sage is a sacred plant used in cleansing ceremonies. Nk'Mip comes from the local Salish dialect and means "place where the creek joins the lake." The winery, with its 20-acre vineyard, is dramatically set in Canada's only desert region. The Santa Fe-style building perches on an arid bench with rattlesnake-infested granite hills as a backdrop, overlooking Lake Osoyoos close to the Washington state border. The Osoyoos Indians entered into a C$7-million joint venture with Canada's largest wine company, Vincor International, to produce four varietal wines—Pinot Blanc, Chardonnay, Pinot Noir, and Merlot, priced between C$13.95 and C$16.95 a bottle. The first vintage was in 2000, and the wines are made by Randy Picton, who spent six years as associate winemaker at British Columbia's CedarCreek Estate.

CHINESE RIP-OFFS

On a recent trip to China for the opening of the wine and spirit fair in Guangzhou, five Ontario wineries presented their Riesling and Vidal icewines to a rapturous reception. Less than 30 ft (10 m) from the booth where the Ontario wineries were presenting their products was a stand under the banner Chez Lee Estate Wine Company, manned by local Chinese pouring an icewine in the familiar elongated half-bottle with a stylized red logo incorporating a maple leaf and a Canada goose! The package looked exactly like an icewine you might find on any liquor-board shelf, except that the label illustration depicted a vineyard with a pagoda in the middle of it. The wine was horrible, a sweet concoction of labrusca juice and alcohol, bearing no resemblance to any icewine I have tasted. The product, as far as I could learn, had been imported from Canada. In the stores around Guangzhou, a modern and prosperous city of almost 7 million people, I spotted other examples of ersatz icewine on display. The local agent for Vineland Estates recounts the story of seeing a bottle of icewine in a Guangzhou department store. He asked the clerk what it was. "That's Canadian icewine," he was told. "In Canada, it's very cold. They have winter all the year except for two weeks in summer when it's warm enough for the grapes to thaw so they can pick them for icewine. It's the only wine they make."

CANADIAN OAK

An enterprising firm called Canadian Oak Cooperage, started by a wine-loving doctor and a professor of biology and geology, is selling barrels made from Canadian oak. The wood is the same species as American white oak, but according to the company, "Our oaks have twice as many growth lines per inch as the American oaks used in commercial wine-barrel production." The first Ontario wineries to use Canadian oak in the 2002 vintage were Featherstone, Daniel Lenko, Malivoire, Thirty Bench, Marynissen, and Lailey.

Opinion:
Get real

In Ontario and British Columbia, as well as the rest of Canada, there is an urgent need to finalize national wine standards that will demarcate wines produced in Canada from wines that are imported from other countries and merely cellared or bottled in this country. Wines labeled "Product of Canada" but grown elsewhere continue to be a vexing and confusing problem for restaurant patrons and wine buyers, as well as distracting from and denigrating the unique character of the true domestic wines.

Official yield

With too much dilute wine around, now is the time for the VQA (Vintners Quality Alliance) to set limits on how much wine can be made per vine plant.

Ban Chablis

The usage of terms such as "Chablis" on labels of Canadian wine should cease. If Canadian vintners want to protect the term "icewine," they should respect the appellations of other regions.

Grapevine

• **No Canadian winery** has yet had the nerve to use screw caps for wines other than plonk, although Venturi Schultze, the maverick winery on Vancouver Island, has been closing all of its fine wines, including sparkling, for several years now with crown caps.

• **Blasted Church** is the name of a born-again British Columbia winery that used to be called Prpich Hills [sic]. The new venture takes its name from an incident that occurred in 1929, when the church in Okanagan Falls was bombed.

• **Nova Scotia** is about to get a new winery that will specialize in sparkling-wine production. Benjamin Bridge (named after the site of an old bridge) will be a gravity-flow facility in the Gaspereau Valley. Raphael Brisbois is consulting. Currently there are four operating wineries in Nova Scotia.

• **Sue-Ann Staff,** Pillitteri Estate's winemaker, was the first woman to win the annual Winemaker of the Year Award at the Ontario Wine Awards competition. She trained at Roseworthy in Australia.

Vintage Report

Advance report on the latest harvest

2002

Ontario—The dry, hot weather during spring and summer meant that yields were slightly down from predicted levels, but the quality and concentration of fruit in the grapes harvested was excellent. Winemakers are predicting that 2002 will be one of the best vintages on record, particularly for red wines.

British Columbia—A cool spring was contradicted by an unexpectedly early bud-break and blossom period, and this favorable early start was followed by an almost seamless summer and autumn with abundant warm temperatures and endless sunshine. It is now likely that 2002 will go on record as being the best vintage yet, surpassing 1998 by having more moderate heat for further flavor development and allowing white wines to retain natural acid balance.

Updates on the previous five vintages

2001

Vintage rating: *Ontario 87 (Red: 88, White: 85), British Columbia 92 (Red: 89, White: 94)*

Ontario—The vintage was compromised by the presence of Asian ladybugs in the vineyards, affecting the flavor of some wines. Some Sauvignon Blanc was harvested almost two weeks earlier than usual. Rains in late September and October slowed down some of the midseason harvesting, which helped the reds.

British Columbia—A high-end vintage for most whites. Red wines also did well, with excellent fruit ripeness and a softer-than-average tannin structure in all but the latest-ripening varieties.

2000

Vintage rating: *Ontario 82 (Red: 80, White: 84), British Columbia 87 (Red: 85, White: 89)*

Ontario—One of the worst years since 1987, but those who gambled and left fruit on the vine were rewarded with a late burst of sunny weather in October. Chardonnay and Riesling performed surprisingly well under these conditions.

British Columbia—September began on the cool side but opened up into a warm, sunny, extended autumn, allowing crops to fully ripen with higher sugar levels than 1999.

1999

Vintage rating: *Ontario 85 (Red: 85, White: 84), British Columbia 88 (Red: 85, White: 90)*

Ontario—Later-ripening varieties, especially Bordeaux red varieties, enjoyed the heat of an Indian summer. Riesling was the only noble cultivar that did not do well in the heat.

British Columbia—A challenging vintage until a very warm September and October allowed all but the latest varieties to fully ripen. Rated very good by growers who downsized their crop of red varieties for the cooler growing season.

1998

Vintage rating: *Ontario 90 (Red: 93, White: 87), British Columbia 90 (Red: 93, White: 87)*

Ontario—One of the longest, warmest, and driest years on record. Long hang time allowed red Bordeaux varieties and Pinot Noir to ripen fully with record sugar levels. The fruit came in clean and unspoiled. Reds showed best; whites tended to lack balancing acidity.

British Columbia—The best and hottest growing year on record, resulting in the best red wines BC has ever produced, remarkable for intensity, ripeness, and heft. White varieties including Chardonnay, Sauvignon Blanc, and Riesling showed almost California-like characteristics, though the heat did decrease acid levels on earlier-ripening Germanic varieties such as Ehrenfelser.

1997

Vintage rating: *Ontario 84 (Red: 81, White: 86), British Columbia 78 (Red: 75, White: 80)*

Ontario—An Indian summer saved the harvest. Cabernet Franc ripened best in reds; in whites, Chardonnay and Riesling did well. The lack of sustained cold weather during December meant some wineries had to wait until March 1998 to harvest their 1997 icewines!

British Columbia—One of the coolest growing seasons recorded, with significant rainfall throughout. The rain stopped in September followed by a long, warm autumn that allowed the full crop to ripen to acceptable levels.

GREATEST WINE PRODUCERS

1. Blue Mountain Vineyards (British Columbia)
2. Henry of Pelham Family Estate (Ontario)
3. Mission Hill Family Estate (British Columbia)
4. Jackson-Triggs Vintners (British Columbia)
5. Sumac Ridge Estate Winery (British Columbia)
6. Cave Spring Cellars (Ontario)
7. Vineland Estates (Ontario)
8. CedarCreek Estate (British Columbia)
9. Inniskillin Wines (Ontario)
10. Château des Charmes (Ontario)

FASTEST-IMPROVING PRODUCERS

1. Daniel Lenko Estate Winery (Ontario)
2. Burrowing Owl Vineyards (British Columbia)
3. Hillside Estate Winery (British Columbia)
4. Thirty Bench Vineyard & Winery (Ontario)
5. Stag's Hollow Winery (British Columbia)
6. Thornhaven Estates (British Columbia)
7. Malivoire Wine Company (Ontario)
8. Peller Estates (Ontario)
9. Peninsula Ridge (Ontario)
10. Hainle Vineyards (British Columbia)

NEW UP-AND-COMING PRODUCERS

1. Lailey Vineyard (Ontario)
2. La Frenz Vineyards and Winery (British Columbia)
3. Pentage (British Columbia)
4. Township 7 Vineyards and Winery (British Columbia)
5. 13th Street Wine Company (Ontario)

6. Maleta Estate (Ontario)
7. Stratus (Ontario)
8. Tawse Family (Ontario)
9. Glenterra Vineyards (Vancouver Island)
10. Nk'Mip Cellars (British Columbia)

BEST-VALUE PRODUCERS

1. Colio Wines (Ontario)
2. Calona Vineyards (British Columbia)
3. Jackson-Triggs Vintners (Ontario)
4. Lakeview Cellars (Ontario)
5. Golden Mile Cellars (British Columbia)
6. Jackson-Triggs Vintners (British Columbia)
7. Mission Hill Family Estate (British Columbia)
8. Sumac Ridge Estate Winery (British Columbia)
9. Magnotta Winery (Ontario)
10. Hernder Estate Wines (Ontario)

GREATEST-QUALITY WINES

1. **Riesling Icewine 2001** Pillitteri Estates Winery, Ontario (C$29.95 per 200 ml)
2. **Shiraz 2000** Jackson-Triggs Okanagan Estate, British Columbia (C$16.99)
3. **Gamay Reserve 1999** Sandstone, Ontario (C$20)
4. **Pinot Noir Platinum Reserve 2000** CedarCreek Estate, British Columbia (C$34.99)
5. **Oculus 1999** Mission Hill Family Estate, British Columbia (C$34.95)
6. **White Meritage 2000** Sumac Ridge Estate Winery, British Columbia (C$19.95)
7. **Unfiltered Merlot 2001** Henry of Pelham Family Estate, Ontario (C$25)
8. **Meritage 1999** Vineland Estates, Ontario (C$125)

9 **Chardonnay American Oak 2000** Daniel Lenko Estate Winery, Ontario (C$19.95)

10 **Pinot Gris 2000** Hester Creek, British Columbia (C$13.90)

BEST BARGAINS

1 **White Meritage 2000** Sumac Ridge Estate Winery, British Columbia (C$19.95)

2 **Gewurztraminer 2000** Château des Charmes, Ontario (C$14.95)

3 **Chardonnay Montague Estate 2000** Inniskillin Wines, Ontario (C$16.95)

4 **Appellation Series Sauvignon Blanc 2001** Mission Hill Family Estate, British Columbia (C$11.95)

5 **Riesling 1994** Domaine Combret, British Columbia (C$14.95)

6 **Pinot Noir 1999** Golden Mile Cellars, British Columbia (C$12.50)

7 **Gewurztraminer 2001** Wild Goose, British Columbia (C$13.95)

8 **Cabernet Franc 1999** Hernder Estate Wines, Ontario (C$13.95)

9 **Dry Riesling** Vineland Estates, Ontario (C$9.95)

10 **Cabernet Merlot 2000** Colio Harrow Estates, Ontario (C$10.95)

MOST EXCITING OR UNUSUAL FINDS

1 **Osoyoos Larose 2001** British Columbia (C$50) *This is the first wine produced in an Okanagan Valley joint venture between Canada's Vincor and the Bordeaux Groupe Taillan, the name being a combination of the adjacent Osoyoos Lake (from the local native name) and Château Gruaud Larose.*

2 **Chardonnay 1999** Temkin-Paskus, Ontario (C$42) *Canada's rarest wine; only a few barrels are made every year. Steven Temkin is a wine writer, and Deborah Paskus the winemaker.*

3 **Red Meritage 2000** Inniskillin Dark Horse Vineyard, British Columbia (C$25.95) *The 23-acre Dark Horse Vineyard is located on the western slope of the valley, north of Osoyoos Lake, one of the warmest parts of Canada, with the country's lowest recorded rainfall.*

4 **Grand Reserve Cabernet Sauvignon Shiraz 2001** Jackson-Triggs Proprieters Okanagan Estate, British Columbia (C$19.95) *Cabernet Shiraz as a blend is rare in Canada and, despite the youthfulness of the Shiraz vines, this is a very good effort.*

5 **Chardonnay 2001** Niagara College, Ontario (C$14) *Made by oenology students under the tutelage of Jim Warren, Ontario's busiest consulting winemaker.*

6 **Rock Oven Red 2000** Kettle Valley, British Columbia (C$28) *The first vintage of a 50/50 Cabernet Sauvignon/Shiraz blend from, respectively, the winery's own vineyard and one they farm.*

7 **Sandhill Barbera 2000** Calona Vineyards, British Columbia (C$24.99) *Calona was the first winery in Canada to experiment with Italian varieties and to produce a Barbera.*

8 **Old Vines Foch 2000** Malivoire Wine Company, Ontario (C$22) *The hybrid Maréchal Foch is generally coarse and rough-edged, but winemaker Ann Sperling has made a sophisticated Rhône-style wine out of it.*

9 **Zweigelt 2001** Lailey Vineyard, Ontario (C$12) *Only a couple of Canadian wineries make a varietal from Zweigelt, an Austrian cross that is usually blended with Gamay in Canada, but English winemaker Derek Barnett has coaxed some subtle flavours out of this grape.*

10 **Baco Noir 2000** Birchwood Estate Wines, Ontario (C$8.95) *A decent drop of wine at a bargain price.*

Chile & Argentina

Christopher Fielden

After many years of comparatively lax wine laws, three measures have thrown the Chilean wine industry into turmoil.

CHRISTOPHER FIELDEN

These are the introduction of Denominaciones de Origen (DO) with the 2002 vintage, the signing of a wine protocol with the European Union, and the compilation of a vineyard register. Many brand names that are used on the Chilean domestic market, such as Corton (Viña Errazuriz) and Rhin and Margaux (Viña Carmen), will have to be abandoned, but the companies have been given a generous 12 years to carry this out. The use of such terms as *reserva* and *gran reserva* on labels is uncertain. One producer told me that the latter was no longer legal, while another denied this, although it is not widely used. The use of *reserva*, on the other hand, is widespread and has no legal meaning whatsoever. For some producers, it suggests that the wine has received some form of oak treatment, while for others it is just part of the name on the label. For Spanish wine producers, particularly, this is a very sore point.

For the vineyard register, growers were offered a choice: either they could declare what all their vineyards were planted with, or they could call in an assessor to carry out a detailed survey. Most of the smaller growers chose the DIY route, since they could not afford the cost of an assessor. The thorny question, of course, concerned Merlot and Sauvignon Blanc. Historically, many of the wines called Merlot have been made from the Carmenère grape and, indeed, many vineyards were planted with a mixture

CHRISTOPHER FIELDEN has been in the wine trade for more than 40 years, during which time he has visited over 100 different countries. On his first trip to South America, he arrived in French Guiana by dugout canoe; he has been fascinated by the continent ever since. He is the author of 10 books on wine, including *The Wines of Argentina, Chile and Latin America* (Faber & Faber, 2001).

of the two varieties. That the difference between the two went unrecognized for so long has always surprised me, given that Carmenère achieves optimum ripeness some three weeks after Merlot. Even if the vines have been correctly identified by a grower, what makes a mockery of the register is that if he has a mixed vineyard, it must be declared under the predominant variety. Thus, a vineyard planted with 60 percent Merlot and 40 percent Carmenère now becomes 100 percent Merlot, even if the individual vines were marked and harvested separately!

Even more troublesome is the problem of Sauvignon Blanc. As has been recognized for a long time, much of what is sold as Sauvignon Blanc has come from a different, and inferior, varietal: the Sauvignonasse. Although a small number of wines are now being sold honestly as Sauvignonasse (or Sauvignon Vert, its synonym), most so-called Sauvignon Blanc wines are, in fact, a blend of the two varieties. Since the growers have been allowed to declare their own vineyards, it is quite possible that Sauvignonasse vineyards will be classified as Sauvignon Blanc, giving growers the ability to sell their grapes under the latter name. However, quite naturally, the wine producers are not prepared to pay the higher Sauvignon Blanc price for what are quite obviously Sauvignonasse grapes. So, having paid the lower price for grapes sold as Sauvignon Blanc, what do they call the resultant wine? All the winemakers I have spoken to on this matter have been unable, or unwilling, to provide a satisfactory answer, but it does not take much imagination to guess what will happen.

Grapevine

• **The first wines** from the smallest and latest DO, San Antonio Valley (south of Valparaiso), have hit the shelf, from the Leyda and Matetic wineries.

• **At Traiguen** in the Malleco Valley, in the extreme south (viticulturally speaking: 38° latitude), 5 hectares (ha) have been planted in an area discovered by oenologist Felipe de Solminihac. The wines are being sold under the Soldesol label by the Aquitania winery, which is owned by Solminihac and his two partners, Paul Pontallier and Bruno Prats.

• **As part of a bid** to upgrade the image of wines from the Colchagua Valley, 25 miles (40 km) of railroad track will be restored. In a joint venture between the government, local growers, and the Carleón Foundation, steam trains will take tourists from Santiago to Pichilemu in the Colchagua Valley. The trains will be met by buses to take tourists around local wineries. At present, trains are running just between San Fernando, on the main line from Santiago, to Placilla, a distance of some 9 miles (15 km).

• **Almaviva,** the joint venture between Baron Philippe de Rothschild and Concha y Toro, has launched a second wine, called Epis, from the 2000 vintage. This wine is composed of lesser parcels of vines and is matured in second-use oak. The retail price will be US$15 per bottle, as opposed to US$65 for Almaviva. Epis will be available only at the winery.

WINES FROM CHILE RESURRECTED

For some years, Chile has suffered from having no national body to promote its wines. Originally, there were two organizations: Viñas de Chile, representing largely the more important producers, and Chilevid, representing the smaller companies. After many years of bickering between the two bodies, they both collapsed and, with no central office, generic marketing ground to a halt. Now the two organizations have amalgamated under the umbrella of Wines of Chile, and Ricardo Letelier has been recruited from Coca-Cola Chile to be its first national director. Unfortunately, this organization receives no financial support from the national government and relies totally on the industry for its funding. Great Britain has been recognized as the export market with the greatest potential, and a Wines of Chile office has been opened under the direction of Michael Cox, who until recently had been responsible for the sales and marketing of Yalumba Wines from Australia.

CHILE: RED-GRAPE PRICES COLLAPSE

Chilean growers are complaining about the fall in prices paid for red grapes in the 2003 vintage. This is particularly true for Cabernet Sauvignon where, according to leading broker Alberto Siegel, basic wine is on sale at just US$0.30 per liter. This is half of what it was two years ago and most probably less than the cost of production.

According to one long-established grower I spoke to, the maximum price he is being paid for his grapes by Valdivieso, whom he has supplied for many years, is CLP 65 per kilo as opposed to CLP 140 the previous harvest. On the other hand, the shippers say that they are often buying grapes they do not need just to keep the growers in business. One beneficial side effect is that the ubiquitous one-liter Tetra Pak on the domestic market is now likely to be full of Cabernet Sauvignon rather than the traditional País.

CHILE: HIGHEST-PRICED WINES

Seemingly encouraged by wineries with either Californian or French investors, the concept of super-premium "icon" wines selling for ever-higher prices appears to have caught on in Chile. Just four years ago, there were 17 Chilean wines that retailed on the domestic market for CLP 12,000 (then equivalent to US$25) or more; now there are 18 that sell for CLP 25,000-plus (now US$35). Similarly, four years ago there were no white wines that sold for as much as CLP 12,000; now there are six that sell for more than that. One consequence, reminiscent of Bordeaux in the early 1970s, is that there seems to be competition between a small number of producers to sell Chile's most expensive wine, regardless of quality. According to Patricio Tapia's guide *Descorchados 2003*, the current leader appears to be Viñedo Chadwick 2000 at CLP 54,900 (US$77).

Opinion:
Wine tourism the way forward

With the collapse of the Argentine peso, many doomsayers forecast the downfall of the country's wine industry, but the companies that sought to concentrate on exports have survived surprisingly unscathed. It has not been easy, with the government deducting its percentage from any money earned abroad, and the initially negative impact of devaluation leading to a certain reluctance by some buyers to trust Argentine suppliers because they were unable to supply goods on time and in the appropriate way. Those wineries that focused on the domestic market lost out in two ways. First, by the devaluation itself; and second, by the fact that such producers were traditionally purveyors of oxidative, old-style wines, and the market was already moving on as the pesos sank. Argentinians now want fresher, more fruit-driven wines—precisely the style that exporters rely on. One unexpected benefit of Argentina's financial difficulties is a significant increase in tourism, particularly wine tourism. Bodega Norton has recently opened a tourist center at its Perdriel winery and is happily surprised by the number of foreign visitors it receives. Other *bodegas* should take note.

Grapevine

• **Miguel Torres Chile** has purchased a 500-ha estate called Matanzas, near Constitución, at the mouth of the Maule River, where the slatey soils and steep hillsides give the potential for producing super-premium reds, hopefully in the style of Priorato.

• **At a ceremony** at the Veramonte winery in March 2003, the Casablanca Valley was formally twinned with the Napa Valley. Local producer Thierry Villard said, "This is just another move in our campaign to get the consumer to recognize the difference between the regions of Chile, and that it is in the Casablanca that the finest white wines are made."

• **Stelvin screws** its way into the Chilean wine market with Concha y Toro subsidiary Cono Sur using it for Riesling 2002 from the Bío-Bío Valley. But Cono Sur's winemaker Adolfo Hurtado has reservations about offering red wines and fuller-bodied whites with a screw cap. Concha y Toro will follow suit shortly with some of its wines in the Trío range.

• **Concha y Toro** is the most important imported wine brand in the US, selling more than 2 million cases a year, more than doubling in just eight years.

• **In the north of the country,** in the Limarí Valley, the pioneering Francisco Aguirre has been joined by a second winery, Casa Tamaya.

• **Following on from the success** of the Colchagua wine route, established three years ago, a similar venture has been launched in the Curicó Valley. Among the wineries behind the venture are Valdivieso, Torres, Viña San Pedro, and Arestí.

Vintage Report

Advance report on the latest harvest

Updates on the previous five vintages

2003

Chile—There is cautious optimism as to the quality. The summer has been cold, but there have been excellent ripening conditions and the grapes are very healthy. The white grapes have been brought in without any rainfall problems. Growers such as Aurelio Montes report excellent fruit flavors. The overall quantity is likely to be less than average. At the end of the harvest, Thierry Villard, with an estate in the Casablanca Valley, describes it as the best vintage he has ever known, although the crop is 20–30 percent down on a normal year.

Argentina—This has turned out to be a very different vintage from expectations. El Niño was expected to bring a damp summer; on the contrary, it was dry and warm with very healthy vines. According to Michael Halstrick of Bodega Norton, this promises to be really exciting for both red and white wines. Flavors should be concentrated as a result of cool nights and warm days in the ripening season. Quantities will be limited as a result of regional frost and hail damage; the quality is perceived to be excellent.

2002

Vintage rating: 95
(Chile: 92, Argentina: 97)

Chile—What might have been an excellent vintage was marred by rain in some regions during the harvest. The rains seem to have fallen as far north as the Colchagua Valley, but they did not affect such premium regions as Maipo, Casablanca, and Aconcagua. In the Casablanca Valley it was a very good vintage, with larger-than-average yields. There must, therefore, be care taken in buying wines from the Colchagua Valley and further south.

Argentina—Considered in Mendoza to be the best vintage for more than 10 years. Abundant snowfall in the Andes assured plentiful water for irrigation. The ripening period was long, with cool, dry weather. This gave wines with concentrated fruit flavors. In the north, in Salta Province, the vintage took place 10 days ahead of normal.

2001

Vintage rating: 94
(Chile: 96, Argentina: 91)

Chile—This was an excellent

vintage, with good wines being made throughout Chile, particularly for Carmenère.
Argentina—Generally considered a good vintage, although the wines lack the concentration of the 2002s. Chardonnays are the most successful wines.

2000

Vintage rating: *92*
(Chile: 90, Argentina: 93)

Chile—A large harvest; red wines are better than whites, due to low acidity.
Argentina—High yields, but while the wines lack some concentration and structure, they are perceived to have good, classic varietal characteristics.

1999

Vintage rating: *97*
(Chile: 97, Argentina: 96)

Chile—A difficult, drought-plagued year resulted in low yields of excellent quality. The red wines are firm and long-lasting, while the whites are lean and elegant. The best vintage for 15 years.
Argentina—The wines are similar in style to those of 2002, although the summer was hotter and drier, giving exceptionally healthy grapes.

1998

Vintage rating: *91*
(Chile: 93, Argentina: 88)

Chile—Overall a better year for reds than whites, especially in the Maipo Valley, where some outstanding reds were made.
Argentina—The year of El Niño gave rainy conditions and a great deal of rot, making conditions difficult for producing quality wines.

Grapevine

• **Santa Helena,** part of the CCU group (Cìa Cerveccerìas Unidas), now has an autonomous position as a winery after long being treated as just a subsidiary of the huge San Pedro operation. Santa Helena has leased vineyards and recently constructed the winery of Viña Siegel—El Crucero in the Colchagua Valley. With more than 800 ha of planted vineyards now under their control, Santa Helena becomes a major player in the region.

• **Pedro Marchevsky,** who has worked with Catena Zapata for more than 30 years and has been largely responsible for developing the Catena family 2,000-ha vineyard estate, has left to join his winemaker wife Susanna Balbo at their own winery, Dominio del Plata. They will work together on developing a number of brands, including Anubis and Benmarco. It appears that tensions were developing between Marchevsky and Nicolas Catena about this venture. Marchevsky has been replaced at Catena Zapata by his former assistant Alejandro Sejanovich.

• **Bodegas Norton** has introduced a range of wines with the world's first lenticular (holographic) wine label. Buyers of Lo Tengo wines will be able to watch the moving legs of tango dancers on their bottles! These should glide in step with the new slogan for Argentinian wine, "Wines with Rhythm."

GREATEST WINE PRODUCERS

1. Viña Montes (Chile)
2. Viña Santa Rita (Chile)
3. Casa Lapostolle (Chile)
4. Bodega Norton (Argentina)
5. Terrazas de los Andes (Argentina)
6. Viña Errazuriz (Chile)
7. Casa Silva (Chile)
8. Bodega Catena Zapata (Argentina)
9. Familia Zuccardi (Argentina)
10. Villard Estate (Chile)

FASTEST-IMPROVING PRODUCERS

1. Cono Sur (Chile)
2. Michel Torino, Bodega La Rosa (Argentina)
3. Santa Helena (Chile)
4. Ruca Malen (Argentina)
5. Antiyal (Chile)
6. Viña Lomas de Cauquenes (Chile)
7. Humberto Canale (Argentina)
8. Viniterra (Argentina)
9. Santa Mónica (Chile)

NEW UP-AND-COMING PRODUCERS

1. Dominio del Plata (Argentina)
2. Ventisquero (Chile)
3. Viñas de Altura (Argentina)
4. Odfjell Vineyards (Chile)
5. Leyda (Chile)
6. Bodegas Salentein (Argentina)
7. Antiyal (Chile)
8. Ruca Malen de Bacchus (Argentina)
9. Matetic (Chile)
10. Viña Von Siebenthal (Chile)

BEST-VALUE PRODUCERS

1. Viña Casablanca (Chile)
2. Trivento Bodegas y Viñedos (Argentina)
3. Casa Silva (Chile)
4. Viña Bisquertt (Chile)
5. Bodega Norton (Argentina)
6. Catena Zapata (Argentina)
7. Viña Montes (Chile)
8. Viña San Pedro (Chile)
9. Bodegas Trapiche (Argentina)
10. Viña Carmen (Chile)

GREATEST-QUALITY WINES

1. **Montes Alpha 'M' 2000** Colchagua Valley, Chile (CLP 45,000)
2. **Don Maximiniano Founder's Reserve 2000** Aconcagua Valley, Chile (CLP 39,900)
3. **Gran Cabernet Sauvignon 1999** Terrazas de los Andes, Argentina (AP 100)
4. **Cabernet Sauvignon 1999** Casa Real Exportación, Chile (CLP 28,000)
5. **Cuvée Alexandre Chardonnay 2001** Casa Lapostolle, Chile (CLP 13,590)
6. **Clos Apalta 2000** Casa Lapostolle, Chile (CLP 55,000)
7. **Almaviva 2000** Chile (CLP 50,000)
8. **Floresta Cabernet Sauvignon 1999** Santa Rita, Chile (CLP 18,000)
9. **Seña 1999** Chile (CLP 55,000)
10. **Norton Reserve Malbec 2000** Argentina (AP 28)

BEST BARGAINS

1. **Montes Reserve Merlot 2001** Chile (CLP 3,600)
2. **Viu Manent Special Selection Malbec 2000** Chile (CLP 5,500)
3. **Chardonnay 2002** Luis Felipe Edwards, Chile (CLP 2,300)
4. **Concha y Toro Trío Sauvignon**

Blanc 2002 Casablanca Valley, Chile (CLP 4,200)

5 **Trivento Viognier 2002** Bodegas y Viñedos Trivento, Argentina (AP 8)

6 **Gato Negro Cabernet Sauvignon 2002** Viña San Pedro, Chile (CLP 1,400)

7 **Morandé Pionero Merlot 2002** Central Valley, Chile (CLP 2,620)

8 **Santa Ana Chardonnay 2002** Argentina (AP A6)

9 **Santa Helena Siglo de Oro Sauvignon Blanc 2002** Central Valley, Chile (CLP 2,000)

10 **Torrontés La Riojana 2002** La Nature Organic, Argentina (AP 8)

MOST EXCITING OR UNUSUAL FINDS

1 **Las Lomas Viñas Viejas Organic Vines 1999** Chile (CLP 2,400) *From 100 percent Pais grown on 80-year-old vines and cropped at just 1½ tons per hectare, this shows that a despised grape can make outstanding, complex wines.*

2 **Verdelho 2002** Don Cristobal, Argentina (AP 12) *This variety is not recognized for Argentina by the EU and therefore cannot be sold in Europe, which is a pity because this is an excellent wine.*

3 **Balbi Barbaro 1998** Mendoza, Argentina (AP 16) *A judicious blend of Cabernet Sauvignon, Merlot, Malbec, and Syrah.*

4 **Greco Nero 2000** Bodegas Graffigna, Argentina (AP 6)

A touch of Argentine viticultural history, this rustic grape was brought over by an Italian immigrant and is rarely found as a straight varietal.

5 **Bodega Tacuil RD 2001** Valles Calchaquíes, Argentina (AP 30) *A blend of Cabernet Sauvignon, Malbec, and regional varieties from a plot that claims to be the world's highest commercial vineyard.*

6 **Black River Merlot/Pinot Noir 2000** Humberto Canale, Argentina (AP 8) *An unusual and, to my knowledge, unique blend of Bordeaux and Burgundy grapes.*

7 **Gillmore Carignan 2000** Maule Valley, Chile (CLP 7,500) *The first successful pure-varietal wine from this grape in Chile.*

8 **Edición Limitada 7 Barricas Uvas Congeladas Chardonnay 2000** Morandé, Chile (CLP 10,000) *A luscious sweet wine made from deep-frozen Chardonnay grapes— a cheap but successful method.*

9 **Orzada Cabernet Franc 2001** Odfjell Vineyards, Chile (CLP 7,000) *A great opener from this new Norwegian-owned winery. In Chile, the Cabernet Franc reaches a degree of ripeness never dreamed of in France.*

10 **Santa Isabel Chardonnay/ Viognier 2002** Nieto-Senetiner, Argentina (AP 8) *A good representative of what is becoming a fashionable New World blend.*

Grapevine

- **One side effect** of Argentina's financial problems has been a dramatic decline in new vineyard plantings. In 2002 there were just 600 ha of new vines planted, compared to 15,000 ha in 2000. The fall in new Chardonnay vines is of particular note, with just 3 ha planted in 2002.

- **Daniel Pi** is now head winemaker at Bodegas Trapiche, part of Peñaflor, Argentina's biggest wine group. Previously he had been overseeing two of Peñaflor's other properties: Finca Las Moras in the Tulum Valley and Michel Torino at Salta. He replaces Angel Mendoza, who has left to establish his own winery.

The Rest of South & Central America

Christopher Fielden

Times are not easy for the major wine companies of Mexico.

CHRISTOPHER FIELDEN

Per capita, domestic wine consumption is small (less than one third of a liter), and while brandy sales are a staple, it is now cheaper to import liquor from countries such as Australia than to distill it in Mexico, so most Mexican brandy is likely to have been produced elsewhere. As a result, a number of Mexican brandy distilleries have closed down. Of the three major wine producers, LA Cetto, with 1,000 hectares (ha) of vineyards in Baja California, appears to be the one that has adapted the best, now exporting to 27 different markets. Santo Tomás, the oldest winery in Baja California, used to sell 300,000 cases of wine a year; it now manages about 80,000 cases. The winery that appears to have the biggest problems is the one with the biggest sales: Domecq. For some years, it has formed one of the most distant outposts of the Allied-Domecq empire, with policy dictated by distillers rather than those with wine interests. Despite being the market leader, it owns no vineyards. Furthermore, because of the uncertainty of grape growing in Mexico, a number of vineyards are uprooting their vines and planting alternative crops. With the fashion for so many things Mexican, such as tequila, beer, and perennially popular Mexican restaurants, there would seem to be plenty of room for an expansion of export sales. Whether the local wine industry is capable of following this through, however, is not clear.

CHRISTOPHER FIELDEN has been in the wine trade for more than 40 years, during which time he has visited over 100 different countries. On his first trip to South America, he arrived in French Guiana by dugout canoe; he has been fascinated by the continent ever since. He is the author of 10 books on wine, including *The Wines of Argentina, Chile and Latin America* (Faber & Faber, 2001).

Uruguay affected by Argentina crash

In the immediate aftermath of the collapse of the Argentine economy, the value of Uruguay's peso halved overnight and the Argentine tourists who used to flock by the thousands to such resorts as Punta del Este disappeared. In addition, demand on the domestic market, in one of the few wine-producing countries to have shown regular increases year on year, fell sharply. As a result, the government has been forced to reduce its promotional support for wine. This has meant the immediate cancellation of a publicity campaign in the UK and an absence for the first time from the Prowein trade fair in Düsseldorf. However, the fall in the value of the peso has enabled Uruguayan producers, who are new to the export market, to compete more readily with the wines of other countries.

Investment-friendly Uruguay

Vinos Finos Juan Carrau was the first to engage in a joint venture (Casa Luntro with J&F Lurton), and more recently it has formed one with Freixenet (Arerunguá). The company also has at the planning stage a joint study of the Tannat and Tempranillo grape varieties with Bodegas Roda of Rioja. Other companies working with foreign wine interests include Cesar Pisano e Hijos, which is working with the Burgundy giant Boisset to introduce a number of new varietals to Uruguay under the Viña Progreso label; Juanicó, working with Château Pape-Clément; and Castillo Viejo, working with a group from the southwest of France.

Grapevine

• **A chance perusal** of Mexico's import statistics showed that substantial quantities of bulk wine from Chile are being brought into the country, and some producers fear that this is blended and sold as Mexican wine. All the major Mexican wine producers have petitioned the government for a law declaring that a wine bearing "Hecho en Mexico" must be made from 100 percent Mexican-grown fruit—all the major Mexican wine producers except, that is, the notable and thought-provoking exception of Domecq.

• **February 2003** saw the visit to Uruguay of a group of growers from Madiran, the one region in France where Tannat is still the major grape variety. Apparently, they were looking at investing in local vineyards!

• **San José-based winery** Castillo Viejo claims to have been the export leader in sales of Uruguayan wines outside Mercosur for the second year running in 2002. The previous year's exports accounted for more than US$1 million of their turnover, with Hong Kong and Iceland among their new overseas markets. Despite this success, Castillo Viejo was one of two top Uruguayan wineries reported to be seeking a deal with their creditors, the other being Los Cerros de San Juan.

Vintage Report

Advance report on the latest harvest

2003

Picking began two weeks earlier than usual in Uruguay, where the quality appears to be good, but volume will be small.

Updates on the previous five vintages

2002

Bolivia—The main wine-growing region in Tarija experienced a poor, rain-affected vintage, compounding industry worries over illegally smuggled wine imports from Argentina.

Brazil—Very good, especially for Pinot Noir and Chardonnay, with low yields due to a wet spring and warm, sunny weather during ripening.

Mexico—The harvest in Baja California was affected by low winter rainfall and is regarded as very special, with low yields and excellent quality. In Monterey, however, it was unusually wet, with fungal disease threatening white grapes, although dry weather returned during harvest for the red grapes. The Parras Valley in northeastern Mexico experienced an extremely hot and dry spring, which caused lots of water stress, producing very small berries and dark, concentrated red wines.

Uruguay—Cool nights in January slowed ripening, enabling outstanding Tannat reds and dry whites to be made. The former show intense color and tannins, while the whites contain moderate alcohol levels and pronounced aromatics. Rain late in the season caused some green tannins in the Cabernet varieties, especially those from later-ripening sites. This is considered one of the best vintages in Uruguayan wine history.

2001

Bolivia—Considered to be very good, especially for reds.

Brazil—Below average due to very wet weather at picking.

Mexico—Baja California produced reds with more obvious fruit and softer tannins than in 2000. Monterey had a quick, hot season, ripening the grapes too quickly. The harvest in Parras Valley was warm and early, with warm nights promoting big, ripe tannins.

Uruguay—Rain affected picking (an occupational hazard in Uruguay's maritime climate), but otherwise it was above average.

2000

Bolivia—Even better than 2001, thanks to extended ripening coupled with relatively low pH levels.

Brazil—Considered normal, with average rain and sun indices throughout the growing season.

Mexico—Baja California produced reds of tannic potential and concentration. Monterey was considered normal. Parras Valley was very hot and dry, resulting in one of the earliest harvests on record, creating rich Chardonnay and Cabernet.

Uruguay—An excellent vintage. Extremely dry weather contributed to significant ripeness and sugar level, especially for grapes grown on the more clay-rich area around Canelones, where heat stressing was minimal.

1999

Bolivia—Normal quality for both reds and whites. Already fading.

Brazil—Sunny weather during ripening produced very good Pinot Noir and Chardonnay for sparkling wines. Also good Cabernet and Tannat for reds.

Mexico—Baja California and Monterey were considered normal. Parras Valley enjoyed a cool summer, which promoted a relatively long hang time for Chardonnay and Merlot.

Uruguay—Normal for both red and white grapes.

1998

Bolivia—Very good, similar to 2000, producing Cabernet Sauvignon with the excellent fruit and tannic structure for wines that continue to develop in bottle.

Brazil—A poor vintage, with wet weather promoting fungal disease and limiting ripeness.

Mexico—Fair and possibly slightly underrated in Baja California, and a normal vintage in Monterey, while the Parras Valley produced aromatic whites and juicy reds thanks to cool nights at picking.

Uruguay—Cooler than 1997, producing good Sauvignon Blanc, but rain affected the reds adversely, provoking green tannins.

Grapevine

• **There used to be no problem** recruiting grape-pickers for the Pinar del Río vineyards of Bodegas Fantinel. Since one of the partners in this joint venture is Coralsa, the Cuban Food Ministry, when the harvest was ready, the army would be called in. Now, it seems, they can no longer be relied on, and they have been replaced by the youth Pioneer Corps. Logistics, nevertheless, are still provided by the army. It is reported that Maria Elena Fantinel, the on-the-spot representative of the Italian half of the partnership, would welcome an early return from exile!

• **Peruvian wine producers** are angry at the lack of support that they are getting from the government in their bid to cut down on fraudulent wine in the country. Research sponsored by the government has shown that 45 percent of all wine and 75 percent of all *pisco* on sale in the country owe their nature rather more to sugar cane than the vine. However, no steps have been taken to prohibit, or even control, this practice. The government seems unwilling to take on peasant power in the cane-growing regions, which are notorious for their militancy.

• **France's leading** international wine consultant Michel Rolland has now extended his activities to Brazil, where he is advising Vinícola Miolo, arguably the country's finest wine producer.

• **With demand** for low-cost red wine in Brazil exceeding by far the supplies from local producers, Aurora, the largest cooperative, has turned to Uruguay, where it has taken over a small cellar that now claims to be the number-one exporter in the country!

• **Brazil's first AOC** has been created. In a bid to upgrade the image of the region, the Vale dos Vinhedos, close to Bento Gonçalves in the Serra Gaucha province, has created its own appellation covering the valley formed by a number of streams running into the Das Antas River. Primarily, the initial legislation covers the geographical area, although it also forbids, for example, irrigation. The wines have to be approved by the control body before they can bear the special neck label.

GREATEST WINE PRODUCERS

1. LA Cetto (Mexico)
2. Château Camou (Mexico)
3. Vinos Finos Juan Carrau (Uruguay)
4. Monte Xanic (Mexico)
5. Cesar Pisano e Hijos (Uruguay)
6. Vinícola Miolo Ltda (Brazil)
7. Bodegas Castillo Viejo (Uruguay)
8. De Lucca (Uruguay)
9. La Concepción (Bolivia)
10. Viña Tacama (Peru)

FASTEST-IMPROVING PRODUCERS

1. Bodega Carlos Pizzorno (Uruguay)
2. Bodegas de Santo Tomás (Mexico)
3. Casa Filgueira (Uruguay)
4. Casa de Piedra (Mexico)
5. Campos de Solano (Bolivia)
6. Cavas Valmar (Mexico)
7. Bodegas y Viñedos Tabernero (Peru)
8. Don Laurindo (Brazil)
9. Adega de Vinhos Finos Dom Cândido (Brazil)
10. Bodegas Pomar (Venezuela)

BEST-VALUE PRODUCERS

1. LA Cetto (Mexico)
2. Cooperativa Vinícola Aurora (Brazil)
3. Bodegas de Santo Tomás (Mexico)
4. Cooperativa Vinícola Garibaldi (Brazil)
5. Establecimiento Juanicó (Uruguay)

GREATEST-QUALITY WINES

1. **Cabernet Franc-Merlot 1999** Château Camou, Mexico (MP 550)
2. **Amat Tannat 1998** Vinos Finos Juan Carrau, Uruguay (UP 550)
3. **Nebbiolo Reserva Limitada 1999** LA Cetto, Mexico (MP 110)

4. **Merlot 1999** Monte Xanic, Mexico (MP 3,000)
5. **Chardonnay Reserve 2001** Vinícola Miolo, Brazil (BR 33)
6. **Family Reserve Tannat 2000** Cesar Pisano e Hijos, Uruguay (UP 400)
7. **Grand Philippe Reserva I NV** Chandon do Brasil, Brazil (BR 80)
8. **Preludio Barrel Select Lote No 35 1997** Establecimiento Juanicó, Uruguay (UP 750)
9. **Casa Luntro 2000** J&F Lurton, Uruguay (UP 500)
10. **Gran Ricardo 1996** Monte Xanic, Mexico (MP 2,000 per magnum)

BEST BARGAINS

1. **Petit Syrah 2001** LA Cetto, Mexico (MP 45)
2. **Gamay 2002** Vinícola Miolo, Brazil (BR 18)
3. **Tempranillo 2000** Cavas Valmar, Mexico (MP 55)
4. **Chenin Blanc 2002** Bodegas de Santo Tomás, Mexico (MP 40)
5. **Ariano Harvest Selection 2001** Ariano Hermanos, Uruguay (UP 200)
6. **Concordia Cabernet Sauvignon-Shiraz 2000** LA Cetto, Mexico (MP 80)
7. **Sauvignon Blanc 2002** Vinos Finos Juan Carrau, Uruguay (UP 180)

MOST EXCITING OR UNUSUAL FINDS

1. **Terranova Moscatel Spumante 2001** Vinícola Miolo, Brazil (BR 19) *From two harvests a year in the tropical São Francisco Valley, this satisfyingly sweet sparkling wine is a gold-medal winner at wine fairs in three continents.*
2. **Platinum Reserve 2001** Angelo Cetto, Mexico (MP 350)

A blend of Cabernet Sauvignon, Aglianico, and Montepulciano designed to marry the New World's favorite red-wine grape to the Italian roots of this bodega in celebration of its 75th anniversary.

❸ Chasselas 2002
Mogor Badan, Mexico (MP 60)
Chasselas might not be a grape you would expect to find in Mexico, but it is the most-planted variety in the Swiss owner's homeland and, considering the hot climate in which it is grown, it makes a wine of a surprising freshness here.

❹ Viñas de Ybytyruzu Blanco NV
Colonia Independencia, Paraguay (PG 24,000) *This is possibly the worst wine in the world!*

Grapevine

• **The Spanish government,** together with the local authority in Bolivia's Tarija province, has established a wine research center called CENAVIT at Pampa Colorada, in a bid to improve the quality of viticulture and vinification in Bolivia. CENAVIT has trial plantings of 20 different varieties, both local and European, and is carrying out research into the ideal rootstock for what are claimed to be the highest commercial vineyards in the world. At present, domestically produced wines are finding it difficult to compete with low-cost imported wines, for the most part smuggled in from Chile.

• **Bodegas Pomar,** part of Venezuela's Polar brewery group, is carrying out extensive trials of 22 grape varieties at El Tocuyo, 30 miles (50 km) south of Barquisimeto, the capital of Lara state.

Here the climate is cooler than at their vineyard in production at Altagracia, close to their winery at Carora. The company has decided that it must move upmarket with its wines because they cannot compete with Chilean imports at the lower end.

• **Although Paraguay** is a fully signed-up member of Mercosur, it has made little effort to introduce the agreed wine legislation that is part and parcel of this South American common market. Indeed, the relevance of any wine law in Paraguay is questionable, since most of the country's production comes from, and is consumed in and around, the community of Colonia Independencia, a village that is better known as the bolt-hole of the Nazi war criminal Mengele.

Australia

Huon Hooke

The collapse of Southcorp's sales in Australia and the UK resulted in a 97 per cent drop in profit for 2002–3.

HUON HOOKE

This followed four successive profit-forecast downgrades, which, not surprisingly, sent its share price into a tailspin, culminating in the sacking of its chief executive Keith Lambert and, in May 2003, the company requesting that it stops trading on the Australian Stock Exchange. Southcorp was Australia's biggest wine producer and exporter, with at least 25 percent of sales before the horrors of 2002–3. Star winemakers such as John Duval and Philip Shaw have left the company, and while discounting is giving wine drinkers a field day, it has forced virtually all sizable wine producers to cut prices or face massive falls in sales. And this at a time when the local wine market is as flat as a bottle of stale fizz.

The great divide

The 2002 sales figures reveal that a huge gulf has opened between the big retail chains and the small and independent retailers, and this has been exacerbated by the discount war. Southcorp and other big producers, desperate to dump stock fast, have offered the big chains great deals,

HUON HOOKE is coauthor of *The Penguin Good Australian Wine Guide*, the country's most respected buyer's guide. He is a wine-marketing and production graduate of Roseworthy Agricultural College, and has been a weekly columnist for the John Fairfax Group newspapers for 20 years. Huon writes columns in the Good Living section of the *Sydney Morning Herald* and the *Good Weekend* magazine of the *Herald* and Melbourne's *Age*. He is also contributing editor of Australian *Gourmet Traveller VINE* magazine and writes for various other publications, such as *Decanter* and *Slow Wine*. He has been judging in wine competitions for 15 years, and judges eight to 10 shows a year in Australia and abroad. Huon has judged in New Zealand, South Africa, Chile, Belgium, Slovenia, and Canada. He currently chairs several Australian competitions and is senior judge at Adelaide and Sydney.

resulting in the small retailers being even less able to compete. Big-company wines are now stocked overwhelmingly by the big chains and sometimes not at all by smaller retailers. Consequently, small retailers are forced to focus increasingly on high-interest, small-output wines that the big chains tend not to trifle with.

Dry cure?

The ongoing drought, which has lasted five years in some areas, has stirred up debate about the use of water and the sustainability of viticulture in this, the driest of all continents. Grape yields have been poor in recent vintages because of the dry conditions, with many growers having to ration water. In some cases, irrigation-water allocations from rivers have been cut by half. The logic of irrigating vineyards and the efficiency of water use have become bones of contention, not to mention the quality implications of pushing new vines hard to produce crops as early as possible. Some growers are turning their thoughts back to dry-growing.

Grapevine

• **Mount Langi Ghiran,** producer of a famous Shiraz in the Grampians region, has been sold to the Rathbone family, owners of Yarra Valley showpiece winery Yering Station.

• **In March 2003,** the American giant Constellation Brands purchased BRL Hardy and in the process overtook E&J Gallo as the world's largest wine company. With just four companies accounting for 70 percent of Australian wine and just two of these now owned by foreign intersects (the other being the Orlando-Wyndham Group, owned by the French Pernod-Ricard group), foreign ownership in the wine industry is a growing concern.

• **The number of wine producers** is still growing at an alarming rate, with around 120 new ones opening for business each year. Out of 1,465 producers in 2002, half were crushing less than 50 tons of grapes a year, which puts them in the microboutique category and ensures they will have huge difficulty capturing the public's attention, let alone the retailers'.

• **Australians love their Chardonnay,** which now accounts for almost 48 percent of white wine sold. Riesling is the next-most important single varietal, but it is less than 7 percent. Blends of Semillon and Sauvignon Blanc are also popular, but reliable statistics are hard to obtain.

• **The dispute over** the Coonawarra regional boundary has finally been settled. Following years of haggling and several court cases, the eventual boundary includes more land than most people ever expected. But the scattered distribution of the best terra rossa soil means no boundary could ever include only the good land. As always, your only guarantee is the producer's name.

• **Andrew Pirie,** founder of Pipers Brook Vineyard, was basically booted out by the Belgian buyers of PBV, Kreglinger, after nearly 30 years of quality-minded hard work. Pirie was quickly snapped up by Sydney's Parker family, who were eager to have him fill the shoes of the founder of Parker Coonawarra Estate, John Parker, who died in 2002.

Rumours, rumours

It is rumored that former Petaluma supremo Brian Croser will (a) buy Penfolds from Southcorp, (b) buy Coldstream Hills from Southcorp, or (c) go and make wine in Europe, specifically Riesling in Alsace. Part of the rumored scenario (a) would entail Southcorp being split up, with Rosemount bought back by the Oatley family, and the rest broken up and distributed elsewhere, perhaps to Lion Nathan or Allied Domecq. It is well known that the founding Oatley family would like Rosemount back, with or without the rest of Southcorp. Perhaps the Oatley family's friends, the Mondavis, would go 50/50 in the buy-back?

Rumor also has it that key shareholders in failed Internet retailer Winepros are looking for a winery that wants a back-door stock-market listing. The original Winepros shareholders, including James Halliday and Len Evans, are no longer financially involved, and Len's daughter Sally is no longer managing director. Winepros, which always lacked a decent revenue stream and made a net loss of A$3.8 million on sales of just A$44,000 in its first year, is still operating on the Web.

Grapevine

• **If you thought** Australia's export boom rested on Southcorp, Orlando, BRL Hardy, and Beringer Blass, think again. The latest sensation is Yellowtail, a Riverina brand made by Casella Wines. In just a couple of years it has grown from nothing to a projected 2 million cases in 2003 in Europe, Asia, the UK, the US, Canada, and South Africa. In the US, Yellowtail is now the biggest imported brand, eclipsing even Riunite and Jacob's Creek, according to AC Nielsen.

• **Australia's love of "tinnies"** cannot be denied. Now we have the dubious distinction of being the first to market wine in aluminum cans since the Brits did it (and rapidly buried the idea) in the 1980s. Queensland winery Gowrie Mountain Estate of Toowoomba has started exporting 250-ml cans of red and white to the UK, with the US and Japan also in its sights. The wine inside is not Queensland wine, but more cheaply produced wine from the major bulk-winemaking companies. Targeted at 18- to 30-year-olds, the wines' benefits are listed as freedom from cork taint and oxidation, and no waste, "because people rarely want an entire 750-ml bottle."

• **Adelaide's beleaguered** National Wine Centre failed to learn the lessons of London's Vinopolis and was in danger of closing due to a lack of visitors, but has been rescued by the University of Adelaide, which has agreed to lease the loss-making center from the South Australian Government.

• **Di Cullen,** the founder, with her late husband Kevin, of Cullen of Margaret River, one of Australia's outstanding wineries, died in March 2003 aged 80. Di planted the first vines in Margaret River back in 1966, was the first winemaker at the family-owned winery, was a champion for women's rights and for conservation and environment issues in Margaret River, and in 1977 became the first Margaret River winemaker to win a gold medal. Her youngest daughter, Vanya, took over as winemaker in 1989 and was voted Qantas/*Australian Gourmet Traveller* magazine Winemaker of the Year in 2000.

Opinion:
Irrational

The law forbids chaptalization, yet winemakers routinely get around this by ameliorating their musts with concentrated grape juice. If cane and beet sugars are banned, surely added grape sugar should be, also. Either that or permit chaptalization with other sugars.

Cellar palate

Overoaking of red wines and some Chardonnays continues in many quarters, and the Australian fetish with wine-show judgings must be partly to blame. But there also seems to be a peculiar kind of oak-blindness among many of our winemakers, which leads them to enjoy dominant oak aroma and flavor in their own wines and when they taste on show panels. I believe repeated tasting of very young wines, especially wines ex-barrel, can inure unwary winemakers to the taste of oak. Fatigued show judges can also display excessive tolerance of new-oak flavor in wines that they would abhor in a real-life drinking situation.

Fizzical dominance

Ed Carr of BRL Hardy is Australia's most awarded sparkling-wine maker. He has a stranglehold on the bubbly trophies at both major and minor wine shows. But he makes a large number of sparkling wines under several brands and, since there are no limits to the number of wines a company may enter (using various subsidiary company names), it is easier for someone in Carr's position to dominate. Carr is a great winemaker and he is just doing what the system lets him. But the system should be changed.

Shows lack the necessary bottle

Some Australian wine competitions continue to permit the entry of unfinished wines that are still in the tank or barrel at time of sampling. This is probably fraudulent, because the wine that wins an award in certain classes of shows, such as Royal Melbourne and Royal Queensland, may not be technically the same wine that later appears on the shop shelf, sporting the medal sticker. At worst, it may have been seriously "stretched" or otherwise modified. Many wine shows have now banned all but finished wines; some still judge barrel samples but refrain from giving them awards. All shows should restrict awards to commercially bottled wines.

Vintage Report

Advance report on the latest harvest

2003

A year of reduced yields caused by general drought, with small bunches of small berries. Rain close to harvest resulted in berry-split, further cutting yields in several regions, stretching from Tasmania to central Victoria to McLaren Vale. Smoke-taint from the terrible January bushfires in the Alpine valleys of North East Victoria added insult to injury. Yet, despite these hardships, the quality is reported to be very good in most areas. Some noted that "big red" regions, such as Heathcote and McLaren Vale, struggled to attain flavor ripeness despite high alcohols, because a hot summer abruptly turned into a cool late summer and autumn, so there may be some reds with unripe tannins. Early reports suggest that the best wines are Shiraz and Chardonnay, with patches of excitement created by Adelaide Hills Sauvignon Blanc, Eden Valley Riesling, Coonawarra Cabernet and Merlot, and Yarra Valley Pinot Noir. The consensus is that 2003 is going to be a red-wine year.

Updates on the previous five vintages

2002

Vintage rating: 93

Record cool temperatures during the summer brought South Australia an outstanding vintage, especially for white wines in Clare and the Barossa—and even McLaren Vale, not noted for fine dry whites. The Riverland had a great year with some fine whites and reds showing superb color and varietal flavor. There is a slight question mark over flavor ripeness for reds in cooler areas like Eden Valley. The Hunter Valley and Mudgee, Orange, Hilltops, and Riverina all had an excellent vintage, while southerly regions like Tasmania and southern Victoria were able to ripen their grapes fully despite a very late harvest, thanks to a long, dry Indian summer. Unhappily, yields were miserly, especially in cool regions such as Tasmania, Yarra, Mornington, and Geelong. Western Australia was less favored, although whites are good.

2001

Vintage rating: 85

In contrast to 2002, this year had one of the hottest summers on record in South Australia, bringing an early harvest of good, rich, ultra-ripe reds. The whites were also remarkably decent because the heat wave preceded *veraison*. A good Hunter Semillon year, although it was a wet harvest for the Hunter, Mudgee, Cowra, and Orange. It is a very good year for southern Victoria and Tasmania—especially for Pinot Noir. It is a special year for Western Australia reds, especially Margaret River Cabernets. Other highlights are in Eden Valley, the Adelaide Hills, and—for big reds—in the Pyrenees.

2000

Vintage rating: *75*

A great vintage for Hunter Shiraz, which are opulent and will be long-lived. Pinot Noir in southern Victoria and, especially, Tasmania are sensational. The Tassie Pinots are like the 1994s: dark, opulent, powerful, and will be long-lived. The big disappointment was in South Australia—all regions had a very ordinary start to the new millennium except Coonawarra, which had a much better vintage and made excellent reds, thanks to its being spared the vintage rain. Central Victoria had a very good vintage of concentrated reds. Mudgee, Cowra, and Orange all had an unusually wet vintage and made dilute wines.

1999

Vintage rating: *85*

The quality of reds, especially in the Barossa and McLaren Vale, turned out to be remarkably high, certainly higher than expected. Coonawarra again was very good. In southern Victoria, a fairly ordinary year, although Bendigo-Heathcote and Rutherglen made good wines. Tasmania was fairly disappointing. The Hunter had a good year, especially for Semillon. Margaret River reds are really outstanding and for long keeping.

1998

Vintage rating: *95*

A great vintage, especially for seriously full-bodied, well-structured, long-keeping reds, in almost every Australian region except Margaret River, where 1999 is much the better year. South Australian reds look immortal, but some were overbuilt, especially in the oak and tannin departments. Whites were less successful—except Clare Riesling, which is very good. Tasmania had a great vintage, especially for Pinot Noir.

GREATEST WINE PRODUCERS

1. Giaconda
2. Southcorp (Penfolds, Seppelt, Wynns, Rosemount, Coldstream Hills, Devil's Lair)
3. Cullen
4. Petaluma
5. Mount Mary
6. Grosset
7. Moss Wood
8. BRL Hardy (Hardys, Houghton, Yarra Burn)
9. Cape Mentelle
10. Penley Estate

FASTEST-IMPROVING PRODUCERS

1. Miranda
2. Brands Laira
3. Hungerford Hill
4. D'Arenberg
5. Voyager Estate
6. Dromana Estate/Garry Crittenden
7. Sandalford
8. Capercaillie
9. Fox Creek
10. Houghton

NEW UP-AND-COMING PRODUCERS

1. Two Hands
2. Kilikanoon
3. Ferngrove
4. O'Leary Walker
5. Tower Estate
6. By Farr
7. Shadowfax
8. Kooyong
9. Thomas Wines
10. Hewitson

BEST-VALUE PRODUCERS

1. McWilliam's
2. Zilzie Wines
3. Orlando Wyndham (Jacob's Creek, Jacob's Creek Reserve, Richmond Grove)
4. BRL Hardy (Stepping Stone, Leasingham Bastion, Banrock Station)
5. Beringer Blass (Jamiesons Run, Saltram, Annie's Lane, Ingoldby)
6. Plantagenet (Hazard Hill, Omrah)
7. Southcorp (Wynns, Seppelt, Leo Buring, Lindemans Bin range)
8. Noon Winery
9. Trentham Estate
10. Miramar (red wines)

GREATEST-QUALITY WINES

1. **Grange 1998** Penfolds (A$350)
2. **Shiraz Viognier 2001** Clonakilla (A$56)
3. **Quintet 2000** Mount Mary (A$82.50)
4. **Cabernet Sauvignon Merlot 2000** Cullen (A$77)
5. **Cabernet Sauvignon 1999** Cape Mentelle (A$57)
6. **Jack Mann Cabernet Malbec 1999** Houghton (A$90)
7. **Museum Elizabeth Semillon 1994** McWilliam's Mount Pleasant (A$30)
8. **Hanlin Hill Riesling 2002** Petaluma (A$24)
9. **Chardonnay 2001** Giaconda (A$120)
10. **Coonawarra Estate First Growth 2000** Parker (A$82)

BEST BARGAINS

1. **Bastion Shiraz Cabernet 2001** Leasingham (A$11.75) *Sold on some export markets as Magnus Shiraz Cabernet.*

❷ Hazard Hill Shiraz Grenache 2001 Plantagenet (A$11) *Sold on some export markets as Hellfire Bay Shiraz Grenache*

❸ High Country Chardonnay 2002 Miranda (A$12.35)

❹ Stepping Stone Coonawarra Cabernet Sauvignon 2001 Stonehaven (A$14)

❺ Semillon 2002 Peter Lehmann (A$9)

❻ Hanwood Chardonnay 2002 McWilliam's (A$10)

❼ Cabernet Merlot 1999 Voyager Estate (A$39.50)

❽ Bin 65 Chardonnay 2002 Lindemans (A$9)

❾ Ninth Island Pinot Noir 2002 (A$23)

❿ Buloke Reserve Sangiovese 2002 Zilzie (A$10)

MOST EXCITING OR UNUSUAL FINDS

❶ Verdelho 2002 Robert Channon (A$18.50) *Could just be Australia's best Verdelho.*

❷ Tempranillo Graciano 2001 Cascabel (A$40) *Tempranillo is a grape that should fit many Australian regions like a glove, but hardly any is planted.*

❸ Geelong Pinot Gris 2002 Provenance (A$25) *Most attempts at Pinot Gris in Australia have been distinctly underwhelming, but this delightful wine probably comes closer than any to a fine Alsatian example.*

❹ Family Reserve Viognier 2001 Elgee Park (A$35) *Viognier is still a very rare varietal in Australia and most are too fat and heavy, too alcoholic, or oaky. This, however, is excitingly similar to a finer style of Condrieu.*

❺ Aeolia Roussanne 2001 Giaconda (A$85) *Roussanne is rare in Australian vineyards, but Chardonnay king Rick Kinzbrunner makes a very complex, layered, barrel-fermented style, the price of which reflects the demand after just two vintages.*

❻ Cossack Riesling 2002 Ferngrove (A$21) *The first crop of wines from this brand-new southwest Western Australian producer are all excitingly good, but none is better than this fragrant, multiple show-trophy-winning Riesling.*

❼ Mesh Riesling 2002 Yalumba-Grosset (A$26.50) *The first vintage of a collaboration between Yalumba and top Riesling maker Jeffrey Grosset, using Yalumba's Eden Valley grapes and blended from batches made separately in both wineries, with an outstanding result.*

❽ Belle Pinot Gris 2002 Madew (A$30) *David Madew has made two superb 2002 Pinot Gris wines from his vineyard near Canberra, this one being a selection from low-yielding vines growing on a bank of gravel.*

❾ Regional Varietal Range Houghton's (A$25) *Every wine in Houghton's new regional range is excellent.*

❿ Viognier 2002 Zilzie (A$14) *To find a good Aussie Viognier at this price is rare enough, but the fact that it is a first release, and grown in the Riverland region, is extraordinary.*

New Zealand

Bob Campbell MW

Vineyards are growing at a heady pace, particularly in Marlborough, Central Otago, and Hawke's Bay, with the price of land and grapes continuing to rise.

BOB CAMPBELL MW

This is despite a growing global wine surplus and a strengthening dollar that threatens the profitability of exports. The situation has led *The New Zealand Vineyards & Wine Industry Review* (2003 edition) to provide a comprehensive analysis of the past, present, and possible future of New Zealand wine, concluding:

• Market pressure is likely to result in greater industry consolidation as small wineries merge or are bought by larger wineries;

• Wineries under financial pressure may be forced to reduce their sights from the premium end of the market in order to make ends meet;

• The price of land for iconic vineyard areas will continue to rise until "they finally succumb to the rigors of economic fundamentals";

• All but the very best New Zealand wine will be vulnerable to irrational marketing and pricing by overseas competitors;

• The industry has been small enough and disciplined enough to maintain a high value for its wine in export markets, but this will be difficult to maintain as production increases.

The authors cite the "Georgia Chicken Effect" as a phenomenon that could threaten the New Zealand wine industry. The Georgia Chicken Effect is named after an incident that took place in Georgia, just after World War II, when an entrepreneur determined that Georgia was a great place to

BOB CAMPBELL MW lives in Auckland, where he is the wine editor for *Cuisine* magazine and coauthor of *Cuisine Wine Country*, a comprehensive annual guide to New Zealand's wineries. He writes for publications in seven countries and has judged at wine competitions in seven countries. Bob established his own wine school in 1986, and 18,000 people have graduated from his wine diploma course.

make a profit rearing chickens. The early players did very well. But news soon spread. Before long, thousands of new farmers entered the business. A shortage of labor and grain drove costs up, while an oversupply of chickens drove prices and profits down. Georgia is still a great place to rear chickens, but Georgia chickens are history. New Zealand is unlikely to stop being a great place to grow Marlborough Sauvignon Blanc or Martinborough Pinot Noir, but the viability of undistinguished New Zealand wine that lacks any real point of difference with undistinguished wine in, say, Chile, Australia, or South Africa may soon be threatened.

Getting screwed

Frustrated by unacceptable levels of cork taint, a handful of Marlborough winemakers banded together to form the Screwcap Initiative in 2000. With the help of sponsorship from suppliers of the two brands of screw cap imported into New Zealand—Stelvin and Auscap—they promoted the advantages of screw cap over cork to their fellow winemakers. A recent report shows that, while only 2 percent of wine was bottled under screw cap in the first six months, that figure rose to 7 percent in the following six months, and then to just over 14 percent in the six months to December 2002 as the number of wineries involved increased to 50, including Montana. While several winemakers have totally embraced screw-cap closures, others are adopting a more cautious approach, particularly with oak-aged white wines and red wines, where the benefits of screw caps have yet to be proven.

Grapevine

- **Kiwis are drinking less local wine.** In 2002 the domestic consumption of New Zealand wine on a per capita basis fell to the lowest level since the late 1970s. New Zealanders drank 8.2 liters of their own wine in 2002, down from a 16.3-liter high in 1986. However, the major reason for this phenomenon is the importation of bulk wine to service the lower end of the market. Many of the larger New Zealand wineries have substituted imported wine for the local product in their wine-cask or lower-priced bottled wines.

- **Beringer Blass,** a subsidiary of Australia's Foster's Brewing Group, purchased Ponder Estate in Marlborough for NZ$11 million. The winery includes a 23-hectare (ha) vineyard and an 11-ha

olive grove. The olive grove was removed shortly after the purchase and will be replanted with vines.

- **Cloudy Bay** has purchased another 56 ha in Marlborough, and this will be planted predominantly with Sauvignon Blanc vines. This was prompted by a "demand for wine styles that are currently beyond our production capacity."

- **American businessman** Ed Aster bought Firstland Vineyards (formerly De Redcliffe) and Hotel du Vin, a well-known hotel, restaurant, and winery complex about 45 minutes' drive south of Auckland. The new owner intends to increase wine production and sales to export markets.

NEW WINE COMPETITIONS

Fifty years ago the country's first wine competition, now known as the NZ Wine Society Royal Easter Wine Show, began awarding medals to the country's better wines. Wine was then judged alongside pumpkins, sheep, and cattle at the annual Agricultural and Pastoral Show. A decade or two later, a second show appeared. Now known as the Air New Zealand Wine Awards, it is run by and for the benefit of the country's winemakers. More recently, four new wine shows have made an appearance. The Liquorland Top 100 International Wine Competition, which is run by a local chain of wine stores; the International Chardonnay Challenge, which is an attempt to measure New Zealand Chardonnay against the same varietal from other countries, and is based in Gisborne, New Zealand's self-proclaimed Chardonnay capital; the Hawke's Bay A&P Mercedes-Benz Wine Show, which is a review of wines from the Hawke's Bay region; and the Bragatto Wine Awards, which recognizes grape growers rather than winemakers. The results from these competitions are posted on www.wineshow.co.nz

FOREIGN INVESTMENT IN NZ VINEYARDS

Unofficial estimates suggest that up to 80 percent of all New Zealand wine is made by companies that are owned offshore. The increasing exposure of New Zealand wines in overseas markets and the relatively cheap price of vineyard land has produced an increasing number of eager offshore buyers. US investors topped the list with 39 buyers, followed by the UK with 27, Singapore 20, Australia 18, and the Netherlands 17. Buyers hail from a total of 13 countries, including New Caledonia (4) and Thailand (1).

HEADING FOR THE HILLS

An increasing number of hillside vineyards are being established to provide better exposure and ultimately better wines. Fromm's Clayvin vineyard in Marlborough is an early example that demonstrated to others the benefits of hillside planting. Escalating prices for the country's best wines have meant that once-uneconomic vineyards are now viable. Central Otago probably boasts the largest percentage of sloping vineyards, thanks to the high price of Central Otago Pinot Noir and the added frost protection afforded by a sloping site.

Opinion:
Undermining New Zealand's reputation

Much of New Zealand's "cheap and cheerful" wine market is satisfied by several large wine producers who import wine in bulk from Australia, Spain, France, Chile, et al. and bottle it for the local market. There is nothing wrong with this practice provided the labels clearly show the origin of the wine. What I do object to, however, is the re-exporting of such wines after bottling. Australian red wine, for example, is imported into New Zealand in bulk before being bottled and re-exported to the UK, where it undermines the premium image that New Zealand wine currently enjoys worldwide. New Zealand winemakers should only export wine that has been made using New Zealand grapes.

Less is best
Oak reacts with the often greener, cool-climate flavors of South Island Chardonnay to produce a resinous character in some wines. I would like to see South Island winemakers resist the temptation to make wine according to perceived market expectations and to use less oak.

Organic licence
Many wineries claim to produce grapes using organic methods, but few (seven at the last count) are certified by Bio Gro, an organization that has clear guidelines and a process to check that those guidelines are being met. Wineries should not be allowed to make any claim about organic status unless they are officially registered as being organic.

Truth in labelling
A label-integrity program is badly needed. Regions, districts, and vineyards need to be defined and the authenticity of labels audited.

Who's who?
Well over half of New Zealand's wine is made from grapes that have been purchased from contract grape growers. If wine is made from grapes grown by the winemaker, that status should be officially recognized on the label.

Verification
All wine producers who enter wine competitions should provide an additional bottle for an official library of samples that can later be used to authenticate the commercial production if necessary.

Vintage Report

Advance report on the latest harvest

2003

Frosts and poor flowering have dramatically reduced the harvest to around half that of the previous year's crop. Rain and generally cool conditions added to many winemakers' woes, resulting in variable quality, although most regions are optimistic that some exceptional wines will be produced. North Island regions were hardest hit, while the more southerly regions had fewer problems and may be expected to produce a larger crop of generally better wines. In Hawke's Bay, red grape varieties have fared better than white varieties, with higher crops and average- to good-quality wines according to the region's producers. Marlborough Sauvignon Blanc, the country's key export wine, is down in quantity, although quality is reported to be above average. A large crop of Marlborough Sauvignon from the previous year will help to compensate for this year's shortage. Ironically, Central Otago, generally considered to be New Zealand's coolest and most frost-prone region, appears to have escaped frost damage and has enjoyed a very good season indeed.

Updates on the previous five vintages

2002

Vintage rating: *North Island 84 (Red: 83, White: 85), South Island 86 (Red: 88, White: 84)*

A long, hot, dry spell of autumn weather resulted in a miracle vintage with many outstanding wines. Gisborne enjoyed a vintage that several winemakers described as the best ever. Hawke's Bay produced many good whites and even-better reds, judging by a recent review of barrel samples. Fears that a high crop of Sauvignon Blanc in Marlborough may result in wide variation in wine quality were not entirely unfounded, although the best wines were exceptional. Canterbury had a cool, late vintage with average to above-average wines, while Central Otago boasted some of the region's best-ever reds amid fears that some grapes may have been allowed to overripen.

2001

Vintage rating: *North Island 68 (Red: 65, White: 70), South Island 84 (Red: 83, White: 84)*

Almost every imaginable malady seemed to afflict this vintage, including fire, frost, hail, rain, and drought. Grape growers would not have been surprised had a plague of locusts descended. It is officially described as a "typical New Zealand vintage, in that there has been a lot of regional variation," although the wines of South Island are significantly superior, while an Indian summer favored later-ripening varieties in the North Island.

2000

Vintage rating: *North Island 85 (Red: 80, White: 90), South Island 83 (Red: 83, White: 82)*

Quality was high in the South Island, but more variable in the North Island, with the later-ripening period favoring red-grape varieties, except in marginal locations, where grapes may have lacked full physiological ripeness.

1999

Vintage rating: *North Island 78 (Red: 78, White: 78), South Island 79 (Red: 80, White: 78)*

The wines in this vintage are of variable quality. The South Island regions fared a little better than those in the North Island.

1998

Vintage rating: *North Island 85 (Red: 85, White: 85), South Island 85 (Red: 88, White: 82)*

This was the year of the drought thanks to El Niño weather, which brought hot, dry conditions and strong winds to most of the country. Some grapes were harvested too late, resulting in slightly overripe flavors and elevated alcohol levels. Wines were more often acidified than deacidified. The major hits of the vintage were Hawke's Bay red wines made from the Bordeaux varieties, principally Cabernet Sauvignon and Merlot. One notable casualty of the hot conditions was Marlborough Sauvignon Blanc, which lacked its usual, pungent, aromatic quality. Curiously, Marlborough Riesling enjoyed an excellent vintage, with many fine wines being produced.

GREATEST WINE PRODUCERS

1. Dry River
2. Ata Rangi
3. Cloudy Bay
4. Felton Road
5. Fromm
6. Te Mata Estate
7. Neudorf
8. Kumeu River
9. Villa Maria
10. Martinborough Vineyards

FASTEST-IMPROVING PRODUCERS

1. Trinity Hill
2. Te Kairanga
3. Greenhough
4. CJ Pask
5. Daniel Schuster
6. Mission Estate
7. Mount Riley
8. Palliser Estate
9. Mills Reef
10. Spencer Hill Estate

NEW UP-AND-COMING PRODUCERS

1. Craggy Range
2. Schubert
3. Escarpment
4. Kaituna Valley
5. Mount Maude
6. Mt Difficulty
7. Carrick
8. Staete Landt
9. Newton Forrest
10. Cable Bay

BEST-VALUE PRODUCERS

1. Montana Wines
2. Drylands
3. Coopers Creek
4. Villa Maria Estate

5. Mission Estate Winery
6. Allan Scott Wines
7. Forrest Estate
8. Hunter's
9. Wither Hills
10. Babich

GREATEST-QUALITY WINES

1. **Le Sol Syrah 2001**
   Craggy Range (NZ$65)
2. **Craighill Riesling 2002**
   Dry River (NZ$32)
3. **Arapoff Gewurztraminer 2002**
   Dry River (NZ$36)
4. **Coniglio Hawkes Bay Chardonnay 1998**
   Morton Estate (NZ$69)
5. **Pinot Noir 2001**
   Ata Rangi (NZ$60)
6. **Block 5 Pinot Noir 2001**
   Felton Road (NZ$60)
7. **Pinot Gris 2002** Dry River (NZ$39)
8. **Riesling 2002**
   Felton Road (NZ$25)
9. **Chardonnay 2001**
   Fromm (NZ$28)
10. **Reserve Marlborough Noble Riesling 2001** Villa Maria (NZ$50 per half-bottle)

BEST BARGAINS

1. **Lindauer Brut** (NZ$12)
2. **Block 14 Syrah 2001**
   Craggy Range (NZ$30)
3. **Gewurztraminer 2002**
   Lawson's Dry Hills (NZ$22)
4. **Sauvignon Blanc 2002**
   Palliser Estate (NZ$21)
5. **Sauvignon Blanc 2002**
   Terrace Hills Estate (NZ$17)
6. **Riesling 2002** Felton Road (NZ$25)
7. **Pinot Noir 2001**
   Mount Maude (NZ$34)
8. **Woodthorpe Chardonnay 2002** Te Mata Estate (NZ$19)

❾ Hawke's Bay Pinot Gris 2002
Morton Estate (NZ$17)

❿ Gravel Pit Red 2001
Red Rock Winery (NZ$20)

MOST EXCITING OR UNUSUAL FINDS

❶ Woodthorpe Viognier 2002
Te Mata Estate (NZ$29) *New Zealand's first Viognier and still the best.*

❷ Tempranillo 2001 Trinity Hill (NZ$25) *New Zealand's first Tempranillo is certain to inspire considerable interest in a variety that appears to be well suited to the warmer wine-growing districts of the North Island.*

❸ Retico 1998 Vin Alto (NZ$120) *A rare Amarone-style wine made from a mix of mostly Italian grape varieties that were allowed to dry on racks for two months after they were harvested.*

❹ Riesling Auslese 2002 Fromm (NZ$17.50 per half-bottle) *A truly Germanic style that is quite unlike any other Riesling, late-harvest or otherwise, made in New Zealand.*

❺ Virtu Noble Semillon 1998 Montana (NZ$38 per half-bottle) *An unusual and outstanding wine proving that New Zealand Semillon has considerable potential for late-harvest styles.*

❻ Le Sol Syrah 2001 Craggy Range (NZ$65) *Syrah is showing considerable promise in New Zealand, particularly in the Gimblett Gravels district of Hawke's Bay. This is the best New Zealand Syrah made to date.*

❼ Hawkes Bay Syrah 2001 Te Kairanga (NZ$45) *An extraordinary wine made from grapes grown in Craggy Range's Gimblett Gravels vineyard. It has received many accolades in New Zealand.*

❽ Te Koko 2000 Cloudy Bay (NZ$35) *A brave and successful attempt to take Marlborough Sauvignon Blanc (and Marlborough Sauvignon Blanc drinkers) out if its (their) comfort zone. Wild yeast, barrel fermentation, full malolactic, extended yeast contact, and bottle age—it's Sauvignon, Jim, but not as we know it.*

❾ Roussanne 2002 Trinity Hill (NZ$24) *New Zealand's first example of Roussanne.*

❿ Kahu Botrytis Riesling 2002 Ata Rangi (NZ$32 per half-bottle) *A great example of botrytis-affected Riesling that combines the lush, honeyed influence of botrytis with the pure and vibrantly beautiful flavors of Riesling.*

Grapevine

• **Lion Nathan** paid John and Brent Marris a top price of NZ$52 million for their high-flying Marlborough Wither Hills winery. The sale included 378 ha of freehold land and 20 ha of leasehold. Brent and John Marris have agreed to continue running the company for a further three years, and they will receive a bonus of up to NZ$8 million if sales targets are achieved.

• **New York businessman** Julian Robertson and Napa Valley vineyard owner Reg Oliver have purchased Te Awa Farm in the Gimblett Gravels area of Hawke's Bay and Dry River in Martinborough. Dry River is New Zealand's leading cult winery. Its tiny production of 2,000–2,500 cases is snapped up annually by mail-order customers who count themselves lucky to be on the winery's A list.

Asia

Denis Gastin

In recent times, perhaps the most convincing statement on the future of the wine industry in Asia has been the high-profile commitment to domestic wine production by beverage-industry leaders.

DENIS GASTIN

In Japan, two of the four brewing giants, Sapporo and Suntory, have launched major new premium, domestic wine brands. In February 2003, Sapporo introduced its Grande Polaire label, the company's new flagship range, featuring 17 wines from four producing locations in Japan (Yamanashi, Nagano, Okayama, and Hokkaido) and one in Washington State in the US. These wines sit above the long-established Polaire range, which encompasses roughly 100 wines, including many that are primarily dependent on imported must, concentrate, or bulk wine. Grande Polaire is thus a statement of confidence in domestic Japanese production. Suntory had made a similar statement with its Yamanashi-based Tomi no Oka premium range in late 2001.

Beverage giant and wine-industry leader Mercian has launched a new range, J-fine, to complement its District and Private Reserve premium labels. With J-fine, Mercian is appealing to the Japanese consumer's

DENIS GASTIN grew up in Australia's northeast Victorian wine regions and has had a lifelong interest in wine. Assignments as an Australian trade official in China and Japan opened up new wine vistas for him and, after leaving the government, he has written extensively about the Asian industry. His particular interests are the more unusual aspects of winemaking, the more remote and least understood regions of the wine world, and the groundbreaking work that some of the industry champions have been doing with exotic grape varieties and new wine styles. Dennis is a feature writer and Australian correspondent for Japan's liquor-industry newspaper, *The Shuhan News*. He has contributed to various other journals and wine reference books, including *The Oxford Companion to Wine* and *Hugh Johnson's Pocket Wine Book* (Mitchell Beazley).

particular palate sensitivities—seeking, as it says, "a sensitive dryness that is specifically Japanese." The range makes a feature of both the local vinifera variety, Koshu, and a popular local hybrid called Muscat Bailey-A, along with Chardonnay and Merlot. Meanwhile, Manns Wine, the wine arm of soy-sauce king Kikkoman, is going upmarket with the launch of its Solaris range, which features individual vineyards, small-scale winemaking, and museum releases. The current release of Solaris Koshu is, for example, from the 1990 vintage. There is a parallel movement under way in China, too. Leading beer company Tsingtao has launched into winemaking with its Kai Xuan winery in Shandong province and released its first wines in late 2002. And the top white-spirit producer, Maotai, has launched a 10,000-ton capacity winemaking venture in Changli county, Hebei province, resolving "to make China's best dry red and dry white wines." These wines have been released under the famous Maotai name.

Grapevine

• **China** is now the eighth-largest viticultural area in the world, with almost 300,000 hectares (ha) of vines, of which around 50,000 ha are wine grapes, and is the world's 11th-largest wine producer. There are over 300 wineries in 26 provinces. Rising domestic consumption is the principal industry driver, having doubled in the last five years.

• **China's Dragon Seal** has reintroduced Rhine Riesling from the 2002 vintage and there is even a Zinfandel on the way, but it has thus far proven difficult to ripen and has ended up in blends.

• **India's agricultural ministry** announced in April 2003 its intention to set up an industry board to encourage the development of the country's emerging wine industry, along the lines of the boards that administer the much larger rubber, tea, and coffee industries. The total specialized wine-grape area is somewhat less than 1,000 ha at present, but that is about to change—perhaps dramatically.

• **The cooperative** Chateau Mani winery in South Korea's Chungbuk province, south of Seoul, has recently introduced a range of dry and sweet wines, including a sacramental wine, and has plans to grow the volume of production and diversify the range as the market for its wine grows.

• **Boon Rawd,** brewers of Singha, Thailand's internationally marketed beer, joined the Asian winemaking fray with its new Khao Yai wine subsidiary. This doubles the number of Thai wineries, the pioneering Chateau de Loei having been established since 1995. A third winery will be added with the arrival of Changyu, China's largest wine producer, which announced in late 2002 that it planned to build a 5,000-ton capacity winery in partnership with its long-standing local distributor, Thai-China Wines.

• **Asahi Yoshu,** the 80-year-old former cooperative winery in Japan's Yamanashi district, is being revitalized and repositioned by its new owners. The young husband-and-wife winemaking team, Tsuyoshi and Junko Suzuki, who were formerly staff at the Grace Winery, initially intend to test new horizons with the local Koshu variety, but ultimately aim to specialize in reds.

CHINA'S WESTERN FRONT

The outstanding development in China in recent years has been the breakneck growth of the industry in the far west of the country—in the Xinjiang Autonomous Region, where the history of the grape can be traced back to 206 BC, and the neighboring Gansu and Ningxia provinces. The pacesetter is Suntime (Xintian), which has come from nowhere in 1998, the year of its launch, to rival the output of traditional industry leaders Great Wall, Changyu, and Dynasty. Its crush totaled just 5,000 tons in 2000, but 57,000 tons in 2002. Suntime now has 10,000 ha of vines in Xinjiang, consisting mostly of classic European varieties, and plans an eventual processing capacity of well over 100,000 tons. It currently operates from two large-scale wineries, with a third under construction, and its premium label, Niya, has become a leading brand in China in a remarkably short time.

Another exciting new winemaking operation in Xinjiang is the revamped Lou Lan winery near Urumqi, the regional capital. Another new player, the Yanqi Xiangdu Sino-French joint venture, declares it is planning an ultimate crush capacity of 30,000 tons. In neighboring Gansu's Hexi corridor, there are now four wineries with a capacity in excess of 5,000 tonnes, the biggest of which is Mogao Winery, with a 10,000-ton capacity. In Ningxia province, the revitalized Yuquan Winery is the province's largest producer. It is significant, also, that major Eastern-based wineries (including Changyu, Great Wall, and Dynasty) are increasingly drawing grapes and wine from the western provinces. They are attracted by the superior ripening and coloring potential in the west (around 2,800 hours of sunshine), the availability of supplementary water, and, particularly, its relative freedom from pests and disease.

OPENING UP CENTRAL CHINA

The first releases from the Shanxi Grace Winery, established in 1997, hit the stores in China's cities in July 2002—and they show real promise. Wine from its first fledgling vintages (1999 and 2000) have been sold in bulk to Great Wall. The winery is located 30 miles (50 km) from Taiyuan, the capital of Shanxi province, a region that is quickly gaining a reputation for premium grapes. It is a joint venture between Frenchman Sylvain Janvier and Hong Kong businessman CK Chan. Because foreigners cannot own agricultural land in China, the venture is entirely dependent on 550 local contracted farmers growing vines on 110 ha of vineyards developed and maintained under winery supervision. The winemaker is Gérard Colin. A *grand cru* range and a premium range will be released late in 2003, but the table-wine range is a fine first-up effort—especially the Loire-style rosé (Rmb70), made from Cabernet Sauvignon, Cabernet Franc, and Merlot. In the table-wine range there is also a Cabernet Sauvignon, a Cabernet blend, and a Chardonnay/Riesling blend.

AU REVOIR?

Following the trend to "localize" ownership, Pernod-Ricard's joint-venture relationship with Dragon Seal was dissolved, while Rémy-Martin now occupies a backseat position in its relationship with Dynasty, leaving operational control in the hands of its local partner. Changyu, on the other hand, has extended its business relationship with French company Castel, completing their very large joint-venture winery and tourist complex near Yantai in September 2002 and opening it in 2003.

TABLE WINE

The much-maligned labrusca/Koshu hybrid Muscat Bailey-A is emerging as one of Japan's truly interesting varieties in the hands of some of its most skilled and innovative local winemakers. Two particularly good examples are available from Tsuno Wines. Other makers have found it works best in blends. Commendable combinations can be seen in Coco Farm's Daiichigakusho and Iwanohara's Vintage. This is good news for grape growers, since this grape is relatively easy to grow in Japan and one of its most widely cultivated varieties, having been planted for the table grapes.

DOTTY INDIAN

When dot-com entrepreneur Rajeev Samant returned to India to set up his Sula Vineyards winery to compete with the longer established Chateau Indage and Grover Vineyards, it seemed to herald a new era for the Indian industry. Wine consumption has tripled in the last five years, albeit from a small base, and the worldly and sophisticated consumption choices of India's very internationalized professional fraternity are a major source of this new demand. This is the main market that Sula targets, although all three companies also have a growing export market in Europe and North America.

BALI SURVIVOR

Moving on from the devastating blow to Bali's vital tourist economy wreaked by the disco bombings in 2002, local wine pioneer Hatten Wines Indonesia continues to forge winemaking history. Under the technical direction of winemaker Vincent Desplat, Hatten's range on the local market has grown to eight wines, including still white, rosé, red, and sparkling wines. The wines are made from the Belgia (white) grape variety, grown in the company's own vineyards, and a virtually perennial supply of Alphonse Lavallée (red) grapes grown by local farmers in the island's north, around the town of Singaraja, just two degrees from the equator.

Grapevine

- **Japan's first national wine show** will be held in Yamanashi in July 2003. A panel of local and international judges will evaluate entries from domestic producers.

- **Obuse Domaine Sogga** of Nagano, Japan, has released Asia's first Sangiovese- Merlot blend (2002 vintage). Akihito Soga, the brains behind this new venture, which has been grafted on to his family's sake operation, has more up his sleeve. Look out for Kerner, Pinot Blanc, Viognier, Barbera, and Gewurztraminer.

Opinion:
Back to the vineyard

The biggest constraint to good wine outcomes throughout Asia is the lack of a genuinely wine-focused viticultural tradition. The largest proportion of vineyard area, by a very big margin, is producing for the table grapes or for drying. Wine represents an increasing end point, and is responsible for most of the recent expansion in vineyard area, but most traditional growers are not yet confident enough to make the commitment to the different viticultural practices that are required for good wine. With heavy investment in modern winery equipment now behind them, the next challenge for most Asian winemakers lies in the vineyards—with yield management and ripeness the priority targets.

Strength in accuracy

In Japan, there is a widespread practice of declaring on labels an alcohol level of "less than 15 percent." In China, one leading company declares almost its total range at 12 percent. This would be an amazing feat of consistency if it were correct, and one suspects that it is, rather, a "default" setting. There should be a labeling law in these countries that ensures a certain minimum accuracy of alcoholic strengths.

Grapevine

• **In Japan,** the most concerted effort thus far in establishing a quality-oriented regional appellation standard is in Nagano prefecture, where a provincial appellation system was established in October 2002. Modeled on the European AOC systems, only wine from grapes grown and fermented in the prefecture can carry the Appellation Nagano Contrôlée, providing it passes a tasting test by a government-appointed jury. With only 12 of the 49 wines reviewed by the jury in April 2003 receiving certification, the signs are that this AOC should be a dependable indicator of quality, not just of origin.

• **In August 2002,** China's National Quality and Inspection Bureau declared Changli county in Hebei province and Yantai in Shandong province as, respectively, the first and second designated AOC regions in China. The focus so far is on superior vineyard practices and production standards, rather than quality in the bottle, but it is an important start.

• **The richly flavored** Graves-style Goichi 2001 Semillon, made by Hayashi Noen in Nagano, is the nation's first commercial release of this variety. In previous vintages, the Semillon had mostly gone into the excellent Chardonnay-based Goichi Kifugoh botrytized dessert wine.

Vintage Report

Advance report on the latest harvest

2003

India—The harvest was over early in Western Maharashtra, with all grapes in by mid-March, following a much earlier start than usual, in late January. Warm weather throughout the ripening period and a weaker-than-usual monsoon season saw fruit ripening early and relatively free of disease. The Sauvignon Blanc and the more aromatic wines will not be as intense as in some previous years, but the red varieties matured perfectly and were picked with high sugars, very good color, and lots of flavor. In Bangalore, where harvesting takes place in April/May, conditions were ideal up to the end of April, and all the early indications are of an excellent year. The weaker monsoon and drier conditions permitted grapes to be left on the vine to reach full maturity. By mid-vintage, the vines had escaped pests and fungal disease, and the early wines are showing real promise.

Updates on the previous five vintages

2002

China—Grapes were very late to ripen in China's Hebei province, but wineries that could delay picking produced wines with good flavor and color. Grape growers in Shandong province, which is farther south and coastal, made even better use of the cooler and drier conditions, achieving desired sugar levels and robust coloring, with very little rot.

Japan—Conditions were very good in Japan's main regions, Yamanashi and Nagano. There were a few typhoons in the early summer, but no damage. With sustained sunshine and little rain late in the season, the vineyards enjoyed much lower levels of rot, encouraging growers to wait for optimal ripeness before picking. Nagano Merlot looks promising.

India—A weaker-than-usual monsoon season delivered drier-than-normal conditions, which favored even ripening patterns and made rot more manageable. The white varieties came off well in Bangalore, as did most of the reds, though some red varieties did suffer insect and fungal attacks. In Maharashtra, it was an excellent year, with good diurnal variations at the critical points, and slow, even ripening.

2001

China—Vintage conditions were generally very good in China. Extended dry spells during a late ripening period in Hebei permitted fruit to develop good sugar levels and color, although some vineyards suffered hail damage. Part of Shandong suffered both late spring frosts and summer hailstorms; consequently, yields were reduced. Shandong also had fungal-disease problems brought on by late rains.

Japan—Both Yamanashi and Nagano had an excellent vintage. The wines are generally softer and more fully flavored than usual.

India—A very good year, with slow, even ripening conditions and a relatively dry harvest period.

2000

China—In Hebei and Shandong, long dry periods during ripening and harvest provided welcome relief for most growers from the usual fungal-disease problems.

Japan—Yamanashi and Nagano had a good year—though it was better in the former than the latter. Nagano's Kikyogahara district, renowned for its Merlot and Cabernet, had only an average year.

India—An excellent year in Bangalore, where light rains in the late ripening period brought temperatures down and assisted flavor concentration.

1999

China—It was a drier year than usual in Hebei and Shandong, resulting in good sugar content and color achieved by most growers. Shandong, however, did not avoid the usual fungal problems.

Japan—Nagano—and Kikyogahara—had an excellent year, with regular weather conditions through the vintage. Yamanashi did not fare so well.

India—It was a very good year in both Bangalore and Maharashtra, although some of the Bangalore reds lacked concentration.

1998

China—Hebei and Shandong had an average vintage. Although it was reasonably dry during the late ripening season, growers still had to battle the usual fungal problems caused by occasional rains, especially in Shandong, encouraging many contract growers to take the fruit early.

For those who waited, average ripeness was achieved.

Japan—For most producers in Yamanashi and Nagano it was a difficult vintage. In Yamanashi there was heavy snow in the winter months, followed by a wetter-than-average "wet" season that continued on well into August. Nagano also had a very wet year, with the Kikyogahara district heavily affected. Underripened grapes and fungal disease were common problems in both prefectures. Surprisingly, however, Nagano's Hokushin district avoided much of the rain and enjoyed one of its best vintages.

India—It was a very good year in Maharashtra, but rains during harvest created fungal problems for some red varieties in Bangalore, where, otherwise, it was a good year.

1997

China—There was nothing particularly notable about this vintage in Hebei and Shandong, with only modest sugar levels and high acid.

Japan—Nagano experienced one of its best years, as museum wines from this vintage recently released by some of its leading producers attest. In the Hokushin district, however, moderate rainfall combined with high temperatures caused a loss of flavor intensity and acidity, and, overall, it was a disappointing year.

India—An average-quality harvest.

Grapevine

- **Wineries in China** paid up to double the price for white-wine grapes in 2002. Prices of white grapes had sunk over the previous five years because of a drop in white-wine sales following a significant swing to red wine as a direct result of the French paradox publicity. White wines have now climbed back and are pushing close to 30 percent of domestic sales, with retail prices firming up. Many growers now regret uprooting or grafting over their white varieties. New plantings are now common.

- **China** has abolished "half-juice wine" as of June 30, 2004. This anomalous product was allowed to be called wine, even though it contained only 50 percent grape juice, for two reasons. First, it recognized the reality that so much of the local grape crop, particularly the local mountain varieties known collectively as *shanputao*, fails to reach even moderately acceptable sugar levels, hence the grapes are picked with huge acid levels, requiring dilution and sugar augmentation if it is to be drinkable. Second, it was an acknowledgment of the need to provide the populace with a drink it could afford, and half-juice wines rarely sold for more than Rmb 10. The law, however, left plenty of room for interpretation on not only the amount of water sugar that could be used, but also for colorants, grain alcohol, and essences of various kinds. Its abolition has received the enthusiastic support of the China Alcoholic Drinks Industry Association, which had become increasingly concerned at the damage this practice was causing the mainstream wine industry.

GREATEST WINE PRODUCERS

1. Château Mercian (Japan)
2. Suntory (Japan)
3. Grace Winery (Japan)
4. Dragon Seal (China)
5. Hua Dong (China)
6. Marufuji Rubaiyat (Japan)
7. Changyu (China)
8. Great Wall (China)
9. Manns (Japan)
10. Indage (India)

FASTEST-IMPROVING PRODUCERS

1. Dynasty (China)
2. Grover Vineyards (India)
3. Izutsu (Japan)
4. Hayashi Noen (Japan)
5. Katsunuma Jozo (Japan)
6. Okuizumo (Japan)
7. Takeda (Japan)
8. Weilong (Grand Dragon) (China)
9. Lou Lan (China)
10. Coco Farm (Japan)

NEW UP-AND-COMING PRODUCERS

1. Tsuno Wines (Japan)
2. Suntime (China)
3. Sula (India)
4. Obuse Domaine Sogga (Japan)
5. Domaine Q (Japan)
6. Shanxi Grace (China)
7. Mogao (China)
8. Fazenda Ouhua (China)
9. Chateau Mani (S Korea)
10. Chateau de Loei (Thailand)

BEST-VALUE PRODUCERS

1. Dragon Seal (China)
2. Tsuno Wines (Japan)
3. Grace Winery (Japan)
4. Marufuji Rubaiyat (Japan)
5. Kitanoro Jozo (Japan)

6. Hayashi Noen (Japan)
7. Grover Vineyards (India)
8. Izutsu (Japan)
9. Weilong (China)
10. Great Wall (China)

GREATEST-QUALITY WINES

1. **Private Reserve Hokushin Chardonnay 2001** Château Mercian, Japan (¥6,000)
2. **Nagano Shiojiri Merlot 1997** Marufuji Rubaiyat, Japan (¥3,500)
3. **Private Reserve Kikyogahara Merlot 1999** Château Mercian, Japan (¥10,000)
4. **Tomi no Oka 1997** Suntory, Japan (¥10,000)
5. **Cuvée Misawa Chardonnay 2002** Grace Winery, Japan (¥6,000)
6. **Unfiltered Chardonnay 2000** Takahata, Japan (¥2,500)
7. **Cabernet Sauvignon/Merlot/ Petit Verdot 2001** Marufuji Rubaiyat, Japan (¥4,500)
8. **Koshu Sur Lie 2001** Marufuji Rubaiyat, Japan (¥1,500)
9. **Cru du Huailai Syrah 2000** Dragon Seal, China (Rmb 300)
10. **Méthode Traditionelle Sparkling NV** Marquise de Pompadour, India (Rp 720)

BEST BARGAINS

1. **Campbell Early Rosé 2002** Miyazaki Tsuno Wines, Japan (¥1,220)
2. **Toriibira Koshu 2002** Grace Winery, Japan (¥1,800)
3. **Riesling NV** Dragon Seal, China (Rmb 35)
4. **Koshu Nouveau Dry 2002** Katsunuma Jozo, Japan (¥1,200)
5. **Cabernet Sauvignon 2002** Dragon Seal, China (Rmb 50)

❻ Merlot Nouveau 2002
Izutsu, Japan (¥1,460)
❼ Sparkling Brut NV
Dragon Seal, China (Rmb 80)
❽ Cabernet-Shiraz NV
Grover Vineyards, India (Rp 450)
❾ Hokkaido Late Harvest Kerner 2000 Sapporo Grande Polaire, Japan (¥1,200)
❿ Dry White NV
Great Wall, China (Rmb 35)

MOST EXCITING OR UNUSUAL FINDS

❶ Cru du Huailai Syrah 2000
Dragon Seal, China (Rmb 300)
First Syrah in China, from very young vines grown from imported French cuttings. Dragon Seal has invested heavily in viticultural improvement, and it shows.
❷ Empery Cupid Wild Grapes Wine 2000 East of Eden, South Korea (Won 25,000) *A sweet red wine made from wild amurensis grape, the only variety grown by this maker and the only wine of its kind in Korea. Virtually organic.*
❸ Sangiovese/Merlot Obuse Domaine Sogga, Japan (¥4,000)
First Sangiovese in Japan, from a young winemaker bent on experimentation.
❹ Koshu Nouveau Dry Katsunuma Jozo, Japan (¥1,200) *An established winery pushing out on new frontiers, Katsunuma Jozo has produced a*

fresh and lively new "persona" for Japan's unique Koshu variety.
❺ Semillon Kitanoro Jozo, Japan (¥1,800) *A new white variety bred from Gros Semillon and Fubuki (itself a cross of Koshu and Mills).*
❻ Muscat Bailey-A/Cabernet Franc/Kainoir 2000 Iwanohara Wines, Japan (¥4,000) *Only 5,000 bottles were made of this intriguing new blend from Niigata, on the west coast of Japan's main island, an emerging new region for wine.*
❼ Goichi Ryugan Taru 2000
Hayashi Noen, Japan (¥1,400)
One of very few pure examples of this variety, a relative of China's Longyan (Dragon's Eye) staple and uniquely oak-aged.
❽ Novo Demi-Sec NV Coco Farm, Japan (¥6,000) *A méthode champenoise blend of Koshu and Riesling Lion (a new variety developed by Sapporo from a crossing of the Koshu-related Sanjaku variety and Riesling).*
❾ Cabernet Gernischt 1997
Changyu, China (Rmb 100)
Apparently a lost Cabernet that is said to have arrived in China in the late 19th century and that, with further work, could emerge as China's signature red wine.
❿ Shanxi Rosé NV Grace Winery, China (Rmb 70) *A new style blend of Cabernet Sauvignon, Cabernet Franc, and Merlot from the exciting, emerging Shanxi region in China's central west.*

Grapevine

• **After a long history** of servicing the bargain basement, Dynasty, one of the giants of the Chinese industry, will be releasing the inaugural 2002 vintage from its new, upmarket winery in Ningxia province, including Cabernet Sauvignon, Merlot, Pinot Noir, Chardonnay, and Italian Riesling. A premium unwooded Chardonnay from an experimental high-altitude vineyard in Ji county, Hebei province, is also scheduled for release in 2003. Interesting sparkling wines are in the works, too.

Organic & Biodynamic Wines

Monty Waldin

Scare stories about 'Frankenstein foods' have meant that, in Europe at least, consumer resistance to genetic modification has remained strong, while sales of organic foods and wines have increased.

MONTY WALDIN

However, GM practitioners seem to be changing tack in an effort to win consumers' approval. A multinational project called the International Grape Genome Program (IGGP), which aims to sequence the genome of the wine-grape vine (*Vitis vinifera*), held its first workshop at the Plant and Animal Genome (PAG) Conference in San Diego, California, in January 2003.

The function of most wine genes is unknown, so the IGGP hopes that, by sequencing the vine genome, the supply of *Vitis* genes with known characteristics will be increased, and more potentially useful vine gene candidates for the genetic modification of vines or vine rootstocks will emerge. One hoped-for spinoff of the IGGP is to create a genetically modified rootstock containing a "gene silencer" from a *Vitis* gene. This could stop viruses from replicating in vine cells if the effect of the gene silencer could systemically migrate from the GM rootstock into the *V. vinifera* scion.

MONTY WALDIN While working on a conventionally farmed wine domaine in Bordeaux as a teenager, Monty Waldin realized that the more chemicals were applied to a vineyard, the more corrective treatments became necessary in the winery. When the opportunity arose to write about wines, he specialized in green issues and now writes a regular column on environmental matters for *Harpers*, the weekly journal of the wine and liquor trade in the UK. His first book, *The Organic Wine Guide* (Thorsons, 1999), is soon to be joined by a guide dedicated to biodynamic producers. Monty's interest in biodynamics was stimulated in 1999 by six months working on a family-owned biodynamic vineyard in California's Mendocino County. Previous winemaking experience in Chile contributed to his latest book, *The South American Wine Guide*, published by Mitchell Beazley in September 2003.

Because the vine scion will not be genetically modified, and only *Vitis* (but not necessarily *V. vinifera*) genes will be used to modify the rootstock, IGGP researchers hope to allay fears of "Frankenstein wines" among some wine drinkers. The specter of Frankenstein wines first arose when GM vines were created using genes from non-vine plants, such as moss (for increased cold resistance) and barley (for increased fungal resistance), although such vines are still several years from commercial production.

The implications for organic producers, who are forbidden to use GM products, are serious if consumers and legislators believe that *Vitis*-only GM technology such as that proposed by the IGGP is acceptable. In other words, a Cabernet Sauvignon wine made from grapes picked from a *V. vinifera* scion grown on a "gene-silenced" GM rootstock would be seen as no different from any "normal" or non-GM Cabernet Sauvignon. The organic lobby feels that GM technology is the agro-industry's unnecessary, irreversible, and potentially dangerous response to problems created after World War II by the agro-industry's own adoption of chemical vineyard treatments.

Grapevine

• **California's Hess Collection Winery** has hired Colombian-born biodynamic consultant René Piamonte to oversee production at its Colomé, Amalaya, and Viñas de Altura estates in the Calchaquíes Valley, Argentina. At 7,808–10,498 ft (2,380–3,200 m), these are the highest-altitude biodynamically farmed (although not yet certified) vineyards in the world. The greatest challenge so far has been to control ants in the vineyards without resorting to pesticides.

• **Certified organic producer Nanni,** based in Argentina's Cafayate region in the Salta province, is regrafting many of its Torrontés vines, which dominate the vineyards, with red varieties—in line with world-consumption trends.

• **At Finca La Colonia** (Alto Agrelo) in Argentina's Mendoza, a 60-hectare (ha) plot of Malbec produced Bodega Norton's first fully certified organic grapes in 2003.

• **The Organic Red Wine of the Year** at the UK Soil Association's Organic Food Awards in September 2002 was awarded to Penfolds Clare Valley Red 2001.

• **Bonterra Vineyards,** the organic brand of Fetzer Vineyards (Brown-Forman Wine Group), is to develop two Mendocino County ranches along biodynamic lines: Butler Ranch, a former fruit farm, planted 100 acres of Syrah, Mourvèdre, Grenache, Cabernet, Malbec, Petit Verdot, Zinfandel, and Petite Sirah; and McNab Ranch, formerly James Fetzer's Ceago Vinegarden, planted Malbec, Cabernet Franc, and Cabernet Sauvignon.

• **In San Juan, Argentina,** Fabril Alto Verde's previously rather lackluster wines have benefited from Master of Wine Angela Muir's consultancy in the Buenas Ondas brand project for UK organic-wine specialist Vintage Roots.

• **In Mendoza, Argentina,** Zuccardi harvested its first fully certified organic grapes from the Fray Luis Beltrán Estate in Maipù for the Terra Orgánica range, which includes an oak-aged Sangiovese.

• **In May 2002,** Santa Emiliana VOE biodynamic and winemaking consultant Alvaro Espinoza began certification of his own Antiyal vineyard at Buín in the Maipo.

BLINDINGLY EFFICIENT INSPECTORS

It is alleged that organic-grape inspectors have turned a blind eye to French growers in the Midi using banned pesticides to counter the *Scaphoideus littoralis* leafhopper, which transmits *flavescence dorée*, an incurable vine disease. Rotenone, a plant extract, is allowed under organic rules. It cannot eradicate *flavescence dorée*, but it can preempt its spread. However, it is difficult to apply and not always successful. Applications must be made over a period of five successive weeks and only at dusk (rotenone is light-sensitive). Louis Delhon of Domaine Bassac, in Puissalicon (Hérault), withdrew some of his vines from organic certification when his rotenone treatments failed and he had to resort to a pesticide; but he was an exception among organic growers in an area considered a *flavescence* hotspot.

FREE AIR-SPRAY

Another issue in the Midi concerning *flavescence dorée* is the forced spraying of vineyards to counter its leafhopper vector. In certain areas the chemicals used are mandatory, and the spraying is supervised by local *chambres d'agriculture* on behalf of the French state. The chemicals are not, however, allowed under organic regulation; and the sprays are often made by helicopter, which can be very imprecise, with chemicals ending up in organic vineyards. But when the organic inspector comes and asks growers whether they sprayed any chemicals on their vines, they can honestly say they did not. So they maintain their organic status even though their "organic" vines are being chemically farmed, albeit to a limited extent and unwittingly. Robert Eden of Comte Cathare is one of the few producers who voluntarily withdrew such vines from organic certification in 2002. Other, less honest, organic growers appear happy with the status quo: their vines get a free spray that protects them from an incurable disease, they maintain their organic status, and they continue to receive subsidies paid by the French state for converting to organics. The system is in desperate need of review.

ECOCERT FRAUD POSSIBLE

French organic inspectors admit that their inspection regimes concerning vineyards in the Midi are open to abuse. "It is possible, probable even, that there is fraud," said Philippe Blais, who liaises between organic growers and Ecocert France, the leading national organic-certification body. "But even with five inspections per vineyard per year, we would not eliminate it totally. We cannot be on the growers' backs 24 hours a day."

NITROFEN SCANDAL

The efficacy of organic inspection procedures came under scrutiny in Germany in 2002 during what became known as the Nitrofen scandal. Organic animal feed accidentally stored in a warehouse containing banned chemical residues ended up in the organic food chain. German wine producers reported no adverse effect on either their reputation or sales.

GLOBAL ORGANIC VINEYARD PLANTINGS

CURRENT STATUS OF CERTIFIED ORGANIC VINEYARDS

Country or region	Hectares certified organic	Percentage of vineyards	Year	Comments
Europe	60,000	1.6	2000	No official statistics exist, but this Swiss-based estimate appears in a paper titled Organic Viticulture in Europe (FiBL). The figure is questionable, since it seems to be based on Italy having 30,000 ha and Spain 20,000 ha.
Argentina	<1,000	<1.0	2003	Based on 100,000 ha of fine-wine vineyards, while Argentina has around 200,000 ha of vines in total.
Australia	<1,100	<1.0	2002	No official figures exist, but unofficial estimates put the total at between 0.5–0.75% of Australia's vineyards.
Austria	700	1.2	2002	The sharp rises in Austria's organic vineyards seen in the mid- to late 1990s have stabilized. No big changes are expected in the near future. Most organic estates are small holdings (less than 3 ha) selling their produce locally.
Bulgaria	0	0	2003	At present no organic vineyards are certified to EU criteria, but Bulgaria is to receive funds from the EU to kick-start its organic agriculture program.
California	6,707	3.0	2003	California Certified Organic Farmers (CCOF), the state's largest organic-certification body, reported that 6,707 acres of wine vineyards were CCOF-certified organic by 2003, a 24% rise on the 2001 figure of 5,441 acres.
Chile	<1,200	1.5	2003	A steep rise since 2000, when the figure was around 0.1%.
France	14,500	1.7	2002	The latest official figures show that the largest concentrations of organic vineyards were found in Languedoc-Roussillon (3,764 ha; 279 growers), Provence (3,186 ha; 209 growers), the Loire (789 ha; 62 growers), Alsace (471 ha; 51 growers), and Bourgogne (372 ha; 52 growers).
Germany	1,600	1.5	2002	The bulk of growers were divided between the following organic bodies: Ecovin (289 members with nearly 1,000 ha), Naturland Fachverband Wein (20 members with 220 ha), and Bioland (130 members with 300 ha).
Greece	700	0.5	2002	Greece's organic vineyards represent 11% of its organic farm area, the highest in the European Union.
Italy	31,000	3.4	2002	Italy does not publish national statistics for its organic vineyards, although the country has over 1.2 million hectares of organic farmland (all crops), and this accounts for more than 25% of EU farmland (all crops). Roberto Pinto (Professor of Crop Science and Agricultural Engineering, University of Udine) estimates Italy's organic vineyards at 31,000 ha, producing 1.3 million hectoliters of wine annually, of which 20% is sold in bulk, 30% sold in Italy, and 50% exported.

Country or region	Hectares certified organic	Percentage of vineyards	Year	Comments
New Zealand	180	<1.0	2003	*This represents around 3% of the New Zealand wine industry's 400-some wine producers.*
Portugal	900	<0.4	2002	*Portugal's first wine domaine to convert to biodynamics was the 8-ha Quinta do Vale Pequeño, in the Ribatejo, in 2002.*
Spain	11,900	<1.0	2001	*Spain's organic vineyard doubled in size between 1998 and 2001, but these figures make no differentiation between growers in the first year, second year, or full organic conversion. La Mancha, Rioja, and Penedès are driving Spain's organic-wine scene, which—like Spain's organic food sector—is entirely geared to exports.*
Uruguay	16.5	<0.2	2002	*Of Uruguay's 3,000 ha of fine wine vineyards, only 16.5 ha were certified organic in 2002. They belong to Vinos de La Cruz, Uruguay's first certified organic-wine producer.*

Grapevine

• **Cono Sur** harvested the first fully certified organic Cabernet Sauvignon and Merlot from a 40-ha plot of its 300-ha Chimbarongo vineyard in the Colchagua Valley in 2003.

• Syrah vines in **La Fortuna's** El Semillero vineyard in Curicó Valley obtained full organic certification in 2003. La Fortuna says all three of its Curicó Valley vineyards should be fully organic by 2005.

• **Chile's** most northerly organic vineyard, Aguatierra, in the Limarí Valley, has announced the launch of a new brand, Punivin, and has hired well-known consultant Felipe de Solminihac (Sol de Sol, Aquitania) to oversee winemaking.

• **Viña Carmen,** producers of Nativa, Chile's first organic brand with EU-accredited organic certification, announced a huge expansion in its organic-vineyard program, from 25 to 125 ha over the next three years.

• **Casa Lapostolle** began biodynamic trials in May 2003 to add to its existing certified organic vineyards (66.6 ha out of 330 ha).

• **Demeter France** reports that for the first time it has certified over 1,000 ha of

vineyards as biodynamic, in 2002, an increase of 350 ha since 2001.

• **Alsace** continued to be France's most biodynamically oriented region with Domaine Charles & Dominique Frey, Domaine Frédéric Geschickt, Domaine Jean-François Ginglinger, and Domaine Martin Schaetzel among the new conversions.

• **Three of Germany's** leading organic estates, Weingut Janson-Bernhard and Weingut Pflüger in the Pfalz and Weingut Brüder Dr Becker in the Rheinhessen, formed a joint-venture promotional body called Signature Wines to raise awareness of organic German wines, and organic Riesling in particular, in key export markets such as the UK.

• **Christine Bernhard** of Weingut Janson-Bernhard said that 2003 would see the first experimental fermentations using interspecific (hybrid) crossings with increased disease resistance like Regent, Johanniter, and Solaris.

• **Charles Back** of Fairview Estate, Paarl, released his first organic *cuvée*, a red called Goat d'Afrique from purchased Olifants River Shiraz.

Opinion:
A call for the recognition of some hybrids

Wines made from fungal-resistant hybrid crossings with the same "unfoxy" quality characteristics as *V. vinifera*, such as those developed in Germany, should be officially recognized across the EU as being eligible for quality-wine status. So far only the Bundessortenamt (Federal Plant Patent Office) in Germany has officially given Regent, Solaris, and Johanniter such status. These vines offer one solution to the use of copper in the vineyard, for which no effective alternative has been found, or indeed sanctioned, by Europe's organic rule-makers. According quality-wine status to Regent, for example, would encourage growers in the New World, whose organic wines are aimed at the European market. Regent might prove very effective in South Africa, for instance, where mildew pressure in the more humid, coastal regions is seen as a real obstacle by would-be organic producers.

Global standards required

A globally recognized and agreed organic grape-growing standard is desirable for those who believe there are too many contradictions and anomalies in the way certification bodies operate: for instance, tolerance of parallel production (when only part of a vineyard is farmed organically) and the use of organic raw materials in compost (manure from animals fed only on organic material rather than on "organic materials where available").

Swiss certification bodies like IMO (Institut für Marktökologie, which certifies the VOE vineyard in Chile, for example) are much stricter over the issue of parallel production than other European certification bodies, setting wider "buffer zones" between organic and conventionally farmed parcels. Sadly, a world organic grape-growing standard is unlikely to appear while growers in European countries continue to argue over, for example, exactly how many kilos of copper per hectare per year may be used to counter downy mildew.

As for a global winemaking standard, this seems even farther away, especially in the EU, where no organic winemaking standard exists, meaning that wines must be described as "made from organically grown grapes" and not as "organic wine." Perhaps the EU could adopt the winemaking rules featured in the US National Organic Program, which do permit use of the term "organic wine" if, for example, no sulfur dioxide is used during winemaking.

Transparent labelling

The listing of aids, agents, and additives should be mandatory on wine labels. This would expose some of the spuriously marketed "natural" wines made by conventional producers, and would indirectly promote the work of the best organic growers, who manage to bottle without fining or filtering wines that remain stable in bottle until consumed.

Grapevine

- **Renate Künast,** the German minister appointed in 2001 during Chancellor Gerhard Schröder's first term of office and a member of the Green Party, reaffirmed her commitment during Schröder's 2002 re-election campaign to make a fifth of German farms organic by 2010 (in wine's case, this would mean over 9,000 new organic vineyards by 2010).

- **English-educated** Nicholas Cosmetatos's eponymously named domaine in Minies, Cephalonia, is the latest Greek domaine to convert to organics, with full certification achieved in 2003.

- **Certified Organic Winegrowers** of New Zealand (COWNZ) is soon due to publish a set of organic grape-growing and winemaking standards and guidelines for current and future organic growers. COWNZ aims to reduce "trial and error" by highlighting the avoidable mistakes that growers often experience when converting from conventional through IPM to organic.

- **James Millton** has developed another 13 acres of steep hillside as a vineyard adjacent to its Naboths Vineyard in Gisborne. Pinot Noir, Viognier, and Chenin Blanc were planted. The Millton Vineyard also released a new wine style, a light semi-sweet Moscato called Muskats @ Dawn [sic].

- **Evert Nijzink** has retaken control of his Settlers' Vineyard in Hawkes Bay, having leased it for five years, and has taken immediate steps to take it back to full organic status. Nijzink says: "It is still showing great natural [fungal and pest] resistance."

- **South Africa** has been slow to develop organic vineyards. Some experimental projects came to grief in 2002, a vintage affected by extreme mildew pressure. However, a number of domaines are emerging in the drier regions of Robertson (despite flash floods in March 2003) and the hitherto undervalued Olifants River.

- **Stellar Organics** in the Olifants River released its first wines from certified organic grapes in 2003. Stellar's winery is also a refrigerated fruit-packing warehouse, so bunches can be chilled and hand-selected before fermentation. (The table-grape season ends just as the wine harvest begins.)

- **The Swiss-owned African Terroir,** formerly Sonop, developed a new winery at its Sonop Estate in Paarl, where it hopes to ferment grapes from 600 ha of organic vineyards in 2004 for its Cape Soleil and Sonop Organic brands.

- **In 2003, Rozendal vinified** certified-biodynamic-estate grapes separately from purchased conventional grapes for the first time in its winery in the Jonkershoek Valley, near Stellenbosch.

- **La Cruz,** Uruguay's first and, so far, only certified organic winery, announced a 100,000-bottle order from a Costa Rican importer for its wines made from organically grown grapes. This was apparently the biggest-ever export order placed for Uruguayan wine.

GREATEST WINE PRODUCERS

1. Domaine Leroy (Burgundy, France)
2. Domaine Marcel Deiss (Alsace, France)
3. Nikolaihof (Wachau, Austria)
4. Domaine Huet (Loire Valley, France)
5. Bossard Domaine de l'Ecu (Loire Valley, France)
6. Millton Vineyard (Gisborne, New Zealand)
7. Cascina degli Ulivi (Piemonte, Italy)
8. Santa Emiliana VOE (Colchagua Valley, Chile)
9. Antiyal (Maipo Valley, Chile)
10. Bonterra (California)

FASTEST-IMPROVING PRODUCERS

1. Jean-Pierre Fleury (Champagne, France)
2. Christine et Eric Saurel (Rhône Valley, France)
3. Domaine Zind-Humbrecht (Alsace, France)
4. Holmes Brothers (Nelson, New Zealand)
5. Bodegas Viña Ijalba (Rioja, Spain)
6. Bodega Biurko Gorri (Navarra, Spain)
7. Cantina di Custoza (Veneto, Italy)
8. Weingut Zähringer (Baden-Tuniberg, Germany)
9. Chapoutier Domaine des Béates (Provence, France)
10. Sedlescombe Organic Vineyard (East Sussex, UK)

NEW UP-AND-COMING PRODUCERS

1. Santa Emiliana VOE (Colchagua Valley, Chile)
2. Christine et Eric Saurel (Rhône Valley, France)
3. Stellar Organics (Olifants River, South Africa)
4. Fabril Alto Verde (San Juan, Argentina)
5. Bon Cap Organic Winery (Robertson, South Africa)
6. Duval-Leroy (Champagne, France)
7. Cono Sur (Colchagua Valley, Chile)
8. La Ferme des Sept Lunes (Rhône Valley, France)
9. Ruiz Jiménez (Rioja, Spain)
10. Reh-Kendermann for Kendermanns Organic White (Rheinhessen, Germany)

BEST-VALUE PRODUCERS

1. Domaine de la Grande Bellane (Rhône Valley, France)
2. Fabril Alto Verde (San Juan, Argentina)
3. Jacques Frélin Vignobles (Languedoc, France)
4. California Direct (California)
5. Stellar Organics (Olifants River, South Africa)
6. Château/Domaine de Brau (Cabardès, France)
7. African Terroir—formerly Sonop (Paarl, South Africa)
8. Perlage (Veneto, Italy)
9. La Riojana (La Rioja, Argentina)
10. Fasoli Gino (Soave, Italy)

GREATEST-QUALITY WINES

1. **Clos de la Roche 1999** Domaine Leroy, Burgundy, France (€510)
2. **Grasberg 1999** Domaine Marcel Deiss, Alsace, France (€31)
3. **Le Haut Lieu Sec Vouvray 1993** Domaine Huet, Loire Valley, France (export only—£15 in UK)

④ **Coyam Red 2002** VOE, Colchagua Valley, Chile (export only—£8.95 in UK)

⑤ **Mâcon-Cruzille Blanc Les Perrières 2000** Domaine Guillot-Broux, Burgundy, France (€9.35)

⑥ **Clos Montirius Gigondas Rouge 2002** Christine et Eric Saurel, Rhône Valley, France (€9)

⑦ **Chardonnay Opou 2000** Millton Vineyard, Gisborne, New Zealand (NZ$24)

⑧ **St Joseph Rouge 2001** La Ferme des Sept Lunes, Rhône Valley, France (€15)

⑨ **Syrah Col.leccio 2000** Albet i Noya, Penedès, Spain (€8.50)

⑩ **Syrah 1999** Bonterra, California (US$25)

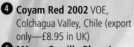

BEST BARGAINS

① **Torrontés La Riojana 2002** La Nature Organic, Argentina (export only—£4.49 in UK)

② **Falerio dei Colli Ascolani 2001** Saladini Pilastri, Italy (€2.90)

③ **Côtes du Rhône Valréas 2001** Domaine de la Grande Bellane, France (€3.66)

④ **Shiraz 2002** Stellar Organics, Olifants River, South Africa (export only—£6.50 in UK)

⑤ **Riesling 2000** Domaine Marcel Deiss, Alsace, France (€11.50)

⑥ **Cabernet Sauvignon 2001** OVC, California (export only—£4.99 in UK)

⑦ **Verdelho 2002** Wilkie Estate, Adelaide Plains, Australia (A$12)

⑧ **Perseus Rioja 2002** Ruiz Jimenez, Spain (€3.35)

⑨ **Grüner Veltliner Federspiel 2001** Nikolaihof, Austria (€6)

⑩ **Mâcon-Villages Quintaine 1999** Domaine Guillemot-Michel, France (€11)

Grapevine

• **Botobolar Vineyard,** in Australia's Mudgee district (NSW), reported organic crops reduced by 80–90 percent in 2003 due to drought conditions, with just four metric tons of Shiraz compared to 15 tons in 2002 and a whopping 35 in 2001.

• **Cabernet de Los Andes,** in Argentina's Catamarca province, launched its first Bonarda, Cabernet, and Syrah from certified organic grapes under the Vicien brand in September 2002.

• **Canada's organic growers,** in conjunction with the International Federation of Organic Agriculture Movements (IFOAM), the German organic viticulture organization Ecovin, and California's CCOF, hosted the 7th International Congress on Organic Viticulture and Wine, Victoria, British Columbia. The two-day congress, held in August 2002, focused on how different methods of soil and vegetation management, vine-protection techniques, and oenological intervention affect the sensory quality of organic wine.

• **Chile's flagship organic project,** Santa Emiliana VOE (Viñas Organicos Emiliana) at Nancagua in the Colchagua Valley, released its first wines from biodynamic grapes under the Coyam and Novas labels in 2003. The wines are blended reds from Mourvèdre, Syrah, and Bordeaux varieties. Also in 2003, Santa Emiliana Voe became the first South American vineyard to gain full certification for biodynamic farming under Demeter, the world biodynamic body. All the preparations were made on site from local materials for the first time, although stag's bladders, needed to make the yarrow preparation (Steiner's 'remedy' for sulfur), had to be sourced from southern Chile, as deer are not found this far north.

Wine & Health

Beverley Blanning MW

Having been commissioned to pull no punches in giving the bad news as well as the good, and with so much hype confusing both sides of the alcohol and health argument, I have special dispensation to summarize the current state of research.

BEVERLEY BLANNING MW

The J curve

Wine has been credited with health-giving properties since the earliest times. With the benefit of modern science, these health effects have been extensively studied, and hundreds of papers have been published on the subject. It is now widely recognized that light and moderate drinkers of any form of alcohol live longer than those who abstain or drink heavily. This relationship is known as the J-shaped curve. The relative risk of mortality is lowest among moderate consumers (the lowest point of the J), greater among abstainers (on the left-hand side of the J), and much greater still among heavy drinkers (on the right). In addition to longevity in general, the J-shaped relationship also exists for cardiovascular deaths, specifically for coronary heart disease and stroke, the leading causes of death in the Western world. For this reason, a great deal of research has focused on the effects of wine and other drinks on cardiovascular health. It is important to note that it is alcohol in general, not wine in particular, that is of paramount importance. Alcohol accounts for at least 50 percent of the beneficial effects concerning heart health, thus its J curve applies to beer, wine, liquor, and all other alcoholic drinks.

BEVERLEY BLANNING MW left a career in advertising to pursue her interest in wine, which she combined with her love of traveling, taking tourists on wine tours across the world. Based in London, she writes for a number of publications, gives lectures, and organizes tasting events. Beverley became a Master of Wine in 2001, specializing for her dissertation on the effects of wine on health.

Good highs and bad lows

Alcohol consumption increases the amount of "good" cholesterol (HDL, or high-density lipoprotein) and decreases the amount of "bad" cholesterol (LDL, or low-density lipoprotein) in the blood. LDL builds up on artery walls, restricting blood flow, while HDL transports LDL to the liver, where it is metabolized and discharged from the body. The balance between HDL and LDL cholesterol is therefore important. This may be the most important beneficial effect of wine. Alcohol can also prevent heart disease by its effects on thrombosis (blood clotting). Alcohol makes platelets, a portion of the blood that contributes to clotting, less sticky, so that they aggregate less. This means that clot formation within arteries is less likely.

The role of antioxidants in wine

There is mounting evidence that wine, especially red wine, has additional cardioprotective benefits compared to other alcoholic drinks thanks to its high levels of antioxidants. Antioxidants are found in many fruits and vegetables, and are present at particularly high levels in wine. Since other foods containing antioxidants have been associated with decreased mortality from coronary heart disease, it has been suggested that wine, with its high level of polyphenolic compounds, may have beneficial effects in addition to alcohol. Phenolics are present in higher concentrations in wine than in other alcoholic drinks. Alcohol alone appears to have no antioxidant role. Antioxidants are important protectors of health because they provide electrons that neutralize free radicals (which have the power to cause degenerative and life-threatening diseases). One of the most important potential benefits of antioxidants is the prevention of oxidation of "bad" LDL cholesterol by oxidative free radicals in the blood plasma. Oxidized LDL leads to swelling of the arteries. It has been shown that wine-derived phenolic compounds are significantly more effective at preventing oxidative damage to LDL than the antioxidants vitamins C and E, which are commonly found in fruits, vegetables, and other dietary sources. There are more than 200 phenolic compounds in wine, and they all have some antioxidant potential; but even when specific compounds can be isolated in vitro, knowledge of how they are metabolized by the body and how they in turn interact with alcohol is far from complete.

BREAST-CANCER FEARS

Breast cancer is the only common cancer often reported to be related to moderate alcohol consumption. Moderate wine drinking was first linked to breast cancer by Viel et al. in 1997, although the long-term Framingham study indicated no link (Zhang et al., 1999).

In 2002, the *British Journal of Cancer* published a paper providing what it claimed to be "the definitive answer" to the question of the link between smoking, alcohol consumption, and breast cancer. The study, which analyzed over 80 percent of the relevant information worldwide on alcohol and tobacco consumption, shows that a woman's risk of contracting breast cancer increases by 6 percent if she consumes just one drink per day. If she drinks three to four drinks a day, this risk increases to 32 percent compared to nondrinkers. In contrast, smoking was found not to contribute to the disease.

As with most research concerning alcohol and health, no distinction was made between different types of drinks, so it is not possible to isolate the effects of wine on breast-cancer incidence. The report concludes that, if the observed relationship is causal, about 4 percent of the breast cancers in developed countries are attributable to alcohol. It also acknowledges that the effect of alcohol on breast cancer needs to be interpreted in the context of its beneficial effects in moderation, a point noted by Dr. Philip Norrie, among others. In March 2003, Norrie stated, "If consuming alcohol in moderation may slightly increase the risk of breast cancer, this is more than compensated by a reduction in vascular disease by up to 50 percent. In Australia, for example, 2,500 women die each year from breast cancer, but 10 times that number die from vascular disease, and for each person who dies from vascular disease, two people survive [but are burdened] with angina, heart failure, and stroke." Nevertheless, the findings are significant, especially for younger women, who benefit less from the cardioprotective benefits of moderate alcohol consumption, as they are at a lower risk of cardiovascular disease. Of additional concern is the discovery that young women are drinking more: in the past decade the proportion of 16–24-year-old women in the UK consuming more than three drinks a day has doubled from 9 percent to 18 percent.

RESVERATROL

A phenolic compound attracting much media interest is resveratrol. Much of this attention is due, no doubt, to resveratrol's rarity as a dietary antioxidant as much as its unique properties. While other antioxidants are widely found in fruits, vegetables, and nonalcoholic beverages such as tea, the only other dietary sources of resveratrol are blueberries, cranberries, peanuts, and beansprouts. Despite resveratrol being present in wine at much lower concentrations than other phenolic compounds (less than 1 mg/l in white wines and 5–10 mg/l in reds, compared to in excess of 200 mg/l for catechins, the basic building blocks of tannin in wine), it is nevertheless considered one of the most potent antioxidants. Resveratrol offers protection against atherosclerosis (a disease of the artery) and coronary heart disease, it has powerful antidiabetic and anti-inflammatory properties, and, according to the *British Journal of Cancer* (February 2002), can be converted by the body into piceatannol, a known anti-cancer agent that can selectively target and destroy cancer cells. Resveratrol is a phytoalexin, a natural plant antibiotic produced by grapes in response to and as a defense against fungal attack and traumatic damage. It should be no surprise, therefore, to learn that it is found in greater concentration in grapes grown in relatively cool, humid climates such as in Burgundy, Switzerland, Oregon, Bordeaux, and Canada. Lowest concentrations have been found in wines from warmer, drier climates such as in Italy, California, South America, and South Africa. Very high resveratrol concentrations have been observed in wines made from Pinot Noir, which in itself might be considered a reflection of this variety's sensitivity to climate and therefore the areas where it is grown. An alternative or additional explanation is that Pinot Noir grapes are thin-skinned and, thus, more prone to fungal infection, which naturally promotes higher levels of resveratrol than other varieties. However, there is no proof (as yet) that resveratrol is the panacea the popular media likes to make out.

Certainly there are some researchers who claim that other phenolics present in larger concentrations show similar, if not greater, antioxidant and anti-platelet aggregation potency (that is, it decreases the "stickiness" of blood platelets and may help blood vessels remain open and flexible) than resveratrol.

REGIONAL OR VARIETAL DIFFERENCES?

Most wine and health watchers focus their antioxidant attention on catechin and epicatechin, which have the highest concentrations in wine. Interestingly, both have been found to be notably higher in wines made from Pinot Noir, especially from Burgundy and Canada. In Burgundian Pinot Noir, for example, concentrations of total catechins were consistently in excess of 200 mg/l, compared with the low levels found in Shiraz, especially from South Africa (38 mg/l), California (44 mg/l), and Australia (43 mg/l). The cooler wine-producing regions fare best in this analysis, although climate has not been proven to explain these differences. Regional differences may depend upon soil and winemaking techniques as much as climate.

PARADOXE BLANC

Since the discovery of the so-called French paradox in 1991, there has been an assumption that it is only red wine that confers health benefits. Most research to date has focused on red wines, because they are known to have far higher concentrations of phenolics than whites (on average, six times more, due to their greater skin and seed contact during the winemaking process). In 2002, a group of winemakers at the University of Montpellier created a white wine, Paradoxe Blanc, containing four times the usual white-wine level of polyphenols by mimicking the winemaking process of red wine. Goldberg et al. measured polyphenols in white wines to try to explain why white wines might have the same potency as reds. The study found that white wines had only 5 to 25 percent of the polyphenols of red wines. Catechin and epicatechin were found in the great majority of wines, but quercetin and resveratrol were undetectable in most. The researchers concluded that the climatic factors that modulate polyphenol concentrations in red wines do not seem to be important for white wines, but they were unable to offer any explanation for white wine's apparent benefits found in earlier studies. Despite far lower levels of polyphenols, white wines have been seen to perform as well as or better than red wine in reducing cardiac risk. One possible answer to this riddle has been put forward by an Australian physicist. Dr. Troup examined the size of the antioxidant molecules in wine and showed that those in white wine are smaller and thus more effective because they can be more easily absorbed. Whether or not this fully explains the research into white wine's benefits, it appears that the positive biological effect of white wines is disproportionately high in relation to its total polyphenol content, and this is certainly an area of research worthy of further study.

WINE, BEER, OR SPIRITS?

Recent research suggests that wine drinkers are at lower risk of death than beer or liquor drinkers, although some observers maintain that the beneficial effects of alcohol are so great that they outweigh any other differences between drinks. A major study of coronary heart disease mortality in 21 countries found that wine was the strongest dietary correlate, offering greater protection than beer or liquor. The Copenhagen City Heart Study found that drinkers of three to five glasses of wine a day had half the relative risk of dying of those who never drank wine. Beer and liquor drinkers had no such advantage; in fact, three to five drinks a day was associated with increased mortality. More recent research coming out of Denmark suggests that moderate wine drinkers appear to be at lower risk of becoming excessive drinkers than moderate drinkers of either beer or liquor. Furthermore, the results suggested that, although high intake of any form of alcohol conveys an increased risk for cirrhosis, wine drinkers are at a lower risk than beer and liquor drinkers.

LIFESTYLE

The Danish Diet, Cancer, and Health Study showed that preference of wine was associated with a healthier, "Mediterranean" diet, higher in fruits, vegetables, fish, salad, and olive oil. New data from the Lyon Heart Study has found that this type of diet, rather than a typical Western diet, combined with moderate wine consumption, may prevent a second heart attack in middle-aged men (aged 40 to 60). Compared to nondrinkers, men drinking two glasses of wine a day reduced their risk of a second heart attack by 59 percent. It is quite possible that wine drinkers are just naturally more moderate in their lifestyles and therefore enjoy better health. Earlier research into the characteristics of drinkers by beverage type has found that wine drinkers are likely to be nonsmokers, well educated, temperate, and generally free of symptoms or risk of illness. In comparison, liquor drinkers tend to be older, heavier drinkers, less educated, and show more risk factors for major illnesses, while beer drinkers fall somewhere between wine and liquor drinkers for most of these traits.

BENEFITS FOR REGULAR DRINKERS

Population research suggests it is regular consumption that is required for cardioprotection. This is the pattern of drinking that is traditionally associated with moderate wine consumption, and it tends to deliver health benefits without the risks associated with heavy consumption. A large study of American male health professionals published in 2003 found that those consuming alcohol five to seven days per week had the lowest risk of coronary heart disease. There was no significant difference in the protection conferred by different types of alcoholic drink, and benefits did not appear to be affected by whether or not the drink was consumed with food, contrary to other research that suggests that food enhances alcohol's positive effects.

PROSTATE CANCER

Researchers in Madrid have found that five different polyphenols inhibit the growth of prostate-cancer cells in vitro. Prostate cancer is the second-deadliest form of cancer for males in the US. If confirmed by larger studies, these findings may help to explain the higher rates of prostate cancer in the US and non-Mediterranean countries.

DEMENTIA

Recent data emerging from two decades of population research in Denmark, the Copenhagen Heart Study, has shown an association between moderate wine consumption and reduced risk of dementia. Moderate consumption of beer or liquor did not have this effect. In fact, beer consumption was associated with a significantly higher likelihood of dementia. A limitation of the study is that it does not take dietary habits into account. Vitamin E, for example, is thought to reduce the risk of Alzheimer's disease. It is possible, and previous studies have indicated that it may be so, that wine drinkers have a healthier diet than consumers of other alcoholic beverages.

RESEARCH ON THE YOUNG

Of all the factors to consider when analyzing risks versus benefits of alcohol consumption, age is perhaps the most important. Heart disease is relatively uncommon in the young, while deaths related to alcohol (such as road-traffic accidents, suicide, and violence) are much more prevalent. There is little research on the effects of wine consumption on the young. It has been generally thought that the benefits of moderate drinking apply only to those at greatest risk of cardiovascular disease, namely men over 45 and postmenopausal women. However, it is known that even though cardiovascular disease may not become apparent until later life, it may be incubated for many years before. A recently published project on nurses between the ages of 25 and 42 showed that the association between alcohol intake and risk of hypertension followed the classic J-shaped curve, which is to say that modest drinkers had fewer high-blood-pressure problems than abstainers, and heavier drinkers had the most problems.

LABELLING AND HEALTH MESSAGES

Producers have almost no opportunity to communicate positive health-related messages about wine on the bottle. Since 1990, the United States has enforced a compulsory warning on all alcohol that pregnant women should not drink, and that alcohol consumption impairs one's ability to drive or operate machinery and may cause health problems. In February 2003, the TTB (Alcohol and Tobacco Tax and Trade Bureau—formerly the Bureau of Alcohol, Tobacco, and Firearms) ruled that producers may put "directional" health statements, such as telling consumers to consult their family doctor or the federal dietary guidelines to learn more about the health effects of wine. To do so, however, producers must include a disclaimer. (This is in addition to the compulsory warning that alcohol may cause health problems.) Furthermore, the TTB insists that any health claim made on a label or advertisement must "disclose health risks associated with both moderate and heavier levels of consumption." It must also outline "the categories of individuals for whom alcohol consumption poses risks." This ruling means that even the previously approved directional statements, which are not allowed to mention any suggestion of benefit, must now be accompanied by two health warnings.

In Europe, no health information at all may be provided on labels. Currently, European law states that unless something is expressly allowed on a wine label, it is forbidden. In August 2003, the European Commission is due to rule on whether or not wine labels should permit additional information that is deemed useful to the consumer on wine labels. This could lead to health-related statements appearing on wine in the EU in the future.

Opinion:
Current practices that should stop

- The widespread Anglo-Saxon cultural acceptance of binge and (to a lesser degree) underage drinking. These practices are injurious to health and their approval or tolerance undermines attempts to communicate the real benefits of moderate consumption of wine and other alcoholic beverages. Binge drinking is on the increase in the Us and the UK.
- Restrictive laws prohibiting labeling of proven health claims about wine.
- In the US, the legal requirement for health warnings on every bottle of wine (especially those that are unsubstantiated or misleading).
- The current ban on ingredient labeling. Given the rise in consumer interest in organic wine and naturally produced food, it would be of interest to many to know what ingredients were used in the production of the wine (even if those ingredients are no longer present).
- Sensationalist media reporting of issues relating to wine and health.

Things that should be happening

- Accurate, up-to-date dissemination of widely accepted information relating to the health benefits of moderate consumption, supported by government and the medical profession.
- Producers should be allowed to include proven, specific, health-related information about wine on their bottles.
- International standardization of the definitions of a unit of alcohol and moderate consumption. Both vary enormously from country to country, causing consumer confusion regarding safe or desirable consumption levels.
- Bottles should indicate the number of units for contents—already practiced by many large retailers in the UK.
- Increased research into the benefits of white wine versus red wine.
- Increased research distinguishing between the health effects of wine versus beer and liquor, especially in vivo research to establish the effects of antioxidants on the body.
- Policies designed to promote sensible, responsible drinking—for example, acceptance of minors in drinking environments to discourage antisocial behavior.
- Cultural unacceptability of excessive consumption and widespread acceptance of the benefits of moderation.

TOP WINE HEALTH BENEFITS

① Increased longevity from moderate alcohol consumption.

② Significant protection against cardiovascular diseases, specifically, coronary heart disease (the number-one killer in the Western world) and ischemic stroke from moderate consumption.

③ Drinkers, especially wine drinkers, have lower risk of diabetes, osteoporosis, dementia, various forms of cancer, and many other diseases, including stress-related illnesses and the common cold.

TOP WINE HEALTH HYPES

① Drinking is good for you— it depends on individual circumstances.

② The benefits of consumption are accrued equally by young and old—most of the proven benefits are to men over 45 and postmenopausal women.

③ Red wine is better than white in providing health-related benefits— actually, the biological effects of white wines appear to be disproportionately high relative to their total polyphenol content.

④ Wine is necessarily a better option than beer or liquor— this conclusion is based on the assumption that in vitro research findings will be replicated in vivo.

⑤ Resveratrol is the most potent beneficial agent in wine.

⑥ The idea that regular, moderate consumption of wine is an acceptable substitute for improving health outcome in place of changing diet and other lifestyle factors, such as regular exercise.

TOP WINE HEALTH DANGERS

① All dangers stem from excessive alcohol consumption—both binge drinking and prolonged, heavy use. There is no danger from moderate consumption. Risks of misuse include:
- alcoholism;
- risk of accidents (especially among the young);
- violent crime;
- domestic violence and child abuse;
- family breakdown;
- suicide and depression;
- severe damage to every major system in the body, including the heart;
- fetal alcohol syndrome in babies born to women who drink heavily during pregnancy.

② Increased risk of breast cancer, even at low levels of consumption. This is of most significance to young women, especially since their consumption levels are increasing.

③ Ignorance of sensible drinking limits, including misunderstanding of what constitutes a binge (approximately six standard drinks).

TOP WINE DANGER MYTHS

① Drinking is bad for you.

② Drinking any alcohol while pregnant increases risk of fetal alcohol syndrome (FAS). Nearly all known cases of FAS involve mothers with chronic alcohol problems. However, controversy continues over whether there is a safe limit of consumption for pregnant women.

Grape Varieties

Dr Richard Smart & Doug Frost MW

Dr Murli Dharmadhikari, the director of the Midwest Viticulture and Enology Center, is working with others in Iowa and Illinois to breed, propagate, and better understand Eastern European grape varieties.

DR RICHARD SMART   DOUG FROST MW

Through a government-supported program called Viticultural Consortium East, run through New York's Cornell University, Murli's group is tending to some new vines. With the harsh winters and torrid summers of middle America similar to those in Eastern Europe, Murli is examining in detail a number of Eastern European vine varieties. Of 78 cultivars originally imported, Murli has identified four or five red varieties that look very promising and two or three white varieties. He plans to work with the original breeders to name and commercialize the vines, and, with UC Davis and Cornell University, he will be creating mother clone blocks of these vines, which will be heat-treated for commercial use.

Heritage clones

Clonal selection was begun and popularized in Europe but ignored in some New World countries, especially the US, until quite recently.

DR RICHARD SMART , "the flying vine doctor," is an Australian vineyard consultant with clients in 20 countries. He began his career in viticultural research in Australia, expanding to Israel, the US, France, and New Zealand. Richard is coauthor of the seminal work *Sunlight into Wine* (Winetitles, 1991) and is considered an authority on canopy management of grapevines. He has a regular column, Smart Viticulture, in *The Australian & New Zealand Wine Trade Journal*, is widely published in scientific and other journals, and is the viticulture editor for *The Oxford Companion to Wine*.

DOUG FROST MW is the author of two wine books, including *On Wine* (Rizzoli International Publications, 2001). He is one of only three people in the world to hold the titles of both Master Sommelier and Master of Wine.

European clonal selectors have had an advantage, since most varieties originated there, and they often have old plantings from which to make selections. Now European growers have access to extensive clone collections from many countries, which move easily across borders without quarantine delays. Nurseries like the Italian giant Rauscedo have clones available from government programs in Europe as well as their own selections. Clonal selection continues in Europe, and some nurseries in the New World are starting to take advantage of their own situation. Most Australian vineyards are not affected by phylloxera; consequently they have not been replanted in the last 80 years or so, thus the country boasts the world's oldest Syrah vines, and maybe Marsanne, too. Recently Narromine Fine Vines, an Australian nursery, has begun to promote "heritage clones" selected from Australia's oldest vineyards. Getting in on this act is the University of California affiliate, Foundation Plant Material Service (FPMS), which is already searching out heritage clones in California and importing the best from Europe, especially from ENTAV in France. In 2003, FPMS had four different Cabernet Sauvignon clones on its list, 26 Chardonnay clones, six Gamay Noir, four Merlot, one Petit Verdot, 29 Pinot Noir, and four Sauvignon Blanc. Italian clones are also on offer.

Grapevine

• **Wineries** in North America's southwest have many different regions, soils, and climatic challenges with which to contend, yet they all face a common issue: unripe and incomplete wines, especially with red varieties. In response to this, many producers in Texas, New Mexico, Arizona, and Baja California are switching from their long-established and cherished Bordeaux varieties to Grenache, Syrah, and other Rhône varieties.

• **All the way** from the northern Baja in Mexico to eastern Texas, nearly forgotten vineyards are springing back to life as growers plant Alicante Bouschet, Carignan, and other Rhône varieties, as well as Tempranillo, and winemakers eagerly exploit existing vineyards to test new options.

• **Craig Parker,** winemaker for Flat Creek Estate in Texas, is happy with his Sangiovese, although he believes that "it definitely requires cooler nights." The varieties that he and his neighbors are planting this year are Portuguese, including Tinta Cão, Tinta Madera, and Souzao.

• **Some Texans** are experimenting with native varieties like Lenoir, the grape that provided El Paso with commercial successes in the 19th century, and Norton, a grape that has done well in Missouri.

• **Red varieties,** even hybrid reds, continue to be problematic in northern US states. New varieties are being created, and plantings with Tempranillo/Riparia hybrids and Sangiovese hybrids, among others, may offer new hope to producers in difficult climates.

• **Vino con Brio winery** of Lodi has released California's first Pinotage, the inaugural vintage being 2002. This grape originates from South Africa, where it was bred, but it has not traveled much outside that country.

OLD VARIETIES BECOME NEW

It seems the interest in "heritage" varieties is becoming more global, extending to Gascony in France, where the local cooperative Plaimont is making *vin de pays* from Petit Courbu, Petit Manseng, Gros Manseng, and Arrufiac, varieties that were almost lost with the swing toward growing grapes for Armagnac. Petit Manseng is also making white wines of distinction for Symphony Wines in Australia's King Valley, which is the only Australian producer of Saperavi, the famous but underrated Russian Federation variety.

NAME CALLING

Cornell University of New York has one of the best-known grape breeding programs in the world, with releases extending back to 1906. Abundance was the name chosen for its newest release in 2003, a red-wine variety. Bruce Reisch, the current breeder, described it as vigorous and productive, with good winter-freeze tolerance, and making good wine with attractive cherry characters. The grape has been grown in trials in New York for over eight years, with the wine proving popular. Less popular, however, was the choice of the name Abundance, which was announced in

Grapevine

- **Carmenère** nearly became extinct. Only a few vine rows were left in Bordeaux when the grape was rescued by its discovery in Chile, where it had been erroneously identified as Merlot. Now it is being planted in Bordeaux, where some producers are insistent that Carmenère will become part of the wine landscape in the Médoc. In Italy, many of the vines thought to be Cabernet Franc have now been identified as Carmenère, particularly in Franciacorta.

- **Petit Verdot** has been on the increase for a decade or so in northern California. A handful of producers is proving that the grape has a great future in this area, with plantings increasing by more than seven-fold. Petit Verdot's growth is evident throughout California's wine country, even in the Napa Valley, where there are more than 100 acres, although the vast majority ends up in Bordeaux blends.

- **Malbec clone 595** accounts for most of the new plantations of this variety in California, and results have not been particularly encouraging, with all but a few wines ending up as blends, although Edgewood Estate, Clos du Bois, and RH Phillips have all made delicious if simple Malbecs.

- **Sauvignon Gris** has the phenolic texture and color of *gris* grapes such as Gewurztraminer or Pinot Gris, but while there are a few old-timers who still have some plots in California, there is not much around. Fred Brander of Brander Vineyards in California's Santa Ynez Valley is pleased with the wine he makes from the grape, but he makes only enough wine to sell at the winery door. As one of America's few specialists in Sauvignon Blanc, other producers may be swayed by Fred's enthusiasm for the wine.

- **Port vineyards** are undergoing change, as Patamares plantings (round-terraced vineyards), which were once all the rage, diminish in favor of more rational vineyard directional schemes. Among the vines, Touriga Nacional is taking over, followed by Tinta Cão and Touriga Francesa. The real victims may be the other 30 to 40 legal grapes in the Douro Valley, which few are eager to replant today. In particular, the white varieties are disappearing.

February 2003. Abundance Vineyards of Sonoma California claims ownership of the name under a registered trademark in the area "Goods and Services—Wine." The Cornell search of US Patents and Trademarks did not turn this up. So the grape reverts to its old nursery name of GR7, while a committee decides an appropriate new name.

SYRAH IS BURSTING FORTH IN SOUTH AMERICA

Brilliant Syrah is grown in Aconcagua and Colchagua and may be found in the easternmost hillsides of Casablanca. Syrah is being blended successfully into Malbecs, Bonardas, and Cabernets in Mendoza. The new Crios 2001 release from acclaimed Argentine winemaker Susanna Balbo is a blend of Bonarda and Syrah. Bodegas Norton has a new Syrah-Cabernet Reserva 2000 blend that shows well. The newest bottling of Argentina's most acclaimed Syrah, Luca 2001, is the best yet. On the Chilean side of the Andes, remarkable Syrah is being grown, from Aconcagua in the north, to Colchagua farther south. The common thread with these bottlings is elevated and well-drained vineyards, but plantings are occurring throughout the country. Viña Errazuriz reports selling over a million cuttings of Syrah to other vineyards in Chile over the past four years. Worldwide plantings have increased from less than 10,000 hectares (ha) to nearly 100,000 ha in the past 20 years or so.

DNA-TESTED GRAPEVINES

In 2002, using DNA identification techniques, FPMS declared that the local US Sauvignon Musque is in fact Sauvignon Blanc, although local winemakers claim that it has different taste from true Sauvignon Blanc. Also recently, it has been confirmed that locally named Sauvignon Vert is in fact Muscadelle, a naming error picked up in Californian importations in Australia. A variety known locally in California as Touriga has now been proven to have identical DNA to Touriga Nacional. The Alvaralheo was also found to be Touriga Nacional, while one instance of Touriga Francesa was found to be correctly named, yet another not. A Grignolino clone was found to be Arneis. Some Roussanne selections were found to be Viognier. Gradually, FPMS is getting the naming of the variety collection in order. Meanwhile, many vines are incorrectly named in vineyards and, of course, sold as the wrong varietal.

ZINFANDEL FINALLY PINNED DOWN

Zinfandel has long been considered California's "own grape," with the name traced back to 1852 importations. The name is uniquely American. It was the most widely planted grape in the 1878–89 wine boom, no doubt because it is a prolific yielder. Yet local scientist Austin Goheen put the cat among the pigeons in 1967 when he suggested that it might, in fact, be the same as

Italian variety Primitivo. This was confirmed by DNA fingerprinting in 1994 by Dr. Carole Meredith of UC Davis. Meredith has continued her studies to look for the European origin of Primitivo, and with the help of Croatian researchers she was able to announce in 2002 that an obscure Croatian variety, Crljenak Kastelanski, is the same as Zinfandel/Primitivo. Interestingly, this same variety is one parent of the distinguished Croatian variety Plavac Mali.

GO SLOW IN MADEIRA

Replantings in Madeira of noble grapes (Sercial, Verdelho, Bual, and Malmsey) are proceeding very slowly, allowing the primacy of lesser grapes such as Tinta Negra Mole or hybrids

such as Baco Noir to dominate. Unfortunately, the same cannot be said for Terrantez, at least at the moment. There are only a few hectares left of the grape, but seemingly scant interest in replanting it. Some in the wine industry talk about changing that attitude, but change in Madeira is still measured in decades, not years. As for Tinta Negra Mole, it is important to remember that Verdelho was not necessarily a respected grape a century ago. Considering Tinta Negra Mole's great success in mimicking the qualities of Bual and Malmsey for the last several decades, is it possible that the grape is deserving of attention and experimentation?

Grapevine

- **Virginia** is doing the most amazing things with Cabernet Franc, mostly due to a new group of clonal selections from northern Italy and France, which have joined the standard clone #1. The Italian clones have quickly offered good results in good vintages, while the traditional clone continues to handle difficult, wet, and cool years. Barboursville's winemaker Luca Paschina is very excited about the new clonal plantings, having felt limited by his reliance on just two clones of Cabernet Franc up until now. In challenging years, such as 2000, he has been disappointed by both clones, but three new promising clones could make his life easier and Virginia's Cabernet Francs more consistent.

- **Petra** is a new variety being grown in Hungary, and it was developed as disease-tolerant as well as very winter-cold resistant. The latter characteristic is

not surprising, since one of its parents is the famed *Vitis amurensis* from western China, which is renowned for being immune to freezing winters.

- **Present-day vine varieties** were generally selected from the wild by early farmers. They were usually seedling vines, being the "children" resulting from natural cross-pollination between different varieties. DNA testing has identified Pinot Noir as a common parent, with offspring that includes Chardonnay, Gamay, and 14 other varieties. The other parent is Gouais, a white variety so mediocre that it is no longer planted in France.

- **Pinot Noir clone** 2A Wadenswil has served the Santa Barbara region well, but newer clones are being found to offer more color, with Dijon clones 667 and 777 becoming popular and some growers preferring 115.

Classic Wine Vintage Guide

Serena Sutcliffe MW

Serena's tenure as head of one of the two most important international wine auction houses makes her uniquely qualified to provide guidance on the current condition of mature vintages of the world's classic wines.

SERENA SUTCLIFFE MW

Together with the greatest wines she has tasted over the past 12 months, the most surprising wines she has encountered, and her best auction bargains, the data in this report will be invaluable intelligence for anyone with such wines in their cellars or who is looking to buy or sell them at auction.

Tom Stevenson

SERENA SUTCLIFFE MW is the head of Sotheby's International Wine Department, with auctions in London, New York, Los Angeles, Chicago, and occasionally Hong Kong. Fluent in several major European languages, she became interested in wine while translating for the UN in France in the 1960s. In 1976 she became the second woman to qualify as a Master of Wine. Serena later served as chairman of the Institute of Masters of Wine. She is a regular lecturer and broadcaster in Europe, the United States, and Asia, and the author of several books on wine. She also writes regularly for publications all over the world. Serena is married to fellow Master of Wine David Peppercorn.

BORDEAUX

1994 Peaked.

1993 Peaked.

1992 Peaked, if you bothered to get them at all!

1987 Peaked.

1985 Peaked, except for First Growths and top seconds.

1984 Mostly unpleasant as well as past their best.

1983 Mostly at their peak, except for gems like Margaux, Palmer, and Pichon Lalande.

1982 Many have peaked, except for First Growths, Super Seconds, top St-Emilions, and Pomerols.

1981 Drink now for optimum pleasure.

1980 Mostly too old.

1979 Peaked, but top wines still drinking well.
1978 Peaked, but top wines still drinking well.
1977 Forget it.
1976 Peaked, except Lafite and Ausone, which are still looking good.
1975 Mostly peaked. Exceptions include Pétrus, Latour, La Mission Haut-Brion, Pichon Lalande, Cheval Blanc.
1974 Enough said!
1973 Ditto.
1972 Ditto to the nth degree!
1971 Peaked, except top Pomerols, which are still glorious, viz. the heavenly, "roasted" Pétrus.
1970 Mostly peaked. Exceptions include Pétrus, Latour, La Mission Haut-Brion, Trotanoy, La Conseillante, Pichon Lalande, Ducru-Beaucaillou, Palmer, Giscours, Beychevelle.
1969 Don't even think about it.
1968 Ditto.
1967 Peaked a long time ago, although Pétrus is still good.
1966 Mostly peaked. Exceptions include Latour, Cheval Blanc, Pétrus, Haut-Brion, La Mission Haut-Brion.
1965 Must be joking!
1964 Mostly peaked. Exceptions include Pétrus, Latour, Haut-Brion, La Mission Haut-Brion.
1962 Peaked, although the First Growths are still good.
1961 Most wines are still wonderful.
1959 The top wines are still magic.

RED BURGUNDY

1994 Drink now, since I think that dry finish will intensify.
1992 Delicious now.
1990 *Grands crus* have further to go.
1989 *Grands crus* have further to go.
1988 The top wines mostly have further to go.

1987 Should have been drunk.
1986 As above. Even Jayer is at its best.
1985 Mostly at, or over, its peak, except for top *grands crus*.
1984 Don't go there.
1983 A very few are hanging on.
1982 As above, for different reasons.
1981 Peaked.
1980 Past their peak. Even those brilliant Jayers should be drunk.
1979 Peaked.
1978 There are still some wonders at the top. They have a signature gaminess.
1977 They were never there in the first place!
1976 Peaked a long time ago, with the odd, rare exception.
1975 Should not be mentioned in polite society.
1974 Unpleasant and old.
1973 Peaked a long time ago.
1972 One or two survivors, viz. de Vogüé's Musigny Vieilles Vignes.
1971 Stay with DRC or similar here.
1970 It is pretty well all over.
1969 Some survivors at *grand cru* level, with scent and finesse.
1968 Should not be mentioned, even in bad company.
1967 Peaked a long time ago.
1966 A few still live gloriously on; Romanée-Conti is mind-blowing.
1964 A few terrific wines at *grand cru* level.
1962 A few top wines are still magnificent.
1961 As above.
1959 As above.

WHITE BURGUNDY

1994 Mostly at their peak.
1993 As above.
1992 As above; they matured faster than many expected.

1991 Mostly at their peak.

1990 Some top wines still have a bit to go, others are glowing right now.

1989 As above.

1988 Mostly at their peak or over it.

1987 Peaked.

1986 Mostly peaked. Some *grands crus* are lovely right now.

1985 Many of the top wines are so fat and full that they will stay around for ages.

1984 Peaked a very long time ago.

1983 Some tremendous wines at the top. They seemed alcoholic and heavy when young, but boy, are they marvelous now. Some of my greatest white burgundies of the last year have come from this vintage.

1982 Virtually all peaked a long time ago.

1981 Peaked a long time ago.

1980 As above.

1979 Most peaked some time ago.

1978 As above, but some gems live on, viz. Chablis Les Clos from Drouhin, which now looks like a Côte d'Or wine.

1977 Peaked.

1976 Peaked, but there are still some stunners about at *grand cru* level.

1973 Peaked, with the odd surprise at *grand cru* level.

1972 Peaked.

1971 Peaked, with some stunners left.

1970 As above.

1969 As above.

1967 It starts getting esoteric from here, but the odd surprise.

1966 Mostly history, but DRC's Montrachet makes history.

1965 You're kidding!

1964 Peaked a long time ago, with a few exceptions hanging on.

1963 You're not kidding?

1962 Peaked, of course, with a few marvelous exceptions.

1961 As above.

RED RHONE

1994 Start drinking up.

1993 Peaked.

1992 Peaked.

1991 Peaked for the south, fine for the north.

1990 Excellent, the best will keep.

1989 As above.

1988 As above.

1987 Peaked or peaking.

1986 As above.

1985 Peaked, although the best will keep.

1984 Peaked.

1983 Peaked for the south, but the top wines from the north still have life.

1982 Peaked everywhere, although the north is better.

1981 Peaked for the north, a few good ones left in the south.

1980 Peaked.

1979 Peaked, but the best are still drinking well.

1978 Mostly at its peak, but with some amazing wines.

1977 Not there in the first place.

1976 Peaked some time ago, but Hermitage La Chapelle lives on to delight.

1975 Peaked long ago.

1974 Ditto.

1973 Peaked.

1972 As above.

1971 As above, but throw in Rayas and Chave's glorious Hermitage.

1970 Peaked, but great Hermitage La Chapelle.

1969 Peaked, but glorious La Chapelle, with Chave and Rayas still there.

1968 Don't go there.

1967 Peaked, but tremendous La Chapelle.

1966 As above.

1965 Don't go here, either.

1964 Peaked, but tremendous La Chapelle.

1963 A bad joke.

1962 Peaked, but tremendous La Chapelle.
1961 The top wines are still out of this world (La Chapelle et al.).
1959 As above.

PORT

1985 Start drinking, but will keep.
1983 As above.
1982 Drinking well now and over the next few years.
1980 As above.
1977 Drinking very well now but will obviously keep.
1975 Drink up fast.
1970 Fabulous vintage; glorious now, but will stay that way for ages.
1966 Excellent wines right now, but will keep, of course. The fruit in them is quite beautiful.
1963 Huge, powerful wines, for drinking or keeping.
1960 Beautiful now.
1958 Mostly peaked, but don't say that to Noval Nacional! Extraordinary wine.
1955 Superb now and not about to fall off the perch.
1950 Drink up, but the Nacional is eternal.
1948 Great now.
1947 Drink now.
1945 Still there, after all these years. Mammoth.

GERMANY

1994 Peaked.
1993 Approaching peak, but the best will mature in splendid fashion.
1992 Peaked.
1991 Peaked.
1990 Excellent and the best will age beautifully.
1989 As above.
1988 As above.
1987 Peaked.

1986 Mostly peaked.
1985 Mostly at peak.
1984 Dreadful vintage.
1983 Mostly peaked, but some wines beautifully present.
1982 Peaked a long time ago.
1981 As above.
1980 Forget it.
1979 A very few survivors.
1976 Tremendous, with a plethora of fantastic wines still vying for top honors.
1975 As above.
1974 Peaked.
1973 Peaked.
1972 Peaked.
1971 Still magnificent in the upper echelons.
1970 Peaked.
1969 Peaked.
1968 Forget it.
1967 Peaked some time ago, but a few stunning survivors at TBA level.
1966 Peaked.
1965 Never there.
1964 Peaked.
1963 Peaked.
1962 Peaked.
1961 Peaked.
1960 Peaked.
1959 At peak, and glorious with it.
1953 Peaked, with a few beauties left.

GREATEST-QUALITY AUCTION WINES

1 **Château Pétrus 1949** Pomerol *Tasted when leading a vertical tasting of Pétrus in the States. Glorious, heavenly ripe fruit, utter sweetness, and allure. Stunning.*

2 **Veuve Clicquot Brut 1955** *Tasted when leading a vertical tasting of Clicquot vintages at Wrotham Park in England. White peaches bouquet, so complex, so long. Such a classic, with pure toast at the end.*

❸ **Riesling Sélection de Grains Nobles 1976** Hugel *Tasted at a Hugel tasting in London. The dream vintage, the dream wine. Pure clover honey, creamy smoothness, luscious but not cloying. A chef d'oeuvre.*

❹ **Chevalier-Montrachet 1962** Bouchard Père et Fils *This was so young at a dinner in Bordeaux. Apricots on the nose, fat and lanolin-smooth, with zests of orange and lime.*

❺ **Heitz Cabernet Sauvignon 1969** Martha's Vineyard *Tasted at a private dinner in Beverly Hills. Inimitably minty on the nose, so fresh and vibrant. The hidden gem between the 1968 and 1970.*

❻ **Château d'Yquem 1959** Sauternes *Generously supplied by a 59er at a private lunch in Singapore, this wine coats the mouth with luscious, balanced, opulent fruit, and is so long and utterly harmonious on the palate.*

❼ **Château La Mission Haut-Brion 1961** Graves *Tasted at a Bipin Desai comparative tasting in Los Angeles. Earthy splendor. So rich, imposing, and thick. Massive, "sweet" wine.*

❽ **Château Lafite 1959** Pauillac *Another feature of the Bipin Desai comparative tasting, this is simply one of Bordeaux's best wines ever. Pure beauty, nobility, and breed, plus complexity and richness.*

❾ **Château Pétrus 1970** Pomerol *At home in London, several times, plus at a Pétrus vertical. This is a winner every time. Sweet, meaty and ripe, superlative. And in double magnum it was just so young and rich.*

❿ **Wehlener Sonnenuhr Auslese 1959** JJ Prüm *Tasted at the same Singapore 1959 lunch. Extraordinary fruit and intensity and "petrolly" complexity, plus silky texture—just slips down.*

MOST EXCITING OR UNUSUAL AUCTION FINDS

❶ **Château La Mission Haut-Brion 1940** Graves *Drunk at home, à deux. After 1½ hours in the decanter, a complete sea change. Nose of rich, scented heather, taste of cedary, sweet leather, and ultimate class. The ripeness of a very hot summer. Totally beguiling. The 1940s were made by women—maybe why I love this!*

❷ **Château Pichon Longueville Comtesse de Lalande 1942** Pauillac *Tasted at a Pichon Lalande vertical I led in the US. Glorious, nostalgic, rich nose. Great wine. So constant, so true. Everything in place. Amazing.*

❸ **Mount Edelstone 1972** Henschke *At a vertical in London given by Lay & Wheeler. Spicy and mature, with wood smoke and raisins on the nose, concentrated and cigarry on the palate. Spearmint and walnuts at the end. An Australian landmark.*

❹ **Montrachet 1951** Bouchard Père et Fils *Drunk à deux at home. Honeyed nose—must have some botrytis and residual sugar. Went well with hummus and… foie gras! The empty glass was redolent of dry sultanas and clementines.*

❺ **Vintage Port 1906** Gonzáles Byass *At a private dinner in Beverly Hills, this was a revelation, since 1906 was not declared. Delicious, with a beautiful, soft, fruity, integrated flavor.*

6 Domaine de Chevalier Blanc 1975 Graves *A tasting I led with Olivier Bernard in Miami. Rich grapefruit/petrol nose, huge full, fruity, round wine. These white Chevaliers last in stunning fashion.*

7 Château La Clotte 1959 St-Emilion *Drunk around the kitchen table at home. Part of my past! Evocative, pure, old-style St-Emilion nose. Cinnamon and licorice, and all the chocolate of La Clotte.*

8 Schloß Rheinhartshausen 1921 Kabinett *Tasted for a London sale catalog, from an aristocratic German cellar. A nose of clover honey, rich, classic Riesling petrol. Endless, honeycomb finish. Okay, so it is 1921, but a Kabinett at this age?*

9 Château Ségur 1911 Parempuyre *The same sale as above. Wonderful warm, spicy wine, with great aromatic intensity and richness. The yields must have been low to produce such longevity in a relatively unknown wine.*

10 Cabernet Sauvignon 1974 Mount Eden Vineyards *A kitchen-table dinner. Almost Port-like, or old Grenache: macerated berries, black-cherry jam. What a wine.*

BEST AUCTION BARGAINS

HAMMER PRICE

1 Montebello Cabernet Sauvignon 1997 Ridge; at the New York November 2002 sale (six bottles: $400) *An absolute steal for this terrific wine. Some idiots only buy full cases!*

2 Château St-Pierre 1989 St-Julien; at the New York September 2002 sale (12 bottles: $300) *An example of the polarization of the market and how only relatively few châteaux are fashionable. Who says classified bordeaux is expensive?*

3 Corton 1995 Bertagna; at the New York March 2002 sale (36 bottles: $700) *Can you believe it? And a very good year, too.*

4 Château Cantemerle 1989 Haut-Médoc; at the New York September 2002 sale (12 bottles: $600) *A wine that melts in the mouth, and from this delicious year. I cannot understand why Cantemerle does not fly.*

5 Château Sociando Mallet 1990 Haut-Médoc; at the London December 2002 sale (six magnums: £320) *A snip at this price. Equivalent to classified-growth quality—and in magnums, too.*

6 Château Léoville-Barton 1996 St-Julien; at the London December 2002 sale (12 bottles: £280) *A lunatic price for this great, long-lasting Léoville. The 1996s are so cheap at the moment.*

7 Pommard Clos des Epeneaux 1999 Comte Armand; at the London November 2002 sale (12 bottles: £280) *Lovely wine in this lovely vintage—how did this one slip through?*

8 Nuits-St-Georges Les Vaucrains 1999 Henri Gouges; at the London November 2002 sale (12 bottles: £200) *The same could be said for this one.*

9 Bonnes Mares 1992 de Vogüé; at the New York March 2002 sale (12 bottles: $600) *Delicious for drinking now. In more fashionable vintages, de Vogüé prices go sky-high.*

10 Savigny Vergelesses 1993 Simon Bize; at the New York November 2002 sale (24 bottles: $550) *Yes, you did read the number of bottles correctly!*

Wine Auctions & Investment

Anthony Rose

Bearing in mind September 11 and the accompanying economic slowdown, it was surprising in the spring of 2002 to find favourable comparisons between the auction market and the unstoppable housing market.

ANTHONY ROSE

In the US, there was talk of "confidence returning." Something had to give, and, sure enough, the bubble burst as the gloomy economic outlook of late summer kicked in. By the start of autumn, prices had started to ease. There was, as it turned out, a justified element of anxiety in Christie's announcement that it was "looking forward to exciting and challenging autumn sales" across its network of European salesrooms.

Bordeaux remains the yardstick for buyers and sellers alike. December showed a further slowdown in the fine-wine market, with a distinct weakening in the Bordeaux section—particularly for 1982, 1990, 1995, and 1996—with selective bidding and less activity from the trade. By the beginning of 2003, a chill polar wind was blowing into the salesroom. The worst Christmas and New Year period for the financial markets in 30 years caused wine merchants to keep their buying powder dry. There is a natural tendency in an increasingly volatile market for investors and collectors to opt for bankers (First Growths from top vintages), especially where factors of quality, rarity, condition, and provenance

ANTHONY ROSE is the award-winning wine correspondent for *The Independent* and writes for a number of other publications, including *WINE Magazine*, *BBC Good Food Magazine*, *Harpers*, and *PLC Director*. He specializes in the auction scene, writing a monthly column on the subject for *Decanter* and contributing to *The Oxford Companion to Wine* on auction and investment. Anthony is married to an Australian wine photographer and lives in London.

are involved. And with the US experiencing a long-overdue adjustment in California wine prices, that is, by and large, the story of 2002.

By the beginning of 2003, the cracks that had already opened up between the drinking vintages of the 1980s and the younger 1990s widened to a chasm. Beyond simply an emphasis on earlier vintages, there was equally throughout 2002 a focus on trophy wines as the tendency to plump for safety—especially Parker-pointed, blue-chip safety—increased. This trend was reinforced by the performance of Yquem at Sotheby's September sale when, despite lukewarm interest elsewhere, a number of lots doubled or even tripled estimates, with £4,140 paid for a single bottle of 1921 and £2,185 for the 1899, 1900, and 1909.

Bordeaux bankers

The Bordeaux 1982 vintage maintained its status as the salesroom darling with Mouton-Rothschild, the first Médoc First Growth to break the £5,000 barrier, at £5,060, while Cheval Blanc had already hit a £7,150 peak. At Sotheby's, Latour broke £5,000, Mouton (in magnum) did the same, while 1982 Pétrus reached £16,500, soaring to £19,550 in June and then £19,800 later in the year for six magnums. If 1982s were not quite mushrooming like house prices, they at least maintained a steady rate of growth. By September, the First Growths could show a 56 percent annual growth rate over their *en primeur* prices, the best performance of any vintage of the past 20 years, although by March this year, that astonishing annual growth rate had dropped back to 46 percent.

In the 1990 vintage, Cheval Blanc and Margaux became the only First Growths to achieve £4,000-plus for the year, with Cheval Blanc leading the pack on £4,830. It was the unclassified Pomerols, however, that remained the star achievers as Lafleur had Le Pin in its sights with an exceptional £5,520 a case. By the summer, prices were on the wane. Large quantities of 1990 Haut-Brion and Lafite sold, at £1,760 and £1,606 respectively, for quite a lot less than their 2000 *en primeur* prices, while Super Seconds 1990 Cos and Lynch Bages failed to reach their reserves. By the autumn, First Growths in 1990 showed an average annual growth rate of 38 percent, which dropped back by March this year to 31 percent. This was still a considerably better performance than the 26 and 21 percent growth posted respectively by 1986 and 1989 and well above the 17 and 19 percent growth rate shown by the 1983 and 1988 vintages in September 2002.

It was a different story for younger vintages in 2002; 1996 remained unpredictable and earlier positive upswings were not repeated. After breaking the £2,000 barrier, Margaux dipped below the £2,000 mark, and by the turn of the year, all four Médoc First Growths took a hammering, as it were, with Margaux and Lafite, the two frontrunners, pegged right back to £1,725. An average annual growth rate of 9 percent for the 1996 First Growths in their first five years since release *en primeur* was slow, to say the least, but this had dropped back by March this year to a mere 5 percent. The 1995s, too, were mired in sticky conditions. Starting from a cheaper base, the 1995s looked in healthier condition with a 22 percent growth rate until September last year, but they too dropped back, to 18 percent, in March 2003.

Meanwhile, attempts to float still-younger vintages (1998 and 1999) of some of the First Growths were ill-timed and, not surprisingly, failed miserably as large quantities of 1998s and 1999s were left on the shelf. The influence of the 2000 vintage is clearly a factor that kicks both ways. On the one hand, its very high *en primeur* prices make the vintages of the 1980s look like good value. On the other, interest in 2000 as it hits the secondary market next year, along with the trickle of excellent 1998 right-bank bordeaux now reaching the market, could detract further from the progress of other good 1980s vintages.

Burgundy

The other major effect of the performance of bordeaux was demand for top burgundy, red and white. The Domaine de la Romanée-Conti was the star, of course, with 1978 La Tâche, for instance, achieving £12,650 and the 1971 £12,320. But it was not all one-way DRC traffic. Henri Jayer was in much demand, with £8,050 paid for the 1996 Vosne-Romanée Cros Parantoux and £7,700 for the 1997, while £6,600 was paid for a dozen bottles of Emmanuel Rouget's 1997 Vosne-Romanée Cros Parantoux. Other top domaines in 2002 included Michel Niellon, Armand Rousseau, Domaine Leflaive, Etienne Sauzet, Lafon, Leroy, and Coche-Dury. In the United States, in particular, the presence of burgundy on the market was given a boost by the generation of collectors who bought bordeaux in the 1980s and California Cabernets in the 1990s turning to top-selling lots from the likes of Leflaive, Lafon, Ramonet, DRC, de Vogüé, Jayer, Rousseau, and Méo.

SUMMING UP

There is no getting away from the fact that, overall, 2002 was a difficult year in the auction room, with early expectations raised in the spring and then repeatedly dashed as time went on. If there is some comfort to be drawn from the year, however, the emphatic message on both sides of the Atlantic was that the strength of the fine and rare area of the market enabled it, up to a point, to resist general market trends, not to mention the buffeting of forces beyond the control of the auctioneers. The auctioneers will be hoping, in that sphere at least, for more of the same in 2003. By corollary, in a buyer's market, this must be one of the best periods in a long time for buying younger, well-regarded classified châteaux for drinking from 2007 onward.

THE BUYER'S PREMIUM

"Please note: a premium of 15 percent plus VAT will be payable on the hammer price." This seemingly innocent footnote tucked away at the bottom of the introductory page of Sotheby's sale catalog for April 24, 2002 raised both eyebrows and blood pressures. Denying that it made Sotheby's any less competitive, Sotheby's Stephen Mould justified the increase recalling that the auction house had not changed the rate since 1984—but, of course, revenues have increased year on year and, with them, so has Sotheby's premium. Christie's declined to make capital out of its rival's PR goof, possibly because it had some inkling that it would be raising its own buyer's premium in

North America on January 1, 2003 from 15 percent to 17.5 percent. Christie's was quick to reassure potential customers that the rise would not affect London or European rates. Not yet, at least, although Amsterdam is already 17.5 percent. Meanwhile, country auctioneers J. Straker Chadwick seized the opportunity to reaffirm that it charges no buyer's premium at all, but rather a nominal £5 per lot.

AUCTIONEERS IN 2002

Christie's reinforced its position as the world's leading wine auctioneer with a worldwide sales total of £20.6 million ($32.9 million) for the year, including premiums. It was down from £23 million in 2001 and £27 million in the millennium year, but it was still an impressive result, given that it was achieved with 34 sales worldwide, which is fewer than average. This comparative success in a difficult year was in stark contrast to Sotheby's performance, which, despite an excellent year in 2001 with a worldwide turnover of £25.5 million, plummeted to just £14.3 million in 2002, with just £5.7 million of this coming from the UK. According to Sotheby's head of department, Serena Sutcliffe MW, this was due mainly to difficult conditions generally and the lack of a big, single-vendor sale. She did not attribute the fall to the fact that Sotheby's raised the buyer's premium from 10 percent to 15 percent in April, even though sales declined more rapidly in the second half of the year. Needless to say, Sotheby's rivals felt that the higher buyer's premium was a factor that had helped them. Evidence that the buyer's premium may well have been a factor came from two other sources. Bonham's Anthony Barne MW and Richard Harvey MW reported a satisfactory 2002 with a turnover on five sales of just under £1 million, up 40 percent on the previous year, while across the border in Wales, J. Straker Chadwick of Abergavenny conducted eight sales for a turnover of almost £1.5 million. Meanwhile, in the United States, Acker Merrall topped the league, turning over $17.2 million, with Christie's in second place ($15.6 million), followed by Sotheby's/Aulden Cellars ($13.3 million). In fourth place came Morrell & Co, with just over $11 million, a remarkable 190 percent increase over the previous year's $3.8 million.

LIFE BEYOND BORDEAUX AND BURGUNDY

Some of the most outstanding performers beyond Bordeaux and Burgundy include:
Commemoration case of 40 years of Henri Krug vintages (24 bottles: £10,925);
Paul Jaboulet 1978 Hermitage La Chapelle (12 bottles: £4,140);
Guigal 1990 Côte Rôtie La Mouline (six bottles: £3,065);
Guigal 1990 Côte Rôtie La Landonne (six bottles: £3,065);
XX Sandeman 1870 White Port Massandra (one bottle: £2,420);
Champagne Krug 1985 (12 bottles: £2,475);
Henri Bonneau 1990 Châteauneuf-du-Pape Cuvée Marie Beurrier (12 bottles: £1,980);
Beaucastel Châteauneuf-du-Pape 1990 Hommage à Jacques Perrin (six bottles: £1,012);
Pingus 1998 Ribera del Duero (12 bottles: £1,760);
Trimbach 1989 Riesling Clos Ste-Hune Vendange Tardive (six bottles: £528).

ITALY AT AUCTION

As the number of fine wines in Italy begins to proliferate, Italian wines have begun to generate growing interest in the salesroom. It is true that there is not as yet a broader secondary market of the type that makes bordeaux the bread and butter of the auction room, but the growing appreciation of Italian fine wines and the sufficient number of wines to feed that interest have led to the appearance in recent times of large sections of Italian fine wines at auction. An example of this trend was the Christie's Fine Wine sale in London on October 24, 2003, featuring 422 lots of Italian wines. Not quite Versace at the V&A perhaps, but huge interest in the collection of rare Biondi-Santi Brunello di Montalcino from the cellar of Tedina Biondi-Santi, sister of the famous "Greppo" estate's owner, Franco Biondi-Santi. Six-bottle lots of the 1945 Riserva sold for £4,950, and of the 1955 for £4,180—prices that would not have disgraced 1961 Bordeaux First Growths. Age and rarity make these niche wines for collectors, and there was further evidence of this in the demand for the traditional *quarto di brenta*, the monster squat bottle that varies between 12 and 14 liters. After the A list of just about anything ending

Solaia, Sassicaia, and Ornellaia—who else bestrides the catwalk in wine's answer to the Milan fashions? Tignanello and Masseto from Tuscany, Gaja from Piemonte, along with Bruno Giacosa, Aldo Conterno, Giacomo Conterno, and Luciano Sandrone, not forgetting Romano dal Forno, Quintarelli, and Case Basse. Names to look out for? Percarlo, Redigaffi, and Soldera.

RECORD PARIS SALE

On September 14, 2002, Christie's held its first wine sale in its Paris salesrooms, where the two *commissaire-priseurs* who took the auction helped Christie's achieve the biggest wine-sale total by any auctioneer in France in 2002. Successful at the higher end of the scale, results were disappointing for vendors further down. A second toe in the water followed in December, when telephone lines buzzed for items from the cellar of the Duke of Windsor, in particular the magnums of 1811 and 1812 Napoleon Grande Fine Champagne Cognac, which each sold for £8,121, and whisky bottles with the Prince of Wales wax seals. Highest price paid was £10,336 for a 50-bottle collection of Château Mouton-Rothschild from 1945 to 1994.

MICHAEL BROADBENT'S 50 YEARS

On October 17, 2002, Christie's held a special tribute sale to mark Michael Broadbent's 50 years in the wine trade. The sale, particularly significant for Christie's since Michael Broadbent founded the Christie's International Wine Department in 1966, saw

Broadbent return to the rostrum in person for the first time this century. Bidding was brisk, not least because Michael Broadbent took the rostrum himself and hammered down the first couple of hundred lots. Perhaps not surprisingly, Broadbent's beloved Bordeaux took all top 10 seats at the auction-room table, with £14,850 paid for a case of 1929 Château d'Yquem and £12,650 for the 1945. Pétrus followed with £12,100 for a dozen of the 1989 vintage and the 1990, while La Mission Haut-Brion reached £8,800 in the 1961 vintage, taking it higher than all the First Growths with the exception of Haut-Brion and Latour.

BORDEAUX 2001

In an uncompromising warning to Christie's customers on the pitfalls of buying 2001 *en primeur*, Anthony Hanson MW, Christie's senior wine consultant, advised Christie's customers that anyone who already owns 1995s, 1996s, and 1997s should be "very prudent" about buying any more young bordeaux, because they have "shown little or no appreciation in value." Hanson went on: "There are two good reasons to buy wine *en primeur*: if a wine is so excellent and rare that it will quickly disappear, and if it looks as if the price is unlikely ever to be cheaper. Be very demanding about price levels before you commit any funds to 2001s. Since the 1995 vintage, château owners have had six years of broadly buoyant *en primeur* sales. Many now have ample cash reserves. They can afford to sell as little as one third of their 2001 harvest and still cover their running costs."

Exceptional growth 1999–2002

			1999	2002	%[1]	%[2]
1.	1978	La Tâche	5,136	15,630	204	44.9
2.	1991	Chave Cuvée Cathelin	2,400	6,996	192	42.9
3.	1982	Lafleur	5,532	15,756	185	41.7
4.	1929	Yquem	5,796	14,850	156	36.8
5.	1982	Pétrus	7,800	19,550	151	35.8
6.	1990	Pétrus	6,540	16,320	150	35.6
7.	1978	Guigal La Landonne	2,736	6,744	146	35.1
8.	1982	Cheval Blanc	3,324	8,112	144	34.6
9.	1989	Pétrus	6,156	14,832	141	34.1
10.	1990	Le Pin	4,944	11,808	139	33.7
11.	N/A	Bio-Reference Labs Inc[3]	0.56	9.20	1,542	154.2

Prices in GBP per case of 12 bottles. **Source:** Christie's, Sotheby's, and Morrell
[1] Percentage growth over July 1, 1999 to June 30, 2002 [2] Annualized growth over
July 1, 1999 to June 30, 2002 [3] Highest stocks and shares growth over July 1, 1999 to
June 30, 2002, courtesy of Jeff Fischer and Tom Jacobs of The Motley Fool (www.fool.com)

Since it would be impossible to track every wine auction price, the examples above
should be regarded as 10 of the wines that have shown exceptional growth, rather
than the 10 most exceptional. An obscure wine in an obscure auction might have
done much better, but the data would be of no practical value, since the idea is to
illustrate the sort of gains that the lucky owners of the above wines might reasonably
be expected to enjoy if the wines had been sold at a major auction house in 2002.

Blue-chip growth: 1998 vintage

		1999[1]	2002[2]	%[3]	%[4]
1.	Le Pin	2,900	6,540	125.5	31.1
2.	Trotanoy	800	1,740	117.5	29.6
3.	Pétrus	3,800	7,520	97.89	25.5
4.	Cheval Blanc	1,150	2,110	83.5	22.4
5.	Lafite	800	1,150	43.75	12.9
6.	Haut-Brion	875	1,090	24.57	7.6
7.	Ausone	1,150	1,420	23.5	7.3
8.	Mouton	780	910	16.67	5.3
9.	Margaux	780	830	6.41	2.1
10.	Latour	780	780	0[5]	0[5]
11.	Johnson & Johnson[6]	49	60.05	22	7.3
12.	Dow Jones[6]	10,970	9,243	−16	−5.3
13.	S&P 500[6]	1,372	989	−28	−8.3
14.	FT 100[6]	6,318	4,656	−26	−8.7
15.	Nasdaq[6]	2,686	1,463	−45	−15

Prices in GBP per case of 12 bottles. **Source:** Christie's, Sotheby's, and Morrell
[1] *En primeur* price 1 July 1999 [2] Auction price 30 June 2002 [3] Percentage growth over 1 July 1999 to 30 June 2002 [4] Annualized growth over 1 July 1999 to 30 June 2002 [5] Not yet on auction market [6] Stocks and shares performance over the same period, courtesy of Jeff Fischer and Tom Jacobs of The Motley Fool (www.fool.com)

While the 'Exceptional growth' table (top of facing page) does illustrate a good weighting toward blue-chip wines (Bordeaux First Growths etc), you would need to be very lucky indeed to have those specific vintages available for auction and to decide to put them up for sale at their peak value. And even luckier to have happened upon Bio-Reference Labs Inc! In this table (bottom of facing page), however, we follow the blue-chip wines on a vintage-by-vintage basis, starting with the 1998 vintage. We track them from their opening price (via retail *en primeur* offers) through to recent auction prices. In the next edition of *Wine Report*, these 1998s will priced at 2003 auction values and a fresh table introduced for the 1999 vintage, and so on (until the number of tables gets unmanageable and we are forced to rationalize). From this data you should be able to discern how reliable the growth is for particular blue-chip wines, especially when from the best vintages.

BEST AUCTION BARGAINS FOR CURRENT DRINKING

PRICES IN GBP PER CASE OF 12 BOTTLES ROUNDED TO THE NEAREST £10.

1 **Riesling Cuvée Frédéric Emile 1998** Trimbach (£210) *Aromatic essence of exotic, lime-like intensity, minerally flavor, and steely acidity.*

2 **Cabernet Sauvignon 1999** Rustenberg (£80) *The top* cuvée *from one of South Africa's best exponents of Cabernet Sauvignon.*

3 **Châteauneuf-du-Pape 1998** Domaine Font de Michelle (£260) *Luscious, powerfully spicy, and rich, dark cherry fruitiness just starting to come into its own.*

4 **La Poja 1998** Allegrini (£295) *A super-Valpolicella made from Corvina with exceptional character and richness.*

5 **Les Forts de Latour 1997** Pauillac (£200) *Classy mini-Latour starting to drink now and over the next five years.*

6 **Château Talbot 1997** St-Julien (£190) *Hugely enjoyable medium-weight classified claret for drinking over three to four years.*

7 **Chassagne Montrachet en Remilly 1996** Colin-Déléger (£290) *Coming into its own now, minerally rich white burgundy from a great vintage.*

8 **Château Grand-Puy-Lacoste 1996** Pauillac (£400) *Deep, dense, dark, complex Pauillac with a youthful core of cassis, fruit, spice, and oak.*

9 **Château Cos d'Estournel 1996** St-Estèphe (£420) *Living up to its Super Second status, a superbly concentrated, stylish claret with a decade's life.*

10 **Bonnezeaux La Chapelle 1990** Château de Fesles (£180) *Remarkable, mature, viscously rich, intense, citrous Chenin Blanc from a great Loire vintage.*

Viticulture

Dr Richard Smart & Caroline Gilby MW

PRD is the new buzz word in vineyard irrigation circles around the world.

DR RICHARD SMART   CAROLINE GILBY MW

It stands for partial rootzone drying, an innovative method of vineyard irrigation developed in Australia by Professor Peter Dry of Adelaide University and Dr. Brian Loveys of CSIRO (Commonwealth Scientific & Industrial Research Organisation). The technique is claimed to improve quality using less irrigation water. Although cost-saving is an important factor, water reduction is an even greater consideration in Australia and elsewhere, where the availability of irrigation water is seen increasingly as a limit to vineyard planting. PRD is generally used with drip irrigation and requires that there are two drippers for each vine, rather than the conventional one. Irrigation is alternated between the two zones, so that the vine always has part of its root zone drying, while the other part is wet. The drying portion sends hormone signals to the vine top to flag impending water stress. This restricts shoot growth, a symptom of mild water stress, and a prerequisite for good quality. Scientists and *vignerons* have long known that a mild water stress helps improve wine-grape quality, especially for reds. The grapes have lower pH, higher acidity, and better color. With PRD, the vine is deceived into "thinking" it is developing a mild water stress by

DR RICHARD SMART , "the flying vine doctor," is an Australian vineyard consultant with clients in 20 countries. He began his career in viticultural research in Australia, expanding to Israel, the US, France, and New Zealand. Richard is coauthor of the seminal work *Sunlight into Wine* (Winetitles, 1991) and is considered an authority on canopy management of grapevines. He has a regular column, Smart Viticulture, in *The Australian & New Zealand Wine Trade Journal*, is widely published in scientific and other journals, and is the viticulture editor for *The Oxford Companion to Wine*.

CAROLINE GILBY MW has an horticultural doctorate in plant tissue and was a senior wine buyer for a major UK retail chain. She is now a freelance writer and independent consultant to the wine trade, including four years on the Wine Standards Board.

maintaining a dry zone. Because the hormonal effect is transitory, it is essential to rotate periodically the root zone that is exposed to drying. This entails alternately watering one side of the vine, then the other. The duration of each application varies according to the climate and soil but is generally about two weeks, so yields do not suffer, yet the fruit is improved. PRD is likely one of the greatest advances in vineyard irrigation since the development of drip irrigation in the 1960s, and will likely put to bed some of the remaining prejudice against irrigated wine grapes.

Commercial interest in PRD is so high that it is being applied worldwide before even experimental evaluation. This is because of the triple benefits of the same yield and better wine with less water. Naturally there is a lot of interest in Australia, where trials are occurring in most low-rainfall regions. But the interest is not limited to Australia. In nearby New Zealand there are trials in the dry Central Otago region. And José Milmo of Parras, Mexico, is using PRD on almost 20 hectares (ha) of new plantings. Spain is a region of great PRD interest. Carlos Falco of Malpica is, as always, eager to trial new technology and has extensive new vineyards of PRD with Syrah. Codorníu is also evaluating PRD in its Raimat estate, as well as at its Argentinian vineyards in Mendoza. Interest is also great in California, where extensive regions are under trial in the Paso Robles area, with reports of PRD installed in up to 240 ha of young vineyards. There also an experiment on the J. Lohr vineyard involving university scientists.

PRD discovered in the 1970s?

When Professor Seguin of Bordeaux University studied the *terroir* effect on Bordeaux vineyards in the 1970s, he found that the supply of soil water to the vine was the most important factor affecting vineyard reputation. The best vineyards experienced midseason water stress, due to infrequent rainfall, but deep roots were able to extract some water from the receding water table. Part of the vine's root system was thus wet, while another part was alternately drying. Sounds like PRD, does it not?

Grapevine

- **Researchers** at the University of Nevada, Reno, have been awarded $3.6 million in 2002 to study which grape varieties grow best in that state. Nevada, with sunny days and cool nights, is claimed to have untapped potential. The researchers will analyze the genes of stressed vines to determine which might be most suitable.

- **In New Zealand,** wine grapes have overtaken every other fruit sector, including the ubiquitous kiwi fruit, according to 2002 census figures. Much of the recent growth has been as a result of overseas investment. Vineyards have increased a dramatic 37 percent in just two years, from 12,200 ha in 2000 to 17,400 ha in 2002.

MARQUÉS DE GRIÑÓN EMBRACES PRD

Carlos Falco, the Marqués de Griñón, has always been one of Spain's most innovative wine growers. By the 1970s, his family estate at Malpica de Tajo, near Toledo, was already planted with a nontraditional variety (Cabernet Sauvignon, dating back to 1963), which was trained to the new Smart Dyson trellis system, and used drip irrigation in a region where no irrigation had been practiced. His was the first vineyard in Europe to adopt the new Australian technique of partial rootzone drying, or PRD (see lead article), and it has now become one of the first vineyards in the world to use electronic dendrometers, devices that measure the minute-by-minute swelling and shrinkage of the grapevine trunk in response to the uptake of water. By observing daily changes in trunk growth, it is possible to determine the degree of water stress experienced by the grapevine and to adjust irrigation accordingly.

PRESSURE BOMBS

A new practice in California for deciding when to irrigate is to use an instrument with the unlikely name of a pressure bomb. This device measures how dry vine leaves are. The grower plucks a leaf from the vine and inserts it inside the pressure bomb, which then builds up pressure until water is released from the petiole (stalk). The force required to the produce a drop of water is called the water potential, and this determines when to irrigate. The technology is 30 years old, but applying it to irrigation has only

recently been advocated by some California scientists. It does, however, have both advocates and critics. Reports suggest that the readings differ on hot days and cool days, and some growers seem to be allowing their vineyards to become too dry before irrigating.

DETAIL IN TUSCANY

Pasquale Forte has established a new 7-ha vineyard on a 110-ha property at Castiglione d'Orcia, near Montalcino in Tuscany. Forte's particular contribution to sophisticated viticulture is in canopy management. Canopy management helps to explain why low-yielding and low-vigor vineyards make some of the world's best red wine, although it has more to do with leaf and fruit exposure (to the sun) than with low yields *per se*. Not content with the fastidious counting and handwork to produce this ideal shoot spacing, Forte has gone one step further and purchased an electronic leaf-area measurement system previously used only in research. He uses this to determine the leaf area on his vines, enabling him to calculate the amount of leaf area for each gram of fruit weight, thereby ensuring that the leaf area is sufficient to mature the crop on the vines. Forte's attention to detail does not stop there. He has purchased another instrument normally used only by viticultural researchers. This instrument, called a diffusion porometer, measures the opening of the microscopic valves on the bottom of vine leaves through which water vapour passes. As the vine begins to suffer water stress, these little valves called stomata) begin to close. A diffusion porometer is able to measure quite precisely the opening of these stomata, so its use gives a very early indication of when irrigation can be applied to avoid water stress. The diffusion porometer can detect water stress in the vine before it is evident to the eye, thereby reducing irrigation to an absolutely safe minimum.

ORGANIC WINE ON THE INCREASE?

With over 2,000 acres of certified organic vineyards, Fetzer is the largest organic grower in California, and the company has announced that by 2010 it will purchase or grow only organic grapes. Fetzer claims a 15 percent annual increase in organic wine sales since 1979 and so regards organic production as economically sustainable. However, it is easier to grow organic produce in the dry summer climate of California than in many other parts of the world, especially in those areas where summer rains cause fungal diseases. It is not clear that the production of organic wine will increase elsewhere at a similar rate, nor, indeed, that the practice will necessarily increase any further in California. Some California wineries offering premium and super-premium wines have embraced organic grape growing, but do not put it on the label. In 2002, there were 141 producers registered with the state. Although others have not bothered with registration and certification, just .6 percent of California's vineyards are registered as organic.

GLOBAL WARMING

Dr. Kathleen McInnes of CSIRO sounded warnings about global warming at the Adelaide Wine Industry Environment Conference in November 2002. She claims that temperature rises of 0.7–3.6°F (0.4–2.0°C) will be in place by 2030. Implications for Australia will mean greater pressure on already scarce water resources. More significantly, perhaps, established patterns of variety suited to particular wine regions might change. This is of concern not only to Australia. There may be changing trends toward cooler regions assuming reputations for what were warm-climate varieties. The grape-growing season will begin earlier, and ripening will take place in hotter parts of the year.

SHARPSHOOTER FUNDS UP FOR GRABS?

It is now a few years since some prophets of doom suggested that California vineyards were threatened by the deadly Pierce's disease, spread by the ever-moving glassy-winged sharpshooter. The insect has indeed spread and is now well established in parts of the Central Valley, especially in vineyards near citrus, where it loves to feed. Dell Hemphill, chairman of the California State Advisory Board on the problem, says that the pest has been kept out of North and Central Coast vineyards. There are over 100 research projects on the pest, but work to prevent the glassy-winged sharpshooter is now itself under threat. Citizens Against Government Waste has set its sights on the $2.25-million funding for the program.

CURE FOR PIERCE'S DISEASE?

UK-based pharmaceutical company XiMed reported in December 2002 that it has developed a cure for Pierce's disease. It is a terpene-based compound that inhibits growth of the bacteria that cause the disease (Xylella fastidiosa). Large-scale field trials in South Carolina have shown eradication of the disease in up to 80 percent of vines, when applied early in the season. Further trials are under way to establish whether the product works under California conditions, and XiMed has just announced a deal with a California company (Arista Biologics) to license the product. In separate news a Brazilian team at the University of Sao Paulo has cracked the genetic code of X. fastidiosa. Researchers hope that this will help in the search for a cure.

MEALYBUG: THE NEXT MAJOR PEST OF CALIFORNIA?

Already under threat from the glassy-winged sharpshooter, California growers now face the prospect of another insect pest. The innocuous-

Grapevine

• **The vines** in Antinori's legendary Tignanello vineyard are now reaching 30 years of age and are gradually being replanted. Replacement vines are a "massale" (vineyard) selection of Antinori's own Sangiovese. At the same time, planting density is being increased from 3–4,000 vines/ha to 6–7,000 vines/ha. Big rocks in the vineyard subsoil are being broken up and laid underneath the vines, both for natural weed prevention and to increase reflected light. Sangiovese can be difficult to ripen fully, so the new system will help guarantee full maturity.

• **Minimal pruning,** which first emerged in Coonawarra, has started trials at Germany's Schloss Johannisberg, in conjunction with Geisenheim, and is showing very promising results with Riesling. Professor Hans Schultz reports that the wines produced are almost always superior to wines from traditionally pruned vines, even when yields are substantially higher. Vineyard management only takes around 300 hours per year per hectare, compared to around 800 hours on a comparable traditionally pruned site.

• **The steep slate slopes** of the Mosel Valley are so well drained that there is no phylloxera, and planting on own-rooted vines is still permitted. Unfortunately, planting subsidies are only available for cuttings on American rootstocks, so own-rooted vines are a costly decision. Ernie Loosen reports that grafted vines here are prone to increased vigor, higher yields, and bunch-stem necrosis, and he prefers to replant using cuttings from old vines. He also reports that own-rooted vines live a longer productive life and allow more hang time, which contributes to higher fruit quality.

• **The Swiss** are working on a cure for the fungal vine diseases esca and eutypa. These infect the vine through lesions and produce toxins that are transported around the vine, eventually causing vine death. The work will look at the nature of the toxins, whether they affect wine quality in the early stages of infection, and identifying microorganisms that can break down the toxins. So far, there are promising results in strains of a fungus called trichoderma, which is already used as a biological control in vines. Trichoderma has recently been added to the list of approved pesticides in Australia and is in use in Chile against botrytis and in France against eutypa.

ounding vine mealybug produces
oneydew on grapes, which attracts
ants, and this unsightly mess is
nown to taint wine. Furthermore, the
oneydew encourages the growth of
ooty mold, while the ants tend to
farm" the mealybugs, which prevent
arasitoids from attacking them. The
nsect is well established in the Central
alley, and has been found in Napa,
onoma, and the foothills of El Dorado
n autumn 2002. It seems likely that
he vine mealybug is being spread
on infected nursery stock. Once in a
ineyard, the insects are easily spread
y machinery and are not always seen
ntil the infection is well established.
hey are difficult to control with
nsecticides, and now there is active
esearch going on about control.

FROST EFFECTS

hampagne expects a 50 percent
ecrease in yield for 2003 due to April
rosts, while growers in Hawkes Bay,
Jew Zealand, were harvesting a
educed crop from frost effects in their
egion late the previous year. Although
prinkler irrigation, frost pots,
ineyard fans, and even helicopters
an combat milder inversion-layer
rosts, man has had little impact on
ery cold advective conditions. In such
ircumstances, nothing can prevent
njury and potential total crop loss.
ortunately, frost is rarely fatal for
he vine, which will grow again
appily, even if a year's crop might
e lost. Exceptions exist, such as
hampagne in 1985, when up to
 quarter of the vines were killed
y frosts of −13°F (−25°C).

NEW FUNGUS A REMOTE THREAT TO AUSTRALIAN VINEYARDS

A massive door-to-door search was
launched for backyard grapevines in
Darwin, Australia, in April 2003. The
authorities are searching for any vines
that may be harboring the grapevine
leaf rust, and all infected plants will
be destroyed. At press time, 197
infected vines had been found.
It is likely that the fungus has come
from Bali or Thailand, or even East
Timor. Darwin, in Australia's top end,
is not a vineyard region, but many
Greek householders use the leaves
for *dolmades* (stuffed vine leaves).
The grapevine leaf rust pathogen
(*Phakopsora euvitis*) has already spread
to vineyards in Russia and North
America. Once established, it is
difficult to control, and the fear is
that the pest might find its way south
from Darwin to major wine-producing
regions; thus, state and federal
governments are sharing the cleanup
cost of A$1 million.

MANAGING CARMENÈRE FOR QUALITY

Now that Chile's Carmenère is no
longer known as Merlot but is
recognized as a wine grape in its own
right, research efforts are going into
improving quality. It is a high-vigor
vine, prone to shatter (*coulure*), high
pH levels, and excessive herbaceous
characters when underripe. It is still
widely interplanted with Merlot, so
leading producer Errazuriz has
painted the vine trunks to allow
separate picking, because Carmenère
needs about four weeks longer on the

vine than Merlot. Pedro Izquierdo at Errazuriz has also been running trials at different light exposures to reduce the herbaceous characters that Carmenère shows when unripe. This trial compares vines with leaf plucking on the morning side of the row only, with fully exposed fruit, and there are clear differences in alcohol, acidity, and flavor profiles.

ANOTHER CASE OF MISTAKEN IDENTITY

The confusion between Carmenère and Northern Italy's Cabernet Franc is perhaps less well known than the Carmenère–Merlot mix-up in Chile, but so much Cabernet Franc has turned out to be Carmenère that growers in Vicenza have even applied for DOC status for it. Currently there

Grapevine

• **Promising results** have been reported for the biological control of the cicadelle leafhopper, which is responsible for transmitting *flavescence dorée*, a vine disease of major concern in France and Italy. The cicadelle was accidentally introduced to Italy from the US, and the Institut de la Récherche Agronomique (INRA) has been experimenting with another American insect, *Neodryinus typhlocybae*, which parasitizes the pest and has dramatically reduced populations in trial release areas.

• **When bush fires ravaged** northeast Victoria, Australia, in the summer of 2003, the region was covered by dense smoke prior to the harvest. The crop looked like a bumper one, with expectations of good flavour and color, but winemakers have claimed that the grapes will be smoke-tainted and offered just A$300 a ton, compared to A$800–900 in previous years. The opportunity to market a "fiery red" has probably been missed.

• **Confusion about organic standards** in the US has been resolved with the new USDA regulations that were issued in October 2002. These defined organic products as free from genetically modified organisms, pesticides, herbicides, and synthetic fertilizers.

• **Is Boerner the ultimate rootstock?** This was bred in Germany as being strongly resistant to phylloxera. It is a cross between the highly phylloxera-resistant species of *Vitis riparia* and *Vitis cinerea*, both originating in the US, homeland of phylloxera. Interest in this new rootstock was high after reports of rootstock failure in California and Germany. While the California outbreak was easy to explain as due to use of a less-than-resistant rootstock (AxR#1), the German one was not. Boerner is now being evaluated worldwide and is performing well in all situations except for wet, heavy soils.

• **Walt Clore** died in February 2003 at the age of 91. He performed variety and site evaluations that formed the basis of what has become the US's second-largest grape-producing state. In 2001, the state legislature named Clore the Father of Washington's Wine Industry.

• **Grapevine detective Carole Meredith** has retired from the University of California at Davis to grow grapes with husband Steve Lagier on Mount Veeder, in the southern Napa Valley. Meredith achieved international fame for her DNA-based studies to determine origins of grape varieties. She identified what ampelographers had long suspected were naming problems in California vineyards, discovering that Gamay was in fact Valdigue, Pinot Blanc was Melon, and Roussanne was Viognier. With her students, Meredith also showed that the Cabernet Sauvignon is the result of a natural cross-pollination between Cabernet Franc and Sauvignon Blanc. More recently, she discovered the origins of California's Zinfandel.

...re no clonal selections available in Chile itself (although two universities are working on this), but one nursery in Italy is reported to offer four clones of Cabernet Franc that are all Carmenère!

BIO-REGULATORS ON TRIAL

There is considerable interest in Germany in the use of bio- (or growth) regulators to control yield. With normal hand-thinning, the vine will compensate with bigger berries and more-compact clusters, which are prone to bunch rot and reduced quality. The aim is to use bio-regulators to maintain the positive aspects of minimal pruning—that is, smaller berries and looser bunches—but also to control yield. Results to date using gibberellic acid (which is already approved for seedless table grapes) are very encouraging. Yields are reduced to around 30–50 percent and sugars increased by up to 40 grams per liter or more, although results differ according to the variety. Professor Schultz and Georg Hill from Oppenheim are organizing a large-scale field trial in Germany, with 50–100 growers across the main wine areas, to look at practical implementation.

Grapevine

• **Who could have imagined** paying €270 for a bottle of Spanish Grenache? Well, that is the price in 2003, and it is all down to the last-decade renaissance of the Priorato region of eastern Spain. Grenache produces powerful wines here, with sufficient color, aroma, and texture to compete with Spain's best wines from more noble varieties like Tempranillo. The secret probably lies in terraced, non-irrigated vineyards, low vine vigor, but not excessive water stress, and a mild climate. Is there a Priorato homoclime in the New World? Many would like to know!

• **The University of Minnesota** recently opened a research facility for winemaking from cold-hardy varieties. This is an area where native riparia grapes grow. There are "local" varieties, one called Edelweiss (Minn 78 x Ont) bred by nearby Wisconsin farmer and self-taught viticulturist Elmer Swenson. Another is called Frontenac (Landot (L.4511) x V riparia), bred at the University of Minnesota and making a red wine similar to Pinot Noir.

• **Chile** has some of the best modern technology in its vineyards and in the last five years has been regulating the use of irrigation and fertilizer. More importantly, its growers are now choosing some of the less deep and fertile soils of hillsides.

• **Late in 2002** the Code of Sustainable Winegrowing was introduced in California. Sustainable viticulture is the key to coexistence. The code book presents 221 questions covering issues from affordable employee housing to community light and noise concerns. By April 2003, growers on more than a quarter of the state's acreage had completed self-evaluation workbooks. Failure to do so can bring vineyard development into conflict with other members of the rural community, as has already happened in Sonoma County.

• **Some 17,000 acres** of California vineyards were grubbed up in the winter of 2002–3 and a further 25,000 acres might be abandoned or removed in the near future, removing the equivalent of 300,000 tons of grapes from the market. This was a result of last season's grape glut. Further testimony to oversupply is the sale of vineyard land by Kendall-Jackson in Sonoma Coast, Mount Veeder, and Santa Barbara, totaling 870 acres.

Opinion:

Research required into the true factors of qualit

Wine consumers are bombarded with ideas about factors affecting wine quality: climate, soil, geology, clones, rootstocks…. The list is endless, and let us not forget the age of the vine—all those myths about older vines making better wine! Bona fide factors that really do affect the quality of wine have been an active area of my research for more than 30 years. The three most important are climate, grape variety, and soil. I often use the analogy of a three-legged stool. If you do not have all three legs the same length, the stool is unstable and topples. And so does wine quality if equal attention is not paid to all three factors. As to other factors that are supposed to affect quality, there are at least two that should be scientifically investigated. I would like to see serious research into:

• Yield control—How much is quality really improved by pruning for reduced yield, green-harvest, or crop thinning? While these practices, particularly the last two, are almost universally endorsed by winemakers, there are few studies to show benefits, given the large number of varieties and regions that need to be explored.

• Old vines make better wine—Surely this is not a difficult area to research. However, I know of no study on the subject. There is much media speculation fueled by those who promote the idea that "old is beautiful." There are few brave winemakers who will admit that often a vineyard's best quality is in its first year or so, then a prolonged middle-age slump before old age may see an improvement.

Vine mealybug control needed

This pest must be controlled and its spread halted. Research must be conducted into how nursery material can be sterilized, the control of ants, and non-insecticide treatments.

Wine Science

Dr Ron Jackson

Although champagne has been the ultimate festive wine for more than three centuries, we have only just discovered how the sparkle that has inspired so much celebration actually manifests itself in the glass.

DR RON JACKSON

Scientists knew that there was insufficient energy in champagne to initiate the spontaneous production of bubbles, since it would require a pressure of around 1,000 atmospheres to force water molecules apart, and a fully sparkling wine has just 5–6 atmospheres. Spontaneous bubbling, or homogenous nucleation, is possible only when the additional energy required is supplied, as it is when champagne is poured into a glass or the bottle shaken prior to opening. After pouring, however, the energy quickly dissipates via this spontaneous bubbling. So how does the wine continue to fizz, albeit at a calmer rate, and where do the bubbles come from?

It has always been hypothesized that carbon dioxide (CO_2) diffuses into microscopic pockets of gas (CO_2 or air) that are created when the wine is poured. Diffusion into existing gas pockets is called heterogenous nucleation, and the energy required for this is of a vastly smaller order than homogenous nucleation, with 5–6 atmospheres being more than ample. The traditional concept has been that these microbubbles are trapped on the rough edges of minuscule imperfections on the surface of the glass, but this was never more than a reasonable suggestion.

DR RON JACKSON is the author of *Wine Science* (Academic Press, 2000) and *Wine Tasting* (Academic Press, 2002) as well as contributing several chapters to other texts and encyclopedias. Although retired, he maintains an association with the Cool Climate Oenology and Viticulture Institute of Brock University in Ontario, Canada, and has held professor and chair positions at the botany department of Brandon University in Manitoba, Canada.

Direct observation has now shown that most bubbles develop on minuscule lint fibres adhering to the glass, not microscopic glass-surface imperfections. The fibres are thought to be cellulose derived from dust or cloths used for drying and polishing. Air is trapped in the hollow broken ends of the fibres when wine displaces air during wine pouring. These microbubbles act as sites for bubble formation and release. Etching flutes (as practised by André Simon) would undoubtedly produce additional sites for fibre attachment.

Bubble behaviour explained

When champagne is poured into a glass, sufficient energy is created to induce what is called homogenous nucleation or gushing, but this energy rapidly dissipates and subsequent bubbling depends on the diffusion of CO_2 into existing gas pockets (heterogenous nucleation). As the nascent bubbles grow, their buoyancy increases to the point where they detach and new embryonic bubbles can begin.

During ascent, the bubbles enlarge (as more CO_2 diffuses in) and their ascent increases. As a result, the bubbles distance themselves from one another and, because they form at a relatively constant rate, delicate chains of enlarging bubbles shimmer their way up to the surface. They initially mound in the centre or collect as a crown around the edge of the glass; but unlike beer, where a stable head of foam is expected, the mousse of champagne remains delicate and refined.

The principal factors affecting foam stability include alcohol content and the amount of surface active components, notably proteins and glycoproteins. Alcohol and several aromatic compounds reduce the surface tension of the bubble, permitting the surface to weaken as the fluid coating of the surface flows away.

Bubble strength is also limited because there are insufficient surface active components to stiffen the bubble's surface (as in the case of beer). These conditions favour the fusion and early collapse of the bubbles, thus the mousse of a champagne is in a constant state of renewal, whereas the head of a beer is far more static.

As a champagne bubble bursts, part of it may be ejected into the air, but most will implode, after which a microscopic column of wine surges upwards from the implosion crater. Because hundreds of bubbles may burst per second, the surface of the wine is laced with these tiny jets, each of which separates into microdroplets that can be propelled up to several centimetres into the air. These events can be detected by sensory receptors on the tongue, the palate, and, particularly, the nose, but their minute size and short duration (a few milliseconds) make them invisible to the naked eye. As the bubbles rise through the wine, aromatic compounds adhere to their surface and are subsequently released into the air as bubbles burst, concentrating the wine's delicate bouquet in a manner that is similar to swirling wine in the glass to promote the release of its bouquet.

SENSORY EFFECTS OF DIFFERENT TANNINS

Recent research has shown that distinct tannin subgroups generate sensory attributes. Catechins, the basic building blocks of tannins, generate bitter taste sensations, whereas different polymers (procyanidins and condensed tannins) induce various rough, grainy, puckery, and dusty-dry textural sensations. Precise knowledge of the sensory attributes of the various tannin subgroups should help winemakers produce more wines that reach the premium category.

INFLUENCE OF LABELS

If you have ever felt that most wine consumers are overly swayed by label information, research from France confirms your fears. Research by Lange et al, published in 2002, found that knowledgeable consumers in Champagne cannot distinguish, under blind-tasting conditions, the various quality grades of champagne. However, when the precise source of the wine was apparent, scores reflected the traditional quality associations. The monetary value ascribed to each wine also reflected perceived prestige. Thankfully, increased wine knowledge tended to reduce this bias.

IS PARKER PREGNANT?

Wysocki demonstrated several years ago that repeat exposure to androsterone (male sex hormone) could improve detection of its odour. It was hoped that this might be a general phenomenon, with experience enhancing sensitivity to other compounds, but further research did not confirm this until Dalton et al published their work in 2002. However, before you expect that practice will turn you into the next Parker, the results show that improved sensitivity applies only to women within the childbearing years! This might explain why females tend to do better in odour tests than males.

CHEMICAL ORIGIN OF BORDEAUX WINE FRAGRANCE

Guth and Sies have discovered an interesting correlation between the perceived quality of several Bordeaux wines and the presence or absence of specific compounds. For example, perceived quality was connected with the presence of ß-damascenone (exotic flower) and eugenol (spicy), but negatively related to the presence of fruit-smelling esters such as ethyl butanoate (apple or pineapple) and ethyl octanoate (sweet, formerly considered an indicator of red wine quality—Marais et al, 1979). The researchers also noted how alcohol markedly reduced the fragrance of several esters and higher alcohols.

RUDDY GOOD

The chemical nature of a wine's red colour changes with time. Initially, it depends on free anthocyanin pigments and their purplish aggregates formed in grapes. During fermentation, the aggregates separate, freeing the anthocyanins and resulting in colour loss. The free anthocyanin pigments subsequently combine with other compounds into more stable complexes called copigments. Finally, anthocyanins bind with tannins to form colour-stable polymers that have brickish shades. To this general picture, Darias-Martin *et al* have shown that caffeic acid (a simple phenolic found in wine) promotes colour stability by encouraging anthocyanin copigmentation.

ACETALS IN WOOD PORTS

Acetals are aromatic compounds formed from a reaction between aldehydes and alcohols. Because acetaldehyde is formed during the oxidative ageing of wood Ports, it would be expected to react with the alcohol groups of glycerol. Glycerol is often the most common compound found in wine after water and alcohol. Data from da Silva Ferreira *et al* confirm the formation of several glycerol–acetaldehyde acetals. After many years, their concentration reaches sufficient levels to generate a sweet, aged, Port-like bouquet.

UTTERLY BUTTERLY

To many people, diacetyl possesses a buttery fragrance. Indeed, it is used by the food industry to make margarine more 'buttery'. Because diacetyl is typically produced during malolactic fermentation, it has been assumed that diacetyl generates the buttery character. But work by Bartowsky *et al* has shown that the connection between a buttery aroma and diacetyl content is far from simple, since a buttery trait is often present when diacetyl is below its detection threshold. This suggests that other compounds are involved in producing the buttery character associated with malolactic fermentation.

LOW-ALCOHOL YEAST STRAIN

Grape growers aim to provide the winemaker with fully ripened fruit. Such fruit produces wines with maximum varietal flavours. Unfortunately, the high sugar content of the mature fruit can lead to wines overly high in alcohol content—producing wines that may be out of balance. This tendency may be reduced as a result of work by Eglinton *et al*, who have produced a yeast strain that converts additional sugars to glycerol (rather than alcohol). Although the increased glycerol content does not directly affect the wine's aroma, the modification can influence other important wine characteristics, usually in a positive sense. For example, enhanced glycerol content can give the wine a smoother, more velvety mouth-feel.

BROWNED OFF

Early (in-bottle) browning of white wines causes significant economic losses to many winemakers. A new electrochemical method of assessing the browning potential of wine has been developed, and this should help producers know if additional fining is needed.

MODIFIED REVERSE OSMOSIS

Grapes may be in perfect condition up to the harvest, only to be ruined by rain. An old corrective measure is chaptalization, the addition of sugar to the juice, which raises the wine's alcohol content, but it does not offset the dilution of grape flavorants. A more modern technique is reverse osmosis, where water is selectively removed from the waterlogged juice. However, this often simultaneously removes essential aromas. Mietton-Peuchot et al report on an improved version of reverse osmosis that can re-establish the original grape sugar content without removing critical flavorants.

GELATINE SUBSTITUTE

For centuries, wine has been fined with gelatine. European gelatine (unlike American) has typically been made from rendered beef products. However, recent scares over bovine spongiform encephalopathy (mad cow disease) have spurred research into substitutes, and Marchal et al indicate that wheat gluten may be an effective replacement.

POLYPLOID NATURE OF WINE YEASTS

Several decades ago, Patel and Olmo showed that grapevines evolved from a sequential crossing (and chromosome doubling) of three distinct species, meaning modern grapevines contain three separate sets of chromosomes. Modern gene sequencing now shows that wine yeasts also contain extra chromosomes, which come from a duplication of its original set. Neither chromosome addition (grape or yeast) is recent, both probably having occurred some 50 to 100 million years ago.

ALTERNATE YEASTS

Historically, yeasts growing on the fruit or winery equipment induced

Grapevine

• **Oenology students** are color-blind, according to a recent study conducted by the University of Bordeaux on 54 of its pupils. In one test, students who were given a white wine that had been colored red described its attributes in terms appropriate for a red wine. Red wine descriptors were used exclusively for the red-colored wine, and only white-wine descriptors for the uncolored sample!

• **In a tasting of 18 wines** from Bordeaux and southern France by eight renowned sommeliers, they could not as a group distinguish statistically between the wines, nor could they differentiate between the supposed quality grades.

• **According to recent** champagne research by Liger-Blair et al, the inception of a new bubble takes just 60 milliseconds; up to 30 bubbles per second can be generated at each nucleation site; bubbles can reach a velocity of almost 6 cm/sec (2⅜ in/sec) as they near the surface; and, perhaps most amazingly, the speed that wine droplets are ejected into the air from a burst bubble can be several metres per second.

• **Goitre** (enlargement of the thyroid gland) was once thought to be caused by alcohol consumption, with Port frequently painted as the villain. However, research has now demonstrated that moderate wine consumption actually reduces the likelihood of developing goitre.

• **Methyl anthranilate,** which is responsible for the so-called foxy aroma of certain indigenous North American grape varieties, is also found in Pinot Noir.

fermentation of the grape juice. This began to change in the late 1960s, with the increasing availability of freeze-dried yeast cultures. It permitted the selective use of strains with known desirable traits (and the avoidance of many 'off' odours). Recently, there has been renewed interest in some of the complexities previously produced by spontaneous fermentations. Research by Henschke et al shows that yeasts such as Saccharomyces bayanus and Candida stellata produce sensory attributes distinct from those generated by the standard Saccharomyces cerevisiae yeast. Their use, alone or combined with standard strains, is another way in which winemakers can produce distinctive wines in an ever-more-competitive marketplace.

CORKED

It is generally believed that the corky 'off' odour of wine is due to TCA (2,4,6-trichloroanisole). However, in a detailed study of 2,400 wines, Soleas et al found that about 50 per cent of 145 wines possessing a corky taint had TCA levels below its detection threshold (2 parts per trillion or 2 nanograms per liter (ng/l) for the tasters used). In addition, 35 per cent of the corky wines possessed TCA concentrations below the analytic detection level of 0.1 ng/l. Of 185 wines closed with a screw cap, none showed a corky taint. In a separate study, where the tasters were specifically asked to identify and rate the degree of corked taint, more than 60 per cent of the wines identified as faulty did not have chemically detectable levels of TCA. These results indicate that compounds other than TCA are implicated in producing a corky taint, and that sealing the bottle with a screw cap avoids such faults.

BELL PEPPERS

It has long been known that the green bell-pepper 'off' odour that contaminates wines made from varieties such as Cabernet Sauvignon and Sauvignon Blanc is caused by 2-methoxy-3-isobutylpyrazine. However, recent research conducted in Bordeaux by Roujou de Boubée et al suggests that this fault is only marginally reduced by manipulating fermentation conditions. This indicates that the only realistic solution must be found in the vineyard and focused on optimal growing conditions, such as full maturation and adequate sun exposure during ripening.

MUSHROOMS

The mushroomy 'off' odour of grapes infected by powdery mildew is partially due to several ketones produced by the causal fungus. These are modified during fermentation to 3-octanone and (Z)-5-octen-3-one.

Wine on the Web

Tom Cannavan

Even after the e-bubble burst, the Web offers an enormously rich seam of wine-related resources.

TOM CANNAVAN

A long, difficult shakeout has worked its way through the world of the Web, where only the best sites remain from the thousands that sprang up during the 1990s. The new watchword is professionalism, and the good news is that quality is higher than ever.

The Internet remains the fastest-growing medium in history. It notched up 50 million users in its first five years, whereas it took television 13 years and radio 38 years to reach the same milestone. The Internet now boasts 600 million users. Since the beginning, thousands of sites indulged the wine-geek's passion for amassing collections, gathering data, voicing opinion, and sharing knowledge. When the Web began, it was frontier country, populated by pioneering enthusiasts. The most obscure corners of wine appreciation were celebrated. Gradually, the establishment took this new medium much more seriously, and by the mid-1990s, e-commerce had become the hottest investment opportunity around. The enthusiasts were joined by a huge array of commercial businesses, including established wine merchants, producers, and publishers who launched their online arms, and a new breed of "pure-play" companies, created exclusively for the Internet.

TOM CANNAVAN has published wine-pages.com since 1995, making it one of the world's oldest online wine magazines, as well as one of the most popular. Updated daily, wine-pages.com contains more than 9,000 pages of content, including over 12,000 tasting notes and the world's biggest BYO directory. According to Jancis Robinson MW, "wine-pages.com should be of interest to any wine lover seeking independent advice" (*The Financial Times*). Robert Parker finds this an "all-inclusive ... superb site ... friendly, easily navigated, with plenty of bells and whistles" (*The Wine Buyer's Guide, 2002*).

Then the new millennium dawned with a cataclysmic loss of confidence. As overenthusiastic forecasts failed to materialize, the Internet bubble burst. In many ways, this was the best thing that could have happened for this fledgling medium. As the spotlight swung away, the child star at last enjoyed a little space to grow up naturally. Now the dust has settled and quality websites are offering tried and tested alternatives to mainstream shopping and information channels.

E-commerce

The original game plan for most online retailers was to pour massive amounts of money into enticing first-time customers. This was a tactic to steal market share from stores: acquiring customers was the priority; cost was almost insignificant. A plethora of promotional vouchers and BOGOFs (Buy One Get One Free) became the norm. As it turned out, this level of discounting proved unsustainable. It failed to establish a loyal customer base, with shoppers cherry-picking the best of the bargains and moving on. Today, most of the pure-play merchants that adopted this ploy have disappeared, and the remaining market is dominated by "clicks and mortar" operators—the online arms of established businesses. With a customer base and logistics already in place, the Internet is seen as just another alternative branch, not as a whole new way of thinking.

Convenience, another watchword

We all love a deal; but as consumers, we have finally realized that convenience is the real beauty of shopping on the Web—not just discounts. *The Guardian* carried a feature about wine on the Net in April 2000. The headline screamed: "What do you save by buying booze online? Answer: Up to 15 percent!" Sadly, of the 15 websites recommended, only five survive today. Many people will now buy online simply to save time and effort, not necessarily cash—as long as quality, service, and choice are first class. The Verdict Research Group forecasts that food and wine home deliveries in the UK will grow by 269 percent to £5 billion by 2007. This would represent the largest sales value increase of any retail sector.

SAY HELLO, WAVE GOODBYE

Though a few wine websites, like price-watching financialwines.com, have disappeared entirely off the radar in the past year or so, many more sail on as ghostly hulks, their upkeep and development having ground to a halt. The once-exciting prospect of winepros.com, a highly professional Australian e-zine that aimed to roll out localized versions across the globe, now boasts "latest news" items from April 2002, and a "latest wine review" dated July 2001. Its forum has some activity, but that's about the only sign of life. Other sites are still active, but seem to have radically downsized their ambitions. Pure-play retailers like chateauonline.com and virginwines.com have reengineered their businesses, and cut back drastically on staff. Staff cuts have also followed at decanter.com, when its parent publishing group was bought by the US giant AOL/Time-Warner. Winebid.com, the online auctioneer, closed its UK operation but is still thriving in its Napa Valley home.

Big-money startups are all but a thing of the past, post-2000. UK retailer Oddbins finally got its act together with a really good dotcom arm in 2002, and the French-based wineandco.com launched, shipping fine wines direct from Bordeaux across Europe. But most of the excitement in terms of new sites is among the independent merchants and small publishers. Niche markets are being covered, like devignewines.co.uk, celebrating

the wines of the Jura, or vines.org, which tracks fine-wine auction prices. Wineinsider.net is part club, part retailer, directly importing wine for its members at prices lower than in stores. It is only in the UK at present, but aims to expand. Enthusiasts continue to offer a surprising breadth and depth of content. Swiss burgundy nut Bill Nanson launched nanson.ch in 2002, a great source of burgundy reviews and features, while Doctor Vino at drvino.net delves into wine politics as well as more orthodox reviews and more. You might even find the Silly Tasting Note Generator at www.gmon.com/tech/stng.shtml an amusing diversion.

LOGISTICAL NIGHTMARES

Barriers to Internet shopping still remain, including the strictures of modern family life, when often there is no one home during the day to accept deliveries. Some companies already offer two-hour delivery slots and evening and weekend fulfillment of orders, but the future may bring more novel solutions. Alternative 24-hour collection points based in gas stations or convenience stores may become community delivery centers, taking in goods for a small fee. We may see the rise of products like BearBox (www.bearbox.com)—secure storage boxes to which you grant access for selected delivery agents.

LEGAL NIGHTMARES

US readers, of course, are still faced with a bureaucratic quagmire in the shape of the "three-tier system." This system, a holdover from the days of Prohibition, seeks to emasculate the wine trade by breaking down the shipping, wholesaling, and retailing of wine into discrete business areas, thereby making interstate direct selling of wine a complex and, in some states, illegal practice. To check out grass-roots movements fighting for change, look at www.freethegrapes.org and www.coalitionforfreetrade.org.

CREDIT-CARD FRAUD

The public perception of how risky it is to type your credit-card details into a Web browser has always been a *bête noir* of online business. But from the outset this logic was flawed: we happily give our card details over the phone, or hand them to a smiling waiter who disappears into the back of the restaurant to do who knows what. Ironically, data encryption and secure servers make online transactions much safer than either practice, and major card companies offer free protection against online card fraud. Confidence in online security is now generally high.

REPETITIVE STRAIN

They may be secure, but payment systems do have their drawbacks and have a long way to go. Hopefully, imminent improvements in technology will alleviate the tedious job of registering and providing personal and payment details for every online transaction. Systems have already been tried and failed, like Flooz and Beenz, which aimed to establish an "Internet currency" that could be

topped up online and spent at participating websites. These were probably before their time and therefore lacked the critical mass of participating websites and customers. It seems certain, however, that Web users will one day end up with some form of online account through which spending will become a one-click process.

THE LAST BASTION OF CHOICE?

One of the most pressing requirements of true wine lovers is choice and diversity. Globalization and the dominance of the marketplace by a handful of big businesses continue to reduce the choice on the high street. Already, supermarkets and multiple chains have drastically cut the range of wines on offer, just as they have done with other commodities, in a concerted effort to "rationalize" wine and increase profit margins.

The boredom that many wine aficionados feel when perusing a big supermarket's shelves might just be the chink in the armor that has let niche players fight back. Independent merchants, specialist importers, and even direct sales from producers can offer almost unlimited choice. The Web offers a wonderful shop window to specialist suppliers, who are often small, local businesses. There are still various pieces of red tape to overcome concerning shipping, taxes, and duties, but the world of choice is wider than ever before thanks to the Web—and despite the shrinking range on the store shelves.

Opinion:
You pays your money

For those aiming to provide sites of top-quality content and service, the legacy of the Web's radical beginnings has been a hindrance. Surfers will pay for their magazines and newspapers, but somehow want equivalent online content to be free. Real quality comes with a price tag, but historically Web-surfers have enjoyed a free ride while the bill was picked up through online advertising revenues. Unfortunately, the past couple of years have seen a massive downturn in the online advertising industry, and many websites that relied on this income have been severely hit. There is a gradual, but definite, shift in attitude toward paying for online content and services, with several pay-for-access wine sites launched in 2002. Hopefully, for both surfers and sites, the message for the early 21st century is that the Internet is finally growing up.

Micro-payments
Now that technology makes the payment of small amounts of money easier and more economical, we might see websites offering specific, valuable information for one-time micro-payments—the first report on a new vintage of Bordeaux, perhaps, or the results of the latest big wine competition before they appear in print.

Sloppy thinking
There is still too much of a tendency to launch a website with much gusto only for it to be left to wither on the vine. Botrytis-affected wine sites are sadly all too common: "Happy Christmas to all our friends!" enthused the home page of one well-known producer in mid-March. Websites that should be crammed with information and advice for loyal consumers are instead littered with "under construction" notices and contact pages where e-mails disappear into the ether. While these businesses make sure that faxes and telephone calls are dealt with promptly, no one is given proper responsibility for the website beyond its initial flush of enthusiasm. The fundamental failure to grasp the potential power of this most exciting medium is frustratingly common.

Using the medium
Some are getting it right, though: haut-brion.com, for example, provides movies on how to decant and serve its wines, cellar tours, and even a stirring rendition of the harvest song in glorious stereo. Other producers'

sites offer chatrooms and forums, plus a rich seam of content. They allow customers to feel as if they are just a little closer to the action, with vineyard webcams so you can witness pruning or harvest as it happens, vintage charts with detailed technical notes, tasting notes, and advice on cellaring. For the wine tourist (an increasingly popular activity) there are sites offering a mass of useful tips, from maps and directions to contact addresses and links to local amenities.

Best of the sites

All sites listed in the first three Top 10s overleaf are free-to-access, English-language sites, unless qualified by the following codes. These codes also apply to the Best Regional Wine Sites, although the primary language for many of these will be the appropriate native tongue.
[S] = paid subscription required for some/all content;
[R] = no paid subscription, but registration required for some/all content;
[E] = non-English-language site, but with English-language version.

Editor's note: I asked Tom not to include his own site, wine-pages.com, in any of his Top 10s because, inevitably, he would either be accused of self-promotion or (more in line with his character) he would not rate his site highly enough. However, I would place wine-pages.com at number two under Best Wine Sites and number one under Best Wine Forums. Although I have a small corner at wine-pages.com, I receive no payment. T.S.

Alexa.com – the world's most popular wine sites

I retain a healthy dose of skepticism when it comes to online polls and Top 100s, since too often there's a strong whiff of vote-rigging about them. (It's usually not too difficult on the Net with a little technical knowledge.) The Top 50 overleaf is compiled by alexa.com, a partner of the Google search engine. Alexa ranks sites according to various criteria, including how often surfers search for them. Though I very much doubt the validity of some of the sites making it on to this list, it is nevertheless a pretty good snapshot of the most popular wine sites in the world, as of spring 2003.

WORLD'S MOST POPULAR WINE SITES

Sites are either Retail [Ret], Information [Inf], or Other [Oth].

1. www.winespectator.com [Inf]
2. www.wine.com [Ret]
3. www.wine-searcher.com [Oth]
4. www.winecommune.com [Oth]
5. www.bbr.com [Ret]
6. www.erobertparker.com [Inf]
7. www.wineaccess.com [Oth]
8. www.wineenthusiast.com [Inf]
9. www.virginwines.com [Ret]
10. www.vitisphere.com [Inf]
11. www.winenara.com [Ret]
12. www.nextwine.com [Ret]
13. www.wine-club-central.com [Ret]
14. www.wine-pages.com [Inf]
15. www.wine-lovers-page.com [Inf]
16. www.verema.com [Inf]
17. www.iwawine.com [Ret]
18. www.reservaycata.com [Ret]
19. www.chateauonline.com [Ret]
20. www.wines.com [Oth]
21. www.majestic.co.uk [Ret]
22. www.wineglobe.com [Ret]
23. www.klwines.com [Ret]
24. www.winebid.com [Oth]
25. www.todovino.com [Ret]
26. www.westcoastwine.net [Inf]
27. www.winebusiness.com [Inf]
28. www.Lavinia.es [Ret]
29. www.oddbins.com [Ret]
30. www.localwineevents.com [Inf]
31. www.zachys.com [Ret]
32. www.decanter.com [Inf]
33. www.MyWineAuction.com [Oth]
34. www.winecountry.com [Inf]
35. www.partywine.com [Ret]
36. www.samswine.com [Ret]
37. www.geerwade.com [Ret]
38. www.winelibrary.com [Ret]
39. www.bacchuscellars.com [Ret]
40. www.wine21.com [Ret]
41. www.primewines.com [Ret]
42. www.wine.co.kr [Ret]
43. www.sherry-lehmann.com [Ret]
44. www.winex.com [Ret]
45. www.laithwaites.co.uk [Ret]
46. www.eswine.co.jp [Ret]
47. www.winepros.com.au [Ret]
48. www.liquorama.net [Ret]
49. www.thewinedoctor.com [Inf]
50. www.winetasting.com [Oth]

BEST WINE SITES

1. www.wine-searcher.com [S]
2. www.erobertparker.com [S]
3. www.winespectator.com [S]
4. www.vine2wine.com
5. www.bbr.com
6. www.decanter.com [R]
7. www.epicurious.com/run/winedictionary/home
8. www.jancisrobinson.com [S]
9. www.wineanorak.com
10. www.gangofpour.com

BEST WINE FORUMS

1. www.erobertparker.com [R]
2. www.ukwineforum.com
3. www.wldg.com
4. www.auswine.com.au/forum
5. www.westcoastwine.net
6. www.groups.msn.com/BordeauxWineEnthusiasts
7. www.enemyvessel.com/forum
8. http://groups.google.com/groups?&group=alt.food.wine
9. www.superplonk.com/forum [R]
10. www.wein-plus.com [R]

BEST WINE RETAILERS ON THE WEB

1. www.bbr.com [UK]
2. www.everywine.co.uk [UK]
3. www.wine.com [US]
4. www.uvine.com [UK]
5. www.winecommune.com [US]
6. www.auswine.com.au [AUS]
7. www.wineandco.com [FR] [E]
8. www.oddbins.com [UK]
9. www.majestic.co.uk [UK]
10. www.wineshop.it [IT] [E]

BEST REGIONAL WINE SITES

Argentina
www.winesofargentina.com [E]
www.argentinewines.com/ing [E]

Australia
www.winestate.com.au
www.winebase.com.au/oznzlink.htm

Austria
www.austrian.wine.co.at [E]
www.weinserver.at

Belgium
www.boschberg.be

Brazil
www.academiadovinho.com.br

Bulgaria
www.winebg.com [E]
www.plancic.com [E]

Canada
www.canwine.com [E]
   British Columbia
   www.winegrowers.bc.ca
   Ontario
   www.wineroute.com

Chile
www.chilevinos.com

China
www.gluckman.com/ChinaWine.html
www.kyoling.com/drink [E]

Croatia
www.hr/wine [E]

Cyprus
www.cyprus-wine.com [E]

Czech Republic
www.znovin.cz
www.vslechovice.cz [E]

Denmark
www.vinavl.dk

Estonia
www.veiniklubi.com

France
www.terroir-france.com [E]
www.abrege.com/lpv
   Alsace
   www.alsacewine.com [E]
   www.alsace-route-des-vins.com [E]

   Bordeaux
   www.bordeaux.com [E]
   www.medoc.org [E]
   Burgundy
   www.bivb.com [E]
   www.burghound.com
   Champagne
   www.champagnemagic.com
   www.champagne.fr [E]
   Corsica
   www.corsicanwines.com [E]
   Jura
   www.jura-vins.com [E]
   Languedoc
   www.languedoc-wines.com [E]
   Loire
   www.interloire.com
   www.valdeloire-wines.com [E]
   Provence
   www.provenceweb.fr/e/mag/
     terroir/vin [E]
   Rhône
   www.vins-rhone.com
   Southwest of France
   www.vins-gaillac.com [E]

Georgia
www.sanet.ge/wine [E]

Germany
www.winepage.de [E]
www.germanwine.de/english [E]

Greece
www.greekwine.gr [E]
www.greekwinemakers.com [E]

Hungary
www.friendsofwine.com [E]

Indonesia
www.hattenwines.com [E]

Israel
www.israelwines.co.il [E]

Italy
www.agriline.it/wol/wol_eng/
  Default.htm [E]
www.italianwineguide.com [E]
   Piedmont
   www.piedmontwines.net [E]
   www.langhe.com [E]

Tuscany
www.chianti.it
www.wine-toscana.com [E]

Japan
www.kizan.co.jp/eng/
japanwine_e.html [E]

Latvia
www.doynabeer.com/wine [E]

Lebanon
www.chateaumusar.com.lb [E]
www.chateau-kefraya.com [E]

Luxembourg
www.luxvin.lu [E]

Macedonia
www.macedonian-heritage.gr/Wine [E]

Malta
www.vomradio.com/website/
features/wines [E]
www.marsovinwinery.com [E]

Mexico
www.mexicanwines.homestead.com [E]
www.montexanic.com.mx [E]

Moldova
www.turism.md/eng [E]

Morocco
www.harpers-wine.com/
winereports/morocco.cfm

New Zealand
www.winesofnz.com
www.nzwine.com

Peru
www.barricas.com

Portugal
www.vinhos.online.pt
www.winesfromportugal.co.uk

   Madeira
   www.madeirawine.com/
   html/nindex.html [E]

   Port
   www.ivp.pt [E]
   www.portwine.com [E]

Romania
www.aromawine.com/wines.htm [E]

Russia
www.russiawines.com [E]

Slovenia
www.matkurja.com/projects/wine [E]

South Africa
www.wosa.co.za
www.wine.co.za

Spain
www.filewine.es [E]

   Ribera del Duero
   www.winesfromribera
   delduero.com [E]

   Rioja
   www.riojawine.com [E]

   Sherry
   www.sherry.org [E]

Switzerland
www.wine.ch [E]

Tunisia
www.tourismtunisia.com/
eatingout/wines.html [E]

United Kingdom
sol.brunel.ac.uk/~richards/wine
www.englishwineproducers.com

United States
www.allamericanwineries.com

   California
   www.napavintners.com
   www.winecountry.com
   www.wineinstitute.org

   Oregon
   www.oregon-wine.com

   New York
   www.fingerlakescountry.com

   Texas
   www.texaswinetrails.com

   Washington
   www.washingtonwine.org
   www.columbiavalleywine.com

Uruguay
www.travelenvoy.com/wine/
uruguay.htm [E]

BEST WINE-SITE LINKS

*These are sites with links to other
categorized wine sites:*
www.vine2wine.com
www.bboxbbs.ch/home/tbm
www.wineweb.com

BEST VINTAGE-CHART SITES

www.winetech.com/html/vintchrt.html
www.bordeaux-vintage-charts.com
www.burgundy-vintage-charts.co.uk
www.port-vintage-charts.co.uk
www.champagne-vintage-charts.com

BEST TASTING-NOTE SITES

www.erobertparker.com [S]
www.tastings.com
www.finewinediary.com
www.winemega.com [E]
www.internationalwinecellar.com [S]
www.stratsplace.com/rogov
www.yakshaya.com
www.superplonk.com

BEST WINE-EDUCATION SITES

www.wset.co.uk
www.wineeducation.org
www.thenoseofwine.com
www.aromadictionary.com

BEST VITICULTURE SITE

www.grapeseek.com

BEST OENOLOGY SITE

home.att.net/~lumeisenman/
   contents.html

BEST SITE FOR GRAPE VARIETIES

www.wine-loverspage.com/
   wineguest/wgg.html

BEST SITES FOR FOOD-AND-WINE PAIRING

www.foodandwinematching.co.uk
www.stratsplace.com/winefood.html

THE FAR SIDE OF WINE

www.winespirit.org
www.winelabels.org
www.thomasarvid.com

The 100 Most Exciting Wine Finds

Each contributor was asked to submit four wines for consideration, which meant approximately 160 wines, give or take the odd extra wine that turned up and a few that failed to arrive.

Only contributors for the emerging or more obscure wine regions were allowed to proffer wines from their Greatest-Quality Wines; the rest had to select wines from either their Best Bargains or Most Exciting or Unusual Finds. The wines below would otherwise be stacked with Pétrus, Krug, and Romanée-Conti, the quality of which most readers will be aware of but few can afford. I then tasted the wines blind, grouped by variety or style, culling almost 40 percent (which is why I limited myself to just two wines from Champagne and two wines from Alsace) to arrive at the 100 below—a veritable mixture of stunning quality, the most amazing bargains, and quite extraordinary finds from countries such as Japan, Lebanon, and Israel. My tasting notes follow the contributors' own notes, for comparison or contrast, or simply for a different take.

Zind Z001 Domaine Zind-Humbrecht (Alsace, €16.09) *An absolutely luscious, effectively dry blend of 50 per cent Auxerrois, 35 per cent Chardonnay, and 15 per cent Pinot Blanc that is 100 per cent Alsace from top vineyards (Rotenberg, Herrenweg, and Clos Windsbuhl), even if it is illegal to say so on the bottle because of its Chardonnay content. Classic barrique fermentation (not new oak) and extended fine lees contact without any of the exaggerated leesy aromas associated with battonage. This wine is dominated by pure, intense fruit.* Tom Stevenson

Le Sol Syrah 2001 Craggy Range (New Zealand, NZ$65) *An extended ripening period paid a handsome dividend, as this intense Syrah testifies. Sweet berry fruit, anise, licorice, floral, and cracked-black-pepper flavors are evident. A wonderfully rich and mouth-filling Syrah.* Bob Campbell MW
Such purity of fruit! And right on, Bob, cracked black pepper, especially on the finish. Star quality. My only worry is – is it built to last? But who cares when it is so delicious to drink now? Tom Stevenson

Tokaji Aszú 6 Puttonyos 1999 Szepsy (Hungary, 9,000 forints) *Simply stunning. Youthful and already gorgeously complex, with notes of dried apricot, citrus zest, honey, and noble rot. Lusciously sweet and very long, but balanced by clean*

acidity. Great keeping potential.
Caroline Gilby MW
Absolutely stunning, I agree. Only the greatest modern Tokaji aszús, like this, have the acidity, sweetness, balance, and purity to go head to head with the best botrytized wines of the Mosel. Tom Stevenson

Solera 1842 Oloroso Valdespino (Spain, €25) *This has long been a special favorite of mine. Although a sweet dessert wine, its initial impact is dry. The sweetness reveals itself in the mouth but finishes dry again owing to the great age of the wines used in blending. Fine nose, revealing the sweetness, and, of course, a very long finish.* Julian Jeffs QC
Classic, off-dry, beautifully matured Oloroso Solera, with just enough young wine to make the palate tingle, yet laid down long enough to build up an almost indelible aftertaste. Classy, and a bargain to boot. Tom Stevenson

Riesling Lerchenberg 2001 J-P & J-F Becker (Alsace, €8.85) *From Becker's excellent organic range, the Lerchenberg vineyard cannot support high yields and is always tremendous quality–value. The 2001 has lovely, citrous-petrol Riesling bottle aromas, classic structure, and a long, dry finish.* Tom Stevenson

Quinta do Monte d'Oiro 1999 Homenagem a António Carqueijeiro (Portugal, €50) *A newcomer made by a man who is passionate about Syrah, this is very northern Rhône in style (José Bento dos Santos adores Chapoutier's Pavillon Hermitage) and an amazing result for an area not known for quality wine. Expensive at €50 a bottle, and now as rare as hen's teeth!* Richard Mayson
A wonderful wine. If the nose matched up to the fabulous palate and finish, it would be grossly underpriced. As it is, it is still a bargain, even at €50. Tom Stevenson

Cuvée No 2 Trilogy 1996 Paul Déthune (Champagne, €50) *The very best of three mystery cuvées sold together (€150). All three are Brut Ambonnay Grand Cru from the same vintage, but their composition differs: one is pure Chardonnay, another is pure Pinot Noir, and finally there is a 50/50 blend. Rich, ripe, and tangy, with lots of strawberry fruit, bracing acidity, and a long finish.* Tom Stevenson

Mâcon-Milly-Lamartine Clos du Four 2001 Comtes Lafon (Burgundy, €12) *Truly great Mâcon from the greatest white-winemaker in the Côte d'Or. The second vintage where Dominique was responsible from start to finish. Even better than the 2000. Lovely, clean, ripe fruit, balanced with very good racy acidity.* Clive Coates MW
Utterly delicious! Tom Stevenson

Lafleur de Quinault 1999 (Bordeaux, €18.50) *After an initial wave of primary fruit, the complexity begins to appear, and the glorious seductive fruit just asks to be drunk. A perfect and irresistible second wine.* David Peppercorn MW
Lovely dense fruit, with nicely developed bottle aromas and some grippy tannins. Tom Stevenson

La Syrare d'Alain Gallety 2000 Domaine A Gallety (Rhône, €11) *From the heart of the Ardèche, where Alain Gallety is by far the most talented winemaker, this Syrah is highly concentrated, rich, and mouth-filling. A brilliant success, like his other wines, such as the Haute Vigne.* Thierry Desseauve
Classic Syrah. Absolutely delicious! Tom Stevenson

Ina'Mera 2000 Juris (Austria, €25) *Good ruby color with an orange rim. Red fruit and delicate hints of wood on the nose. Beautifully balanced on the palate, not overpowering. Good tannic structure underpinning mulberry*

and tobacco notes. Wood used sparingly and well, extract sweetness on the length. Dr. Philipp Blom
So beautifully balanced that the concentrated fruit here seems as light as a feather. What class! Tom Stevenson

Henriques & Henriques 15-Year-Old Verdelho (Portugal, €35) *H&H's 10- and 15-year-old Madeiras are standard-bearers, and the quality at this level is second to none. This Verdelho is very impressive; fragrant, incisive, and, above all, clean as a whistle. A glimpse of true Madeira.* Richard Mayson
Such purity and finesse. Impressive indeed! Tom Stevenson

Bopparder Hamm Feuerlay Riesling Eiswein 2001 Weingut Didinger (Germany, €36 per half-bottle) *Perfect harmony between exotic fruit and racy acidity. Finely structured, mouthwateringly delicious.* Michael Schmidt
Classic eiswein, by which I mean pale in colour with electrifying acidity, not the amber-brown TBA lookalikes that have become commonplace among eisweins in recent years. Tom Stevenson

Warre's 1992 Traditional LBV (Portugal, €25) *A fantastic LBV, bottled unfiltered from a very good vintage by some. This is as good as many Vintage Ports, but—with the extra time in wood before bottling—it has developed more quickly. Good now and will keep. A bargain: poor man's Vintage Port!* Richard Mayson
Classic Port bottle aromas followed by substantial, juicy, oak-infused fruits on the palate, and Christmas spices on the finish. Tom Stevenson

Syrah 2001 Gentilini (Greece, €17.50) *Better balanced than the 2000, this vintage has lovely ripe fruit, a Rhône-like nose, and real lift from its 10 percent Mavrodaphne grape, which gives the wine its sour-cherry flavor and higher acidity than the Syrah.*

Well-managed oaking. Surprisingly good now, best after 2005. Nico Manessis
Is it the Mavrodaphne that adds the hot, minty-spice dimension? Big fruit balanced by grippy tannins, which give a really dry finish despite the fruit. Excellent! Tom Stevenson

Riesling Steinhaus 2001 Ludwig Hiedler (Austria, €10) *Perfect definition, almond and green apples, more delicacy than power, gracious on the palate, transparent fruit staying on the palate for a long time. Very fine.* Dr. Philipp Blom
Yet there is a lot of power there, just beautifully balanced. And it is, perhaps, three to five years away from when we should seriously consider drinking this wine. Tom Stevenson

Hazard Hill Shiraz Grenache 2001 Plantagenet (Australia, A$11) *Sold on some export markets as Hellfire Bay Shiraz Grenache, this wine is unashamedly at the big, bold end of the style spectrum. This gives a lot of bang for your buck: concentrated, exaggerated flavors of plum jam, dark chocolate, and almost Porty sweet fruit.* Huon Hooke
Good God, Huon, you have the nerve to propose such a brash, jammy wine — just the sort of thing I object to. But, damn it, the darned stuff's lovely! Tom Stevenson

Palafreno 2000 Querciabella (Italy, €25) *Deep, almost opaque, youthful Merlot/Sangiovese blend from vineyards in Greve. Ripe raspberry/strawberry fruit with subtle hints of oak on the nose, opulent yet elegant fruit on palate, soft and forward, but with underlying firmness on the finish.* Nicolas Belfrage MW
Oak dominates from start to finish, but there is plenty of classy fruit, excellent, grippy tannins, and fine acidity. An opened bottle retasted a few days later revealed more fruit than oak, a definite sign that we should keep a few bottles, Nick. Tom Stevenson

NV Cuvée aux 6 Cépages Moutard (Champagne, €22.50) *In addition to the classic Chardonnay, Pinot Noir, and Meunier, this includes three other little-known Champagne varieties: Pinot Blanc and the ancient, obscure Arbane and Petit Meslier. Very soft and smooth, with a touch of oak, this is a great success, unlike Moutard's pure Arbane varietal.* Tom Stevenson

Masseria Maime Negroamaro Salento 2000 Tormaresca (Italy, €18) *Explosive nose of soft red summer fruits, particularly strawberries and raspberries. Rich, smooth palate of great concentration, ripe berry fruit with tobacco and dark chocolate. Very sexy.* Nicolas Belfrage MW *Definitely great concentration, and I get the dark chocolate, Nick, but I think the tobacco comes after the sex. The fruit is packed so tight, and there is a bitterness of undeveloped extract (which will go sweet), that we should really cellar this for at least five years.* Tom Stevenson

Les Ailes de Berliquet 1998 (Bordeaux, €18) *Simply made to please! Has welcoming, elegant, ripe fruit on the nose, then delicious, sweet, ripe-fruit flavors. A perfect second wine, conveying the breed of the cru, yet perfect drinking now.* David Peppercorn MW *Elegant fruit with soft and supple tannins for a touch of class. Ridiculously easy to drink.* Tom Stevenson

Grand Reserve Cabernet Sauvignon Shiraz 2001 Jackson-Triggs Proprietors (Canada, C$19.95) *Winemaker Bruce Nicholson's first attempt at an Australian-style blend is a winner. Dense purple-ruby color that holds to the rim; on the nose is all cedar, smoke, vanilla, and crushed blackberries; spicy, well-extracted fruit with a tarry note, fleshy and oaky with an evident spine of acidity. Although only 25 percent Shiraz, this grape does tend to dominate the palate.* Tony Aspler *Maybe the wine has changed since Tony tasted it, but although the Syrah seems to provide the structure and the pithy fruit with grippy tannins on the finish, it was the menthol character of the Cabernet that dominated the mid-palate when I tasted it. Menthol finesse on finish, with oak overwhelming both grapes on the aftertaste. Superb first attempt.* Tom Stevenson

Gaia Estate 2000 Gaia Wines (Greece, €18) *This wine is unfiltered and needs decanting. Black cherries on the nose and palate. Smooth tannins, long finish. Agiorgitiko essence. A superlative, vintage-good extract and 14 percent ABV.* Nico Manessis *An amazing display of power and elegance. Black cherries indeed, Nico, and they are covered in rich, dark chocolate.* Tom Stevenson

Coteaux du Layon Selection de Grains Nobles 1999 Domaine Delesvaux (Loire, €28) *The latest harvest in Anjou, end of November, in a very difficult year for Chenin. Very sweet, creamy with an excellent and very long acidity (green lemon and mineral touch). Drink over the next 15 years.* Antoine Gerbelle *Takes on Sauternes at its own game … and wins!* Tom Stevenson

Tempranillo Graciano 2001 Cascabel (Australia, A$40) *Spanish-Australian Susana Fernandez made just 160 dozens of this exciting blend in McLaren Vale. It is a richly concentrated, chunky wine smelling of compost and barnyard, with underlying cherry-plum flavors, and a dense, savory palate finishing with authoritative, drying tannins.* Huon Hooke *You must have mighty fine compost down under, Huon! What I find astonishing about this wine is that it could very well be Spanish under blind-tasting conditions. I most definitely* *would not guess Australia! I love the way that the rich fruit in this wine is cut by pithy tannins.* Tom Stevenson

Blandy's Alvada 5-Year-Old Madeira

(Portugal, €8) *A new wine launched in 2002 representing the new face of Madeira. Packaged and marketed as a dessert wine, this is a rich, suave blend of Bual and Malmsey. None of the old cheesy character here. This is approachable and easy to drink.* Richard Mayson *Sweet, rather than intensely sweet, with excellent acidity and an amazing retronasal (not a term I use very often) perfume of dried candied-peel spiced with fresh lemon zest. Quite extraordinary.* Tom Stevenson

Bierzo 1999 Descendientes de

J Palacios (Spain, €25) *Excellent structure without the heavy acidity often associated with Mencía, and good fruit. The thread of acidity that runs through the mid-palate throws the fruit into sharp relief, rather in the manner of a Cru Beaujolais. Probably needs a further year in bottle.* John Radford *There is also a fair bit of oak, but it does indeed have excellent structure and the underlying fruit is very serious quality. Very good tannins. Impressive.* Tom Stevenson

Pinot Noir 2001 Ata Rangi (New

Zealand, NZ$60) *Ata Rangi Pinot Noir has always been famous for its drop-dead gorgeous silken texture and mouth-filling richness. Since 1998, the wine has had more structure with greater complexity, particularly after a few years' bottle age. New Zealand Pinot Noir does not get much better than this.* Bob Campbell MW *Magic, Bob!* Tom Stevenson

Côte Rôtie La Brocard 2000

Domaine François Villard (Rhône, €36.59) *In few years, François Villard has brought this cuvée to the top:*

black in color, very oaky but not drying out; powerful body with compact tannic structure, but soft and refined with length and density. Drink in five to eight years. Thierry Desseauve *Nowhere near ready to drink. Great wine, but no, Thierry, I do not think it is particularly oaky. There is more than enough going on in this wine not to notice the oak, and over time the fruit will swell in the bottle and the oak will diminish. But yes, Thierry, it is definitely not dying out and it is indeed refined with great density.* Tom Stevenson

Domingos Soares Franco Colecção Privada 2001 Touriga Franca

(Portugal, €17) *Touriga Franca is the most-planted grape in the Douro (where it comes a distinct second to Touriga Nacional in terms of quality), and this is one of the first examples of a wine made from this grape outside the Douro region. Very floral aromas, plums, and morello cherries. Good structure as well. Shows what can be done.* Richard Mayson *Lovely, sappy, pithy fruit, nicely structured, with good but not obtrusive tannins. Serious quality.* Tom Stevenson

Bürgstadter Centgrafenberg Frühburgunder Trocken "R" 1999

Weingut Rudolf Fürst (Germany, €54) *A nose reminiscent of dried fruit and ripe blackberries; on the palate it is chocolaty, full-bodied, loads of fruit, underpinned by a firm tannin structure.* Michael Schmidt *Beautifully sweet and sensuous Pinot fruit from nose to finish.* Tom Stevenson

Savigny-Lès-Beaune La Dominode 1999 Domaine Jean-Marc Pavelot

(Burgundy, €15) *Pavelot is one of the few growers in Savigny whose wines capture the inherent volume of the village terroir without being too rustic. Indeed, they are remarkably rich and civilized. Of his five premiers crus, this, from 70-year-old vines, is*

368 | WINE REPORT 2004 | GLOBAL REPORTS

my favorite. Clive Coates MW
Surprising tannin and power after
such a floral-perfumed Pinot aroma.
Do not even think about drinking
this until 2007. Tom Stevenson

San Leonardo 1997 Tenuta San
Leonardo (Italy, €45) *A Bordeaux blend,*
mainly Cabernet Sauvignon with Cabernet
Franc, Carmenère, and Merlot. Very ripe,
refined fruit on the nose, blackcurrant,
cranberry, blackberry and some "lead
pencil." An aristocratic wine made by an
aristocratic maker. Nicolas Belfrage MW
A massively dense, opaque colour with very
fresh, sweet-herbal, white-pepper aromas
of great finesse on the nose. The nose
is so beguiling that the ripe, tangy black
currant fruit on the palate appears to
be relatively simple. Tom Stevenson

Riesling Beerenauslese 2000
Hirtzberger (Austria, €40) *Immense*
depth. Stone fruit and purity. A new
and wonderful face of Riesling, the
sweetness merely serving to underscore
the aromatic richness of apricot,
peach, and green tea. Delicate and
very, very long. Dr. Philipp Blom
Peach, apricot, and yes, Philipp, I even
get the green tea, which seems to be
lifted up by the acidity on the finish.
This would be too liquorous in texture
but for a tiny amount of residual gas.
Tom Stevenson

Reignac Bordeaux Supérieur 1999
(Bordeaux, €16.50) *Not just luscious*
and delicious fruit, but also remarkable
length and sheer originality of flavor. A
revelation of what can be achieved in
a good Entre-Deux-Mers vineyard
with old vines and complete
dedication. David Peppercorn MW
Sweet Merlot aromas followed by
sweet, elegant fruit. Tom Stevenson

Osoyoos Larose 2001 (Canada,
C$50) *Winemaker Pascal Madevon, a*
Bordelais, has blended 70 per cent

Merlot, 20 percent Cabernet Sauvignon,
and 10 percent Cabernet Franc to
produce a robust wine in St-Emilion
style. Opaque, dense purple in color,
the nose is a mix of cedar, vanilla, black
currant, and blueberry; richly extracted
fruit, full-bodied, with an opulent mouth-
feel, the wine shows unctuous flavors
of dark chocolate and blackberries
with a floral grace note. Tony Aspler
Creamy oak and gamey aromas on
the nose, followed by tannins that
would be sandpaper-dry but for the
big, inky fruit. We need to taste this
in a few years, Tony. Tom Stevenson

Emeritvs 1999 Marqués de Griñón,
Dominio de Valdepusa (Spain, €55)
Carlos Falcó's innovative mix of older-
vines Cabernet Sauvignon, Syrah, and
Petit Verdot shows impressive structure,
warm, ripe fruit, and increasing complexity.
The length is characterized by an
elegant balance between fruit and
soft tannins that should see the wine
improve for several years. John Radford
Purple-hued, silky-soft Syrah dominating,
with smooth tannins, lovely depth, and
a perfumed finish. Tom Stevenson

Le Mistral 2000 Joseph Phelps
(California, $25) *Classic Grenache blend*
with black pepper, fresh cranberry,
and plum aroma, and a superb
balance of fruit and tannin. Outdoes
Châteauneuf-du-Pape. Dan Berger
Soft, sweet oak from nose to finish,
but packed with lovely ripe fruit along
the way. Some spice, with hot peppers
on the finish. I am with you on the
black pepper, Dan. Coarse ground! But
definitely more Syrah than Grenache.
Good tannins. Elegant, despite its
14.1 per cent alcohol. Sweetness
builds in the mouth. Tom Stevenson

SMV 2001 Fairview (South Africa,
R116) *A first from the Cape: a blend*
of Shiraz, Mourvèdre, and Viognier.
Not a brash statement, but Shiraz

plays the lead role, with hints of Rhône-like spice and pepper. A palate-warming wine, with easy tannins, promising overall elegance in a year or two. Mourvèdre and Viognier are not very apparent (yet), but half an hour with the wine reveals pleasantly varied dimensions. John Platter
There is a touch of jam here, but the wine has such elegance and class that I can accept it, as will anyone else who is lucky enough to drink it. Tom Stevenson

Dolcetto d'Alba Tiglineri 2001 Enzo

Boglietti (Italy, €15) *Pure Dolcetto – selected fruit from three different vineyards. Very deep ruby tending to purple, almost inky. Upfront nose of plums, blackberries, and small black fruits generally. Firm, muscular fruit on the palate; mouth-filling and challenging; considerably more grip, in terms of acidity and especially tannin, than most Dolcettos; capable of aging well, unlike most. Uncompromising, impressive stuff.* Nicolas Belfrage MW
Dolcetto for grown-ups! Tom Stevenson

Château Belá Riesling 2001

Egon Müller (Slovakia, 520 koruny) *Renowned Mosel producer Egon Müller has turned his hand to Slovakia. His first vintage shows a lovely, clean, mineral nose, with touches of lemon and white peach. It is sweet, yet elegant, with flavors of acacia honey and apple blossom, backed by vibrant mineral acidity.* Caroline Gilby MW
This has already developed some lovely Riesling bottle aromas. It really is quite sweet (top end of Spätlese level), but no one can deny that it represents a beautifully clean rendition of Riesling. Tom Stevenson

Riesling Exklusiv Novemberlese

2001 Günter Brandl (Austria, €13.50) *On the nose, beautifully dense with hints of dried apricot and apples. Concentrated and deep, just a little*

residual sugar. Exotic fruit on the palate, always focused, concentrated, and long. Dr Philipp Blom
From the nose alone it is clear that opening this any time over the next three or four years would be infanticide. Tom Stevenson

Bourgogne Pinot Noir 1999

Domaine Michel Lafarge (Burgundy, €7.50) *From vines barely 30 ft (10 m) away from appellation Volnay. From this stable – not unexpectedly – rather better than the vast majority of villages wines. Quite full. It has all the succulence of this excellent vintage. Will still keep.* Clive Coates MW
Serious burgundy for a not very serious price. Drinking well now, but best kept until 2005. Tom Stevenson

Westhofener Morstein Riesling Trocken, Großes Gewächs 2001

Wittmann (Germany, €20) *Unique combination of power and elegance with a firework display of fruit, with great complexity on a long finish.* Michael Schmidt
Rheinhessen Riesling at its best! But keep it a few years, please. Tom Stevenson

Premier Cru Merlot 2000 Wölffer

Estate (Atlantic Northeast, $100) *This wine is all about muscle, complexity, and high extraction. Very French-like, earthy, and smoky. Low cropping and severe selection of berries have resulted in concentrated flavors and a finish that is nothing short of tremendous.* Sandra Silfven
I find more elegance than muscle, but it does not have the structure, finesse, or tannins to warrant the price. However, price to one side, this is a very good red, although the ripeness and roundness of its cassis-like fruit is more Carmenère than Merlot. Does Long Island have the same mistaken-identity problem as Chile? Tom Stevenson

Vinya 2002 José Maria da Fonseca (Portugal, €7) *A new wine blending Syrah with the local Aragonez (Tinta Roriz). Big, ripe, and fruit-driven, with a touch of oak. Relatively inexpensive, this wine illustrates why I have nominated José Maria da Fonseca as one of the fastest-improving producers.* Richard Mayson *Fresh, sappy fruit, with chocolaty tannins and a soft, almost sweet, aftertaste. Perky.* Tom Stevenson

Sergio Rosso Veronese 1998 Michele Castellani (Italy, €15) *This is a light style of Amarone, a "drinking" style, as distinct from the massive "meditation" style. The color is quite deep, showing no signs of oxidation (a constant danger of Amarone). Nose of morello cherries, almost cherry liqueur. Medium-rich palate, ripe, or slightly surmature, cherries, plus ripe figs and raisins, hints of Christmas spices, smooth tannins, good acidity, quite long finish. Moreish.* Nicolas Belfrage MW *I confess that I am not an Amarone fan, principally because of the high concentration of acetaldehyde. If you are an Amarone aficionado, you must try this, but if you are not, then you really should take the plunge here. It is not too oxidative and has the spiced-cherry complexity of dry-concentrated grapes that is overwhelmed in 'real' Amarones.* Tom Stevenson

Quinta do Mouro 1999 (Portugal, €19) *Old, dry-farmed vines. A really intense, concentrated old-fashioned wine. (Most Alentejo vineyards are now irrigated.) A touch rustic, perhaps, but none the worse for that in a world that is becoming increasingly sanitized. In a country that has priced trophy wines, this is still good value at €19 a bottle.* Richard Mayson *I might have used the term rustic, but now that Richard has, I think it is probably unfair. It certainly is not old-fashioned. Old-fashioned Portuguese reds used to be as dry as dust, with so much pepper it would make you sneeze. This has a really good density of fruit with a sweetness of ripe grapes on the finish, although it is technically dry.* Tom Stevenson

Oloroso Solera Especial Dry Sack Williams & Humbert (Spain, €20) *A classic dry Oloroso, 15 years old. Although dry, it has that generosity given by its natural glycerine: the old pata de gallina style. It is a great joy to find it. A generous wine with a very smooth finish and enough acidity to make sure it is not unctuous. Very satisfying. Great length.* Julian Jeffs QC *Sensational stuff, but I beg to differ – there is genuine sweetness: about 20 grams of sugar per litre by my reckoning.* Tom Stevenson

Villány Cabernet Sauvignon Barrique 1999 Attila Gere (Hungary, 3,575 forints) *Hungarian red that is not just "a best of Eastern Europe" but can stand up against international standards. Ripe fruit with cassis, subtle vanilla, and hints of coffee. Good depth and varietal intensity without being overextracted. Real finesse and balance, though still a baby.* Caroline Gilby MW *Not a blockbuster, but it does have an elegance that some higher-profile international reds lack in their quest for power and concentration. However, I think the fruit probably had more freshness and finesse than has been captured in the wine. A case of very good, but the vineyard has the potential to do better.* Tom Stevenson

Fontalloro 1999 Fattoria di Felsina Berardenga (Italy, €50) *This IGT Toscana is 100 percent Sangiovese, partly from within the Chianti Classico zone, partly from just outside, hence not eligible for DOCG. However, this is the top wine of a top producer. A wine of power and elegance, with a penetrating*

palate of cherry-berry fruit mixed with tobacco and herbs. Firm but perfectly ripe tannins provide a long sweet finish. Destined for a long life from an excellent vintage. Drink between four and 15 years. Nicolas Belfrage MW
This is indeed an excellent wine, but if it was a tad riper, it would be even better. Tom Stevenson

Classico 2001 Flam (Israel, NIS 65) *Call this the second wine of this small winery if you like, but this is a wine that has no need to stand in anyone's shadow. The blend, of 50 percent each of Cabernet Sauvignon and Merlot, spent seven months in small oak casks. Medium-bodied, with smooth tannins and tempting flavors of currants, plums, wild berries, and spices, this is a well-balanced and seductive wine. Drink between now and 2005.* Daniel Rogov
Merlot currently dominating the smooth yet dense fruit in this gorgeous blend. Tom Stevenson

Craighill Riesling 2002 Dry River (New Zealand, NZ$32) *A dense and complex wine that rises way above the simple but appealing lime flavors of the average New Zealand Riesling. Delicate floral aromas (I found orange blossom); a suggestion of stone fruit and spice adds complexity to the wine's lime/citrus backbone. A taut and powerful wine with an ethereal texture and a lingering finish.* Bob Campbell MW
Although a delightfully dry Riesling to drink now, we really should not think of opening this wine for a few years, when that tautness, minerality, and ethereal character will benefit from the effects of bottle-matured aromatics. Tom Stevenson

Château Mourgues du Grès Terre d'Argence 2001 (Rhône, €7.50) *This cuvée is the middle of the range at the Château Mourgues. With its dark-ruby color, it is a wine that straightaway expresses rich fruit. It is full and fresh* on the palate with good balance. Thierry Desseauve
Floral, full, firm, intense. Almost inky, but has the acidity and freshness to lift it into a much more elegant style. Tom Stevenson

Old Vines Red 2001 Brampton (South Africa, R44) *Merlot-Cabernet blend, second label from one of the Cape's oldest estates. Easy drinking; some juicy sweetness offset, complemented by drier, heather, and bramble flavors. Finished in oak.* John Platter
Clever combination of sweet, sappy fruit and nicely dry, tingly tannins. Tom Stevenson

Alfred C Portugieser Trocken 2001 Deutzerhof (Germany, €17) *Nose of preserved red berries and cherries complemented by deep, toasted aromas. On the palate velvety texture, fine fruit, soft tannins, harmonious, finishing on a spicy, toasty note.* Michael Schmidt
The nose was outclassed in the company I tasted this, but there is no denying the seductiveness of the succulently soft fruit on the palate. Tom Stevenson

Tempranillo 2000 Abacela (Pacific Northwest, $22) *Abacela pioneered Tempranillo in the Northwest. Three different clones are used for this wine and all are estate-grown. There is a lovely scent of wild clover and very tart, dark fruit, with a structure that is designed to age.* Paul Gregutt
Sweet, perfumed fruit underpinned by grippy tannins. Tom Stevenson

Cru du Huailai Syrah 2000 Dragon Seal (China, Rmb 300) *The grapes are from imported Rhône cuttings grown in Huailai county of Hebei province, close to the Great Wall. The wine has an attractive, raspberry-dominated, red-fruit bouquet, with plump vanillan oak aromas and flavors. Its most unexpected and appealing feature is* the spicy white-pepper character and intense color—a much more cool-climate characteristic than this region would normally deliver. Denis Gastin

Fresh, elegant, smoky Syrah. Definitely not Shiraz style. And Denis is spot on with his white-pepper observation. A sign of things to come from the Sleeping Giant? Tom Stevenson

Z de l'Arjolle 2001 (Vins de Pays, €11) Sturdy berry fruit on nose and palate, ripe and rounded, with some spice and tannin. The surprise of Zinfandel/Primitivo in the Midi. Rosemary George MW

Opaque. A wine of substance. Leans more to a very good Primitivo than a Zinfandel, although, of course, the grapes are the same. Plenty of tannins, but good spicy fruit too. Despite its size, this is not a wine of great longevity. However, it should develop nicely for two or three years. Tom Stevenson

Merlot 2000 Margalit (Israel, NIS 125) An unusual wine for Margalit, who is most famed for his Cabernet. Rich, ripe, and concentrated, with layer after layer of currants, plums, and black cherries, all with generous hints of tobacco, smoky oak, and vanilla. Remarkably tannic for a Merlot, this full-bodied wine will start showing its best only in 2004–5. Daniel Rogov

The fruit has a touch of VA-lift, but this is more than made up by the chocolaty-spicy fruit and grippy tannins. Tom Stevenson

Bastion Shiraz Cabernet 2001 Leasingham (Australia, A$11.75) Sold on some export markets as Magnus Shiraz Cabernet, this is a slice of genuinely gutsy Clare Valley red at an astonishingly low price. Dusty, earthy, buried plum aromas and real intensity and richness in the mouth. There is no pretense to elegance, but it has depth and fleshiness, concluding with a long and satisfying carry. Huon Hooke

Definitely in your face on the palate, if not the nose, with typical Aussie mystical mastery of welding together oak and fruit. Great value. Tom Stevenson

Merlot Reserve 2000 Flam (Israel, NIS 130) After 15 months in small oak casks, this wine is already showing deep, concentrated, and luscious black fruits all overlain with generous mocha, chocolate, and vanilla flavors and aromas, as well as a pleasing sensation of herbaceousness that comes in on the long finish. With smooth tannins and excellent balance, this mouth-filling, ripe, and elegant wine will drink well from its release and then cellar well until 2005–7. Score 93. Daniel Rogov

Smooth, chocolaty-menthol fruit of some finesse. Tom Stevenson

Le Soula Blanc 2001 Domaine Gauby (Languedoc-Roussillon, €12) Pale gold, yet shot with green, it has citrus and other more exotic fruits on the nose, a substantial palate, with Chenin adding a crispness that is almost Loire-like in character. While absolutely true to its terroir, it would be difficult to place this wine blind. Paul Strang

Flinty, lovely acids. A revelation! Tom Stevenson

Pinot Noir 2000 Domaine de Valmoissine, Louis Latour (Vins de Pays, €10) Lovely, sweet Pinot Noir, with ripe fruit and refreshing acidity. This is unexpectedly good Pinot Noir from the south, albeit from a cooler part of the south. Rosemary George MW

Ripe Pinot fruit with more than a touch of class. Perfect for current drinking. Tom Stevenson

Château Plaisance 2001 (Southwest France, €6) The red-fruit nose is typical of the Négrette grape, but it is seasoned with pepper and spices from Syrah, Cabernet, and Gamay. A shortish maceration results in an uncomplicated wine that does not need long keeping, but its nickname 'the Beaujolais of Toulouse' does not do it justice. A delicious summer red that is also perfect with a wintry cassoulet. Paul Strang

You are right, Paul. The structure alone does not do justice to its nickname. Furthermore, there is no banal banana, let alone plain pear-drop. I agree – a good country wine that would be marvellous with a cassoulet. Tom Stevenson

Verdelho 2002 Robert Channon (Australia, A$18.50) *This new producer in the Granite Belt has for the last two consecutive vintages of this wine picked up the only gold medals at the Sheraton Queensland Wine Awards. This astonishing wine is a rich, buxom, opulent, tropical-fruity wine that could just be Australia's best Verdelho.* Huon Hooke

Passion-fruit freshness. Tom Stevenson

Curious Grape Bacchus 2001 New Wave Wines (Great Britain, £5.99) *Bacchus at its best; sherbert and citrus on the nose, with a long, balanced off-dry finish. This wine is one of the freshest, fruitiest examples of this grape. Stephen Skelton*

Underripe Bacchus can be a real cat's-pee stinker, while overripe Bacchus will be so full of exotic fruit that it can result in an overkill; but catch this grape with just the teeniest bit of underripeness and you can achieve something that all lovers of the freshest, crispest Sauvignon Blanc will adore. This is one such wine. Tom Stevenson

Lledoner Pelut 1998 Domaine de la Colombette (Languedoc-Roussillon, €11) *Very dark garnet color, but not soupy, since the wine manages to combine power with elegance and is not at all heavy despite its 14 percent alcohol. Hints of wild plants from the garrigue on the nose, with cherries and crushed-fruit richness on the palate. Some chocolate and spices later. Part-*

raised in newish wood, but the oak is not obtrusive. A good long finish. Paul Strang

This wine has an elegance and freshness that belie its alcoholic strength. Very floral, with a touch of sweetness to the fruit. Tom Stevenson

Baco Noir 2000 Birchwood Estate (Canada, C$8.95) *The early-ripening Baco Noir may be a lowly hybrid, but with careful winemaking it can produce a budget-priced red of some complexity and elegance. This one is deep ruby in color, with a hint of violet. The nose suggests blackberries, leather, and wet earth; in the mouth, medium-bodied with lively bramble and green-plum flavors and driving acidity that follows a soft, fruity middle palate. Could be mistaken for a Côtes du Rhône-Villages.* Tony Aspler

Rich, plummy red, with a hint of smoke on the nose, ripe, round cassis fruit on the palate, and fresh, clean acids on the finish. Good oak, not too obtrusive. An excellent-value red that can cock a snook at 50 per cent of French AOC red wine. Tom Stevenson

Attitude Sauvignon Blanc 2002 Pascal Jolivet (Vins de Pays, €12) *I was not paying attention to the label when I tasted this and automatically assumed it was Sancerre and liked it, and then I discovered it was a mere vin de pays. Good stony crisp nose, with firm flinty mineral flavors on the palate.* Rosemary George MW

Attitude is the right name for this in-your-face Sauvignon. Tom Stevenson

Altozano Tempranillo 2001 González Byass (Spain, €4.50) *Nicely constructed hot-climate Tempranillo, with enough fruit to balance the heat and a whisper of tannin to add complexity. Freshness and fruit prominent – another excellent everyday red. John Radford*

A fruity guzzler that is a steal at this price. Tom Stevenson

Cabernet Sauvignon Reserve 2000

Flam (Israel, NIS 130) *A blend of 90 percent Cabernet Sauvignon and 10 percent Merlot, this wine has spent 15 months in oak casks, resulting in a well-focused, well-balanced wine of enviable structure and enormous promise for the future. So deep you feel you can get lost in it, with traditional Cabernet flavors and aromas of red currants, ripe red fruit and spices, this is a wine that will be enjoyable in its youth, yet promises to cellar comfortably until 2008–10.* Daniel Rogov
Classic Cabernet fruit with lovely aromas and a hint of menthol finesse from nose to mid-palate, but to be super-critical, it is let down on the finish, where the elegance and class bleed away to reveal a certain rustic character on the aftertaste. However, it is a very nice wine. Tom Stevenson

Spirale Passerillé sur Paille 1998

André & Mireille Tissot (Jura & Savoie, €24 per half-bottle) *An amber or almost-tarnished bronze color. The nose is extremely enticing, with honey and dried fruit. It is very sweet, but this is balanced by sufficient acidity to give a clean, dry finish. Overall, this is a beautifully delicate, but honeyed, style that works better with dessert than with foie gras. A good reason to change the Vin de Paille laws.* Wink Lorch
I agree: the glycerol texture would make this wine too cloying with the foie gras, but it also would not go with many desserts. This wine is reminiscent of a TBA in texture although not in acidity, which is far softer; but like a TBA it should just be sipped on its own. Tom Stevenson

Vintner's Pride Encore 1998

Pellegrini Vineyards (Atlantic Northeast, $28.99) *High extraction, good weight, and a nice stuffing of red-berry fruit make this wine so appealing (65 percent Cabernet Sauvignon, 4 percent Cabernet Franc, 28 percent Merlot, and 3 percent Petit Verdot).* Sandra Silfven
Sweet blackcurrant. Like one of the old great Svitchov Cabernets from the 1980s. Tom Stevenson

Johannisberg Riesling Reserve 2001

Dr Konstantin Frank (Atlantic Northeast, $24.95) *This classic, off-dry Riesling has a nice, mineral character with notes of citrus and slate, elegant racy acidity, and a long, delicious finish.* Sandra Silfven
Early-developed bottle aromas make this Riesling stand out from its peers in the Finger Lakes, but it would have much more finesse if these aromatics took longer to form. Tom Stevenson

Private Reserve Kikyogahara Merlot 1999

Château Mercian (Japan, ¥10,000) *This was the best red in a line-up of the 128 Asian wines I tasted for Wine Report. It is very well made, highlighting all the sweeter and softer Merlot characteristics, with good concentration, fine balance, and a long, firm finish. Should age well.* Denis Gastin
Not a classic wine by any means, but it does have a typical plum-tomato Merlot aroma and nice, clean, medium-weight fruit that leans more towards Bordeaux than the New World. Tom Stevenson

1730 Palo Cortado

Pilar Aranda (Spain, €38.60) *Real Palo Cortado, with a nose like an Amontillado, but bigger and deeper. On the palate it is smooth, but with a bite. A wine of conspicuous maturity, plenty of body, and enough acidity to ensure excellent balance.* Julian Jeffs QC
Leans towards an Amontillado that is itself leaning too much towards the Fino it once was, but there is no denying well-aged elegance. Tom Stevenson

Martinez 1997 Vintage Port

(Portugal, €90) *Martinez has been making excellent Vintage Ports during the 1990s, but they are undervalued.* Richard Mayson
Very soft and easy to drink. Tom Stevenson

Extract of Styria 2000 Kupljen (Slovenia, 1,500 SIT) *A wonderfully harmonious blend of Pinot Gris, Chardonnay, and Riesling, part-fermented in French oak. The grapes blend together beautifully, with a nicely subtle touch of oak.* Caroline Gilby MW
A cleverly blended white, exotic with good acids. No gaps. But this is for drinking, not keeping. Tom Stevenson

Fläscher Riesling x Sylvaner 2001, Weingut Davaz (Switzerland, SF 14.50) *Very aromatic, typical Riesling x Sylvaner (Müller-Thurgau), with aromas of ripe fruit, honey, and roses. Slightly dry finish with mineralic aromatic. For many years Davaz has produced one of the best examples of this aromatic grape.* Chandra Kurt
As good as this grape gets in the dry to off-dry format. Tom Stevenson

Private Reserve Hokushin Chardonnay 2001 Château Mercian (Japan, ¥6,000) *Very good varietal fruit concentration, this wine has received restrained oak treatment. It gets better if left in the bottle, and is still sound five days after opening!* Denis Gastin
Elegant, if ubiquitous, pear, melon, and pineapple rendition. Soft, gentle, and as clean as a whistle. Tom Stevenson

Muscadet de Sèvre-et-Maine Etiquette Blanche 2002 Château de la Bidière (Loire, €6) *Old vines of Muscadet (55 years) vinified out of barrel. It has an incredible mentholated nose; roasted, lemon taste and creamy. A dry and very rich mouth at the same time, and a crystallized lemon finish that recalls the Petit Manseng of Jurançon.* Antoine Gerbelle
Very fresh banana-peel aroma, with correctly lean structure and typically good acidity, but atypically rich fruit for Muscadet, with some zesty lemon on the finish. Tom Stevenson

Chenin Blanc 2002 L'Avenir (South Africa, R40) *Lovely whiffs of botrytis over an array of ripe fruitiness—peaches, apricots—give this humbly priced, just off-dry white some width and intrigue.* John Platter
Like biting into a juicy green apple. Tom Stevenson

Vin de Lune 2000 Clos Triguedina (Southwest France, €15) *A deep, vivid, almost linseed-oil yellow. Because of the exotic fruits with a hint of ginger picked up on the nose and carried through to the palate with a long barley-sugar finish, most tasters might think this dessert wine has been made from Petit Manseng, but it is 100 percent Chenin Blanc. The grapes were hand-picked in late November and the wine aged in oak for 18 months.* Paul Strang
Elevated VA, but deliciously rich and different on the palate, with a slightly toasty sweet finish. Tom Stevenson

Verdelho 2002 Wilkie Estate (Organic, Australia, A$12) *This intensely crisp, dry white puts traditional and flabby Australian Chardonnays to shame.* Monty Waldin
Exotic fruit, not heavy, good acids. Tom Stevenson

White 2002 Domaine Gerovassiliou (Greece, €8) *Citron-lime nose riding on the assertive mineral backbone of Assyrtiko. Crisp and lingering, this is one of the few good wines produced in the rain-plagued 2002 vintage. Best over the next two or three years.* Nico Manessis
The ideal wine for Sauvignon Blanc lovers looking for an introduction to Greek wines. Tom Stevenson

Heritage Rosé NV Sparkling Wine Valley Vineyards (Great Britain, £7.99) *Light and lively on the palate, with gentle strawberry fruit on the nose.* Stephen Skelton
Ripe strawberry fruit, tiny bubbles, and

soft acidity on the finish. Tom Stevenson

Roque-Sestières Vieilles Vignes Blanc 2001 (Languedoc-Roussillon, €5)
The bouquet develops in the glass to suggest wild flowers and pineapple. Dry on the palate, but with more underlying pineapple and some exotic fruits. Surprising depth of flavor, and stylish at the end. Paul Strang
Very fresh, particularly on the palate. This is a food wine of some substance. Tom Stevenson

Comte de M 1998 Chateau Kefraya (Lebanon, LL 42,000) *The Kefraya flagship Comte de M defines the new generation of Lebanese wines from arguably its most adventurous and dynamic producer. Those who have not been won over by Serge Hochar's creations will be pleasantly surprised by this wine's correct, consistent, and robust character. A blend of Cabernet Sauvignon, Syrah, and Mourvèdre, this has notes of tobacco, chocolate, berries, and spice.* Michael Karam
Couldn't agree more: tobacco, chocolate, berries, and spice. Tom Stevenson

Grand Estates Chardonnay 2001 Columbia Crest (Pacific Northwest, $10) *A stunning, ripe, screamingly delicious Chardonnay that frequently sells for even less than the quoted $10 tag. Bursting with fruit and zippy acids, plus the kind of sweet, nutty oak rarely found at this price.* Paul Gregutt
I do not know how many bags of coffee-flavoured, medium-toast oak chips they slung in this, but it certainly hits the spot for most American Chardonnay drinkers. Tom Stevenson

Grenache Blanc 2001 Beckmen (California, $20) *Subtle earth-spice and pear complexity in a rare opportunity to see the white Grenache grape at its best, with no oak to obliterate its profile.* Dan Berger
Well, I can smell some oak, Dan,

but it certainly does not dominate. Good, high acids. Tom Stevenson

Soave Classico Superiore Ca' Visco 2001 Coffele (Italy, €20)
Penetrating, almost piercing, palate, beautifully balanced between sapidity and acidity. Long, remarkably fine finish. There is nothing loud about this wine, but it evinces an amazing purity and finesse. Nicolas Belfrage MW
Classy Soave. Tom Stevenson

Chardonnay 2000 Chateau Ksara (Lebanon, LL 18,000) *The outstanding white of recent years; many have initially blanched at the price only to be won over by a wine that is subtle, complex, and at times straining at the leash. Floral, buttery, and oak notes all combine to make a balanced and consistent wine, one that should do well on the international market.* Michael Karam
Fresh, clean, and elegant, with an admirable lack of oak influence. Tom Stevenson

Arbois Naturé 1999 Frédéric Lornet (Jura & Savoie, €8.50) *A distinct green tinge to the mid-yellow color. An intense nose combines pithy citrous flavors with creamy oak. The palate is dry with high, but balanced, acidity giving great freshness. Again, there is a tangy citrous note, but combined with a spicy and mineral character too. Medium-full with great balance and length of flavor, it reminds me strangely of a well-made Sémillon and shows the true character of Savagnin, never revealed in vins jaunes or traditional oxidized whites.* Wink Lorch
I agree; lemon-edged Sémillon-like, and definitely no oxidative character! Tom Stevenson

Roussette de Savoie Marestel 2000 Domaine Dupasquier (Jura & Savoie, €6.80) *The nose still remains relatively closed, but a spicy peach character is emerging. The dry palate reveals*

more, with an excellent acid balance and superb richness. Nutty and spicy with intense yellow-fruit character. Not yet quite integrated, but everything is there in abundance to meld together in the long term. This highly regarded wine proves that some Savoie whites are built to age well and to match a sophisticated cuisine. Wink Lorch
Fresh, creamy fruit with cashew nuts and a touch of chewy sweetness on the finish. A serious Savoie. Tom Stevenson

Campbell Early Rosé 2002
Miyazaki Tsuno Wines (Japan, ¥1,220) *From the Campbell Early, a labrusca hybrid grown in the very marginal wine-grape territory of Japan's Miyazaki prefecture, where conditions are closer to Florida than Bordeaux. This rosé is sweetish, but not in an anti-food sense, with an intriguing spicy bouquet and loads of flavor. It must be served cold, and goes well with local delicacies like black boar hotpot or sashimi wild deer.* Denis Gastin
Not as cloying on the nose or as sickly sweet on the palate as most Campbell Early or, indeed, labrusca wines in general tend to be. However, its extremely aromatic, highly floral, strawberry-jelly aroma will come as a shock to the uninitiated, and this is not so much reflected as cloned on the medium-sweet palate. Tom Stevenson

Selection 2001 Massaya (Lebanon, LL 14,000)
The Ghosn bothers have produced a thumping-good plummy red. Cinsault, Syrah, Cabernet Sauvignon, and Grenache all combine to produce this gutsy and energetic red, one that threatens to garner more plaudits than Massaya's Reserve, its senior stablemate. Mulberries and oak notes dominate a wine that smacks of the Bekaa, but one that will also go down well with New World fanciers who like their wines full-bodied and playful. Excellent value. Michael Karam
As Michael says, a thumper! Very gluggy indeed. Tom Stevenson

Fleur de Crussol 2001 Domaine
Alain Voge (Rhône, €9) *This prestigious cuvée is vinified in wood and represents the height of Alain Voge's ambition: a fresh and ample wine with a strong floral nose and a rich, deep, smooth palate.* Thierry Desseauve
This butter-oaky white with its oily fruit is not the greatest wine I have encountered, but it is the best St-Péray I have tasted. Tom Stevenson

Amat Tannat 1998 Vinos Finos Juan
Carrau (Uruguay, UP 550) *A chunky tannic wine that will last. This shows what the Tannat grape can do when it is fully ripe and barrel-aged (here a mixture of French and American oak). Red fruit blended with tobacco, toast, and leather.* Christopher Fielden
Pleasant, if obvious, oak on nose, fresh sappy fruit on the palate, and a clean, crisp finish. Easy drinking. Tom Stevenson

Touriga Nacional 1999 Tiger
Mountain Vineyards (Other US States, $25) *Slightly herbal notes to a rich blueberry and cassis nose and mouth. Earthy, tannic, and fairly short, but intriguing.* Doug Frost MW
Fascinating to find a reasonable rendition of this classic Douro grape in Georgia, but the aldehydes indicate that it is peaking. Probably much better a year or two ago.
Tom Stevenson

Index